Fire in the Cane Field

The Federal Invasion of Louisiana and Texas,
January 1861–January 1863

Fire in the Cane Field

The Federal Invasion of Louisiana and Texas,
January 1861–January 1863

Donald S. Frazier

State House
Press

Buffalo Gap, TX

Library of Congress Cataloging-in-Publication Data

Frazier, Donald S. (Donald Shaw), 1965-
    Fire in the cane field : the Federal invasion of Louisiana and Texas,
January 1861-January 1863 / Donald S. Frazier.
      p. cm.
    Includes bibliographical references and index.
    ISBN 978-1-933337-36-4 (cloth : alk. paper)
    1. Louisiana–History–Civil War, 1861-1865–Campaigns. 2. Louisiana–
History–Civil War, 1861-1865–Naval operations. 3. Texas–History–Civil
War, 1861-1865–Campaigns. 4. Texas–History–Civil War, 1861-1865–Naval
operations. 5. Secession–Louisiana 6. Secession–Texas. 7. United States–
History–Civil War, 1861-1865–Campaigns. 8. United States–History–Civil
War, 1861-1865–Naval operations. I. Title.

E470.7.F73 2008
973.7'309763–dc22

                                2008005191

State House Press
P. O. Box 818, Buffalo Gap, TX 79508
www.mcwhiney.org/press

Printed in the United States of America.

Distributed by Texas A&M University Press Consortium
(800) 826-8911
www.tamu.edu/upress

ISBN-13: 978-1-933337-36-4
ISBN-10: 1-933337-36-2

10 9 8 7 6 5 4 3 2 1

Book designed by Rosenbohm Graphic Design

This work is dedicated to the sacred memory of the late
Judy Capone,
and in honor of her devoted husband
Andrew Capone.

They are the best examples of all that is great about Louisiana.

CONTENTS

PREFACE

Your work should be a contribution to the field.
—Dr. Grady McWhiney

I remember the first book I ever bought with my own money. The purchase occurred at a Scholastic Book Fair at Springdale Elementary School in Macon, Georgia. The title I purchased: *The Golden Book of the Civil War.* Later, as she watched my classroom maturation, my fifth-grade teacher, Jo Beth Grenga, made an offhand comment that, when I grew up, I should be either a historian or a journalist. I've worked as both.

This book purchase, that teacher's encouragement, launched me on the great hunt of my lifetime. The muse of history was calling, and I searched my surroundings for the source of its urgings. One place I looked was in the oldest cemetery in Macon, which, for a kid from West Texas, was a great adventure. The memorial parks I had visited before in my brief lifetime had been populated with flat headstones, neatly arranged, where riding lawnmowers could manage their perpetual care. I had never visited a cemetery with crumbling brick vaults, kudzu jungles, and magnificent glowing angels gazing down with stony stares of pity and remorse from their sepulcher perches. Neither had I seen the graves of Civil War soldiers until that summer day at the Rose Hill Cemetery.

There, amid the sprawl of a well-used city burial ground, was a section marked, rather modestly, with a metal sign, as "Confederate Square." Row upon row of white arched-top stones marked the final resting places of hundreds of dead Confederates, all casualties once cared for at the military hospital in the city. Instinctively—for a Texan at least—I surveyed each row for an indication of where these men had come from and recorded the names of every one of the Lone Star fallen. At my father's urging, I sent this list to the archives in Austin to see what I could learn about the lives and deaths of these Americans. In due time, I received a response.

This exercise revealed two things. First, these troops had never fought in the battles that I—as an eleven-year-old kid—had heard of. My new book had readable text and excellent battle maps illustrated with little painted soldiers moving across rugged landscapes, but I could not find my Texans in the book. They had not been at Gettysburg or Vicksburg. Instead, their service records from the archives revealed only alien names, such as Rocky Faced Ridge, Chickamauga, and, most curiously, Arkansas Post. In the process, I had also unwittingly met my first Rebels and made my first intellectual investment in the lives of people who had made history. It was a history I had not yet heard of, and one where these dead Texans seemed to be out of place. One in particular stood out. Jonathan B. Craig, Company E, 15th Texas Cavalry, in row 12, grave 534. So, I began reading everything I could about his life and times and in the process became a researcher.

This effort, the first of my *Louisiana Quadrille*, is a similar attempt. The more I studied the Civil War, the more I learned of the subtle nuances and obscure military events that defied efficient entry into such general texts as *The Golden Book of the Civil War*. These were the places where Texans tended to fight. Somehow, these little-known places and issues held an allure for me that often-discussed issues, such as Lee's strategy with the Army of Northern Virginia during his invasion of Pennsylvania, did not. I was drawn to the Arkansas Posts of the Civil War. I call this four-book scholarly campaign a "quadrille" for good purpose: the maneuvers of the Union and Confederate armies and navies in the western gulf country, as well as that of their politicians, remind me of a crafty card game bluff or a spirited dance with ever changing partners—*quadrilles* all.

After a false-start career as a features writer for the Arlington *Citizen–Journal* and as a defense industry drone for General Dynamics, I attended graduate school at Texas Christian University. I aligned myself there with Professor Grady McWhiney, an important scholar of the South and the Civil War. When he asked me what I wanted to write about—he insisted that his students write book manuscripts instead of dissertations—I mentioned Texans in the Civil War. I was leaning toward studying Granbury's Brigade, since Private Craig and most of the Confederate Texans in that Macon cemetery had all served in this outfit. "Doc," as he was called by his students, declared that topic unacceptable because of the amount of literature already published on the subject. "Your work," he advised, "should make a contribution to the field" —not duplicate it. I then mentioned a passing interest in Henry Hopkins Sibley's Brigade of Texans. He agreed to the topic.

At first I intended to write a fairly conventional "muster-in to muster-out" history of the brigade as it campaigned from New Mexico to Galveston to Louisiana. As I delved into the story of this unit and the men who composed it, however, I encountered yet another aspect of the Civil War that I had never heard of. Eventually, instead of taking this command from 1861 to 1865 and describing the where and how of its military operations, I found myself fascinated by the "why" questions. "Why New Mexico?" became the first big pursuit, resulting in a dissertation that, true to Doc's urgings, became *Blood and Treasure: Confederate Empire in the Southwest,* published by Texas A&M University Press in 1995.

Other books and articles followed. I penned *Cottonclads: The Battle of Galveston and the Defense of the Texas Coast,* published in 1996, as a popular narrative introduction to what, at the time, I believed to be an interesting but not terribly important episode in Texas Civil War history. Then Sibley's Brigade moved to Louisiana, and for me this changed everything.

Here, for the first time, I was confronted by a bundle of all the salient issues of that great violent spasm of American history that has been known most commonly as the Civil War. Union armies seized New Orleans and vied for control of the Mississippi River while Confederates struggled to do more with less. Profound and complicated political dimensions complicated the story, including Abraham Lincoln's view of the war versus the reality on the ground. Issues surrounding secession, including the questions of technique and legitimacy, swirled among the military considerations. Slavery, the big issue, became more stark and immediate the deeper I dove in the murky pool of Louisiana history. In the end, I discovered in microcosm a place that presented the entire sweep of issues facing Americans in the mid-nineteenth century, including those that bedeviled them before the shooting started and those that plagued them in the wake of plundering armies.

My investigations into Louisiana revealed other profound features of American civilization. This book, and the three to follow, describe what I can only call a messy, dangerous, and ultimately devastating experiment in democracy. The issues dividing the nation were to have winners and losers, majorities and minorities. The resulting secession movement and war demonstrate simultaneously all that is noble and base about Americans, all that is generous and mean. Ultimately it brought into bold view all of the shortcomings and excesses of the experiment called the(se) United States.

Growing up in the South and heading into my career as an academic historian, I had heard all the other monikers for the conflict, ranging from regional favorites of "The War Between the States," "The War of Yankee Aggression," and "The Late Unpleasantness" to more antique terms like "The War of the Rebellion," "The Second American Revolution," and "The War of Secession." The more I investigated the events in Louisiana and Texas, the more I decided that none of these titles really fit. The war really seemed to be a War for Southern Independence—a war that failed catastrophically.

This series of four books is my attempt to tell the American saga of those destructive years using Louisiana's story as the door through which we approach the larger issues of sectionalism, capitalism, wealth, power, character, courage, race, virtue, leadership, ingenuity, class, society, and loyalty. *Fire in the Cane Field* introduces the story by describing the advent of secession in Louisiana and its immediate consequences, including invasion by Federal forces. It also describes why the Battle of Galveston on January 1, 1863, was one of the great turning points in the Trans-Mississippi. Subsequent titles, *Thunder across the Swamp: The Fight for the Lower Mississippi, February 1863–May 1863; Blood on the Bayou: The Campaigns of Tom Green's Texans, June 1863–February 1864;* and *Death at the Landing: The Contest for the Red River and the Collapse of Confederate Louisiana, March 1864–June 1865,* will continue the tale and propel the narrative chronologically until the end of the war, whatever name you choose to call it.

This body of research is intended to be a solid introduction to the topic. There are hosts of books on the war in Louisiana and Texas, ranging from general histories to monographs on specific and varied topics, including battles, labor, economics, units, and campaigns. My offerings are not intended to supplant or duplicate them. Instead, I have attempted to weave this amazing scholarship from a wide variety of fields into a comprehensive story placed in the larger American context. Any successes I have in this endeavor, more than a decade and a half in the making, I owe to the intellectual pioneers who have preceded me. Any failures are, of course, my own.

I owe a debt of gratitude to so many people over so many years that there is not time or space to mention them all. I am grateful first, of course, to my close professional colleagues, including Robert Pace, the late Grady McWhiney, Robert Maberry Jr., and Steve Hardin. Others include Art Bergeron, Larry Hewitt, Marvin Schultz, Ed Cotham, and Judy Schaeffer. Members of a variety of organizations listened patiently as I described my research journey, including the Baton Rouge and New Orleans Civil War Roundtables; the Young-Sanders Center; the Houston, Austin, Brazos Valley, and San Antonio Civil War Round Tables; and the Louisiana Historical Association and the Texas State Historical Association. Their comments and observations proved invaluable.

One of the joys of this project has been the cloud of friends I have made along the way, including LaFourche District Louisianans Andrew Capone and his late wife, Judy. Glenn and Angela Falgoust and Chris Peña have been extraordinarily generous with their time and resources, and Denis Gaubert let me have a crack at his photo collection. There are also Florida Parish Louisianans, Molly Wiggins and her late husband, Bob, and Teche Louisianans, the late Billy and Margie Shinn. Most of these folks have either hosted me overnight in their homes or have unflaggingly and unselfishly aided me with materials, photos, maps, guide services, meals, and a whole host of support, encouragement, and inspiration. A number of friendly Texans bear thanking as well, including Josh Winegarner of Amarillo and Dan Laney of Austin for their interest in my work, and Martha Hertzog of Austin for her constant reminders to get this project into print. There is also to thank, of course, my wife Susan for her patience and support and my daughters for their appreciation of Louisiana as a research destination. The ink on these pages is remarkably inadequate to convey the depths of my gratitude to all of those mentioned for their assistance and camaraderie.

My boon companions bear special attention. Dr. Robert Pace read this manuscript thoroughly and commented extensively. Susan worked the images and index. Amy Smith, of course, has my undying admiration. Thank you all.

Soli Deo Gloria.

CHAPTER ONE

SECESSION

*The battle for the right to govern ourselves and control our
own institutions had to be fought with the fanatics
of the north at some time.*
Tom Green, Texan

Flashes of lightning and the rumble of thunder warned the gray
uniformed soldiers that they were in for another long evening.
Then, to emphasize the point, high winds gusted up in a hurry
that night of April 10, 1862. The usually benign breezes from the Gulf
of Mexico shifted and turned fearsome as they howled across the low-
lands of Louisiana and rocketed across the swamps and tidal marshes
near the mouths of the Mississippi River. They roared about, carrying
with them rain and destruction, making soldiers walking their beat as
pickets and guards lean into the storm, longing for shelter and safety
from the elements.

For the Confederate troops battened down at forts Jackson and St.
Philip, this was just the latest assault by the weather. A wet winter and
spring had caused the river they had been charged with defending to
overflow its banks a few weeks before, cresting the levees and pouring
a yellowish ooze into the works. Stout-looking cannon emplacements
and barracks flooded with equal felicity. Since then, the discouraged

men had spent their time mucking out the brick citadels. Now this windstorm promised more ill. The locals knew it was too early for a hurricane, but the thunderstorm that burst upon them that night certainly felt ominous—a harbinger of violent times ahead.

Nature seemed arrayed against them. The surging waters of the last few months had been more destructive than any act of war so far. A huge chain and log obstruction blocking the passage of enemy vessels on the Mississippi once lay draped below forts Jackson and St. Philip, but debris carried on the mighty current had destroyed that effort by catching on the chain in vast rafts until, finally, the barrier had parted. The defiant river had again flowed freely to the sea. Resolute against shot and shell, the mighty redoubts now seemed to slump under the grinding decay of water and mud.

Confederate engineers, determined to have their way, launched a counter attack against this wild geography. After the flooding troubles and the loss of the great chain, Confederate Brigadier General Johnson K. Duncan had taken a different approach to obstructing the river and had ordered workers to lash a series of abandoned schooners by the bow, stern, and amidships facing the current in a three-cabled gate across the Mississippi. As proof of his concept, flotsam from the river had indeed gone gliding neatly by. Satisfied with his ingenuity, he no doubt had looked on with satisfaction as the salvaged sailing vessels had a neat look, their spars and rigging trailing in the current like jellyfish tendrils designed to snare enemy paddlewheels and propellers. Their rusted and oily binding chains had draped symmetrical in a great arc across the flood, a great bowed shield against any enemies bold enough to come up the river.

The storm troubled him. The next morning General Duncan, a native of Pennsylvania, resident of New Orleans by predilection and choice, and Confederate commander of the Mississippi River defenses, surveyed his positions and checked for storm damage. As he rode along the river, first light revealed that the once trim lines of the schooner and chain obstructions now lay hopelessly tangled. The wind had done its work better than any Union flotilla. The once graceful curve sat bent, skewed, and askance as forlorn vessels twisted in the current of the river, some listing with the weight of water below decks. Chains once believed invincible had become unpinned, sundered, and sunk. These imaginative obstructions, once an image of engineering efficiency, now looked shabby and broken.

Nothing, it seemed, was going as planned. Duncan needed this barrier intact to delay the enemy long enough for his gunners to blow them to pieces. Without it, the powerful sloops of war might speed by his forts with nothing more than a passing exchange from broadside and battery. Duncan also knew that Federal warships, lurking just a few dozen miles downstream, would catch wind of his misfortune make short work of what remained of this first barrier to invasion. His forts just upriver, he believed, could still hold without the obstructions, but he was far from certain that the Yankee fleet could be stopped.

Discouraged, he returned to his headquarters to prepare his report, no doubt reviewing the fevered days that had whipped by over the past eighteen months and the circumstances that had brought him to this day. For this man of plans, schematics, and numbers, the events of the past year and a half had once formed a chain that had appeared logical, sensible, and well designed. Now that chain of events—of which he and his men formed a span—now looked battered and tenuous, much like his damaged river obstructions. Intentions, he mused, rarely survive contact with reality.

Duncan may not have realized that he served at the end of a chain of history whose first link had been hammered on November 19, 1860. That day, Governor Thomas O. Moore of Louisiana had been at his desk in the crenellated, fort-like capitol at Baton Rouge preparing to sign a momentous document. The recent U.S. election had brought Abraham Lincoln to the presidency and had capped years of increasingly venomous debate as to the nature of the constitutional compact that governed the nation and the future of slavery, and most southerners believed the results to be truly unacceptable.

Moore reviewed the document, casting his eyes upon a sentence pregnant with conflict. "Whereas, some of our sister States, aggressive like ours, are preparing measures for the future security and for the safety of their institutions and their people, and both patriotism and self preservation requires us to deliberate upon our own course of action," the parchment read. The Governor scanned a little further on, then, scratching his signature upon the bottom, he had the secretary of state affix the state seal upon it. He had decided. The legislature would meet in special session in less than a month to determine a course of action. He had a pretty good idea what it would decide. He hadn't always been so certain.[1]

Before Lincoln's election, Moore had assumed his fellow Louisianans were fairly rational about the national crisis. When asked his opinion as to the need for disunion should the Republicans triumph, Moore had answered no. "I shall not advise the secession of my state," he had written Governor William H. Gist of South Carolina. "I do not think the people of Louisiana will ultimately decide in favor of that course." The Pelican State would be circumspect yet firm in this crisis. Moore refused to be stampeded.[2]

As ordered, the elected representatives of the people of Louisiana gathered at noon on December 10 in Baton Rouge. Governor Moore, described by one observer as "a tall spare man between fifty and sixty years of age, of a quiet unobtrusive manner, and of a rather homely disposition, and very different from the fiery spirits that surrounded him," addressed the joint assembly. He declared that a special convention should meet that would determine whether the Pelican State would accept the verdict of the recent elections, and, if not, what course of action they should take. "If I am not mistaken in public opinion," Moore declared, "a convention will decide that Louisiana will not submit to the presidency of Mr. Lincoln." The assembled politicians thundered in approval. "The Northern mind is poisoned against us, and it no longer respects our rights—or their obligations." Of all the Deep South states, Louisiana had the warmest affiliation and closest commercial ties to the North, yet now the momentum favored the secessionists.

The Governor tried to reign in these hotspurs. Interested in protecting protocols and making sure that processes were observed, Moore directed lawmakers to retire to their respective houses and pass a bill making such a convention legal and binding. The governor also appointed Lafourche Parish planter and Mexican War hero Braxton Bragg as military aide-de-camp and convened a board of military commissioners to oversee the arming of Louisiana's militias. He would certainly be a sober and steady hand at the task. A day and a half later, the special session adjourned, its work completed. Instructions went forth to each of the state's representative or senatorial districts to elect delegates on January 7 for a meeting to discuss the national crises to be convened on January 23, 1861.[3]

With these instructions placed in circulation, the Christmas season of 1860 saw many Louisianans preparing for war and some hoping for peace. The winter months had always been lively in New Orleans, with the fear of Yel-

Louisiana's first Confederate governor, Thomas Overton Moore. State Library of Louisiana.

low Fever dissipated and the arrival of Northern friends seeking to avoid the brutality of a New York winter. This year, though, militia companies drilling in fields, lots, and in the streets lent an additional festive and expectant atmosphere. At a St. Barbara's Day banquet on December 4 a smartly dressed militia officer, Colonel James B. Walton, addressed his assembled men, their ladies, and city leaders. Raising his glass, the man bellowed, "Gentlemen, the time for talking has passed; the time for action has come. Let one word be sufficient. The Orleans artillery is ready." Hurrahs filled the chamber as the toast received a warm reception. Scenes like this played out daily across the state during that troubled December. Meanwhile, lively debates raged regarding who should attend the convention as delegates and whether or not Louisiana should act alone or in concert with other Southern states, or perhaps wait to see what developed.[4]

Electioneering by would-be convention delegates was lively that Christmas season as well, and two distinct camps emerged. The most vocal and radical camp wanted immediate secession. Their opponents, dubbed "cooperationists," ranged from those wishing to only follow the lead of the rest of the South to outright Unionists.

The vote to choose delegates proved close. Candidates from the radical camp swept most of the elections, but returns indicated a close race. Of the popular votes cast, only 52 percent went to the radicals. In most of the sugar parishes, as well as the Florida parishes across the Mississippi River, cooperationist delegates received the nod.[5] Sugar, after all, was booming. Planters had produced almost 300,000 hogsheads annually on average for the past decade, but the 1861 crop promised to be half again more. The 1,291 Louisiana sugar estates composed an industry worth more than $200 million, including the value of the land, sugarhouses and their steam-driven grinders, vehicles, animals, and some 140,000 slave families. Capitalists had invested heavily in the business over the past thirty years. The general economy in New Orleans relied on the robust growth of the sugar industry. The sugar planters, sensible men with much to lose, could not afford rashness and intemperance. Immediate secession, they feared, would bring ruin to all they had built.[6]

Surely cool heads would prevail, but the signs were troubling. Time and rashness, these capitalists believed, worked against the interests of all Louisiana sugar planters and New Orleans banks that funded them. While they debated these sober concerns and campaign for positions at the conclave, the momentum of disunion rumbled along well beyond the state's borders. On December 21, 1860, South Carolina voted to secede and sever its ties with the United States, increasing pressure on other southern states.[7]

Despite their immense wealth and influence, the sugar planters fought a losing battle to stem this national current. The new year brought more signs that Louisiana, too, would soon declare its independence. Fearing violence from among some of the more vituperative partisans, and in a clear attempt to slow the momentum or political anarchy, Governor Moore sought to head off a spontaneous outbreak of civil war in his state by seizing and controlling the U.S. military arsenals, forts, and depots to keep their contents under state control. On January 9 and 10, militia units from New Orleans seized army installations in the city and

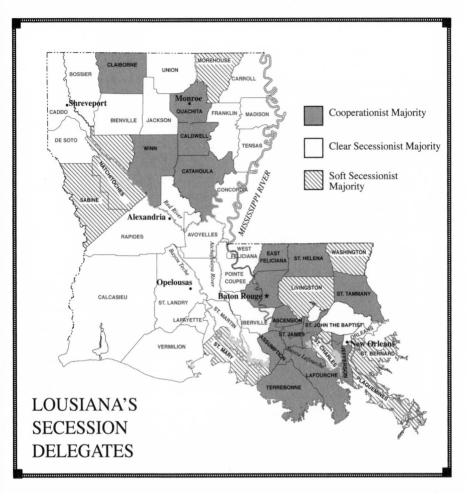

LOUSIANA'S
SECESSION
DELEGATES

Cooperationist Majority

Clear Secessionist Majority

Soft Secessionist
Majority

fanned out to Baton Rouge and other posts in the state. They also captured Forts Jackson and St. Philip, guarding the Mississippi approaches from the Gulf of Mexico. Meanwhile, Colonel Bragg and the military commissioners authorized the enrollment of some five hundred Louisiana regulars for service to the state. If Louisiana were to leave the Union, it would do so with order and dignity.[8]

Governor Moore began to accept the verdict of history even as he leaned against secession. "I could see that the Governor, who was not a great politician, but a man of considerable standing in the state, had no great heart in the movement, but was altogether overruled and goaded on by those around him, and had to go with the political current," observed William Watson, a Scottish merchant.[9]

One of Louisiana's hotspurs, Colonel James B. Walton was a veteran of the Mexican War and leader of the famous Washington Artillery of New Orleans. He would later serve with distinction with the Army of Northern Virginia. State Library of Louisiana.

Economics, not politics, drove the governor toward secession. He was a cotton planter and had long objected to the chokehold Northern merchants seemed to have on his commodities. Not only did they mark up his crop, make huge profits, and manipulate his prices, but they also sold him items that appeared terribly overpriced. Of course, slavery remained an issue. Northerners clearly profited from the institution, yet lectured the South on its evils, Watson wrote. "I could see that he had a strong sense of the position in which the South stood with the North in regard to trade, and it was no doubt a little irritating." On this point Moore and the sugar planters agreed. Northerners who opposed tariffs in the 1850s favoring the cane industry sneeringly referred to south Louisiana capitalists as "Sugar Nabobs." Moore believed that these Yankees needed to be taught some manners.[10]

Without the South—and all of its peculiarities—northern businessmen and their crusading abolitionist neighbors would suffer, predicted Watson. "The Southern planters were the real producers of the country," the Scotsman continued. "They were enduring the toils and privations of a backwoods life. They were bearing the odium of being slaveholders. The North was pocketing the lion's share of their labours, living in ease and luxury, and maintaining an exterior of virtue and sanctity." From his vantage point as a foreigner and commercial captain, Watson remarked that even the self-righteous reformers of the North paid for their pews at church and their Sunday dresses with

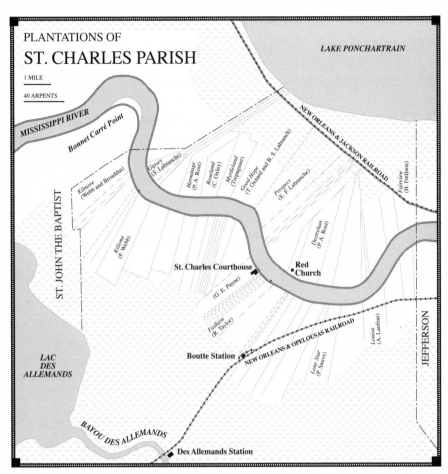

PLANTATIONS OF

ST. CHARLES PARISH

1 MILE

40 ARPENTS

LAKE PONCHARTRAIN

MISSISSIPPI RIVER

Bonnet Carré Point

NEW ORLEANS & JACKSON RAILROAD

ST. JOHN THE BAPTIST

Kilmore
(Webb and Broaddus)

Gipsey
(S. Labranche)

Hermitage
(P. A. Rost)

Roseland
(C. Oxley)

Myrtleland
(Trepagnier)

Good Hope
(T. Oxnard and B. S. Labranch)

Prospect
(E. F. Labranche)

Fairview
(H. Frellson)

Killona
(F. Webb)

Destrehan
(P. A. Rost)

St. Charles Courthouse

Red
Church

(G. E. Payne)

Fashion
(R. Taylor)

NEW ORLEANS & OPELOUSAS RAILROAD

Louisa
(A. Lanfear)

JEFFERSON

Boutte Station

Lone Star
(P. Sauve)

LAC
DES
ALLEMANDS

BAYOU DES ALLEMANDS

Des Allemands Station

This map is based on the 1858 map *Norman's Chart Of The Lower Mississippi River By A. Persac. Published by B.M. Norman, New Orleans, La. 1858. Entered ... 1858 by B.M. Norman ... Louisiana. Engraved, Printed & Mounted By J.H. Colton & Co. New York.* It shows the property lines of Mississippi River plantations, a few of which are labled above. Based on French and Spanish surveying conventions, property lines were measured in arpents of approximately 191.8 English feet. Sugar plantations usually included between two to eight arpents of river frontage but claimed forty, sixty, or more arpents in depth. Often fields ended when tillable soil gave way to the swampy "*marais*" beyond. Growers contained the Mississippi with a levee system, crested with a road providing land communications between properties. A secondary, "forty arpent" road usually crossed fields in the interior, giving additional lateral transportation access for cane carts besides tracks leading to the levee along the field margins.

money "often derived in a pretty direct way from the products of the Southern planter with all the horrors of slavery upon it."[11]

The furor and question at hand remained complicated. "Although I could see nothing to justify the secession movement, still the remarks of the Governor reminded me that a question may be looked at from many points of view," Watson concluded. "It was questionable if the Northern Abolitionists came into court with clean hands."[12]

Just three weeks into 1861, amid martial and momentous stirrings, delegates to the special convention began arriving in Baton Rouge. One of the first was Alexander Mouton, a veteran statesman. He had represented Lafayette Parish in the statehouse as a young man, and in his thirties he had served in the U.S. Senate. In 1843 he left the nation's capital to assume his newly elected role as governor of Louisiana, and he served for four years at the state capital in New Orleans. At the end of his term, when he was forty-two years old, he retired from public service to his palatial home, Ile Copal, near Bayou Vermillion to resume his private affairs as a planter.

At age fifty-six Alexander Mouton re-entered public life, this time to participate in something truly extraordinary. Louisiana's representatives, clamoring for a political break with the United States, had authorized a convention to meet and decide the secession issue. They asked Mouton to serve as the president of the meeting, based on his experience and wisdom.

He agreed, determined to model the dedication to public service he had sought to instill in his children. Upon his retirement from politics a decade and a half before he had arranged for his oldest child, Alfred, to enter the United States Military Academy at West Point, class of 1846. A French-speaking Acadian, the awkward seventeen-year old dutifully followed his father's instructions, despite his lack of English skills, and assumed a military career. Little could father or son know that this decision would one day bring Alfred back to Louisiana as a soldier under circumstances neither could have foreseen.

Now, in the opening days of 1861, the conventioneers who had summoned the elder Mouton back into the public eye proceeded rapidly, with secessionists eager to win their way. After brief opening ceremonies on January 23, a select committee adjourned to draft an ordinance of secession. Three days later, on January 26, the statement of disunion passed, 113 votes to 17. Clerks passed out golden pens to the signatories who affixed their names to the document. Once the revolutionary ink dried, Mouton declared the connections binding Louisiana to the

United States to be dissolved, the first four days of his second political career complete. Amid joyous clamor, a squad of picked men proceeded to the flagpole in front of the capitol and hoisted a Louisiana flag as symbol of its rediscovered sovereignty. When word arrived in New Orleans, most citizens of the Crescent City exploded with joy. Others looked on, nervously.[13]

Governor Alexandre Mouton at the time of secession.
Photo from ancestry.com.

Thirty-one-year-old Julia LeGrand regretted the new banner she now saw flying near her Garden District home. "I feel that we should have retained the old flag," she confided to her diary. "We alone held fast to the Constitution. The Yankees have no right to it; they have been persecutors and meddlers even from the witch-burning time until now."[14]

Representatives from New Orleans came forward to invite the secession convention to leave the statehouse in boring Baton Rouge and reconvene in their city. The delegates accepted, and on January 29 they resumed their work in the Lyceum of City Hall to packed galleries and a general buzz among New Orleanians. There were decisions to be made—in less than a week representatives from the Deep South planned to meet in Montgomery, Alabama, to form a cooperative coalition of seceded states or, more likely, to launch a new nation in opposition to the sundered United States. The secession convention chose six Louisiana delegates to be the voice of the people in new political entities that might emerge, including the rumored Confederate States of America.[15]

As these men sought ties with the rest of the South, Richard Taylor, chairman of the Committee on Military and Naval Affairs, introduced an ordinance organizing Louisiana's army and navy, declaring that the state lay "utterly defenseless."[16] Young men throughout the state rushed to enlist in what most believed would be a great frolic. For the next two months, state officials reassembled militia rolls and unlocked arsenals to arm and create something akin to a respectable army. Everyone anticipated that Louisiana would take its place among the other seceded states in some type of southern Confederacy. The patriots of 1861, however, did not necessarily equate disunion with war. Showing that they were prepared to resist political coercion, they believed, was only prudent.

For the six Pelican State representatives in Montgomery, finding common ground with the rest of the indignant South proved harder than anticipated. They had witnessed the creation of the Confederate States of America and watched the ascension of former Mississippi senator Jefferson Davis as its first president. Having returned to New Orleans, they wanted to know if Louisiana would formally join the new Confederacy. The state secession convention languidly reconvened on March 4 to debate the question, but the sessions proved less bellicose and one in four of the once ardent delegates never even bothered to attend. They may have found New Orleans too hospitable, too entertaining. When the Confederate constitution came before the more diligent members of that body, they rejected the document.

Secessionists and pro-Confederates were shocked. This defeat of their ambitions resuscitated old passions and shook the most militant of their members out of the bars and casinos, igniting a hot argument as Southern partisans demanded that Louisiana citizens should vote on the measure in a statewide plebiscite—a clear attempt to bypass the verdict of the convention. Opponents of joining the Confederacy grew equally bellicose. "The whole secession movement and the action of this convention were characterized by a total disregard of the voice of the people," screamed delegate Joseph Rozier, exposing a weakness in his opponents' arguments. Why now, at this late date, had secessionists suddenly discovered a passion for the *vox populi*? Why had the state taken the radical step of declaring its independence only to quickly surrender it to another power? Was all of this agitation about the good of Louisiana, after all, or as many suspected a cabal designed to create a southern nation?

The answers to these questions drowned in a tidal surge of emotional and bellicose harangues. Trying to breast this current, Rozier

This image from Frank Leslie's Illustrated Newspaper *shows the port city of New Orleans occupying a great bend of the Mississippi. Without question, it was the most important city in the South. Lake Pontchartrain is in the distance; St. Louis Cathedral and Jackson Square are to the right.*

continued to argue that a plebiscite at this late stage would be inherently flawed and not reflective of the actual will of average citizens. His appeals to reason failed fast. After days of political deal making, hallway arguments, and back-room negotiations, the conventioneers turned against Rozier and his supporters. Despite the first outcome, officials reintroduced the Confederacy question to the more fully awakened and assembled body, and Louisiana joined the new nation on March 21, 1861, linking its fate to the other seceded states: Texas, Mississippi, Alabama, Georgia, Florida, and South Carolina. Joyful secessionists convinced themselves that the people had spoken.[17]

Perhaps. For many Americans across the South, the complex issues of the winter of 1860–1861 distilled into a simple elixir. With war enthusiasm stirred up, many southerners accepted secession and the Confederacy as, if not inevitable, certainly a useful vehicle for defending their honor and that of their states against a perceived conspiracy of northern politicians, abolitionists, and generals. "The battle for the right to govern ourselves and control our own institutions had to be fought with the fanatics of the north at some time, and I expect it had as well be by us as our children," wrote Texan Tom Green. "We are no doubt better prepared for the fight than our children would have been and will bring more nerve to the conflict that they would as the injuries received from the nasal twanged, self righteous, witch killing fanatics are more recent and fresh with us." If there were to be a showdown, it might as well happen now.[18]

With the issue decided in Louisiana, Pelican State patriots boasted that they would do their part for their new nation. Officials transferred public property seized by state forces to Confederate control. The Confederate government responded warmly to this declaration of affection. Leading Louisianans like Braxton Bragg and P. G. T. Beauregard joined the ranks of the new nation's high command while other offices and patronage flowed from Montgomery to Baton Rouge. When the Confederacy issued its first wave of army commissions for officers, one notice traveled to the banks of Bayou Vermillion in Louisiana. Alfred Mouton, the West Point-trained son of the president of Louisiana's secession convention, had become a Confederate captain.

From South Carolina to Texas and from Maine to Florida, trainloads of enthusiastic young men left their homes for the adventure of their lifetimes and a chance to answer the great national questions of their age. Leaders both North and South drew their battle lines as armies gathered in the heady spring days of 1861. When Confederate forces opened fire on Fort Sumter in mid-April, the issue of open warfare between the states seemed foreordained.

President Abraham Lincoln answered this challenge to U.S. control by calling for seventy-five thousand volunteers to suppress what he described as rebellion. Four more states—Virginia, North Carolina, Tennessee, and Arkansas—responded to this projection of presidential power by leaving the United States and joining the seceded South. Kentucky declared its neutrality, but Missouri and Maryland quickly became contested ground. With this new addition to the nation, the Confederate capital moved to Richmond to make the most of its well-established cadre of bureaucrats and its industrial and hospitality sectors.

With secession thus expanded, an April 1861 *New York Times* editorial revealed a sinister agenda: "It is about time now that Virginia . . . should be opened up for the occupation and settlement of free white men," the writer asserted. "By inviting immigration to her town and cities, and by guaranteeing and protecting the homesteads of all who will manfully and loyally labor for her regeneration." Northerners also appeared eager for the contest. Neither side could have anticipated that the nation had become locked in a titanic struggle that would, before long, engulf even the most remote and humble citizen of the country. No one would be spared. The hopes for compromise would be destroyed—by fire and sword.[19]

As the southern insurgency gathered momentum, the leadership of the United States faced a defining moment. In Washington, D.C., President Lincoln, inaugurated just seven weeks before, sought to understand what he was facing as the Confederate tempest brewed. He clearly saw rebellion. "By the affair at Fort Sumter . . . they have forced upon the country the distinct issue, 'immediate dissolution or blood,'" he said in an address to an emergency joint-session of Congress on July 4, 1861. "And this issue embraces more than the fate of these United States. It presents the question whether discontented individuals, too few in numbers to control administration according to organic law in any case, can always, upon the pretenses, or arbitrarily without any pretense, break up their government."[20]

Lincoln and his advisors doubted if the secession movement that had swept the seven Deep South states had even been a legitimate expression of the will of the people. A disgruntled minority, they believed, had misused the political machinery to impose its will on the people of the South or had somehow duped them into agreeing to this reckless course. "It might seem, at first thought, to be of little difference whether the present movement at the South be called 'secession' or 'rebellion,'" Lincoln continued. "The movers, however, well understood the difference." The president argued that southern demagogues had convinced otherwise law-abiding citizens to take a radical stand. "They knew their people possessed as much of moral sense, as much of devotion to law and order, and as much pride in and reverence for the history of their common country as any other civilized and patriotic people. Accordingly, they commenced by an insidious debauching of the public mind. They invented an ingenious sophism which, if conceded, was followed by perfectly logical steps, through all the incidents to the complete destruction of the Union."

In short, Lincoln believed that southerners had ceased thinking for themselves and had fallen under the control of those who sought disunion. "With rebellion thus sugar-coated they have been drugging the public mind on their section for more than thirty years, and until at length they have brought many good men to a willingness to take up arms against the government." With southerners having struck a blow against the U.S. government at Fort Sumter, Lincoln believed that Federal armies had to break the trance.[21]

At the same time the national crisis revealed the limits and weaknesses of the Republic and its political machinery. The hypnotized southerners, Lincoln argued, had assumed the inevitability of the situation "the day after an assemblage of men have enacted the farcical pretense of taking their state out of the Union." The conventions that claimed to have spoken for the people were bogus, and without such illegal gatherings, Lincoln believed, average southerners would have been immune to the lure of rebellion.[22]

In his mind, U.S. regulars and volunteers would assemble in great patriotic armies and return national prestige into the troublesome states. The democratically oppressed would welcome them as liberators; they would serve as stern schoolmasters for the politically naïve. "It may well be questioned whether there is today a majority of the legally qualified voters of any state . . . in favor of disunion," Lincoln concluded. "There is reason to believe that the Union men are the majority in many, if not every other one, of the so-called seceded States. The contrary has not been demonstrated in any one of them." Faithful Federal soldiers would encourage these Unionist populations to rally to the flag and throw off the yoke of the Confederate pretenders. The government would, with the backing of these liberated southerners, rebuild and designate a legitimate state government that could repair the political damage done by fire-eating rebel demagogues.[23]

At any rate the fire of war would also serve to convince even strident rebels to repent. Those few ardent secessionists, Union planners believed, would lose faith in their revolution as their new government proved inadequate to see to the safety and welfare of its citizens. The early success of Federal arms would see to it.

Other northerners, though, believed that militarized politics served as only a partial solution to the national crisis. Abolitionists and like-minded reformers believed that the roots of southern evil lay in their dependence on slavery and what many suspected was a decadent lifestyle. Secession, whether legitimate or not, was only a symptom of a diseased member of the body politic that needed the drastic inter-vention of a national physician armed with bayonet and sword rather than lancet and scalpel. These upright social engineers sought to un-pin the very foundations of the South and reorganize the civic fabric of the rebellious states, thus making future secession or constitutional crises unlikely. Abolitionist William Lloyd Garrison predicted that "the death grapple with the southern slave oligarchy" would eventually destroy slavery itself and overthrow the existing order of southern so-ciety. "Stand still, and see the salvation of God," he quoted.[24]

Without the sin of slavery, these northerners argued, the South could remake itself along more conventional national lines. There would emerge a national homogeneity that would celebrate the same-ness of the American people and their institutions, and eradicate points of difference and contention. In essence, the South would be healed of its terrible maladies only when it came to mirror the North. "I do not doubt that the ordeal the country's now passing through will tend to give us the nationality we seek," wrote Union General Thomas Williams to his family, "and restore . . . the virtue, public and private, and the love of country for which our sires of the first revolution were so distinguished. The chastisements and chastenings of eternal wis-dom and mercy can never fail of their purpose."[25]

Even the most optimistic of the Yankee pulpit and print philoso-phers knew that this magnificent transformation of the South would not take place without its share of scuffles. Southerners who would not embrace bayonet enlightenment would face the wrath of a venge-ful North. Those who persisted in rebellion would suffer political dis-enfranchisement and seizure of property. They would be hunted as criminals. Treason would not go unpunished. Naturally those with wealth and power would be the greatest resisters, this reasoning declared, and the destruction of this obstructive and obstinate block of tyrants would allow liberty and freedom to blossom in a re-imagined South. Perhaps the importation of wholesome Yankees would help. Some viewed a prostrated Dixie as the United States' next territorial conquest. "The South," former New York Senator Hamilton Fish told friends, "would be splendid colonies to the North."[26]

Lofty reform rhetoric did not translate easily into hard military strategy. Men in charge of enforcing these idealistic views using soldiers, cannons, and horses, endorsed a firm yet less apocalyptic approach. Lieutenant General Winfield Scott, commander of the army of the United States, ordered a blockade of southern ports and stressed the importance of seizing the Mississippi River. "The object being to clear out and keep open this great line of communication . . . so as to envelope the insurgent states," he wrote, "and bring them to terms with less bloodshed than by any other plan." The key to success in the national effort was the capture of the South's greatest city. "It will be necessary," Scott urged, "that New Orleans should be strongly occupied and securely held until the present difficulties are composed."[27]

Scott believed that the hardheaded southerners were more determined in their course than many in the North credited. Any large invasion would be strongly resisted and would probably only exacerbate sectional issues. Southerners who might otherwise quietly sit the fence on these great national issues would be forced to choose a side, and they would naturally follow the lead of men of influence, their friends, family, or the side with the largest battalions. Only a steady, coercive, yet subtle approach would work to blunt the fury of secessionists. Like an anaconda strangling its prey within the steady constrictions of its coils, the power of the United States should be used to wear down the rebellious South and win through exhaustion, not conquest. Scott argued that rash and reckless action could prove disastrous. "The greatest obstacle in the way of this plan—the great danger now pressing upon us," he continued, was "the impatience of our patriotic and loyal Union friends. They will urge instant and vigorous action, regardless, I fear, of consequences." Any invasions of the interior would result in massive casualties. These deaths need not occur, he argued, because southerners will abandon secession when it became economically and commercially untenable. Their passions would cool with time, Scott argued, and eventually Unionists could reassert themselves in local elections.[28]

The old general, as events revealed, could not turn the tides of war. As southerners became more bellicose, and northerners more self-righteous, Scott's conservative approach—while remaining a central tenet to the Union plan—was transformed into a more comprehensive and aggressive strategy. Federal planners wanted more rattlesnake and less anaconda, and hoped to see Confederate armies crushed on the battlefield and its capital captured. They wanted to deliver a lesson. They wanted blood.[29]

Even Lincoln expanded on Scott's strategy. The president believed that his general was perhaps too cautious and that the upstart Confederacy could simply not resist constant simultaneous advances by Federal armies. The North should attack "with superior forces at different points at the same time," he wrote to one of his commanders, "so that we can safely attack one, or both, if he makes no change; and if he weakens one to strengthen the other, forebear to attack the strengthened one, but seize and hold the weakened one, gaining so much." The so-called Confederacy, once punctured, would collapse and, balloon-like, emit its stale air with a harmless hiss.[30]

Meanwhile, Southerners believed that a good sock to the northern nose would cause the bully to end its badgering so that reason could be restored. Confederate war planners, faced with sizable territory to defend, sought to demonstrate their resolve. The Confederate coast would need to be defended, the Mississippi River held inviolate, and invasion repelled to keep southern institutions unspoiled. Most importantly, though, Confederate armies must dramatically and decisively defeat the Federals on the battlefield and make the butcher's bill too high to be supported by the northern public.

These Confederates, echoing their enemy General Scott, counted on a war of exhaustion. Southern society had to outlast the patience of their northern antagonists. While Confederate troops killed Union troops on the battlefield, southern political institutions would have time to assert their legitimacy and authority. They had to convince the

A Harper's Weekly *image depicting a naval reconnaissance of Confederate Forts Jackson and St. Philip, with the chained hulks crossing the river. Notice that they are shown (inaccurately) to be turned broadside to the current.*

people of the South that their new government would ensure the protection of their property and wellbeing. In order for the Confederacy to gain its independence, its government had to prove its legitimacy.

For Louisiana, this required—above all else—a successful defense of New Orleans. With the majority of Louisiana's troops in training for service elsewhere, Governor Moore doubted that the government at Richmond was paying enough attention to needs on the Gulf Coast. New Orleans's leaders continued making arrangements for local defense within their limited power, but they expressed uneasiness at the state's lack of preparation. "Louisiana was still lying apparently dormant," an official report concluded. It would soon be nudged awake. On May 26, 1861, the first rumblings of the Crescent City's future arrived in the form of the USS *Brooklyn,* enforcing the blockade of the mouth of the Mississippi River and releasing Scott's anaconda. A Confederate commander, seventy-five-year-old General David Twiggs, arrived in New Orleans five days later to energize a defense for an attack that most realized must now surely come. The elderly veteran of the Mexican War, while still serving the United States, had become notorious with his superiors for authorizing the surrender of Federal property in Texas during the secession spasms of the previous February. Now the old warrior, wearing the uniform of a Confederate, did his best to organize the defenses of New Orleans.[31]

Citizens of the Pelican State grew uneasy at the prospects of their homes and farms becoming a theater of war. New Orleanian Claude LeGrand had gone to Texas to make his fortune in the late 1850s but had returned home to enlist in the 7th Louisiana Infantry when the call

went out. He now served in Virginia and faced the real prospects of imminent combat. He also urged his sisters in New Orleans to move to a
safer location. "God grant the rascals will not molest you, if you are still
in the city," he wrote. "I wish to God you had gone to Texas in time. Do
go to Texas as soon as you can." He signed his letter, "Your very uneasy
brother, Claude."[32]

The first summer of war passed with the Confederate authorities
paying little attention to the potential threat against Louisiana, especially with the echoes of battle resounding across Virginia from the
banks of Bull Run. Within this vacuum of national leadership, officials
in the Pelican State charted their own courses. Governor Moore dallied
on issues of New Orleans fortifications, siding with landowners who did
not want their fields and homes desecrated by redoubts and trenches,
insisting instead on clarification from Richmond as to private property
rights in such cases and receiving silence in return. Meanwhile, entre-
preneurs in the Crescent City outfitted privateers, blockade runners,
and even an ersatz ironclad for personal gain, but heavy guns for the
defense at Forts Jackson and St. Philip remained a rare commodity—as
did gunpowder. A small government-funded gunboat fleet sprang to
life but remained without enough cannons to make it formidable.

The Confederacy eventually turned its attention to New Orleans
that fall as military campaigning in Virginia subsided. General Twiggs,
feeling his years, resigned his command, and Major General Mans-
field Lovell arrived to take his place. This new officer watched as work-
men laid out two large ironclads, CSS *Louisiana* and CSS *Mississippi,*
for service on the Gulf Coast. These leviathans would surely ward off
anything the Federals might bring against them, but this promise
would only be realized, Lovell knew, once they were armed and afloat.
Instead, both seemed plagued by shortages of materials, armaments,
and bureaucratic clarity. Like the Confederacy they were to defend,
the broad scope and great promises made by the boats' designers relied on dwindling resources and disorganized lines of supply.

Nor had the Federals forgotten New Orleans. An early October 1861
dustup between the Confederate river defense fleet and increasingly
bold Union blockaders at the head of passes downstream revealed to
most observers that Louisiana's ordeal fast approached. Even though

A Harper's Weekly *image depicting the gathering of Admiral David Glasgow Farragut's fleet at the mouth of the Mississippi River in 1862. The Confederates hoped they could resist this naval juggernaut.*

the Confederates succeeded in driving the Federals out to sea, the blockade remained in force. A month later, a sizable fleet of northern war steamers under Commodore David Glasgow Farragut and nearly ten thousand soldiers under Major General Benjamin Butler gathered at Ship Island off the coast of Mississippi. A second armada, including several sizable ironclads, assembled in faraway St. Louis. Meanwhile, rumors circulated about a flotilla of mortar schooners under construction in New York. "The scales of success will most apt to incline to the side which has the steam or iron sides," wrote Union Brigadier General Thomas Williams from aboard the transport *Great Republic.* "I allude to combined land and water expeditions. That side will be the side which has the most money. Money is called the sinews of war," he added. "I suppose the enterprise and skill and daring which put the sinews in motion may be called Mars' nervous system."[33]

New Orleans, already feeling the pinch of the blockade, would soon feel the blast of battle as 1861 drew to a close. With luck, Forts Jackson and St. Philip would hold back the Union fleet, and Confederate forces could stave off a land attack, but the hoped-for ironclads remained unfinished well into the New Year. As news of Confederate military disasters began arriving with increased regularity in 1862, serious doubts lingered as to Louisiana's ability to resist invasion. The editors of the *New Orleans Daily Crescent*, a local newspaper, asked the question on most citizens' minds. "The Yankees are coming in great force . . . are we prepared?"[34]

CHAPTER TWO

THE YANKEES ARE COMING

They brought a cannon, but said it would be unnecessary
as they could have taken the town with brickbats.
Elisa Bragg, Thibodaux, Louisiana, 1862

They were not.

A little more than a year after secession, in April 1862, Confederate New Orleans lay dying. Billowing smoke rolled off of the Crescent City's levee and across the dark waters of the Mississippi as tons of cotton, baled and stacked, smoldered at the riverfront. The smell and the smoke hung heavy in the humid air. Near the river alarmed citizens filled the boulevards as crews of workers—black and white—loaded wagons and any available conveyance with the luxuries of life and the tools of war. A reminder of their dashed hopes passed by, almost noiselessly, amid the bedlam: the hulk of the unfinished ironclad CSS *Mississippi*, abandoned and ablaze, drifted with the current. Once hailed as the sure defender of New Orleans, the ship served now as a mocking reminder of the boasts made by the Rebels of the Confederacy's largest and richest city.

Prominent citizen George Washington Cable, a southern soldier at the time, recalled the heartbreaking scene. "The alarm-bells told us the city was in danger and called every man to his mustering-point," he wrote. "The children poured out from the school-gates and ran crying to their homes, meeting their sobbing mothers at their thresholds." The entire town felt the doom upon it, as the soldier explained, "you have seen, perhaps, a family fleeing with lamentations and wringing of hands out of a burning house: multiply it by thousands upon thousands; that was New Orleans, though the houses were not burning."[1]

Amid the melee of evacuation and destruction, lookouts announced the arrival of dreaded visitors. Downriver, coming around the bend, steamed Commodore David Farragut's black ships. "I will never forget the long, dreadful night," Julia LeGrand wrote in her diary, "when we all sat with our friends and watched the flames from all sorts of valuables as the gunboats were coming up the river." In close order the tall Federal ships glided past the perishing *Mississippi* and took their stations near the shore. High water in the river increased their stature until the decks of the vessels towered over the streets, and bluejacketed crews waited by their guns to open fire against the city's Rebels, if needed. A rattle of chains marked the dropping of the navy's anchors as the ships reversed their engines and churned to a halt while, as though weeping in sympathy with the South, the leaden clouds released a downpour.[2]

One of the vessels slowly lowered a boat until it smacked the river's surface. The black oaken craft cast away from its host as the crew unfolded its eight oars and pulled hard for shore, a white truce flag hanging limp from the stern in the saturated Louisiana air. On April 25, 1862, New Orleans, Queen City of the South, had most decidedly fallen.

As the Union boat unloaded its passengers, a Confederate observer was astonished at the personal courage of the Union invaders. "Two officers of the United States Navy were walking, abreast, unguarded and alone, looking not to right or left, never frowning, never flinching, while the mob screamed in their ears, shook cocked pistols in their faces, cursed and crowded, and gnashed upon them," Cable wrote. "Through the gates of death those two men walked to the City Hall to demand the town's surrender. It was one of the bravest deeds I ever saw done."[3]

A sketch by Union Dr. Daniel T. Nestell of the arrival of the U.S.S. Hartford *at New Orleans. Notice the burning wrecks of Confederate ships in the river, and the water level nearly even with the levee. The artist served aboard the U.S.S.* Clifton. *Courtesy of the Nestell Collection, Nimitz Library, U.S. Naval Academy, Annapolis, Maryland.*

The U.S. Navy had arrived to tamp out secessionist sparks just a year after the fall of Fort Sumter. During those first four seasons of war overreliance on forts had caused the Confederates' undoing on a number of fronts, and now the two brick citadels—Forts Jackson and St. Philip eighty miles downriver from New Orleans—had also failed. The Union fleet simply sprinted past, guns blazing. The Confederate river flotilla, too, had failed, as had the bizarre looking war-turtle, the ironclad CSS *Manassas*. The Federal capture of New Orleans, unthinkable just months before, struck a blow against the independence of the Confederacy.

Along Bayou Lafourche, away from the pandemonium of New Orleans, wealthy plantation owners—the so-called "Sugar Nabobs" much maligned by competing northerners—braced for the aftershocks of this shift in secessionist fortunes. Clarissa Grant Hewitt, wife, plantation mistress, and cousin to Union general Ulysses S. Grant, found herself awakened from a sound sleep by her son Richard. "He had ridden for twenty-four hours, only stopping to change horses; as he brought us the fatal and dread tidings that New Orleans was in the possession of the enemy." The other members of the household gathered in the kitchen. "We were a sad little group that gathered around the breakfast table, each one trying to cheer the other with the hope that our fate may not in reality be as dreadful as we anticipated."[4]

Union sailors aboard a ship's boat. Courtesy of Andrew D. Lytle Collection, Mss. 893, 1254. Louisiana and Lower Mississippi Valley Collections, LSU Libraries, Louisiana State University, Baton Rouge, Louisiana.

The tidings seemed out of step with the lovely April day. The Hewitts' Crescent Plantation sat just three miles down Bayou Lafourche from its junction with the Mississippi River at the town of Donaldsonville. The grounds were resplendent with the blooms of the season. "This beautiful spring morning, the season of the year when the dear old place is at its best with a great abundance of roses of many varieties . . . make a lovely scene, such as one is loath to leave," Clarissa recorded in her diary. Flowering vines twined around railings and pillars, bringing splashes of bright color among the dark tropical foliage. Hearing the news of New Orleans's surrender made her own surroundings seem all the more precious to her: "Never did the old typical Southern home, in its simplicity and comfort, seem so attractive, with the large rooms, high ceilings, and all that tends to make a home beautiful and comfortable, filled with interesting souvenirs of the many places that we have visited in our extensive travels." Clarissa and her husband, James, counted 176 slaves among their estate, as well as a second plantation near Louisville, Kentucky, and a town home in New York. The wealthy belle sensed that the coming of Federal troops would mean the end of her world. "The most insignificant article seems to have a special value, and as I look upon it all, I feel

A postwar depiction of the brave march of Federal naval officers through the streets of New Orleans. Battles and Leaders.

instinctively that I shall never see it again. It was impossible not to feel the foreshadowing of the evil days that must inevitably come to us with the fall of New Orleans."[5]

Wealthy southerners were correct to worry. The capture of New Orleans ushered in a host of new problems for their fledgling nation and a new order that would destroy the old establishment. Some of the richest plantations on earth lay in this region, along the "Coast," as locals called the stretch of Mississippi River between New Orleans and Baton Rouge, and also along bayous Lafourche and Teche. That year, 1862, promised to surpass even the bumper sugarcane crop of the year before. Millions of dollars' worth of productive agricultural commodities, ranging from sugar and cotton to livestock and corn, now awaited the fortunes of war.[6]

Besides the obvious financial, psychological, and political impact the capture of the city had on the Confederacy, the arrival of Union troops on the lower Mississippi also opened a new military front: Federal sailors and soldiers had reshaped the southern nation. For Louisianans, the capture of New Orleans held immediate implications. The enemy now walked among them, and each new day seemed to bring additional disasters, like aftershocks from a tremor.

On the night of April 27, sixty miles downstream from New Orleans, most of the Confederate soldiers garrisoned at Fort Jackson rebelled against their own officers, overpowering those who stood in their way. After having been bypassed by Farragut's dash upriver and abandoned to suffer a grinding siege at the hands of General Benjamin Butler's small Union army, these desperate Rebels bowed to the verdict of war just two days after the surrender of the city they were charged with defending.

The mutineers communicated the uprising to their comrades across the river at Fort St. Philip, while others drove files and spikes into the touchholes of their once-feared cannons to render them temporarily inoperable. The conspirators, many of whom were foreigners pressed into Confederate service, had already endured several nights of continual bombardment and, with the news of New Orleans's fall, they had simply reached their limit. After damaging the guns, they fled the fort. Only one unit, St. Mary's Cannoneers of Franklin, Louisiana, stood fast. At first light on April 28 Confederate commander Brigadier General Johnson Duncan surrendered his remaining troops, keeping his personal honor intact. Later that day Union soldiers took posses-

New Orleans under the guns of David G. Farragut's fleet. Notice the depiction of Confederate wrecks and burning cotton along the levee. The iconic spires of St. Louis Cathedral appear in the center of this image. From The Soldier in Our Civil War, *vol. I.*

sion of the pitted bastions—not as a result of a brilliant assault, but because their adversaries had simply given up and fled.[7]

For northern war-planners the events of April exceeded even the most optimistic expectations and pointed to an early end for the Confederacy. General George B. McClellan marched onto the peninsula of Virginia and threatened Richmond from the east. Union armies had secured Kentucky, Missouri, and parts of Arkansas. Federal enclaves on the coast of North and South Carolina provided beachheads for military and political operations in those states. The hard-won Union victory at Shiloh, early in the month, finalized the Federal capture of Tennessee. General Don Carlos Buell had pinned the defeated Confederates inside their works at Corinth, Mississippi. General Henry Halleck, the architect of strategy in the western theater, advanced Union forces down the Mississippi River from Missouri and Kentucky.

CONTROL OF THE
MISSISSIPPI RIVER
APRIL 15, 1862

"The Rebels say they're going to try another battle . . . in which, if failing, they intend to give up rebelling," crowed Union General Thomas Williams from just below New Orleans. "So mote it be, that they be again disastrously beaten, and at last into submission to good government, into law, loyalty, and order."[8]

On May 1 cheerful yet vigilant Union soldiers and sailors commanded by Major General Benjamin Butler finally arrived from downriver to capitalize on Farragut's actions of the previous weeks, and they sent ashore a garrison to occupy New Orleans. Infantrymen from six Federal regiments disembarked from their transports and assembled near the waterfront as an angry crowd insulted them.[9] The rumble of wheels and the clatter of hooves on gangplanks marked the arrival of three field batteries and two companies of cavalry—useful for crowd control in case the mood turned worse.[10] These sturdy Midwesterners and New Englanders nervously fingered hundreds of triggers as they formed lines along the docks, eyeing the jeering mob through which they must pass.

Occasional shouts of "Hurrah for Jeff Davis" and "Hurrah for Beauregard" seemed pitiful in light of the circumstances. After a short wait, the order for movement came. As musicians played "Yankee Doodle," the regimental columns marched down the boulevards toward the tangible symbols of authority in the conquered city—the Customs House, the Mint, Lafayette Square, and city hall. General Benjamin Butler, the cagey master of the army compo-

David G. Farragut, commander of the West Gulf Blockading Squadron. His daring and skill in capturing New Orleans led to his promotion to admiral. Library of Congress.

nent of Farragut's offensive, ordered his troops to remove old flags from the city's public places in an effort to erase the memory of the yearlong Confederate tenure'. Corporal Rufus Kinsey of the 8th Vermont could not believe how easily the city had fallen. "When the events of today shall have become History," he scribbled in his diary, "posterity will be amazed that the Crescent City, Queen of the South and mistress of the Gulf . . . should surrender to the despised Yankees, without striking a blow."[11]

The small Union army moved quickly to exploit its victory. Across the Mississippi, the 21st Indiana shouldered their Merrill rifles and moved through the streets of Algiers with less fanfare and commotion, hurrying toward the New Orleans and Opelousas Railroad yards. They would seize the facility and use it as a tool for subduing the bayou hinterland.[12]

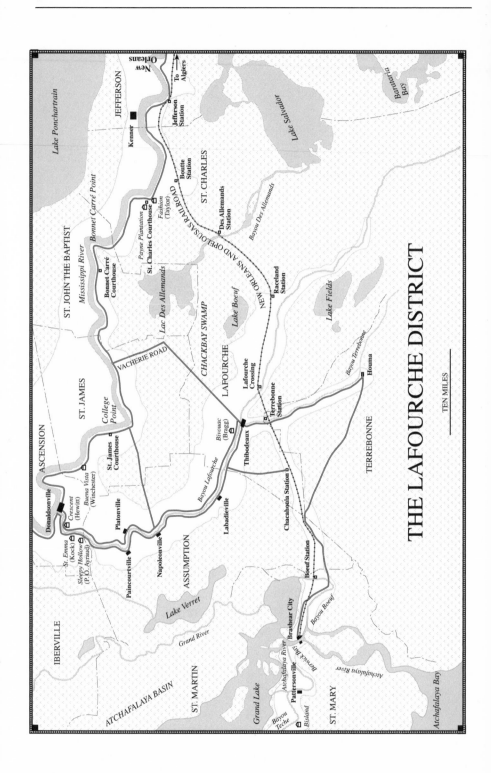

THE LAFOURCHE DISTRICT

TEN MILES

In the city Butler quickly revealed his attitude toward the defeated enemy. Shortly after arriving he issued a proclamation outlining his administration's policies and ordered the *New Orleans True Delta* to publish the piece. When the newspaper's editors refused, Butler replaced them with one of his soldiers, Captain John Clark, a former editor of the *Boston Courier*. Butler now had a Unionist newspaper—and a convenient mouthpiece.

On May 2 the general sent for Mayor John Monroe to explain the new regime. The politician responded by requesting special consideration, claiming that the river metropolis should enjoy a status more favorable than that of a "captured city." Butler agreed that New Orleans had not been captured by assault or siege but insisted that the municipality was, semantics notwithstanding, a conquered city. "Else how did we get here, and why are we here?" the general asked. "Did you open your arms and bid us welcome? Would you not expel us if you could?" Butler then informed the mayor that he was no longer in charge, and that martial law would be enforced. "I warn you that if a shot is fired from any house, it will never again shelter a mortal head," Butler growled. "If I can discover the perpetrator of the deed, the place that knows him now shall know him no more forever."[13]

Residents of the surrounding area also experienced the Union occupation firsthand. Helen Dupuy, a French-speaking teenager at the Sleepy Hollow Plantation on Bayou Lafourche, noted with horror the arrival of Federal troops. "The first Yankee gunboats passed Donaldsonville May 4 at 11 a. m.," she wrote in her diary. Living just a few miles from Donaldsonville, she heard that Union sailors were confiscating sugar, cotton, and other spoils of war in town: "Then began the most awful pillaging."[14]

The New Orleans and Opelousas Railroad took the first land invaders into the region's western interior. Lieutenant James B. Kinsman of Butler's staff arrived seventy miles away at Thibodaux shortly after the fall of New Orleans to announce the arrival of Federal authority and to demand good treatment for local Unionists. A few days later, on May 5, the 21st Indiana loaded onto a train and traveled this iron route from New Orleans and captured the 12 locomotives, 12 passenger cars, 5 baggage cars, 2 express cars, and 209 freight cars at Brashear City on

The inland port of Brashear City, Louisiana, had connections via the Atchafalaya River to the Mississippi as well as through Berwick Bay to the Gulf of Mexico. Its strategic position made it key to strategic planning by both sides during the Civil War. From Harper's Weekly.

Berwick Bay. In the following days this fast-moving regiment continued its reconnaissance-in-force by rail and on foot, dispersed budding militia units gathering haphazardly, and tramped from south to north along Bayou Lafourche, gathering spoils from the fat, unguarded plantations. Their reports delighted Union commanders.[15]

Elisa Bragg, the wife of one of the Confederacy's rising commanders, General Braxton Bragg, watched as the Hoosiers passed her farm near Thibodaux. "A detachment came [to town] searching for arms and ammunition," she wrote her warrior husband. "They brought a cannon, but said it would be unnecessary as they could have taken the town with brickbats." After obtaining keys to the public buildings, the U.S. troops conducted a search but found nothing of importance. "They say they will return in a little while to seize cattle," wrote Elisa. She went on to describe a more immediate concern: "We can get nothing from [New Orleans], and no place is provided with provisions. The households have no supplies." For civilians in the newly occupied region, a host of troubles loomed, including the possibilities of privation and hunger.[16]

Crescent Plantation house near Donaldsonville, the home of James and Clarissa Hewitt. They abandoned their house and farm and lived as refugees for the duration of the war. From Frances Fern, ed., Diary of a Refugee.

Alarm spread along the banks of Bayou Lafourche, in advance of the Federal troops, driving the inhabitants into a frenzy like rabbits before a brush fire. "My son's news of the fall of New Orleans was confirmed . . . by a man on horseback, riding rapidly down the Bayou road, calling out as he went by, 'The Yankees are coming!'" wrote Clarissa Hewitt of Crescent Plantation. At the landing that fronted the Creole-style mansion, the steamers *Lafourche* and *Mary T* lay waiting, their fires up, ready to carry the family and about half of the farm's sugar crop to safety. "It was a sad little group that left the dear old home. We were so overcome with sorrow and terror as to our future fate that we gave no thought of what we were taking with us. The Negroes were far more thoughtful for us; one picked up my husband's favorite sofa, another his chair, one even went so far as to sweep the silver on the breakfast table into a handy clothes-basket and carry it on board."[17]

For most of the slaves in the region, the events of April must have been bewildering. Some, like members of the Hewitt's domestic staff, went into exile with their masters and mistresses. Others—field hands mostly—tried to make sense of their changed circumstances amid much uncertainty. Were they to continue laboring, and if so, who would give the orders? How would they eat? Who would see to their needs? What would the arrival of Federal troops mean for them? Was freedom at hand? If so, what would that mean? Great crowds of slaves milled around at plantations in the region, trying to make sense of these events amid an atmosphere of panic and confusion.

For one Louisianan, the emergency of the moment made his duty abundantly clear. Richard Hewitt refused to join his parents' exodus and instead headed back to his regiment. "My heart was torn at the separation from my son . . . who had returned to join his company,"

Clarisse Hewitt wrote. He was a lieutenant in William R. Miles' Louisiana Legion, forming north of Lake Pontchartrain. "We Southern women need all our strength and courage to give up our sons and loved ones, our homes are taken from us, and we must become refugees!" Her youngest son, Louis, served in the 7th Louisiana Infantry, and her oldest boy, James Hewitt Jr., in the 2nd Kentucky Infantry.[18]

The Hewitts were not alone in their desire to escape Union occupation. "When we entered the Mississippi River, it had become a seething mass of craft of all kinds and description . . . to carry away the terror-stricken people who were flying from their homes with their loved ones and treasures," Clarissa recalled. "[They were] all making a mad rush for the mouth of Red River."[19]

Not every Confederate vessel received timely word of New Orleans's surrender. On May 7 the blockade runner *Fox* arrived at Bayou Grand Caillou completing the fourth of its round trips importing supplies from Cuba bound for the South. This time the ship's hold carried an astonishing 350,000 pounds of powder, 4,500 rifles, and a wide variety of medicines and military stores as well as Confederate diplomatic correspondence. The *Fox,* however, found no one ready to receive its weapons and supplies. The fast-moving 21st Indiana took a train to Terrebonne Station then led it overland to cut off the vessel before its skipper could figure out what was going on in Louisiana. Within a week this rich prize fell into the hands of the Union army, succeeding where the navy had not.[20]

Amid all of these maneuvers, only sporadic, symbolic, and ineffective resistance had been mounted against the Union invasion. In Houma Rebel partisans ambushed four invalids from the 21st Indiana returning unescorted to the hospital in New Orleans, killing two on May 16. Their Hoosier comrades marched to the town within hours to exact justice o. When Houma's inhabitants refused to produce those responsible, Indiana privates applied torches to the suspected bushwhackers' houses—and those of the town's leaders—and destroyed their property. The columns of smoke over Houma that day proved that the Federals would project their power into the region at will.[21]

The 21st Indiana became a forceful deterrent in the region against any hopes of a secessionist resurgence. Colonel James W. McMillan

An example of a prosperous and extensive Louisiana sugar operation, as portrayed in Harper's Weekly. *Such agricultural wealth made this region quite a prize to Union planners.*

placed troops along the railroad at key bridges and junctions, including the Lafourche crossing near Thibodaux, Raceland, and the crossing of Bayou des Allemands. Even though his four hundred troops were scattered along sixty miles of track, the Hoosier officer believed he could hold that line using captured locomotives and cars to rush reserves to any threatened point.[22]

For Union observers, the next move appeared obvious. "After . . . New Orleans we shall probably endeavor to get up beyond Baton Rouge, or as far as the point of the Red River's entrance into the Mississippi," observed General Williams. A careful glance at the map revealed a huge Union army under General Don Carlos Buell poised to capture Corinth, Mississippi, and then to push inland from the north as Butler consolidated his gains from the south. The end of the war might very well be at hand, Williams believed. "The purpose of [our movement] is to cut off supplies," he continued, "and make a demonstration in favor of General Buell."[23]

Across the South the implications of a Union presence in southern Louisiana also shone clearly. "New Orleans is gone and with it the

Confederacy!" Mary Boykin Chesnut of South Carolina wrote in her diary. Even from her far-away perch she could see the dangers of an unopposed Union army operating in the Pelican State and cutting off access to the Gulf of Mexico. "Are we not cut in two? The Mississippi ruins us if it is lost."[24]

CHAPTER THREE

BEHAVIOR THAT WOULD SHAME A COMANCHE

*It seems from the last news that it requires us all to drive
the enemy from out of the heart of our country*
Sergeant Frank Starr, Sibley's Brigade

With New Orleans captured, Federal forces moved swiftly to finish their seizure of the lower Mississippi. David Farragut had wanted Benjamin Butler to garrison the Crescent City while he moved back to sea and struck against Mobile, but Gideon Welles, the Secretary of the Navy, changed his plans. Instead, Farragut's fleet of deep-draft, ocean-going warships would continue bucking the Mississippi's brown current and head upstream. On May 9 Union sailors and marines from the USS *Iroquois* captured Baton Rouge without a shot, taking possession of the U.S. arsenal and barracks and mocking the pageant of secession that had occurred there sixteen months before. Farragut followed with the bulk of his fleet, including transports loaded with fifteen hundred infantrymen needed to hold the town. By May 13 Federal ships had pushed on, scouting northward and capturing Natchez, Mississippi. Arriving at Vicksburg four days later, the Union vanguard demanded the town's surrender, hoping to crown their lightning campaign with a rapid victory before Confederates could fully fortify the strategic heights.

Rebel Columbiads disappointed the Union sailors. Sensing the emergency, all Confederate troops that had evacuated New Orleans, along with those in garrisons at various places in Mississippi, had rushed to occupy Vicksburg and to man a dozen heavy guns overlooking the river. On May 18 Farragut and the rest of his squadron arrived at the city, and he demanded its surrender. The commander of the post, Lieutenant Colonel James L. Autry, replied, "Mississippians do not know, and refuse to learn, how to surrender to an enemy."[1] Foiled after ten days of demonstrations against the Rebel fort, Farragut and most of his fleet retraced their route to Baton Rouge to regroup, impotent and unable to deter Confederate excavations.

This reversal agitated the expedition's Union officers. "Our combined force, though equal to a profitable diversion in behalf of our army at Corinth is unequal to the capture and holding of Vicksburg," General Thomas Williams groused. "Instead of 2,000 men, I ought to have at least 10,000. It's provoking, isn't it?"[2]

At the same time, Farragut sensed that the southerners downstream had recovered from the shock of the invasion. Rebel bullets drove home the point. On May 28, as Union troops returned to Baton Rouge from the frustration at Vicksburg, Confederate partisans fired at a boat party coming ashore. Incensed, Farragut ordered the big guns of USS *Hartford* and USS *Kennebec* to shell the town. The panicked residents of the surrendered city fled the maelstrom, which killed a woman and caused two other citizens to fall into the river and drown. Farragut would not tolerate such behavior.[3]

To be so close to achieving a major war aim frustrated the Federals. After a month of stirring action and unfettered success, the crews of Farragut's fleet paused to catch their breath. Hindered in their attempt to complete the capture of the Mississippi, the Federal navy had to content itself with simply a profound penetration into Rebel territory and the capture of Louisiana's capital. When the ironclads and rams of

A Harper's Weekly *image showing U.S. warships on station at Baton Rouge. The crenellated state capitol occupies the hill beyond.*

Captain Charles Henry Davis's Mississippi Flotilla worked their way down from the north, fresh from their own successful capture of Memphis, Tennessee, on June 6, Farragut decided to try again. He called for Commander David Dixon Porter's mortar flotilla to add their weight to the bombardment, and the slow cumbersome bomb ketches made their way upstream, towed by an escorting collection of gunboats including the USS *Clifton, Westfield,* and *Harriet Lane.*

Marine private Henry O. Gusley of Lancaster, Pennsylvania, served aboard *Westfield,* a converted New York ferryboat, and marveled at the country he was seeing on his journey up the Mississippi. He found the river towns charming. "The majority of them . . . are beautifully situated on bends of the river," he scribbled in his diary. "There is a picturesqueness about them that leads a passer by to suppose that they are pleasant places to live in, and the trees which line the streets add much to their beauty and unquestionably to their comfort." Between towns, though, he could not believe the splendor of the river plantations. "From New Orleans to Baton Rouge they seem like one continued city," the leatherneck continued, "the thriving lands and beautiful levees mark it as one of the more desirable places for one to lead a happy life."[4]

This trip also provided the marine with his first glimpse of slavery. What Gusley saw surprised him. "The much talked of hardships of the Southern slave have been to us proven a chimera by this trip up the great Mississippi through the hot bed of slavery," he wrote, rather un-

CONTROL OF THE
**MISSISSIPPI RIVER
MAY 15, 1862**

sympathetically. The twenty-four-year-old Pennsylvanian was in-clined to see life aboard the *Westfield* as being a great deal harder than life on the Louisiana plantations. While the sailors and marines kept to a steady routine of duties and followed strict rules of conduct, the field hands ashore spent hours gawking at the Yankee ships, leaning on their implements. At the end of the day, while Gusley pulled guard duty, he watched enviously as the slaves lounged near their cabins. "We have noticed them at evening sporting around their neat cabins, their rude singing proclaiming them happy," he noted. "Their condi-tion as compared with the free Negro of the North is a Paradise."[5]

In contrast, and as though to confirm their belief that they were close to ending the war, U.S. sailors and troops also saw evidence of panic and chaos among the slave-owning planter class. All along the Mississippi levee, smoldering and blazing cotton bales lay in disarray at every town and landing. Near Donaldsonville, hogsheads of sugar bobbed in the river, their saccharine contents ruined. Signs of devastation lined the invasion route as Louisiana and Mississippi planters had destroyed their crops—some out of patriotism, others by fear of the law—to keep them out of enemy hands. Millions of dollars of wealth and dreams vanished because of desperate acts by a seemingly defeated people. "These secession people must see that their principles lead to nothing but loss and ruin," expounded Williams in a letter to his family, "and yet, they appear to be

David Dixon Porter commanded the mortar fleet in the initial campaign for the lower Mississippi while his stepbrother, Farragut, oversaw the overall operation. Naval Historical Center.

as enamored of Secession, as if she promised them every good. Strange madness! Calamity, I fear, is the only thing that can restore them to their senses."[6]

In Louisiana the urgency and alarm showed how unprepared the Pelican State had been for a Union invasion. Self-assured Confederate planners, believing no harm could come to this Rebel heartland, had divided the state three ways militarily, with the Florida Parishes east of Baton Rouge administered from Jackson, Mississippi; the sugar parishes and Acadiana, north to Alexandria, served from Houston; and the northern parishes aligned with the army headquarters in Little Rock, Arkansas. This arrangement placed all of Louisiana west of the

The Union mortar boats added necessary weight to the bombardment of Vicksburg but still couldn't force the citadel to yield. Battles and Leaders.

Mississippi at the fringes of military districts. Far from the centers of command, men and matériel had been siphoned away to face the enemy on distant fronts until literally none remained beside an unmotivated, somewhat timid militia. The citizens of Louisiana, thus unprotected, lay at the mercy of the Union invaders once they took Forts Jackson and St. Phillip.

This lack of defense forced planters in the western parishes to face difficult choices. As long-time Whigs, many of the sugar growers along Bayou Lafourche saw the arrival of the Yankees as a event that fell short of the disaster bewailed by their pro-Confederate neighbors. Shrewd businessmen among them sought immediate contact with U.S. troops to safeguard their plantations and to guarantee a market for their crops. Instead of burning their cotton and dissolving their sugar like some Louisianans, they cached it away to await events and to appreciate in value. Others, however, trusted neither the Union invaders nor their neighbors and, like those at Crescent Plantation, abandoned their homes and estates to become refugees. Even so, ardent secessionists, defiant in the face of a turbulent situation, clung confidently to their property, secretly hopeful that some Confederate would come to their rescue.

In New Orleans Butler, the droopy-eyed architect of occupation, revealed his genius as a pragmatic administrator. "[Butler] is a remarkable-looking man," wrote one observer. "Stout in person, nervous and

A PLANTER'S HOUSE AND SUGAR PLANTATION, ON THE MISSISSIPPI RIVER.

The wealth and scope of the Mississippi River plantations astounded many of the Northern soldiers, sailors, and marines trying to end the rebellion in Louisiana. Harper's Weekly.

peculiar in manners, he has a large head and a striking profile not wanting in dignity and greatness. His manner is affable and his conversation bright and agreeable." He was also one of President Lincoln's most notorious political appointees. Hardly an ideologue, Butler was a master politician who arrived at creative solutions to advance political agendas and humble his opponents. He fancied himself a soldier, but the Massachusetts general's war record proved otherwise. Butler possessed an uncanny aptitude as a military governor, however, and he had arrived in New Orleans ready to work.[7] Butler believed military necessity required that a firm hand be applied to the entire region, and he moved to control as much of Louisiana as he could, as rapidly as possible, to exploit the region's momentary defenselessness.

Butler also had a great talent for personal financial advancement and harbored a sincere love of profit. With the aid of his brother, Andrew, the general initiated a scheme for a quasi-legal plundering of their conquered domain. Within weeks, the two were speculating heavily in rum, sugar, salt, cotton, and even Texas beef cattle, employing soldiers and sailors to carry contraband of war to New Orleans for auction. Loyal planters, who affiliated themselves with the Butler

Major General Benjamin Butler became the great architect of Union policy toward conquered Louisiana. His defeated enemies dubbed him "Beast Butler," but his iron rule kept New Orleans under Federal control. Library of Congress.

brothers through the judicious use of bribes and kickbacks, sent their goods to the city and into Union lines without fear.[8]

"'Set a thief to catch a thief,' is an old adage," one Butler critic noted, "and so it may be said 'employ the devil to punish the devil.'" The Union general was determined to make New Orleans come to heel. "He was not embarrassed by any sensitive feelings," the observer continued. He also acknowledged that Butler was not known for his martial prowess. It did not matter, however: "If he had no skill or strategy in military matters he certainly possessed both, to a high degree, in political and criminal matters; and if he could not organize or command an army of soldiers, few could equal him in organizing an army of spies and detectives."[9]

Butler used intimidation and a force of clandestine agents to intimidate the city's residents. William B. Mumford, a denizen of New Orleans gambling dens, had desecrated an American flag shortly after the Yankees had arrived. Butler ordered him hanged in front of the flagpole from which he had ripped the flag. After a local merchant made light of Union casualties in Virginia battles, spies reported the incident, and Butler commanded the businessman's incarceration in a military prison on Ship Island. When a woman snickered at the passing funeral cortege of a Union officer dead from disease, authorities ordered her to Ship Island as well. Local clergy were not immune from Federal retribution; officers trundled several Episcopal clerics out of town after they violated Butler's General Order No. 33, requiring them to modify their liturgy and pray for the president of the United States. Another shopkeeper refused to trade with Federal troops. Soldiers seized his store and sold his entire inventory at auction.[10]

Many women of New Orleans defied the Yankee occupation, and their rude remarks and disrespectful gestures brought Butler's wrath. When inhabitants of an upper-story residence emptied a chamber pot on Farragut as he passed below their window, Butler decided it was time to act. He issued General Order No. 28, a directive that, in short, branded all rude or unescorted women as whores. This affronted southern pride across the Rebel nation. "We hardly expected from Massachusetts," Mary Boykin Chesnut of South Carolina noted in her diary, "behavior that would shame a Comanche."[11]

Citizens who appeared before Butler for an audience were conscious of his contempt. "He lay back in his chair and retorted with a provoking smile or ironical politeness," one resident observed, "which acted strongly upon the temper of his opponent."[12]

Butler did not limit his sarcasm and affronts to women and overt secessionists. He also enraged the sizable foreign population of New Orleans. Consuls complained bitterly to Secretary of State William Seward of Butler's suspension of civil liberties and other diplomatic affronts, leading to a government investigation. Aggravating this issue was Butler's genius for destroying the old order of New Orleans by hitting the financial system. He effectively devalued all Confederate currency, including deposits in New Orleans banks, and then levied a contribution upon individuals and businesses equal to the amount they had pledged to support the Confederacy. Those who did not comply—including foreign subjects—saw their property seized and sold at public auction.[13]

The general's genius for causing his opponents discomfort was unexcelled. He used the more than $1.2 million raised through these means to support the poor and needy, and he employed thousands as government employees. If proper though spiteful ladies hated Butler, the poor did not. He now had a loyal constituency. Even so, he issued the following warning lest they forget their benefactor: "The hand that cuts your bread," he declared, "can cut your throat."[14]

Confederates within the city had few options. Citizens of New Orleans unwilling to take a loyalty oath to the United States would have to identify themselves as "registered enemies." Butler planned to evict them from New Orleans at a future date. Meanwhile, most could not escape the signs that the occupation would be long-lived. "Yankee troops are drilling and parading in our streets," LeGrand moaned. "We have lost our city, the key to this great valley, and my opinion is that we will never, never get it more, except by treaty. About their having the whole river, that is of course only a question of time. Poor New Orleans!" she added, "What has become of your promised greatness!"[15]

With their plans for immediate control of the Mississippi River stymied, Butler and his staff officers unrolled their maps to plan their next conquest, from their headquarters at the Customs House. To observers from Washington, D.C., to Canal Street, Vicksburg's defiance could cause the campaign for the Mississippi to be long and torturous. But once the river was in Union hands, the lands along its banks would have to submit to the overwhelming and unassailable power of the U.S. Navy. A northern-imposed peace could be brought to the region, and it could once again become productive and useful.

The land west of the river especially intrigued, and troubled, Butler and his fellow gazers. Southwest Louisiana fell into a number of easily discerned avenues along the great Atchafalaya Basin. This forty-mile-wide swamp harbored numerous streams and bayous that mingled and twined around the Atchafalaya River, which in turn connected the Red River to the Gulf of Mexico more than one hundred miles away. At its heart was Grand Lake, a sizable but shallow gathering of the waters of the great swamp. Few places in the Atchafalaya Basin's interior lay above the surrounding waters. Alligators abounded. "Louisiana," wrote a Massachusetts soldier, "seems at least one whole geologic age behind the rest of the world."[16]

Even so, not all of Southern Louisiana was a primeval swamp. Corridors of dry land lay between the basin and the Mississippi River to the east and Bayou Teche to the west. An added feature was Bayou Lafourche, which had at one time been the main channel of the Mississippi. It left the Father of Waters at the commercial center of Donaldsonville and proceeded south by southeast to the Gulf of Mexico while the Mississippi made its great bend east toward New Orleans. The lands bordering Bayou Lafourche composed the so-called Lafourche District, an area known for huge mansions, fabulous wealth, and some of the most valuable acres on earth.

The geography of the region revealed obvious strategies for Yankee and Rebel alike. The Federal invaders realized quickly that the Atchafalaya Basin would serve as a natural no man's land, shielding Union ambitions along the Mississippi. Everything east of that point was within reach of the U.S. Navy. West of Bayou Teche, however, lay the Attakapas Prairies, an uninterrupted sea of grass that led toward the supplies and reinforcements of Texas. The keys to the region were certainly the tenuous strips of land that hosted farms, towns, and roads along the major streams. Huge plantations lay side by side for miles, and millions of dollars in agricultural commodities had yearly flowed from that area in happier times. Cattle and horses flourished, as did other forms of wealth, including some 21,500 slaves in the Lafourche District alone.

Prior to 1860 travelers and writers had struggled with hyperbole as they sought to describe the fantastic features of the area. "The stranger," T.B. Thorpe of the *Harper's New Monthly Magazine* observed, "is filled with amazement, and gets an idea of agricultural wealth and profuseness nowhere else to be witnessed in the world."[17]

For middling Americans of the day, these great estates defied description. The large houses sat at the back of level lawns. Sugarhouses stood nearby, conveniently located for cartloads of cane to be bought in from the fields and hogsheads of sugar to be trundled to landings and piers. Slaves and overseers worked the steam-powered machinery to grind, press, and cook the cane. This process extracted the brown liquor that was cooled in long wooden troughs and refined into sugar. These slave laborers lived in an area called "the quarter," usually a single or double row of whitewashed cabins. In addition, other buildings—barns, stables, gristmills, icehouses, churches, dairies, tanneries, smithies, hospitals, jails—dotted the premises as well. Behind the dwellings and workshops lay the great fields of cane, claimed from the swamps by drainage canals and protected by networks of levees. The sugar planters were lords of a self-contained, self-sufficient world. These marvelous estates would soon be battlefields.

This opulence was, of course, built by forced labor. Sugar cultivation was not economically feasible for small planters, and as a result most of the individual cane operations in the Lafourche District and along Bayou Teche involved scores of slaves. Black people, therefore, composed more than half of the population in most of these parishes. This highly valuable commodity—enslaved workers—would prove to be a strategic target in time of war.

Union war planners realized that the human and physical geography of Southwest Louisiana offered an opportunity for Confederates to mount a creative defense. Mobile enemy forces could use the swamps and bayous to harass the invaders and impede, if not prevent, any successful navigation of the Mississippi by Yankee shipping. A small group of Rebels, thus employed, might cause trouble for many times their number.

Even with the peculiarities of the region's geography, there were two obvious keys to its control. Donaldsonville served as the upper gateway to the region. Brashear City, on the banks of an Atchafalaya estuary called Berwick's Bay, served as the lower gate. Both of these positions could be easily reinforced by water. Union gunboats covered Donaldsonville from either the Mississippi or Bayou Lafourche. Meanwhile, a saltwater route allowed the U.S. Navy to approach Berwick's Bay from the Gulf of Mexico by running up Atchafalaya Bay and passing up that river into the interior. This route, however, was subject to tides and shallow soundings.

In more peaceful days, engineers and investors had also struggled with the geographical challenges of the area, and they had partially overcome these natural obstacles by constructing the New Orleans and Opelousas Railroad. A marvel of design for its time, the "Opelousas Railroad" stretched from the Mississippi River at Algiers, opposite New Orleans, to Berwick's Bay, eighty miles away. Its unfinished roadbed stretched for miles beyond that point, a reminder of postponed prosperity. Traversing trembling prairies and outright swamps for most of its way, this well-built railway provided a convenient and reliable route into the southern reaches of the Lafourche country, as the raid of the 21st Indiana had already proven. Soldiers, weapons, and rations would now travel the rails, replacing the sugar, cotton, and livestock for which the railway was originally intended.

While Butler set up his operation in New Orleans, word of the invasion of Louisiana rippled around the globe. In London U.S. Ambassador Charles Francis Adams used the news to discourage British supporters of the Confederacy from their bellicose positions, for they understood what control of the lower Mississippi implied for the future of a viable Southern nation. The news so stunned them that they could hardly accept it. "It took them three days," Adams wrote home, "to make up their minds to believe it."[18]

Across the English Channel Louisianan John Slidell had been trying to convince Emperor Napoleon III to side with the Confederacy. The French said they would follow Great Britain's lead, but Edward Thouvenal, French Minister of Foreign Affairs, wanted to hear the Louisiana diplomat's assessment of events. "I replied . . . that it was a heavy blow for us and would give the enemy the command of the Mississippi and its tributaries," Slidell reported. The French official responded with disappointment. "Although he did not directly say so, it left me to infer," Slidell continued, "that if New Orleans had not been taken . . . our recognition would very soon have been declared."[19]

Both Union and Confederate military leaders understood that events in Louisiana affected their strategic situations. General Robert E. Lee, defending the Confederate capital at Richmond, Virginia, understood that hopes for southern independence might be undone by events at New Orleans and along the Mississippi. "The loss of the city is a very severe blow to us," he penned, "and one that we cannot fail to feel most sensibly." Below Vicksburg Union commander David Dixon Porter unwittingly agreed with Lee's assessment, and he realized the implications of his colleague and foster brother David Farragut's accomplishment. "New Orleans' falling seems to have made a stampede in secessia," Porter crowed to his friend, Assistant Secretary of the Navy Gustavus A. Fox. "You may put the rebellion down as 'spavined,' 'broken backed' and 'wind galled.'"[20]

The rebellion seemed doomed to failure on every front. Even events in the faraway desert Southwest had resulted in Confederate disaster.

While Union naval men gloated over their Mississippi successes, Rebels on the Rio Grande, more than a thousand miles to the west, understood that they had been whipped in their bid to extend their control to the Pacific. How could these men have known at the time that events in far-off Louisiana would soon control their destiny?

For the moment at hand, under the crystal blue vault of a far West Texas sky, these one thousand bedraggled Confederate veterans watched as brigadier general Henry Hopkins Sibley explained the causes of his recent failed campaign to conquer the West. Far from the steamy and miasmic atmosphere of his native Louisiana, Sibley looked out upon his Army of New Mexico while it stood in formation under a brassy sun. The parched desert plain stretched shimmering in every direction for miles, studded by jagged rockpiles, before it faded into the purple mountains on the western skyline. So vast and timeless a landscape seemed indifferent to the presence of so small a gathering of soldiers. Indeed, the sheer magnitude of this desolate land seemed to dwarf all works of man and to mock human ambition.

On this hot, dusty parade ground of Fort Bliss in Far-West Texas, in the brooding shadow of Franklin Mountain, Sibley addressed his soldiers. "It is with unfeigned pride and pleasure that I [congratulate] the Army of New Mexico upon the successes which have crowned their arms in many encounters with the enemy during the short but brilliant campaign which has just terminated," he said. Though the offensive had failed, his Texans had a right to be proud of their behavior. In the previous months, while Federal forces had captured New Orleans and raided the Lafourche District, the men of Sibley's Brigade had endured a demoralizing defeat. Sibley tried to put a positive light on the episode.[21]

He needed to boost their morale somehow. He was about to leave his troops, who were in the process of quitting the region themselves. "Called from your homes . . . you have made a march, many of you over a thousand miles." Gazing out into the masses of bearded and sunburned faces, Sibley understood that these bedraggled men felt defeated and had little fight remaining in them. As they looked back at him, they believed that their commanding general had misused them, was worse than inept, and was probably a coward.[22] "The boasted valor of Texans has been fully vindicated," the Louisianan continued, looking past their obvious disdain for his leadership. "ValVerde, Glorieta, Albuquerque, Peralta, and last, though not least, your successful and almost unprecedented evacuation . . . over a trackless waste of a hundred miles through a famishing country, will be duly chronicled." Sibley went on to state that the invasion of New Mexico would "form one of the brightest pages in the history of the Second American Revolution." [23]

For Union troops operating in Louisiana, the terrain appeared to be an impenetrable jungle in many places. This fanciful sketch from Harper's Weekly *captures the impression of the region's swamps.*

Indeed, as the general's native state was suffering invasion, ragged clusters of exhausted Texas soldiers returned from New Mexico, many of them thoroughly sick of war. Sibley's veterans counted themselves lucky to have survived. Hundreds of their companions had not, and scores were being held captive in northern prisons. While Union warships had been bombarding Forts Jackson and St. Philip, these troops had been plodding along the road from Santa Fe to Albuquerque. As Butler's troops raided the Lafourche District and Farragut's ships shelled Vicksburg, the Texans had been abandoning Confederate Arizona. As smoke spiraled skyward from the destruction of Donaldsonville that August, the end of the Texan column snaked along the road back into San Antonio.

Despite urgent needs for Confederate manpower, officers ordered Sibley's army dissolved and the troops sent home. The loss of their equipment, their poor physical condition, and their lack of horses or transportation made them more than worthless to the war effort now. Likewise, while the rank and file returned to their families, the leaders of the New Mexico Campaign turned on each other, their government, and their commanders as public opinion distributed blame and reward. Even to casual observers, though, Brigadier General Sibley, the leader of the expedition, owned the brunt of the blame. Many knew him to be a drunk. His men had watched him abandon sick and wounded comrades to an uncertain fate. Some of his officers pressed charges of drunkenness, outright cowardice, and misappropriating confiscated goods during the campaign. A charismatic man in his younger days, Sibley found his reputation in tatters. So he packed his belongings and headed east from San Antonio, but not for home. Instead, Sibley rode for Richmond, Virginia, to defend himself to the Confederate government.

Sibley's soldiers had followed the events in Louisiana and elsewhere through letters and newspapers even while in a remote region of the war. "Last evening's mail brought the news that New Orleans had fallen into the hands of the enemy . . ." wrote First Sergeant Frank Starr, on the brigade staff. "Those gunboats seem to be terrible things," he added prophetically. The perceptive Sergeant Starr began to suspect the course of his, and the brigade's future. "It seems from the last news that it requires us all to drive the enemy from out of the heart of our country."[24]

CHAPTER FOUR

MILITIA

*How much longer is Louisiana to be considered without
the protection of and beneath the consideration of
the Confederate government?*
Governor Thomas O. Moore

Cooperation among Louisiana Confederates would not be forthcoming during the summer of 1862, despite the best efforts of some of its state officials. Governor Thomas O. Moore, finally recovering from the shock of Union invasion, grew furious over the enemy molestation of his homeland. Forced west of the Mississippi River by the events of early May, Moore defiantly rallied resistance to the invasion by authorizing the creation of three new military training camps, one at Monroe in north Louisiana, another—Camp Pratt—between Spanish Lake and New Iberia, and a third within a short carriage ride of the relocated state capitol at Opelousas. Moore anticipated the day when his state's citizens, armed and drilled, could protect and reclaim their homes.

Moore's most obvious need was manpower. Two pieces of national legislation assisted him as he raised his army. The first, the Conscription Act of April 1862, mandated that men between the ages of eighteen and thirty-five serve in the Confederate national military, with few exemptions. Passed within days of that law was the "Act to organize bands of partisan rangers." By using Partisan Ranger companies—semi-irregulars exempted from conscription into regular volunteer units because of age, health, or wealth restrictions—Moore hoped to keep the Yankees from taking more of his state by using guerilla warfare tactics until more disciplined reinforcements arrived, at which point conscripts could be gathered and the militia organized. Within days several companies of these semi-legitimate Partisan Ranger bushwhackers made their way along bayous and swamps toward the enemy and the promise of trophies taken from the Yankee dead. They would also help bring in reluctant conscripts.

About two thousand militia answered the summons that summer. These teenagers, homebodies, and family men responded haphazardly. "Many bad patriots refused to enlist, giving as a reason the misery in which they would leave their families," Helen Dupuy wrote in her journal. "They would not listen to anything, and revolted against the officers of the militia. They fled to the woods and prepared to resist those who would try and capture them." As further embarrassment President Jefferson Davis informed Governor Moore that not all conscripts gathered would defend Louisiana but instead would fill out the state's regiments wherever they served. Unfortunately for Moore most of them went elsewhere.[1]

In a letter to Moore Davis wrote, "With respect to conscripts, the law of Congress does not allow new regiments to be formed from their number." They were to be drilled, organized, and formed into an army, but they could only be used for local defense under dire circumstances. Undoubtedly some would be used to bulk up Louisiana units eventually returning to serve in their home state, but their return depended upon Confederate commanders releasing regiments from the eastern theater for Trans-Mississippi service. Davis promised to send a general to organize the defense of the Pelican State and begged Moore for patience while the Confederate grand design had a chance to work. "In the mean time," Davis continued, "I trust that the new commanding general, with your assistance and cooperation of the patriotic citizens of Louisiana, will be able to keep the enemy in check and afford protection to the greater portion of the state until we shall be able to drive the invader altogether from the soil."[2]

As Moore grappled with the reality that the national government expected him to round up the timid and export them out of state, while Union invaders hovered nearby, he realized he was governor of province on the far margins of Confederate strategic concern. General Earl Van Dorn had seized the war matériel saved from New Orleans and had employed it in the defense of Vicksburg. To compound Moore's problems, the Confederacy had announced the creation of the Department of the Trans-Mississippi in May, with headquarters in Little Rock. Its commander, General Thomas C. Hindman, had promptly appropriated all military property in Alexandria. War planners in Richmond also created within the department the District of West Louisiana and Texas, naming General Paul O. Hébert of Louisiana as its commander. He headquartered in far-off

Paul Octave Hébert was a native of Iberville Parish, a West Point-trained engineer, a Mexican War veteran, a former governor of Louisiana, and a wealthy sugar planter by the time the Civil War erupted. His first assignment was to see to the defenses of New Orleans. The Confederate government then posted him to Texas, hoping he could make Galveston ready as well. State Library of Louisiana.

Houston. Moore—left in the middle void between these two military headquarters—demanded better support from the Confederate government, requesting that officers be sent from Virginia to focus attention on Louisiana. In the meantime he ordered detachments of his untrained and unenthusiastic militia levies to guard the mouth of the Red River and to patrol the west bank of the Mississippi.[3]

The beleaguered governor, uncertain how he would make do with the scarce resources at hand, felt the hard political pinch of State's Rights. Confederate officers had authorized the removal of Louisiana property without permission, and weapons and materials paid for by Louisianans now served on distant battlefields. "Am I never to get even my own property?" lamented Moore to Secretary of War George Randolph. "The Confederacy has never sent me a musket. Let it not

Major General Thomas C. Hindman was one of the leading Arkansas proponents of secession. When his state left the Union, Hindman abandoned his seat in the U.S. House of Representative and tried unsuccessfully for a posting with the government of the new Confederacy. Instead, the Mexican War veteran returned to his home at Helena, Arkansas, and raised a command that would become the 2nd Arkansas Infantry. He led a brigade at the Battle of Shiloh, where he was slightly wounded. By the time of his appointment to the District of the Trans-Mississippi, he had earned promotion to major general and received instructions to protect Arkansas from invasion. Old State House Museum.

take what I have paid for. It is hard to bear invasion," he continued, "and at the same time . . . to have taken from me what I had provided without help." Even though the Confederacy claimed to be a nation, Moore discovered, each state was on its own when money was scarce and trouble was near.[4]

To make matters worse, Confederate foragers stationed in Arkansas, under orders from Hindman to round up supplies, commandeered them in Louisiana. Troops from the newly raised 24th Texas Cavalry pressed Confederate and state property in Shreveport as well as the hogs, poultry, and personal possessions of its residents. Drifting 125 miles south down the Red River, they visited the same kind of vandalism on Alexandria before returning to Arkansas.[5]

Moore fumed at this latest outrage. "I have not even been informed that General Hindman has any command over any portion of my State," he roared in another letter to Randolph. The arrival of foragers from Arkansas had surprised him, but their conduct had been infuriating. "A party of armed men," Moore sputtered, "seized private property, entered houses of private citizens, brutally practiced extortion and outrage, and with bullying and threatening language and manner spread terror among the people and disgraced the service. Nothing prevented our citizens from resisting," Moore added, "but the desire of our people now and at all times to pay due respect to the authority of our Government." The governor went on to announce that he had taken measures to avoid a repeat of these offenses against Louisianans. "With Butler below and

Hindman above, each . . . committing the same outrages, I am forced to self-protection," he warned. Militia would not only resist foragers and arrest Confederate detachments on such errands, but cannons would sink any steamers used to carry away property. In addition, he wanted the offending officers from the 24th Texas Cavalry cashiered. "You can refuse to dismiss them," Moore threatened, "but my marksmen may save you the trouble if they come again."[6]

Exasperated by the lack of attention from the Confederate government, Moore forced the state militia to fight the Union invaders. In the last week of May he ordered butternut Louisiana infantry from Camp Pratt into the Lafourche District, in an attempt to force the militia to answer his call. The raid started out well. Lieutenant Edward Fuller, who had helped organize the St. Martins Rangers as part of Lieutenant Colonel Valsin Fournet's brand-new 10th "Yellow Jacket" battalion only days before, now helped lead his untrained friends and neighbors into action when they crossed Berwick Bay. "We went to [Brashear] City, then in the hands of the Federal Government and captured the few officers and men in charge of the place," he wrote. "We then waited until all of the railroad trains came in, captured the officers in charge of them." The bloodless haul induced the Confederates to push deeper into Union-held territory. For the next few days, the Confederates plowed down the line of the New Orleans and Opelousas Railroad. By the end of May Fuller's men had succeeded in bloodying a few Union outposts in sporadic gun battles and minor scuffles, burning the bridge over Bayou des Allemands, destroying a few lengths of track, and breeching the Mississippi levee in a half dozen places before heading back toward Rebel lines.[7]

The Federals quickly repaired the damage, but before long the Confederates tried to press their advantage. The 8th Vermont arrived in June to replace the 21st Indiana in this war of outposts, while Fournet's soldiers invaded the Lafourche District with the balance of his command from beyond Berwick Bay.

Governor Moore urged these troops to succeed and thereby to convince the militia it was safe to fight. The Confederates struck in the dark morning hours of June 17, near Thibodaux, setting fire to the Lafourche bridge before retreating from the Union response. Even so, the Federal troops abandoned their bridgehead and fell back to Bayou des Allemands, just thirty-two miles from New Orleans, conceding the Lafourche country to the Rebels. "We . . . came to the conclusion that our force was not sufficient to hold so long a road, in the heart of a country filled with guerillas," recorded Corporal Rufus Kinsley of Vermont. The Federals also moved to divest themselves of a growing population of freed slaves who were swamping their ability to feed and house them by forcing them away from their camps, out of their lines, and back into Confederate controlled regions.[8]

The Federal retreat and growing discomfiture emboldened Fournet. On June 22 a Union train left the safety of Federal lines at Des Allemands and ventured toward Thibodaux to return slaves to the plantations they had left. On the return trip Fournet's men ambushed the expedition at Chitimahaw Station, near Raceland, killing and wounding nearly a dozen Union soldiers. "They were fired into by a band of guerillas concealed in the cane-brake," Corporal Kinsley reported. The New Englander did not believe they should have been returning anyone to slavery and had brought down God's wrath on the enterprise. "As I look at it, they were engaged in bad business," he continued, adding a flourish of scripture from the Gospel of Matthew: "'Verily I say unto you, they shall receive their reward.'" He also paraphrased Deuteronomy: "Thou shalt not return him again to his master." The Federals, acting snake-bitten, hunkered down at their Des Allemands redoubt, abandoning their claims on the Lafourche for the time being.[9]

Despite these bold Confederate moves, the secessionist ardor of the locals remained tepid. On June 25 militia Captain William B. Ratliff rode to see if Fournet's troops would remain along the Lafourche long enough for him to rally his men. "[Fournet] stated that he was ordered to come here for five or six days and expected the Malitia [sic] to be drawn out of the parishes to keep this country free from the enemy," related the officer. Confederates expected local men in the parishes to protect their own homes and plantations. Fournet and his men had provided the muscle to drive away the Federals. Now it was time for those who would to rally to the Confederate flag.[10]

This brief foray by gray-clad soldiers did not raise the confidence of Lafourche residents. In fact, the 10th Louisiana Battalion was actively preparing to evacuate the region and return to Camp Pratt, with Fournet declaring his mission accomplished. Ratliff's spirits plummeted as he explained to Fournet the severe shortages of weapons, ammunition, and supplies. "I stated . . . that it would be impossible to get out the Malitia [sic] here without a force." Unmoved, Fournet fell back to Brashear City with all of the recaptured rolling stock and locomotives of the Opelousas Railroad. He crossed his men over into the Teche country, reporting to his superiors that the Lafourche militia had refused to cooperate.[11] Three days later Colonel J. K. Gaudet of the St. James Parish militia regiment reinforced this perception by writing "it is in my opinion entirely impracticable to attempt any thing . . . . We are as completely under control of the Federal forces as [New Orleans] itself."[12]

The militia leadership in the Lafourche believed that their government had lost touch with reality. "It is not difficult . . . to be two hundred miles from the enemy penning proclamations and orders," Gaudet fumed, "but when they involve such momentous consequences to a large community who are defenseless, a moment of sober thought should prevent them from being promulgated."[13]

Moore's military strategy had backfired. With only temporary Confederate support like that exhibited by Fournet, the militia commanders remained insubordinate, often making their own policy and countermanding orders from the governor. Very soon the important citizens of the Lafourche District, especially those along the Mississippi River, made clear to the state leadership that without a substantial infusion of weapons and troops, the militia would stay out of the fight. "It would be unwise to invite, by a vain display of our meager resources, the attack of a ruthless enemy who would not hesitate to spread desolation over our land and deprive our women and children of shelters," declared Colonel W. W. Pugh of the Assumption Parish militia. "If our militia is to be called into active service, there should be a supporting force of sufficient magnitude to give it . . . the semblance of a successful resistance . . . . There is a serious doubt, whether the militia as a body can be brought into active service without aid of a sustaining force from some other quarter."[14]

Governor Moore answered this exasperating demand by dispatching two mounted companies of irregulars to Donaldsonville. Perhaps they

One of the first depictions of a Texas cattle drive, published in Harper's Weekly. *During the Civil War, tens of thousands of these range beeves made their way from Texas to hungry Confederates. In October 1862, sixteen-year-old Goliad County resident W.D.H. Saunders helped push a herd of eight hundred animals from his home, across the Sabine River at Orange, and on to Opelousas, Louisiana, merging with another herd of three hundred head along the way. "When we reached the Mississippi a thousand of the beeves took to the water and easily swam across," he wrote. The cowboys passed Port Hudson and then sold their herd at nearby Woodville, Mississippi. Saunders didn't get back home to Texas until January 1863. From J. Marvin Hunter, ed.,* The Trail Drivers of Texas: Interesting Sketches of Early Cowboys and Their Experiences on the Range and on the Trail During the Days that Tried Men's Souls--True Narratives Related by Real Cow-punchers and Men who Fathered the Cattle Industry in Texas, *268-269.*

could make a bolder statement than Fournet. These Partisan Rangers, though, refused to answer to the command of mere militia officers, and took positions along the Mississippi to harass passing gunboats, inventing strategy as they went. In addition to inviting retaliation from the U.S. Navy, these gunmen were also the authors of notorious depredations against their fellow citizens, driving some to the Federals for refuge. Fearing Federal retribution, the mayor of Donaldsonville begged the Confederates to stop their activities in the area. Partisan Captain James A. McWaters simply replied that he would take it under advisement with the governor.[15]

Back at Opelousas Moore tried again to awaken officials in Richmond to the plight of his state and by extension, the nation. "How much longer is Louisiana to be considered without the protection of and beneath the consideration of the Confederate government?" he roared. "When am I to have a general, as long ago promised? The army of the Mississippi valley is wholly dependent for supplies on keeping open our communications with Texas." The governor believed that Butler would soon realize his advantage and send his army to interdict shipments of Lone Star beef and grain. General P. G. T. Beauregard's Confederate army at Tupelo, and General Earl Van Dorn's garrison at Vicksburg, would starve. The only thing that had prevented it from happening, to date, was his creative use of militia and conscripts to keep the Federals off balance. "The whole army," he scoffed, "dependent for their supplies of beef on the activity and vigilance of . . . ragged and half-armed militia"[16]

CHAPTER FIVE

TOTAL WAR

Every time my boats are fired upon, I will burn
a portion of your town.
Admiral David Glasgow Farragut

While detachments skirmished in cane fields and on the bayou banks of the Lafourche District, Commodore David Farragut and Captain Charles Henry Davis made a second attack against Vicksburg, convinced that a victory there would end the war. The combined Union fleets pounded the Confederate gun positions, but their heavy iron availed nothing. Farragut's fleet ran past the Rebel batteries on June 28 in an attempt to gun down the enemy at closer range, but still the southern fortress held. The navy, with a massive fleet consolidated upstream and Porter's mortars below, faced a stalemate. The army, though, continued to toil on at Vicksburg. Brigadier General Williams, unwilling to quit simply because the navy had, turned to science and the spade, attempting to cut a canal across De Soto Point on the Louisiana shore opposite and thus cause the great river to bypass the fort. Short of receiving large numbers of reinforcements from the Union army occupying Memphis, the Federals could accomplish little else. Farragut and his commanders saw their hopes for an end to the war dwindle away in the summer heat.

Captain Charles Henry Davis commanded the Union fleet coming south down the Mississippi from St. Louis against Vicksburg. Naval Historical Center.

What had promised to be the last year of the war and the triumph of Union arms crashed to a halt in every theater. Not only had Federal ships failed to crush Vicksburg, but the North's largest army, commanded by General George B. McClellan, had fallen back from Richmond with heavy losses. Two men, General Earl Van Dorn on the Mississippi and General Robert E. Lee in Virginia had, through their victories, surprisingly saved the Confederacy from collapse, breathing new life into the struggle. The soldiers and sailors of the United States had come within days of ending the entire war. Now strategists on both sides grappled with how to proceed.

The Federals, denied a swift victory on the Mississippi and having failed to take Richmond, feared that a year of purely military attempts at suppressing the rebellion had amounted to only half measures—the suppression of the rebellion not pursued with enough vigor. At the urging of more radical elements, politicians and generals urged a new style of warfare.

In Washington, D.C., Lincoln summoned Major General John Pope to build a new Union army in northern Virginia to protect the seat of government and to move against the Confederate capital. This hero of western campaigns convinced the panicky president that desperate times called for unorthodox measures. Pope ushered in an era of total war aimed at destroying military targets as well as southern society's desire and ability to fight by targeting civilians in his area of operations–with Lincoln's blessing. In addition the U.S. War Department called for three hundred thousand additional volunteers, while dispatches arrived before northern governors requesting three hundred thousand militia for nine-month's service. Radical politicians celebrated the new energy displayed by the president, and most predicted that the war would not end until the South lay crushed. Some among them renewed the call for emancipation of all the slaves; some wanted to use the freedmen as soldiers, to fill out their ranks and to help punish the Confederacy.[1]

In mid-July President Lincoln and Congress took steps to help conduct his new style of warfare. On July 11 Lincoln appointed General Henry Halleck as general-in-chief of Union armies, unifying the command of the nation's forces and declaring a mandate to bring the Rebels to heel. Congress, meanwhile, passed the Second Confiscation Act and the Militia Act. The first law allowed the seizure of private property, including slaves, from those unwilling to swear loyalty to the Union. The second allowed African Americans to serve in the U.S. military. "That those who make a causeless war should be compelled to pay the cost of it," Lincoln declared to Congress, "is too obviously just, to be called into question."[2]

For many secessionists, this new Federal policy revealed what they had always thought were the true intentions of northern extremists. Julia LeGrand, writing from New Orleans, observed that "the radicals, knowing that they have the reins of Government in their own hands, are determined to press the war and overwhelm us before the Democrats come into power." Their tactics, she argued, played as dangerously as had the Reign of Terror in the French Revolution. "These dreadful radicals are the Jacobins of America and their cry is like the old one, 'More Blood.'"[3]

The Confiscation Acts also greatly expanded the Butler empire. Already trading with loyal planters and coercing others to comply with extortion-like protection schemes, Andrew and Ben could now target the homes and estates of Confederate soldiers as forfeitures to the Republic. Unionists—including many of Butler's cronies—spent the end of summer seizing abandoned plantations and convincing former slaves through intimidation and reward to continue raising crops, which were sold in New Orleans and shipped by sea to the North. The middlemen in this scheme made money by trafficking war-rare staples to eager Yankee merchants and factory owners. In Louisiana this meant U.S. troops supervised the workers on government-run plantations, and the Butler brothers used their position and access to make money as government backed brokers of strategic commodities.[4]

With military officers from general to private looting the occupied land, eager to claim their portion of the spoils of war, the discipline of Union troops in south Louisiana eroded. Many field officers, with the implicit approval of Butler and the confiscation acts, helped themselves to furniture, silverware, art, and other valuables, as certain line officers and the their commands took livestock, crops, and anything unguarded. For many Federal soldiers, the unaccustomed access to sugar and rum was bewildering and delightful. Despite orders issued by provosts and regimental commanders to halt the thievery, the plundering of south Louisiana proceeded steadily, fueled by the ambiguity inherent in the concept of total war. Many of the troops simply could not distinguish between government sanctioned looting and wanton pillaging.[5]

Some northerners saw this ruin as a military necessity but lamented the consequences. "The Confiscation Act . . . of recent passage must bring the Southerners to their senses, or culminate in their destruction," General Williams wrote. "If the war continues a year longer, I don't see how they will escape a servile war. The negroes are flying from their masters in all directions, and have become thoroughly impressed with the idea of being free. The doom of slavery is already written, unless the South stop the rebellion." This Detroit-born officer could not understand while the people living in Louisiana would allow themselves and their fortunes to be wasted. "They began the rebellion to establish a great slave empire: they must stop the rebellion to save their country from destruction and servile war, and perhaps themselves from negro domination and a Black Republic. What a terrible punishment."[6]

By early July the Federals were merely keeping their eyes on Vicksburg from above and below, unable to do much else, conscious that they had come tantalizingly close to inflicting a mortal blow to the rebellion. Farragut, recently promoted to rear admiral, and the recently advanced Commodore Davis had been unable to overtake the Confederate earthwork on the Mississippi. The objectives and keys in this new theater of war were crystallizing. "Today the rumor is rife that we are to proceed down the river to New Orleans, and in confirmation of the rumors our mortar vessels have been taken in tow by the steam-

CONTROL OF THE
MISSISSIPPI RIVER
JULY 1, 1862

ers," observed marine private Henry Gusley. "This immense naval demonstration of ours is to end in the fizzle now so apparent."[7]

Vicksburg had remained unbroken. General Williams's engineering scheme to dig a canal to divert the river away from the Rebel fortress failed, resulting in scores of Federal soldiers dead from disease, exposure, and exhaustion. As though to emphasize the point that the Yankees had limitations, the CSS *Arkansas* cut its way through the combined fleet north of the town in mid July. The ship provoked Farragut's flotilla into charging down the Mississippi after it, without success, causing the West Gulf Blockading Squadron to fall back below Vicksburg. Davis sent his own ironclad, the USS *Essex,* and a fast ram, the USS *Queen of the West,* on a raid to destroy the Rebel warship, but

The Union ironclad U.S.S. Essex *went hunting for the C.S.S.* Arkansas, *but the Confederate warship found refuge under the guns of Vicksburg. The Federal warship continued down the Mississippi, serving between Baton Rouge and New Orleans. Naval Historical Center.*

the *Arkansas* remained docked beneath the protection of the fortress's guns. The *Essex* sluggishly steamed on and joined Farragut's fleet— Davis's brown-water ugly duckling among the saltwater swans. The *Queen of the West* headed back up river.

This setback, coupled with the surge of Rebel energy, put Union forces in a foul humor. When Captain James McWaters's gunmen fired at navy vessels passing Donaldsonville in their operations against Vicksburg, Farragut simply stated, "Every time my boats are fired upon, I will burn a portion of your town."[8] When the attacks continued, he made good on his warning and directed the mighty USS *Brooklyn* and USS *Cayuga* to shell the town on August 9 and 10 before sending ashore troops to enhance the destruction. A third of the buildings burned. "Barbarous as these proceedings may appear," Private Gusley remembered, "they are but just retaliation of the infamous and cowardly acts of the rebels, and no doubt will serve as wholesome warnings to citizens in other towns who aid and abet guerilla practices."[9] Louisiana militia officers, caught

The powerful USS Brooklyn *could bring a broadside of ten 9-inch Dahlgren cannons to bear on a target, making it a formidable force on the Mississippi and the Gulf of Mexico. Library of Congress.*

between Union and Confederate fires—but judging the Federals to be the greater threat—moved to end Rebel activities in the area. By mid-August state militia troops arrested McWaters and another partisan captain in response to what they considered irresponsible behavior.[10]

This event attracted Governor Moore's attention. By now resigned to his abandonment by the Confederacy, he curtailed his aggressive yet ineffective military operations in favor of more benign measures to regain the support of the Lafourche citizens. He banned trade with Federally controlled areas. He then began organizing relief drives to help the indigent, especially soldiers' families. Later Moore promoted Confederate Associations to encourage patriotism and a sense of loyalty to the Rebel cause. Eventually his work began to have an effect. The situation in the Lafourche country stabilized, and the Federals failed to exploit their advantage. Nevertheless, in Moore's opinion and that of pro-Rebel partisans in the sugar parishes, the Confederate government remained negligent.[11]

The screw steamer Cayuga *had fought against Forts Jackson and St. Philip and headed upstream with the rest of the Union fleet. Its 11-inch pivot gun and 24-pounders could rake the banks of the Mississippi and keep it clear of Confederate sharpshooters. Naval Historical Center.*

Butler had not been more aggressive in ushering in the disasters Moore had predicted because he and his Federal colleagues had larger issues at hand. June and July had been aggravating months for the Union. The lack of coordination from the massive Union army in northern Mississippi only compounded Union frustrations. Although the navy and a token force of infantry bashed themselves bloody against Vicksburg, Confederate movements toward east Tennessee and, ultimately, Kentucky had caused Federal commanders to disband the army that had won the Battle of Shiloh and parcel it out to other theaters of war instead of striking what might have been the decisive blow. Union armies around Corinth, Mississippi, and Memphis, Tennessee, went on the defensive. To further complicate the strategic situation on the Mississippi, when Farragut and Williams had quit menacing Vicksburg and had fallen back to Baton Rouge, Confederate general Van Dorn sent a Rebel army and their war craft *Arkansas* after them.

On a hot, humid August day, the Confederates proved they remained dangerous. An army under General John C. Breckinridge

Farragut made good on his promise to shell Donaldsonville when Confederate parti-sans continued taking shots at his ships. The charred remnants of the town's principal buildings reminded the locals to mind their manners. State Library of Louisiana.

violently attacked the Federals at Baton Rouge on August 5 and man-aged to bludgeon the Union garrison, kill General Williams, and star-tle Butler with the ferocity of their onslaught. Some speculated that only the loss of the *Arkansas,* due to mechanical failures, prevented a total Union rout. Others credited the personal bravery of the fallen Williams, along with the valor and bayonets of the 21st Indiana, with saving the day for the Union. Unsuccessful in their designs to destroy the U.S. garrison at Baton Rouge and threaten New Orleans, the Reb-els backed off and withdrew to the imposing bluffs at Port Hudson, a day's march upriver. There they would create another citadel to hold the Mississippi and protect the stream of Texas supplies flowing down the Red River and into Rebel hands. At the same time they would continue to pose a potential offensive threat against northern gains in Louisiana. With this brief campaign, the Confederacy won back a critical length of the Mississippi and again dashed Union hopes for a quick end to the war.

Despite Breckinridge's bold attack, the construction of the new fort at Port Hudson, and the awakening of Rebel resistance, a terrible fate befell Baton Rouge. General Butler ordered the town destroyed and his

A Harper's Weekly *sketch of the Battle of Baton Rouge, a surprise blow that fell against Union forces on August 5, 1862.*

exposed garrison withdrawn to New Orleans to protect that city from the newly energetic enemy. Even though the general reconsidered his brutal sentence and officially countermanded his orders to burn the city, by August 21 soldiers had sacked the town anyway, cut down its massive shade trees, plundered its homes, and crated up its public art for shipment to New Orleans. A third of its homes lay burned, Butler's attempts at clemency notwithstanding. This terrifying destruction had its desired effect. Frightened citizens feared Union retaliation and tried to keep from provoking the invaders.[12]

General Butler, haunted by Breckinridge's assault and his own lack of progress in seizing the Mississippi, shifted to defensive tactics. Of primary importance was defending New Orleans, and he began to handle that task by enlisting all available manpower in the city. Within weeks Butler raised twelve hundred recruits, filling the ranks of his existing regiments and adding a full regiment and a half of loyal Louisiana infantry to his command. Needing mounted troops to counter the Confederate partisans west of the river, Butler ordered officers to collect several companies of cavalry from among the white unionists and other pro-northern refugees in New Orleans and the surrounding region. Butler projected that his summertime recruiting efforts would increase the size of his army by twenty percent.[13]

To build the new units, Butler considered applications from his junior officers eager to raise their commands and possibly gain promotion in rank. Captain Frank Godfrey, formerly a second lieutenant with a battery of Maine artillery, opened a storefront recruiting office in New Orleans and began assembling his command. "The recruits are mostly foreigners, or men of Northern birth," he wrote home about his enlistees. "They will fight as well for one side as another." By October three new companies took the field. "I recruited my company in a little over three weeks," Godfrey noted. "The men are nearly all Germans, a few Irish, and some Americans."[14]

Butler granted a Federal army commission to Major Harai Robinson, described by one Confederate as a "renegade Texan," contingent on his ability to fill out his regiment. With experience, the Louisiana Union troops would became a valuable tool for Federal operations in southwestern Louisiana.[15]

Other Texans enlisted in Butler's army as well. Refugees from the Lone Star State had made their way to Matamoros, Mexico, or had risked tide and surf in small boats to reach Union blockaders—all in an effort to escape the Confederacy. Two among them, Edmund J. Davis of Brownsville and Andrew Jackson Hamilton of Austin, had made their way separately to New Orleans and became vocal advocates for a Union invasion of Texas in speaking tours in Washington, D.C., and New York. Their efforts earned Hamilton a brigadier general's commission, and Davis became a colonel. By the end of October enough of their fellow Unionists had arrived to organize the first company of what would become the Federal 1st Texas Cavalry. All this new unit lacked was recruits, but more arrived daily.[16]

The unorthodox Butler also enlisted African American soldiers. The first of these organizations was the 1st Louisiana Native Guards, "1,000 strong . . . the darkest of whom will be about the same complexion of the late Mr. [Daniel] Webster," he wrote, an obvious reference to "Black Dan's" swarthy complexion but indicating a clear preference for lighter skinned blacks in belief that they were more intelligent and

CONTROL OF THE
MISSISSIPPI RIVER
SEPTEMBER 1, 1862

easy to train. This action encouraged the abolitionists in Butler's army. "They are just as good . . . as white men," Captain Godfrey wrote to his parents. "As to how they will fight I cannot tell. The majority of our officers whom I have heard say anything about it seem to think they will fight well. I think they will try them pretty soon and determine the question as regards the American Negro's fighting propensities."[17]

Butler was not an abolitionist, but he was practical. Ironically, he had been a Breckinridge Democrat in the election of 1860 and was at that time even somewhat sympathetic to the South. Later, while serving as a Union officer in Virginia, Butler had coined the term "contraband" to refer to the slaves who found themselves behind Union lines or who sought the protection of Federal soldiers, classifying them as spoils of war. His clever manipulation of the unsettled wartime status of slaves, designed mostly as a political barb at the Rebels rather than a humane solution to the black refugee issue, made him an accidental hero to his more liberally minded countrymen. "If I tried hard I think I could find quite a number of flaws in him," Captain Godfrey wrote. "But one thing is certain . . . there is not a governor of a state, or a general in the army, that has done so much towards the abolition of slavery as he."[18]

This adoring New Englander's comment aside, Butler felt no genuine obligation to the freed slaves and was amazingly innocent of any moral conscience regarding their well being. In New Orleans Butler ordered that most runaways be turned away from the city and Union lines, considering them an unnecessary drain on resources. Those who appeared useful were allowed in and put to work in exchange for rations.

When the Rebels threatened, Butler was prepared to meet them with an army reinforced by black men. In mid-August after the Battle of Baton Rouge and amid rumors of a follow-up Confederate attack against New Orleans, Butler remained steady: "If it becomes at all imminent, I shall call upon Africa to intervene, and I do not think I shall call in vain."[19]

As the supply of black labor increased, Butler's use of these refugees widened. Soon large teams of newly freed slaves worked on such general maintenance issues as digging fortifications, clearing brush, chopping wood, and maintaining latrines. Freedwomen served as laundresses and cooks for Union troops. Butler also pressed black labor to repair public works, including levee repair, a task vital to the wellbeing of south Louisiana's agricultural economy. As one historian wrote, "wherever menial and hard labor existed, Federal forces found a place for runaways." For the freedmen and freedwomen, life among Butler's Yankees was remarkably similar to life as slaves on the sugar plantations. Although the contrabands were neither whipped nor traded, they were conscripted, moved against their will, and assigned tasks at the will and whim of Federal authorities.[20]

President Lincoln's views on Louisiana soon made Butler's cavalier attitude toward this displaced population obsolete. The Pelican State was to be the laboratory of Reconstruction. Aside from the ravages of war, the largest problem facing the occupation government was the disruption of plantation routines, causing economic chaos. Slave laborers dropped their hoes and shovels to join the columns of U.S. troops as they tramped along the Louisiana roads. Crops remained unharvested, and rations became scarce. The state would never be successfully rebuilt while in the middle of such a social and economic war-born maelstrom.[21]

There remained no doubt that political reconstruction could not take place without economic reconstruction. Vital to this recovery would be a workable, long-term solution to the labor issue. With workers back in the fields, the plantations could resume their operations. The return of a semblance of the normal rhythms of life would encourage political stability. This, in turn, would allow Lincoln's plan for Louisiana to come to fruition as satisfied planters worked within the new order to restore their state to the Union. Butler's task was to plan and execute his solution to the issue of labor in Louisiana. Clear success in this endeavor would elude him.[22]

Throughout the summer and into the fall of 1862, both Union and Confederate planners faced unexpected challenges on the Gulf Coast. Butler, instead of earning military laurels for taking the rest of the Mississippi, busied himself with the task of imposing Federal will on the citizens of New Orleans and its littoral. However unwittingly, he also became one of the early architects of emancipation and a prophet of a new order in the South. For the Confederacy the fall of New Orleans had been a severe shock to dreams of independence.

Back in Virginia, the immediate danger that summer played out a few dozen miles to the east of the Confederate capital at Richmond. Even as calamity visited Confederate Louisiana, Union general George B. McClellan, commander of the ballooning Army of the Potomac, had marched up the Virginian peninsula, driving back Confederate forces under Joseph E. Johnston. The Battle of Seven Pines, followed quickly by news of determined fighting in the Shenandoah and later by the savagery of the Seven Days Battles, occupied the attention of Confederate leadership, who could heard the thump of artillery from their Richmond offices. The total war depredations of John Pope in northern Virginia ceased only when Generals Lee and Thomas "Stonewall"

Jackson routed him at Second Manassas on August 30. President Jefferson Davis and Secretary of War George W. Randolph, consumed with nearby events, could not respond to the military anarchy on the Mississippi until late summer.

Confederate politicians asked General P. G. T. Beauregard to comment on the feasibility of recapturing New Orleans. They also wanted him to lead the expedition. "Of course I should be both proud and happy to drive from my native state the abolitionists who are now desecrating its soil," the Creole veteran had replied, but there would be a cost. "We can retake New Orleans but we cannot hold it without subjecting it to destruction . . . and its destruction would be attended with a degree of human misery frightful to contemplate, without a proper return of evil to the enemy." The famously ambitious hero of Manassas and Shiloh declined to endorse or lead an offensive against Butler. Recapturing New Orleans, he replied,

North Carolinian Theophilus Holmes was a decorated Mexican War veteran but resigned his commission when Southerners fired upon Fort Sumter. He served as a major general under Robert E. Lee during the fighting around Richmond in the summer of 1862 before heading up the Trans-Mississippi Department. Largely deaf, he earned a reputation for being well-intentioned but cantankerous; his troops dubbed him "Granny." National Archives.

"would not even give us the command of a single foot of ground along the Mississippi, much less the river itself; hence, why make the sacrifice?"[23]

This answer satisfied Jefferson Davis. He ordered his commanders to scour their armies for any spare troops they could find and dispatch them to Louisiana to answer the carping of its bristly governor and to help in its defense. Davis also ordered a friend of his, a general in the Army of Northern Virginia—General Theophilus Holmes—to replace the mercurial Hindman in Arkansas, reorganize the Confederate Department of the Trans-Mississippi into a unified command, and provide leadership. When Holmes arrived, he divided up his vast realm into various operational districts to help him with his task. He refashioned the Confederate District of Louisiana out of the parishes west of the Mississippi river, leaving Hébert with the District of Texas, New Mexico, and Arizona in recognition that efforts in the Far West had in theory created another theater of war. These strategic moves finally gave Louisiana the military authority and legitimacy it needed and that its governor had long desired.

Randolph remained unsatisfied, though, with a purely defensive stance in the Pelican State. Perhaps Beauregard was right in thinking New Orleans could not be retaken, but perhaps an effort should be made to divert the Federals from their ambitions upriver. Randolph wanted to make the effort. He requested that another friend of the president—in fact a former brother-in-law—command the new District of Louisiana: General Richard Taylor.

CHAPTER SIX

RICHARD TAYLOR

The right man in the right place
General Braxton Bragg, Commander, Army of Tennessee

O ther soldiers headed toward Louisiana as well. Some Texans, their horses laden with supplies, headed to war in July 1862, answering the cry for help issued by Governor Thomas O. Moore. Lieutenant Colonel Edwin Waller, Jr., a veteran of the early days of the New Mexico campaign, had returned to Texas to raise his own command and expand the Rebel successes in the Far West. With strategic circumstances out there now changed, the New Mexico adventure in shambles, and the enemy closer at hand, he would ride east to answer Louisiana's call while his former comrades in Sibley's Brigade scattered to their homes to rest and refit for the future. Waller's command, designated the 13th Texas Cavalry Battalion, would be among the first, and few, to answer Louisiana's call.[1]

Waller, the thirty-six-year-old son and namesake of a signer of the Texas Declaration of Independence, advertised for men in typical Lone Star State style. He sought soldiers who "were at home on horseback, who ride like cowboys, who hit the bull's eye with rifle or pistol, and go anywhere and stand anything like a regular Ranger." Since the New Mexico campaign was over, he had wanted to lead his men east

Colonel Edwin Waller Jr. first saw war as a child, fleeing the oncoming Mexican army in 1836 while his famous father helped form the new Republic of Texas. A farmer and merchant, Waller was one of the first to the front when the Civil War erupted; he served in the New Mexico campaign before returning to Texas to raise his own command. Instead of heading west, though, his new outfit headed east into Louisiana. Texas State Library and Archives.

of the Mississippi River where, he promised recruits, they would serve in the very "teeth of danger" like the famous Terry's Texas Rangers. He exhorted young men to join "a service that Texians delight in. Come with me, and I will lead you right [where] your habits and disposition will enable you to make the best fight in your power." By the time he had built his battalion, New Orleans had fallen and the Confederacy required his unit fill the new gap in the national defenses.[2]

On July 1, 1862, having supplemented his numbers with conscripts, Waller ordered the five companies of the 13th Texas Cavalry Battalion to head for Louisiana from their camps around Hempstead. "We . . . travelled along at a good gait but very dusty," wrote Private William Craig. "Horse pretty well packed." Unlike the impressive scenes that accompanied troops the year before, this unit started out amidst modest fanfare. As the battalion headed to war, clusters of local girls and women escorted the troops along the way. "Several ladies visited camp this morning to take a farewell glimpse at Waller's Battalion," Craig added. As the soldiers passed the residence of a local notable, "ladies waved their handkerchiefs at us and three or four of them followed along behind about 3 miles."[3]

The battalion's route of march passed just north of Lake Charles and across the Attakapas Prairies to Vermillion Bayou where, Craig wrote, they went into "the best [camp] that we have ever had before." Drill, parades, and training in dismounted tactics occupied the men's time as their leaders learned where they could best be used. Many visited the nearby towns of Lafayette and New Iberia. "A great many people live around here and are very kind," Craig wrote. "Most all are French." More good news

*A sketch of the homestead of Captain James Belvarde Pope January, 13th Texas
Cavalry Battalion. This hardscrabble farm near Victoria, Texas, was a far cry from the
opulent Louisiana plantations where he and his men would be fighting. Victoria
College Special Collections.*

arrived with the appearance of Captain J. C. Terrell's company from Fort
Worth, which brought the battalion to six companies.[4]

Waller's men occupied "Camp Texas," as they dubbed their bivouac, until late August, when orders came for them to proceed toward
Brashear City. "This looked like active service," Craig later wrote. "The
Battalion took up the line of march in good spirits and moved off with
alacrity."[5]

After ferrying across Berwick's Bay to Brashear City, the unit moved
on to Thibodaux in search of the enemy. A local priest, commenting
on these newcomers, found them quite different from the Louisiana
troops who had passed through a month before. "One finds charming,
polite, and honorable young men, who come from good families and
who are obliged to take up arms whether they liked it or not," the cleric
wrote of the Pelican regiments. "Among the Texas soldiers who come
here it was difficult to meet one who was a good sort. They seemed
uncivilized. What struck me was that in spite of their coarseness, they
were devoted to one another."[6] Unknown to the chauvinistic priest at
the time, it was these westerners and hundreds more like them who
would fight for Confederate Louisiana.

Major General Richard Taylor was the son of a president, the former brother-in-law of the Confederate president, and protégé of General Thomas "Stonewall" Jackson. A Yale graduate, this wealthy and politically savvy officer was already an accomplished student of war but quickly revealed he could put his book learning to good use in the field. Library of Congress.

As these Texans left their homes behind, Richard Taylor was returning to his native state. Indeed, Taylor's transfer from the Army of the Valley was far more than a mere change in station. He went west with a specific mission, endorsed enthusiastically by Secretary of War Randolph. Simply stated, Taylor was to threaten or retake New Orleans as a means of thwarting Union ambitions against Port Hudson and Vicksburg. Confident in his ability to accomplish this task, Taylor rowed across the Mississippi on August 19, heading for a reunion with his family, who had taken refuge in the cotton town of Washington. After a few hours' visit, he headed six miles down the road to Opelousas. After consulting with Governor Moore there, Taylor moved eighty miles north to Alexandria and established his headquarters on the Red River, closer to the center of the state.[7]

Taking over the control of military affairs from the harried Governor Moore, the newcomer wasted no time in putting a military offensive into motion. The Federal troops in Louisiana, he believed, were inexperienced and perhaps vulnerable to a determined push by Confederate veterans. The fact the Butler had not acted decisively in the region smacked of Union weakness. Confederate Secretary of War Randolph had endowed Taylor with sweeping powers to commandeer troops from Texas, Mississippi, and Alabama, and he intended to do so; this gathering would undoubtedly include seasoned combat veterans. "I am about to undertake an expedition which I anticipate will place me in possession of the Opelousas Railroad up to the vicinity of Algiers," he wrote to Brigadier General Daniel Ruggles at Port Hudson on August 20, Taylor's first day back in Louisiana.[8]

A view of the fortified bluffs at Port Hudson, looking from the west bank of the Mississippi. Harper's Weekly.

The defenders at that Mississippi citadel had a vested interest in Taylor's success. Beef cattle driven in from Texas, accompanied by Louisiana produce, would feed the troops at Port Hudson as well as those at Vicksburg, and the Red River would be the conduit of supply, the umbilical cord that fed the expanding forts a steady diet of red meat and corn. To ensure close cooperation between the forts and their line of supply, Taylor further requested a string of couriers be established to facilitate communications up and down the Mississippi and from his headquarters to Richmond. The Union might control most of the Mississippi, but Taylor would see that the western edge and what remained would stay in Confederate hands.[9]

The only son of President Zachary Taylor, Richard had enjoyed a prewar life of privilege at his stately home, Fashion Plantation, in St. Charles Parish. An aristocratic and well-heeled gentleman, Taylor had been an early supporter of secession in Louisiana. He had also been an active advocate of a strong defense for his state, but overconfident state officials ignored his urging and shipped troops to other theaters of the war. He, too, had left for distant fields after being elected colonel of the 9th Louisiana. In the Shenandoah Valley Taylor quickly earned promotion to brigadier general, in charge of a Louisiana brigade, under generals Richard S. Ewell and Thomas J. "Stonewall" Jackson. He won accolades for his performance in Virginia and advanced in rank to major general.[10]

Taylor's military career was exemplary and noteworthy. Unlike many of the Confederacy's high command, the Louisianan had never attended West Point. He was, however, a natural soldier, according to close friends. Taylor had served as an aide on his father's staff in Mex-

Baltimore native Joseph Lancaster Brent left his home in present-day Glendale, California, to join the Confederate cause, giving up a booming career as a lawyer and rising politician. He learned to manage artillery and heavy ordnance while serving on the staff of John B. Magruder in Virginia. He followed Richard Taylor to Louisiana, a region for which he had a special affection. Once there, he did what he could with what he had. Courtesy Special Collections Room, Glendale Public Library, Glendale, CA.

ico. He had also studied abroad and had earned a reputation for being extremely erudite, especially in regard to military history and tactics. Like many of the South's warriors, he suffered from chronic illness. Rheumatoid arthritis occasionally debilitated him. A former brother-in-law of Jefferson Davis by the president's first marriage, Taylor also enjoyed a certain amount of access to the executive. His bravery under fire, his excellent leadership in the Shenandoah, and his ties to the president all marked him for transfer to Louisiana in the role of a Rebel knight-errant and champion.

General Braxton Bragg, a rising star in the Army of Tennessee whose home lay within Taylor's new jurisdiction, had great confidence in the officer. Bragg remarked to a fellow Louisianan that Taylor was "the right man in the right place. If anybody could do anything in Louisiana, he would."[11]

Major Joseph L. Brent, an ordnance officer, accompanied Taylor from Virginia to ensure that the army in Louisiana Taylor was to build and lead would have adequate weapons, ammunition, and equipment. Brent established machine shops, arsenals, and depots at New Iberia, Franklin, Monroe, and Alexandria. To obtain items his department could not produce, he contracted with a foundry at Shreveport. Brent also cultivated relationships with his counterparts east of the Mississippi, helping to ensure their cooperation should he need to requisition supplies from outside his command. This talented soldier did much to offset the inadequacies of arms and munitions.[12]

Brent was perfect for the job. He had been a promising attorney in Los Angeles, California, before the war, but he went east to join the fight. He had been on the staff of General John Bankhead Magruder but applied to accompany Taylor to Louisiana because of family ties in the region. Taylor had great confidence in his chief of artillery and ordnance. "A lawyer by profession, Major Brent knew nothing of military affairs at the outbreak of the war but speedily acquainted himself with the technicalities of his new duties," he wrote. "His energy and administrative ability were felt in every direction."[13]

Volunteers stepped forward to help as these talented officers formed a useful army in the District of Louisiana. Among them was Confederate captain E. W. Fuller, already a successful leader in skirmishes against the Federals, whom Taylor described as "a western steamboat man, and one of the bravest of a bold, daring class." The boat-captain turned partisan offered *Music,* a small river steamer he had captured, as a gunboat and dispatch vessel to courier messages between the mouth of the Red River and the growing fortress at Port Hudson. An infantry company Fuller had raised, the St. Martin's Rangers, would operate as its crew. Cotton bales served as armor for its machinery, and three field pieces served as its battery. The *Music* would also carry supplies and equipment to the Rebel troops digging in above Baton Rouge. "We remained there until fall, keeping up a constant communication with the east side of the river and providing arms, ammunitions, and supplies of all kinds for the army then organizing," wrote Lieutenant Edward T. King. "It was during this period that we crossed 30,000 beef cattle to the east side to feed the armies of the Confederacy."[14]

Taylor tried to close the Federal door of opportunity Farragut had opened by capturing New Orleans. Upon close inspection, the new commander of the District of Louisiana found conditions extremely poor. His tiny army was certainly not ready for an offensive, despite his earlier bold plan. He also lacked significant artillery. Confederates had dumped ten heavy guns into the waters of south Louisiana during the panic that followed the Yankee invasion. Shortly after his arrival Taylor ordered the old 32-pounders and 24-pounders fished out and repaired. Major Brent saw that they were returned to service. These guns, brushed and oiled, served aboard cotton-clad gunboats and through embrasures from behind earthen walls.[15]

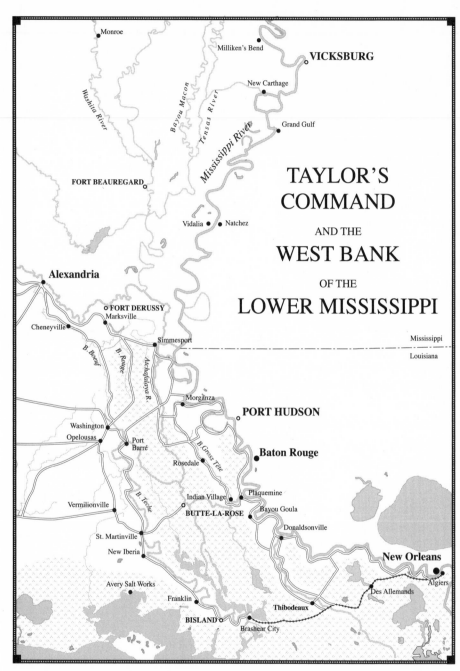

The general also faced a chaotic social challenge among his friends and neighbors in the occupied parishes. Northern forces had raided the southern fringes of the state, thoroughly disrupting life for its inhabitants. The most obvious reminder was the crowd of Lafourche District refugees who had fled to Alexandria and packed its hotels, rooming houses, and restaurants.

As times grew harder, the citizens of Louisiana began to turn on each other. Clarissa Hewitt, along with six family members and eighteen slaves, had been living aboard the steamers *Mary T.* and *Lafourche* since leaving their plantation in May. They had trouble finding safe harbor along the Red River. "We are refugees and in a part of the country that has been drained of much that it produced, and the white laboring man has joined the army, leaving the fields but scantily cultivated," she confided to her diary that summer. "We begin to feel the want of food." The Hewitts and their entourage found themselves facing scowls and shotguns when the steamers stopped at plantation landings, traditional hospitality now a casualty of war. The once-pampered aristocrats were soon forced to subsist on slave rations: sweet potatoes and corn bread. "After months on board the steamboat, with bad water as well as a lack of proper food, we are all beginning to feel the affects," she concluded. With two teenage daughters suffering from typhoid, the party headed to Alexandria, as so many others had, hoping to find shelter.[16]

Amid this chaos surrounding his headquarters in Alexandria, Taylor studied maps and made plans. He identified Brashear City as strategically vital to the region, but vulnerable to Union attack by both rail and sea. Federal naval domination of the Mississippi had essentially made the Lafourche District an indefensible *cul-de-sac* for the Confederates, and the partially finished Opelousas Railroad allowed U.S. troops rapid transportation and reliable supply lines for any campaigns in the area. After the skirmishes of the summer, the Union garrisons had fallen back from Brashear City to New Orleans, but they had returned to occupy key control points along the iron alley into the under-defended heartland of the sugar parish. Union soldiers now actively patrolled the railroad near Boutte Station and fortified the important crossing at Bayou des Allemands, defending the west bank approaches to New Orleans while keeping their offensive options open.

The circumstances seemed familiar to General Taylor. The maps revealed similarities between southwest Louisiana and the theater of

A Library of Congress image of a 24-pounder on a siege carriage in a fortified emplacement.

operations where Taylor had learned the art of war. Like the glens and vales of the Shenandoah Valley, southern Louisiana had clear lines of movement and transportation, with the complicating terrain feature being swamps instead of mountains. Like General Jackson, though, Taylor might be able to use these various avenues of approach to his advantage. He might surprise and confuse his enemies as he defeated them in detail. Control of the rivers and bayous would be crucial.

The major shortcoming was that Taylor was no longer among the highly motivated soldiers of Virginia. The apathetic troops in the District of West Louisiana shocked him. "I can assure you that at times I am almost disheartened by the want of patriotic feeling here," Taylor wrote to a friend in Virginia. "They are unwilling to do anything to defend themselves. In the lower part of the state this feeling is almost universal."[17]

This gunboat sports an old-fashioned 32-pounder served by a crew of seven sailors and a dog. This cannon was one of the most common heavy guns at the start of the Civil War. Naval Historical Center.

Despite this gloomy assessment, Taylor's arrival in the area returned hope to Governor Moore and many of his militia generals. They respected this fighting Louisianan and, spurred on by a new feeling of assurance, the men of the various parish commands confidently turned out as summer passed into fall. Those that did not would be conscripted—the energetic and decisive Taylor would see to it. Within a few weeks, these militia believed, an embryonic Confederate army would come to Thibodaux, justify the confidence of the citizens of the Lafourche District by destroying the enemy outposts and garrisons, and finish a glorious campaign by pushing the invaders back to the city of New Orleans. This rosy scenario ended with the state militia, filled with a renewed patriotic ardor, joining their victorious Confederate allies in a triumphal entry into the Crescent City.

Of course, there would be Butler's thirteen thousand men to contend with.

CHAPTER SEVEN

Plundering Armies

The arrival of General Richard Taylor, the renewed Confederate activity in the sugar parishes, and rumors of Rebel reinforcements from Texas caught the attention of the vigilant Yankees, who moved quickly to extinguish the resuscitated sparks of secessionist resistance. On August 28 a hundred men from the 8th Vermont Infantry, seventy from the 2nd Massachusetts Cavalry Battalion, and a section of artillery left the New Orleans vicinity on a raid through St. Charles Parish. After traveling by rail twenty-four miles from Algiers to Boutte Station, the column detrained and headed north toward the Mississippi River and Bonnet Carré point to investigate rumors that the Louisiana militia had begun to assemble. Nearly four miles from the tracks, the Federals marched onto the grounds of Fashion Plantation, Taylor's home.

The New Englanders made short work of the place. "It is one of the most splendid plantations that I ever saw," wrote one Vermonter to

Austin Harrison Ward was a twenty-one-year-old from Brattleboro when he enlisted in Company I, 8th Vermont. He survived the war, eventually earning the rank of sergeant. Courtesy of Denis Gaubert, Thibodaux, Louisiana.

his hometown newspaper. "I wish you could have seen the boys plunder." After they gathered the livestock, soldiers ordered Taylor's 175 slaves to empty the house. Union troops sat in the yard and feasted on the contents of Taylor's larder, as "hundreds of bottles of wines, eggs, preserved figs and peaches, turkeys, chickens, and honey in any quantity" emerged. One solider carried away the kettle and frying pan Zachary Taylor had used in the Mexican War. The New Englanders ransacked the former president's private papers, too, scattering important historical documents across the yard like litter. "I have one letter of his own handwriting," boasted one Vermonter. "The camp is loaded down with plunder—all kinds of clothing rings, watches, guns, pistols, swords, and some of General Taylor's old hats and coats, belt-swords—and in fact, every old relic he had is worn about camp." After this desecration, the writer cautioned his Vermont audience that "you and every one may be thankful that you are out of the reach of plundering armies."[1]

The New Englanders moved on another mile and camped near St. Charles courthouse, only to awaken at four o'clock the next morning amid reports that the enemy militia—at remarkable strength—had gathered only eight miles away. Confident and eager to scatter these amateurs, the Massachusetts troopers mounted up, the infantry quick-timing behind. By mid-morning the Federals located their quarry, three hundred men of the St. Charles Parish militia, in a bend of the river two miles above Bonnet Carré. They attacked immediately.

Shocked and surprised by the onslaught, the southerners panicked. Rebel pickets dutifully fired, dropping two of the approaching Federals, before they fled. While the infantry and cavalry deployed into line,

A Harper's Weekly *sketch of an activity euphemistically called "foraging," which often amounted to government-sanctioned pillaging as an instrument of war.*

the Union artillery swept the camp with canister shot, wounding one of the few remaining militiamen and frightening two more into surrendering. After this brief exchange the remainder of the St. Charles Parish militia crashed into the surrounding cane and swamps, heading for their homes.

The Yankees, having drawn blood and embarrassed their skittish enemy, returned laurel-crowned to their cars at Boutte Station. Along the way the mounted troops flushed three more prisoners out of the canebrakes, while the infantry looted all the plantations along the line of march. "From appearances, the sprit of plunder seems to have taken complete possession of their soldiers," reported one southerner traveling in their wake. "They prefer to steal, rob, and insult defenseless men, women, and children, rather than fight brave men on the battlefield," he added—a spurious claim, since the Yankees had tried to do just that, but the Rebels defenders had run.[2] Before long, a plunder train three miles long snaked its way back to the railroad. Five hundred freed slaves aided the army in ushering along the booty, which included more than one thousand head of cattle and half that number of sheep, mules, and horses.[3]

Undaunted, perhaps even motivated, by this Yankee raid, Taylor pushed ahead with his plans. He remained confident that, with a few regular Confederate soldiers among them, the militiamen would find their mettle and turn out *en masse* to liberate New Orleans. If not, they could be coerced. Taylor made sure that local provosts enforced Confederate conscription laws, sending out squads of troops to round up shirkers when necessary. After issuing another appeal to Richmond for more Confederate regiments, from whatever quarter, Taylor decided to make a tour of his department to inspect the troops he had on hand.

The soldiers he visited were of mixed quality. At Opelousas five new companies of Partisan Rangers drilled under the watchful eye of Governor Moore and would soon join the rowdy band near Donaldsonville operating on the Lafourche. Lieutenant Colonel Valsin Fournet's 10th "Yellow Jacket" Infantry Battalion, which Taylor suspected was little more than a few companies of apathetic Cajuns from St. Martin's Parish, drilled in the immediate vicinity of New Iberia. "The men were without instruction, and inadequately armed and equipped," Taylor noted after inspecting the troops. He lectured their commanders on the "importance of discipline and instruction," then promised to find weapons for them.[4]

There were promising signs as well. As Taylor continued his journey down the Bayou Teche road toward the Lafourche country, a courier announced that the Shiloh veterans of Lieutenant Colonel Franklin Clack's 12th "Confederate Guards Response" Battalion had arrived in camps near Opelousas, having transferred from duty with the Army of Tennessee in response to Louisiana's plea for help. Most were from New Orleans and eager to liberate their homes. Although only two hundred strong, the presence of these practiced warriors might lend courage to their compatriots in the region. At the same time Taylor passed squads of conscripts and militiamen coming into instruction camps, the fruits of Governor Moore's earlier efforts. Some would serve nearby and aid in Taylor's plans. The majority, however, would fill out Louisiana units on other fields and thus prove useful while safely removed from the temptations of deserting back to their nearby homes.

A man with an eye for order, Taylor reorganized some of his forces. McWaters's men would be combined with the other Louisiana horsemen in the Teche country to form the 2nd Louisiana Cavalry under Colonel William G. Vincent, a capable Confederate officer. Taylor also called for the tiny but tough 12th Infantry Battalion to fold in with the unsteady 10th to form the 33rd Louisiana Infantry.[5]

Taylor needed artillery in the region. All he had on hand were the paroled members of the St. Mary's Cannoneers. Commanded by the son of a wealthy Teche planter, Captain Florian Cornay, the cannoneers had already been under fire at the Fort Jackson garrison. Now they waited at camps near Franklin, paroled in accordance to prisoner protocols worked out between Union and Confederate leaders. Now they waited to rejoin the war until learning of their exchange for a like number of captured Federals. Major Joseph Lancaster Brent made sure these troops, including those on hand and anticipated to arrive, had all the tools of war. "Batteries were equipped, disciplined, and drilled," Taylor wrote. "Leather was tanned, harness made, wagons built, and a little workshop, established at New Iberia by Governor Moore, became important as an arsenal of construction."[6]

Other units were on the way. Captain Oliver J. Semmes, younger brother of Raphael Semmes, the famed future skipper of the CSS *Alabama,* was coming west from Port Hudson with his plucky, red-shirted 1st Regular Battery. These steady gunners had performed excellent service at the Battle of Baton Rouge and would be valuable to Taylor as well. Captain George Ralston's Battery H, 1st Mississippi Light Artillery would cross the river from Port Hudson to help.

Passing into the Lafourche District, Taylor visited the camps of troops who had served in the region all summer, including James McWaters' five companies of rambunctious partisans who ranged between Donaldsonville and Thibodeaux. The general appreciated these fighters but needed many more like them. While traveling along Bayou Lafouche, Taylor came upon what he hoped were the first rumblings of an avalanche of new troops. Colonel Waller and his three hundred Texans of the 13th Texas Cavalry Battalion reported to their new commander near Thibodaux. "The men were superbly mounted, well armed, and thoroughly equipped for war," a Louisianan observed. "Altogether it was as gallant an array as ever marched under any flag."[7]

Taylor, with a personal score to settle, now searched for opportunities to punish the invaders and decided to push against the enemy at two points. Militia leaders in the Lafourche country had urged an expedition to strike back at the enemy. The most logical point would be the railroad crossing at Bayou des Allemands, which served as the principal Union garrison in the region. From here, Butler's New Englanders and Midwesterners could pivot southwest along the railroad as far as Berwick's Bay or head northwest to Thibodeaux. The capture of this position would accomplish three goals: the immediate enemy threat would be eliminated, the railroad would be open to Algiers, and captured weapons could arm the militia. By cutting this land link to New Orleans, the Confederates would restrict Federal troops attempting raids along the Lafourche to amphibious landings from the Gulf of Mexico or the Mississippi River and road marches from Donaldsonville. Anticipating those possibilities, Taylor, who held no dread of gunboats, planned to follow up his railroad raid by disrupting shipping on the Mississippi with artillery positions cut into the levee. With these projects clear in his mind, he ordered his subordinates to execute them.[8]

There may have been another reason Taylor was anxious to launch his offensive and challenge Federal control of the Lafourche region. Rebel armies were gathering or on the move across the South. In Virginia nearly a month before, General Thomas J. Jackson had bloodied a Union army under the command of Nathaniel P. Banks at Cedar Mountain, a battle followed up two weeks later by General Robert E. Lee's sound thrashing of General John Pope at Second Manassas. In the Confederate heartland, meanwhile, generals Braxton Bragg and Edmund Kirby Smith invaded Kentucky while smaller armies under Sterling Price and Earl Van Dorn threatened the Federal stronghold of Corinth in Northern Mississippi. The southerners even regained lost ground in Northwest Arkansas as General Thomas Hindman and a force from Fort Smith erased Union gains of the previous Spring. Taylor would now make his contribution to this Rebel resurgence.

Taylor counted around fifteen hundred men on hand for the Bayou des Allemands raid. This strike force included McWaters's companies of mounted Louisiana partisans; the Terrebonne, St. John the Baptist,

The many hidden paths and byways through the marais, *swamps, and marshes provided Louisianans with ways of moving unseen by the enemy.* Harper's Weekly.

and St. Charles parish militias; and Waller's 13th Texas Cavalry Battalion. Militia General John Pratt led the Louisianans, but Taylor indicated that he wanted Waller, a regularly appointed Confederate officer, to serve in overall command of the raid.

This army counted on surprise and knowledge of the local terrain for success. The railroad crossing at Bayou des Allemands fronted a half-mile wide stretch of water and therefore could only be attacked from behind. This would cause the southerners, however, to place themselves between the garrison and potential Federal reinforcements coming up from New Orleans. Pratt decided that the risk was worth the gain, and he ordered his militia to improve the rough local road across the Chackbay swamp by felling trees and building bridges. By traveling at night and taking this infrequently traveled road through the mire to the Mississippi, the Rebels would pass northeast around the head of Bayou des Allemands and turn back south and get behind the Union position. Next, they would block the railroad at Boutte Station and cut communications with New Orleans, thus isolating their prey. With stealth and security, Waller's Texans and Pratt's Louisianans could then fall upon the Federal rear before the Yankees

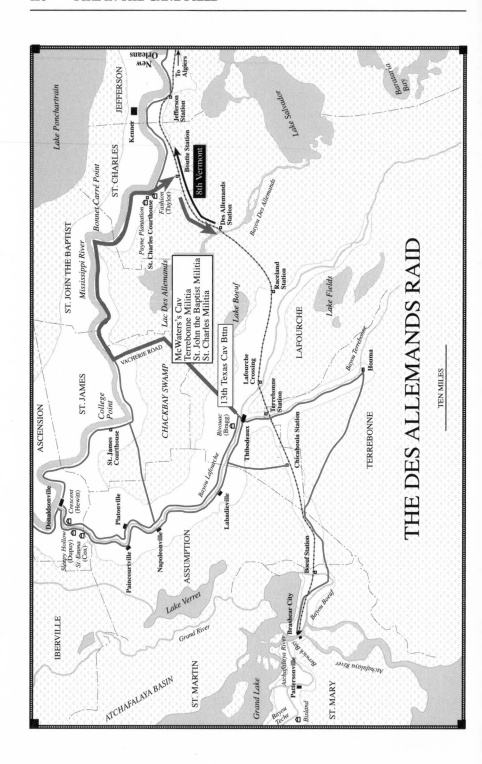

THE DES ALLEMANDS RAID

in New Orleans could rescue them. The militia would lead the way; the Texans would follow close behind.[9]

Emerging from the Chackbay, Pratt's column passed through the once-rich St. Charles Parish and viewed sites of destruction that confirmed the rumors about their enemy. "It was one continual scene of desolation and sadness," wrote a Louisiana militiaman. "Nearly every place on the route had been despoiled and plundered—even to the huts of the poorest creoles." The soldiers found Taylor's home in shambles, "the furniture smashed, the walls torn down, pictures cut out of their frames," the Louisianan continued. The personal papers of President Zachary Taylor lay scattered across the floor as the soldiers toured the scene. "The barbarians had respected nothing but the portrait of General [Winfield] Scott upstairs."[10]

Convinced now more than ever that these invaders needed to be checked, the first of the raiders arrived unopposed at Boutte Station on the morning of September 4. Finding the railroad buildings vacant, the militiamen and partisans concealed themselves on either side of the tracks to ambush any Union trains that might arrive while they waited for the Texans. To further confuse the enemy, the Rebels threw the switch to shunt any arriving locomotives onto a siding and into a sure collision with an empty passenger car. Should the Yankees come, those not killed by Louisiana bullets might be killed in an old-fashioned train wreck.[11]

Although Pratt's men were in place, Waller's inexperienced Texans remained nowhere to be seen. "When General Pratt reached my camp, he expressed great anxiety on Waller's account," wrote Colonel George B. N. Wailes of the St. Charles and St. John the Baptist Militia. "He was known to be in our rear somewhere, moving toward us, but was ignorant of the country and the route." Lieutenant Achille Bougere, a local boy detached from the 30th Louisiana Infantry at Port Hudson, went back to find the Texans.[12]

Evidently not sharing the same sense of urgency gripping their Louisiana compatriots, the Texans were dawdling. Waller and Pratt may also have been at odds over who should actually be in command. Upon reaching the Mississippi River, the Texans had gone into camps and lingered for a day and a half while Pratt's militia had moved on to

Boutte. Instead of moving up, Waller's undisciplined horsemen had instead fallen two days behind in their march and had been further delayed when their advance elements reached the Mississippi and began seizing passing vessels. The Texans helped themselves to any useful cargoes but allowed those vessels not employed in Federal service to proceed to New Orleans. This would prove to be an amateur's mistake, as these ship captains reported the Rebel presence, compromising the security of the operation. Federals in New Orleans began plotting to catch these saucy newcomers.

Events now conspired to speed up the Rebel timetable. General Pratt, his trap ready, received word that an unsuspecting Federal escort train was en route from Bayou des Allemands to meet the regularly scheduled supply train from New Orleans. With Waller wasting time on the river, the militia officer had no choice but to take charge. He ordered his men to spring the ambush as planned—without the Texans.

Several miles westward down the tracks, the Federal garrison at Bayou des Allemands continued its usual routine, unaware of the snare that lay athwart its line of communications. The regular pulse of occupation called for supplies to come by rail from Algiers. The ration and ammunition train ran unescorted for much of the way but was met by a guard train at the double tracks of Boutte Station, the only siding on that part of the line. From Bayou des Allemands came a second train of mostly empty cars with an escorting force composed of a company from the 8th Vermont and a single 12-pounder howitzer. At the rendezvous point, workers swapped the empty cars for the full supply cars, and the loaded supply train shuttled the rations and soldiers back to the garrison while the empty cars returned to Algiers to await the next trip. The Federals' failure to permanently occupy the station and protect its critical siding and switch would prove to be a critical mistake. The location of Pratt's ambush was well chosen.[13]

What had started as a mundane guard mission for the train-riding Vermonters quickly turned bloody. As the armed escort approached Boutte Station, a slight jolt rocked the cars when the train unexpectedly slid off the main line onto the siding. Within moments, dozens of shotguns and rifles flashed in a ragged volley. Buckshot and bullets

This photo of a Civil War train, while not taken in Louisiana, does include a flatcar, a passenger car, and freight cars similar to those on the train ambushed at Boutte Station. Notice the soldiers standing on top, and the second locomotive at the head. Library of Congress.

swept the boxcars and flatcars, knocking many of the New Englanders off the train. All twelve crewmen of the cannon fell immediately. When the train collided with the idle passenger car, those Yankees still standing fell hard. More were tossed to the ground while the cannon careened off its platform, crashing end over end into a heap by the side of the tracks.[14]

Amid this chaos of steam, soot, and shot, Private Lewis J. Ingalls of Belvidere, Vermont, regained his senses quickly enough to try to save the situation. He "jumped from the car and adjusted the switch, little dreaming he could regain his place but hoping to save the few left alive," reported Corporal Rufus Kinsley. Ingalls ran ahead of the train to the siding's far end and corrected the track. A Rebel rifleman noticed the movement and shot a bullet through the Vermonter's neck, but the New Englander completed his mission despite this and three additional wounds received in rapid succession. His quick action allowed the train to push the blocking car onto the main track, allowing the remaining troops aboard the train to escape. "He sprang for the train, and reached the rear car just in time to escape," Kinsley continued. "When you hear the trump of fame sounding the name of some great general, who had secured for himself some safe place, where he could see his soldiers capture a city or win a battle, just you remember Lewis Ingalls, will you?"[15]

Having slipped the Confederate snare, the surviving Federals rolled along on their battered, bullet-riddled train toward New Orleans, lucky to be alive. The engineer could barely see past the car in front, but he had sense enough to bring the train to an abrupt halt a few miles down the track. His vigilance, as well as that of the engineer on the on-rushing locomotive from Algiers, barely avoided a head-on collision between the two trains. Relieved at their good fortune and the intervention of pluck and luck, one engineer reversed his engine while the other followed behind, both trains heading toward Algiers and safety. Back at Boutte Station, thirteen Federals lay dead, two others were dying, and twenty more suffered from wounds. Those that had fallen from the cars found themselves surrounded by Rebels and facing an uncertain fate.[16]

With scenes of pillage and destruction fresh on their minds, the Louisiana militia was not inclined to be charitable. Irate soldiers committed atrocities, slashing and harassing their captives with sabers and bowie knives, but leaving them alive. Some Confederates burned the buildings at Boutte and tore up the tracks while their comrades robbed the prisoners and confiscated their equipment. Pratt assembled the captives and marched them at the head of his westbound column toward Bayou des Allemands, the ultimate target of the raid.[17]

Major McWaters and his mounted men neared the Union outpost first, and the wily partisan resorted to a *ruse de guerre*. Secreting his men in cover within sight of the Union positions, McWaters forwarded a flag of truce for a parley. Captain Edward Hall of the 8th Vermont, answering the flag, sent forward a detachment to determine the Rebels' intentions. When these men did not return, he sent forward a second detail. Confederates seized both squads and, along with the prisoners just arriving from Boutte, marched the Union men in front of the militia column toward the Federal position. Hall, unwilling to massacre his own soldiers in order to fire at the Rebels, ordered his two Ellsworth rifled cannon thrown into the bayou and then surrendered his command.[18]

The outing had been a complete Confederate success. The day's fighting had killed more than a dozen invaders, wounded a score more, and made prisoners of another 155. Pratt's men exchanged their converted flintlocks for the Springfield rifles of the Vermont soldiers. The militia counted three cannon—one from the train and two fished out of the bayou—as new additions to their forces.[19]

The future looked gloomy for the captured Yankees. An escort guarded most of the prisoners as they headed down the railroad toward Berwick's Bay, New Iberia, and captivity. Pratt's command accompanied them as far as Thibodaux, and turned them over to others to exact revenge. The victors identified seven of their captives as deserted militiamen; their pleas for mercy fell on unsympathetic ears. Rebel bullets settled the matter and a track-side ditch became the turncoats' open grave.[20]

The following day, September 5, General Butler ordered the survivors of the 8th Vermont, along with the 2nd Massachusetts Battery, to take another train and retrieve the regiment's honor. In addition, the 21st Indiana would proceed up the Mississippi and block the Confederate line of retreat via St. Charles Courthouse. The U.S. troops headed out, but thirteen miles from Boutte Station, the locomotive struck a cow, derailing many of the cars and injuring several more soldiers. "We formed in line of battle at once, supposing of course the enemy had thrown us from the track, and were in readiness to gobble us up," Corporal Kinsley wrote. No Confederates appeared, but, unable to proceed, this portion of the expedition returned humiliated to New Orleans. Orders went out recalling the 21st Indiana as well. The next day, Federal pickets withdrew to within twelve miles of Algiers, as nervous planners searched for a way to strike back and regain the lost ground. Since coming to Louisiana, the 8th Vermont had lost more than three hundred men killed, wounded, and captured in little swamp skirmishes.[21]

Had the Union attack carried forward, the Vermonters would have certainly fallen in with Waller's Texans and added to their list of woes. Late for Pratt's ambush, the Texans finally emerged at Boutte Station at noon on September 7. "Here we remained about two or three hours in walking around and looking at the place," wrote Private William Craig. "The Depot that was fired . . . was still burning." The militia had been thorough in its destruction. "The place was entirely deserted—not so much as a dog or chicken left," added Lieutenant C. C. Cox. "Only a heap of ashes." After word arrived that the Union troops had been spotted coming up the tracks, Waller did not wait for a fight but instead ordered his men to mount their horses and retrace the route to the Mississippi, so that he might continue his private war against the river's shipping. He would soon regret his decision.[22]

CHAPTER EIGHT

BONNET CARRÉ

Col. Waller knew when to run. He learned about that part of war there
Overton (Texas) Sharp Shooter
May 31, 1888

A t two o'clock on the afternoon of September 7, Lieutenant Colonel Edwin Waller's Texans rode their horses atop the Mississippi levee near the St. Charles courthouse, bent on mischief. "We saw two schooners slowly coming down the river," Private William Craig of the 13th Texas Cavalry Battalion wrote afterward. Waller ordered his men to dismount. The horse holders went to the rear and into a nearby cane field, and the rest climbed the levee with their weapons ready. The vessels, U.S. flags flying from their sterns, innocently came alongside the Texan position after being hailed from shore, unaware that St. Charles Parish was back in Rebel hands and that they were being lured into a trap. Once the ships had tied up to the landing, armed Confederates pushed aboard the vessels and informed the skippers of their mistake. Aboard were tons of sugar and a cargo of liquor. Waller's men took what they wanted and then applied the torch to the rest. "The Star Spangled Banner . . . was torn into atoms," Craig recalled. "By this time, the two schooners were wrapt in flames." After securing seven prisoners from the ships' crews, the

A Harper's Weekly *image of cargo schooners burning and adrift.*

Texans returned to a pleasant camp at G. E. Payne's Plantation near St. Charles Courthouse, satisfied with their day's work.[1]

Late that afternoon, thirty of Waller's bolder men decided to ride down the levee toward New Orleans and attack a large ship rumored to be aground near Algiers. Leaving camp amid high expectations, the detachment received a shock as they prowled the shores that evening across the river from the New Orleans suburb of Carrollton. At about 10 p.m., the Texans spied Union troops tramping aboard four steamboats while the powerful steam frigate USS *Mississippi* idled nearby. Correctly guessing that the expedition was intended for them, the Texans' horses raced the Union steamers upriver. The Rebels arriving at Payne's Plantation about daybreak, barely ahead of their enemy.[2]

Having just risen, Colonel Waller acted unconcerned about the report of imminent attack, but the senior captain of the unit, fifty-two-year-old James Belvarde Pope January, was worried. A veteran of the wars of the Texas Republic and the Mexican War, he had fought Comanches and Mexicans in his day, and he sensed a trap. He "went to Col. Waller, and expostulated with him to get him to move," remembered one Texan. "Waller refused to stir. The officer of the day went to him, and, as was his duty, suggested to him the propriety of moving. Waller refused to stir." Another tried to persuade him to leave the camp: Lieutenant Reid N. Weiseger recommended that the command

The USS Mississippi *was one of the more powerful warships in the Union navy. This steamer's distinctive profile made it easy to recognize, even in the dark. G. H. Suydam Collection, Mss. 1394, Louisiana and Lower Mississippi Valley Collections, LSU Libraries, Baton Rouge, Louisiana*

at least move upriver ahead of the gunboats, strike a perpendicular road, and hide in the cane until the danger passed.[3]

The badgering irritated the proud Texan leader. "Colonel Waller replied that every officer in the battalion seemed to be trying to command him; that he had not come down there to run, and he was not going to do it," a soldier recalled. "But there is as much in knowing when and how to fight as there is in being willing to fight. A very wise king in the olden times said 'there is a time for all things' and that being true, . . . there is a time to run. But that time Colonel Waller had not learned. He learned it pretty soon, however, that day at Bonnet Carré."[4]

When pickets reported warships coming upriver, confirming his men's reports, Waller finally heeded his officers' advice. He ordered his men to mount their horses as a precaution. Soon Federal transports carrying the 21st Indiana and a section of the 1st Maine Battery glided upriver past the Texans' position. Unable to ignore the danger now, Waller ordered his men into the cover of a narrow lane in the canefield to hide until the Federals either went away or landed for a fight.[5]

Hoping to use the cover of the sugarcane to surprise the enemy, Waller's men blundered into a trap. Additional U.S. troops had unloaded, undetected, below the Texan camps. While the 21st Indiana, 4th Wisconsin, and part of the 1st Maine Battery moved down the river road from their landings near Bonnet Carré point, the 14th Maine, 6th Michigan, 9th Connecticut, and the rest of the 1st Maine Battery had moved up the river road from the other direction. With several miles between them, neither element of the Union force could see the other across the canefields, the marshy, wooded *marais*, and sprawling plantations, but they knew that the Confederates lay unseen somewhere between them. They would have to flush the enemy into the open like a covey of quail.[6]

Unaware of the scope or gravity of the danger, the Texans bided their time until a picket on a lathered horse announced that it was they who were hunted. Stunned, Waller ordered his men to proceed up the river road to what he hoped would be escape, trusting that by some good fortune the Union troops he had seen pass by earlier were on a different errand. Instead, his advance guard encountered the 21st Indiana's skirmishers, deployed as the anvil awaiting the beating of the Union hammer from below. A squad of Texans from the advance broke ranks and rode down upon the scattered infantry, thinking them easy prey and expecting to force their way to freedom. Instead, three Texans in the lead were felled by well-disciplined fire from the Hoosier's breechloaders. Surprised that the enemy would not be pushed away as easily as he had hoped, Waller ordered his column to turn around and head back the way they came. He now realized that he had blundered badly.

"Consternation seized the command," Lieutenant Cox remembered. "We countermarched on the double quick—or being cavalry I should say trot." When the Texans arrived near the intersection of a work road running perpendicular to the levee, they came under fire from the USS *Mississippi* in the river off to their left. Every few seconds, heavy shells whizzed overhead. "The only effect of her fire was to accelerate our movement," Cox wrote later. Behind them the two 12-pounders accompanying the 21st Indiana moved into their firing positions as well.[7]

Trapped on three sides, the Texans spun to their right and trotted down the road toward the swamp. At the *forty arpent* road, the Texans dismounted and deployed into line facing the river and preparing to ambush their pursuers. To their front lay a cleared field, forty yards wide. Behind them, dense sugarcane grew for three hundred years until giving way to the wooded *marais* beyond. Waller ordered his horse holders to move into the cover. Hiding along the road and fronting the open field, the Rebels waited anxiously for the Federals to emerge where they could be cut down like so much wheat. Despite the shells and grapeshot passing overhead, the Texans hunkered down in their line, waiting for the first glimpse of a blue uniform to break free from the waving wall of green sugarcane.

James B. P. January. This rugged veteran of the Texas frontier came to Louisiana to do his part but quickly grew frustrated with his inexperienced commander. He would later resign his commission and return to his farm near Victoria. Special Collections, Victoria College.

Unable to bear the suspense, one man succumbed to buck fever. The tenderfoot discharged his weapon, blowing the Texan ambush. Converging Federals, thrashing blindly through the tall cane, heard the shot and were now quite alert to their danger. The infantry backed out of the canefields to let the artillery and navy probe for the sneaky Rebels.[8]

The Texans tried to hold their ground during this blind pounding. Despite their lack of experience and the growing ferocity of the attack, "the men stood fast," Lieutenant Cox remembered. Before long, though, the outcome appeared obvious; the Federals clearly knew their location. "Waller gave the orders to fall back to our horses amid shells and balls," private Craig recorded. "Some horses had got frightened and run off, and some men took most any horse they first met with." Outnumbered and with their cover blown, Waller's command would have to try to outrun the Federals.[9]

Sugarcane grows densely in the field and can present a seemingly impenetrable wall of vegetation. Colonel Edwin Waller's Texans learned all about fighting under these conditions at Bonnet Carré.

One Texan later gave credit to his colonel for being an apt pupil of war. "Then, Colonel Waller learned there was a time to run; but unfortunately he had no where to run except the boggy swamp behind them. You can bet that, from that day on, Col. Waller knew when to run. He learned about that part of war there. . . ."[10]

The Federal infantry moved cautiously through the cane as the Texan battalion dissolved into clusters of panicked men followed a drainage canal through the cane and thrashed deep into the wooded swamp behind the tree line. The big guns of the USS *Mississippi* continued firing toward the thrashing sounds of the retreating Confederates. Captain January of Victoria, turning to face the enemy, drew his sword, and refused to run farther. He and fifty of his men, after putting on a brave show, surrendered. In the mire Waller ordered his

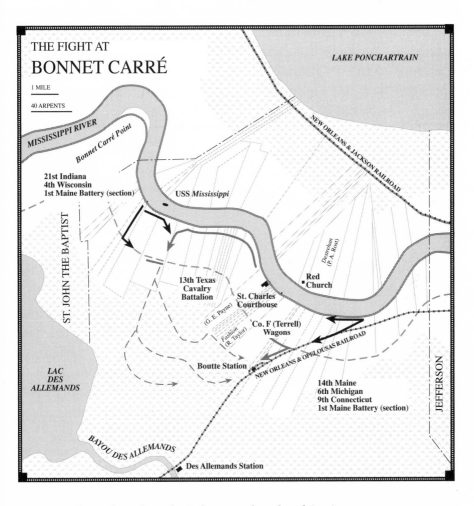

THE FIGHT AT
BONNET CARRÉ

1 MILE

40 ARPENTS

LAKE PONCHARTRAIN

MISSISSIPPI RIVER

Bonnet Carré Point

NEW ORLEANS & JACKSON RAILROAD

21st Indiana
4th Wisconsin
1st Maine Battery (section)

USS *Mississippi*

ST. JOHN THE BAPTIST

*Destrehan
(P. A. Rost)*

Red
Church

13th Texas
Cavalry
Battalion

St. Charles
Courthouse

(G. E. Payne)

Co. F (Terrell)
Wagons

*Fashion
(R. Taylor)*

LAC
DES
ALLEMANDS

Boutte Station

NEW ORLEANS & OPELOUSAS RAILROAD

14th Maine
6th Michigan
9th Connecticut
1st Maine Battery (section)

JEFFERSON

BAYOU DES ALLEMANDS

Des Allemands Station

command to abandon their horses, but by this time most were not
around to take heed of such advice. The Rebels plunged deeper into
the timber, a "regular stamped[e]," according to Cox. "The music the
shot and shells made among the trees was scary." Not content that
the Texans had dispersed, the Union infantry from the 4th Wisconsin and 21st Indiana emerged from the cane into the clearing just vacated by the Texans, and they formed their lines of battle as the guns
of the 1st Maine Artillery peppered the woods with shell, shot, and
canister. After tearing up the vegetation for a few minutes to smoke
out any renewed chance of ambush, the cannons ceased firing. The
two infantry regiments advanced, moving past the splintered trees
and following the horse tracks deep into the mire.[11]

With the sounds of cannon blasts and gunfire in their ears, Waller's panicked soldiers thrashed deeper into the swamp as best they could, determined to stay beyond enemy reach. Those still in the saddle struggled as their mounts bucked and lurched through the bog. "We rode our horses as far as they could go," Lieutenant Cox remembered. "The water was a foot to 18 inches deep, the ground filled with cypress knees, and the bottom very soft." With the rattle, shouts, and commands of five hundred Union soldiers coming from the margins of the timber only two hundred yards away, the Texans abandoned their forlorn mounts. "I took one last fond look at my good horse, saddle, and accoutrements, and struck out on foot . . . without coursing or compass." The Texans undoubtedly heard the triumphal shouts of their enemies as the Federals rounded up the bogged horses and led them back as trophies.[12]

Lieutenant Achille Bougere, the Texans' Louisiana guide dispatched by Pratt, had arrived that morning just in time to take part in the rout. He led one band of novices deeper into the swamp. When their horses became stuck, the men faced an unpleasant duty. "In order to prevent them from falling into the hands of the Federals, they cut the throats of each others horses," wrote one veteran. "Not one of them had the heart to kill their own horses."[13]

Weak from illness, Lieutenant Reid Weisiger hid in the roots of a fallen cypress tree, unable to go further. Although scores of Federals passed nearby, he remained undiscovered. After dark he emerged, dodged between pickets, and made his way to where the battalion wagons had been parked near the St. Charles courthouse, still undiscovered by roving Federals. As the first survivor of the disaster to emerge and relate the news, Weisiger respectfully urged the wagons and their escort to make their way to Thibodaux. These teamsters prudently followed his advice.[14]

All that day squads of Texans pushed their way through the sucking mud of the swamp. Lieutenant Cox fell in with a cluster of officers, including Waller. "It was the blind leading the blind," Cox would write later. "I think we boxed the compass a dozen times—we could not keep a course but kept going as our strength would permit. Much of the time one could not travel over a hundred yards without stopping to rest." As officer and enlisted man alike struggled in the mud, the tragic humor of the disaster became evident. "Hungry and tired and humiliated as we were, the plight we were in was so ludicrous that we could but laugh and try to make a joke of our mishap," Cox wrote. "There was one consoling reflection: we had so far escaped being taken prisoner."[15]

The scattered Texans slowly made their way to friendly lines. "We came through a swamp that never was trod before by man," Private Craig recorded. "In some places water and mud was waist deep and some come very nigh giving up." This solider finally broke free of the morass by emerging onto the grounds of Taylor's Fashion Plantation, having made a huge half circle. He and his comrades were "all wet and hungry and remarkably tired. Some came in with no shoes on, no hats, and some with hardly any clothes." That evening the troops helped themselves to the corn growing in the field before skirting the edge of the timber back toward the Opelousas Railroad. By first light the bulk of the battalion had reached the ruins of Boutte Station. From there they headed down the railroad line toward their comrades at Bayou des Allemands and beyond.[16]

For the rest of the day on September 9 bedraggled Texans appeared in camp. The Louisiana militia made much of their allies' misfortune. "Our little band of Texians [was] in a bad plight," Cox recounted. "Our humiliation and discomfiture in the presence of the victorious Kageans was very mortifying." Next Taylor's Texans headed for a general reorganization at Terrebonne Station, suffering the further embarrassment of being dubbed the "Cane Cart Cavalry," after their new mode of transportation. "Men were coming in . . . gangs all day," Private Craig noted. "All went to the hotel and got breakfast and got clean clothes and looked once more like people." Only one company, Terrell's, which had missed the September 8 disaster at Bonnet Carré by being detached to escort the wagons, still had horses. Without mounts or weapons the 13th Texas Cavalry Battalion appeared eviscerated, even though they had only suffered three killed and fifteen captured. Taylor's hopes for a viable army shivered.[17]

CHAPTER NINE

A CONFEDERATE ARMY

What a happy time we passed
Helen Dupuy, Sleepy Hollow Plantation

The disaster at Bonnet Carré proved to be more annoyance than decisive in Richard Taylor's mind, and he moved ahead with plans to resist the Federal invasion—now less one battalion. Despite the wrecking of Waller's command, the Confederates remained determined to follow their raid on Des Allemands and Boutte stations by moving a small force toward the Mississippi River and contesting its control with the Federals. The strategic junction of Lafourche Bayou and the Mississippi was the key to control one end of the Lafourche District, and Taylor directed his troops to scour burned-out Donaldsonville and its environs to turn out the parish militia and keep the enemy at bay. On September 10, shortly after making their camps at St. Emma Plantation a few miles west from Donaldsonville down the Lafourche, several dozen troopers of the newly designated 2nd Louisiana Cavalry rode to a point where locals reported that fugitives of the Ascension Parish militia were hiding. "The Confederates

A present-day image of the restored plantation house, St. Emma, near Donaldsonville, Louisiana. Owned by German immigrant Charles A. Koch, it was part of a magnificent sugar empire that included the nearby Belle Alliance plantation. This home would serve both Confederate and Union masters during the war. Courtesy Kay Frazier, Abilene, Texas.

told then that if they surrendered no harm would be done them," wrote Helen Dupuy from her nearby home at Sleepy Hollow Plantation. Instead the scofflaws opened fire, killing two Confederate officers and wounding an enlisted man. The cavalrymen shot back, killing one and scattering the rest. Five surrendered. Forcing the Confederacy's will on the population of this portion of the Lafourche region would continue to prove problematic.[1]

The Confederates faced other challenges for control as well. Following up on their successful rout of Waller at Bonnet Carré, Union troops shifted their focus away from the Opelousas railroad and toward Donaldsonville. On September 11 troops aboard three transports, escorted by the USS *Katahdin,* landed at the town to seize sugar and other contraband of war. While the warship hovered off shore, infantry scrambled down gangplanks and began their mission. For several hours troops rolled hogsheads of sugar onto the waiting steamers, and scores of Unionist refugees escaped secessionist persecution and sought asylum aboard with the Yankees. Before long Federal soldiers also began looting.

The dismantling of one household caught the attention of Lieutenant Francis Roe, commander of the *Katahdin.* "I received positive information that a company of these troops had entered a large mansion . . . had pillaged it in a brutal manner, and carried off wines, liquors, silver plate, and clothing belonging to the ladies," he wrote in disgust to the officers who had ordered the expedition. "I respectfully request instructions if the guns of the *Katahdin* are to be used for the protection of soldiers upon a marauding expedition, and if I am to use them in the protection of drunken, undisciplined and licentious troops in . . . wanton pillage."[2]

The USS Katahdin *was a 691-ton screw steam gunboat, one of the more active warships on the lower Mississippi. She returned to the open sea in 1863 and patrolled the Texas coast. She was nearly identical to the USS* Cayuga, *hence the large number "8" on her funnel as an identifier. Naval Historical Center.*

While the troops had been ransacking Donaldsonville, Rebels from Vincent's 2nd Louisiana Cavalry skulked along the edge of the woods behind the town, seething. Roe ordered his gunners to shell the Confederates out of their cover and succeeded in driving them away. He almost wished he had not. "I opened my fire upon guerillas hovering in the rear, apparently occupied in preventing such acts of the United States troops," he reported. "I feel quite ready to place the *Katahdin* and her guns under the fire of an enemy. I am desirous of encountering enemies and injuring them in every manly manner, but I cannot further prostitute the dignity of my profession, as I conceive I have done to-day. . . . It is disgraceful and humiliating to me to be ordered on guard duty of soldiers employed in pillaging ladies' dresses and petticoats."[3]

When the note reached Butler, he responded bluntly and incredulously. "The acts of the troops in pillaging (if true) are without palliation or excuse," he wrote. But certainly soldiers in the army of the United States would not stoop to such misdeeds, he argued. Insolent naval

Francis Asbury Roe, a native of Elmira, New York, was one of the more capable of the naval officers serving on the lower Mississippi, despite being described as a "rhodomontade of a sub-lieutenant" by General Benjamin Butler. He commanded the USS Katahdin *in all of its actions until transferring to command USS* Sassacus *on the coast of North Carolina, where he fought ably against the ironclad C.S.S. Albermarle. He enjoyed a long postwar career and retired at the grade of rear admiral. Naval Historical Center.*

officers, on the other hand, were not to be tolerated. The conduct of the infantry, even if proven, paled by comparison to the "bombastic, and ridiculous rhodomontade of a sub-lieutenant of the Navy," he wrote.[4]

Donaldsonville, devastated by naval guns, partially burned, and now ransacked by infantry, became a desolate no-man's-land. U.S. troops returned to their transports and departed for New Orleans, leaving behind a trail of broken furniture and shattered glass. The Confederates of the 2nd Louisiana Cavalry, perhaps feeling vindicated by the rough treatment the Federals delivered to the lukewarm citizens of the region, returned to their scouting and picket duties, mindful to maintain a safe distance from the Mississippi and its threat of amphibious raids by the U.S. Navy.

Taylor, meanwhile, had returned to his headquarters in Alexandria, where he received news about hoped-for reinforcements. Secretary of War Randolph had continued urging commanders to shake loose any units they could spare. From the defenses of Mobile, Alabama, came Colonel Leopold Armant's 18th Louisiana "Creole" Regiment, veterans of Shiloh and largely native to the sugar parishes. Confederates on the Alabama coast also promised to send Colonel George McPheeters's 24th Louisiana "Crescent" Regiment. This command had been a New Orleans militia organization before being mobilized and sent to the bloodbath at Shiloh. After their enlistment had expired, the men had joined other units. Now, the 24th regiment was to be reformed and reorganized at New Iberia, and the men serving abroad would be brought home. Additionally Randolph urged that Sibley's Texas Brigade, three more shadow regiments, be sent from the west.[5]

The Confederate high command issued other orders designed to aid Taylor. Instead of protecting the entire state west of the Mississippi, Taylor would now only be responsible for all the territory west of the Red River. To the north lay the District of Arkansas, and west of it the Indian Territory. West of Louisiana, leaders subdivided General Paul O. Hébert's vast District of Texas, New Mexico, and Arizona into several sub-districts. Although Taylor asked for reinforcements from anywhere in the Confederate Department of the Trans-Mississippi, the closest and most important supplier would be the Eastern Sub-District of Texas, headquartered at Houston. This jurisdiction stretched from the Louisiana border and along the coast to Matagorda Bay, encompassing the important positions at Sabine Pass and Galveston.

Taylor eyed the idle forces in Texas greedily. Besides a regiment of heavy artillery, four field batteries lay semi-dormant west of the Sabine. German craftsmen in New Braunfels continued refitting and repairing the famous Val Verde Battery, composed of ordnance captured at that namesake battle and including two 6-pounders, two 12-pounder howitzers, and a mountain howitzer than had been manhandled back from New Mexico. The rest of Sibley's veterans, although furloughed, could be reconstituted as Randolph had suggested; at least a half-dozen other cavalry regiments and nearly that many infantry regiments were available and might be sent to Louisiana without endangering the Texas coast. In addition, a new brigade of cavalry, dubbed the "Arizona Brigade" because of its now obsolete mission, gathered near Hempstead. If most or all of these Texas troops joined his Louisiana forces, Taylor reasoned, he would whip the Yankees and recapture New Orleans. He wrote to Hébert to see if any of these troops could be spared.[6]

Good news continued to arrive in Alexandria: Brigadier General Jean Jacques Alfred Alexander Mouton reported for duty. This wealthy son of Alexander Mouton, former governor and secession convention president, had earned his stars in combat as colonel of the 18th Louisi-

General Jean Jacques Alexandre Alfred Mouton was born into privilege as the son of Louisiana Governor Alexandre Mouton. He spoke French as a child, and spoke English with difficulty. A graduate of West Point, he served valiantly at Shiloh before returning to Louisiana to recover from wounds and help defend his home from the Federal invasion. The Acadian Museum, Erath, Louisiana.

ana Infantry. "Modest, unselfish, and patriotic, he showed best in action," wrote Taylor, "always leading his men" and "ever proved faithful to duty." Seriously wounded at Shiloh, the thirty-three-year-old Acadian officer returned to his home near Lafayette to recover. Once there, he received news of his promotion to brigadier general and his assignment to command a brigade in the Army of Tennessee. After spending the summer convalescing, Mouton transferred to Taylor's command instead, literally to defend his home.[7]

The Department of West Louisiana had too few men to defend too many important positions. Even so, the Yankees faced similar challenges. Taylor understood that the thirteen thousand Union troops in Butler's Department of the Gulf were preoccupied with holding coastal towns from Key West to Pensacola and with defending New Orleans. The countryside, as had been proven by the attack at Bayou des Allemands, might be won back. Taylor ordered as many units as were fit to travel into the Lafourche District.

Mouton would command. Taylor ordered the general to establish his headquarters at Thibodaux, "secure early information of the enemy's movements, and to provide a movable floating bridge by which troops could cross [Bayou Lafourche]." From there Mouton was to supervise the defense of both Bayou des Allemands and Donaldsonville, each site about thirty miles away in different directions. Should a Union invasion occur, Mouton would enjoy interior lines, and troops from either position could reinforce the other.[8]

Mouton split his forces as ordered. Colonel Vincent of the 2nd regiment operated from his headquarters at St. Emma Plantation near Donaldsonville. The crack gunners of Oliver J. Semmes's 1st Louisiana

Regular Artillery joined him there. Captain Thomas Faries's Pelican Artillery, a company formed in part from men in St. James and Ascensions parishes, camped nearby with three small obsolete bronze guns. Eight companies of the newly formed 33rd Infantry operated from Winchester Plantation on the Mississippi. At nearby Napoleonville the portion of the Ascension Parish militia still loyal to the Rebel cause drilled and trained.[9]

Mouton's men also deployed to the south and east of Thibodaux. The Lafourche Parish militia, aided by the balance of the 33rd Infantry, watched the recently captured post at Bayou des Allemands. Detachments from the St. Charles and St. John the Baptist militias observed the Vacherie road, the Mississippi, and Boutte Station. The Lafourche militia at Raceland and Ralston's Mississippi Battery at Thibodaux served as Mouton's reserve.[10]

Also near Mouton's headquarters were Waller's shamefaced Texans, busily trying to rebuild their battalion. "We are on foot—dismounted and degraded to the infantry service," Lieutenant C. C. Cox wrote. "Colonel Waller was very sore over the condition of his command." Fearful of being permanently converted to foot soldiers, a delegation from the battalion asked Taylor to let them remount themselves, at their own expense. Taylor agreed. He ordered an officer from each of the six companies to return west of the Sabine and replace the horses lost in the Bonnet Carré debacle.[11]

Secessionist sympathies in the region remained far from universal. The struggle to marshal even this tiny army confirmed Taylor's suspicions of the lukewarm nature of South Louisiana's Confederate patriotism. In all, Taylor reported some 4,600 men ready for duty and another 1,100 away from their commands for various reasons. Confederate provost officers identified a staggering eight thousand men in his district as deserters or fugitive conscripts. The few committed Rebel defenders of the sugar parishes would be constantly tested in the coming weeks.[12]

The Federals continued to keep their eyes on Confederate movements in the region. On September 22 Butler dispatched another Union raiding and reconnaissance force to Donaldsonville. Sugar awaited transport, and a steamer chugged north from New Orleans to pick it up. Meanwhile the 21st Indiana landed to patrol the vicinity to probe Rebel strength in the area, especially Vincent's Louisiana horsemen at St. Emma. The gunboats USS *Sciota, Itasca,* and *Katahdin* covered the landing and the loading operation.

For the next two days the Hoosiers skirmished with Confederates from the 2nd Louisiana Cavalry, the Acension Parish militia, and elements of the 33rd Louisiana Infantry. Aboard the *Katahdin,* officers reported "a good deal of brisk skirmishing . . . in the rear of town." Heading down Bayou Lafourche, the 21st Indiana brushed against Rebels on the afternoon of September 23 but without significant effect. That night Rebel troops concentrated in the vicinity of Colonel Vincent's headquarters at St. Emma Plantation. The next morning the Hoosiers attacked that location but fell back to Donaldsonville under heavy pressure after inflicting a few dozen casualties. Two Union troops had died, a third fell wounded, and Confederates captured an Indiana lieutenant. That evening, the tired and footsore infantry loaded aboard the transports and returned to New Orleans, their knowledge of Rebel troop strengths fairly won. The gunboats followed on September 25.[13]

Mouton worried that this incursion had been a reconnaissance in force and presaged a full invasion. Four days later Colonel Waller left Thibodaux with fifty of the men in his command who were still mounted. He scouted for five days down the Mississippi, looking for signs of trouble, but he returned having found nothing to indicate an invasion. Even so, Mouton ordered him to gather his command and reinforce Vincent and the forces near Donaldsonville in case the Federals returned. "The cavalry went up the right hand side of the Bayou, and the Cane Cart Cavalry on the left," Craig scribbled in his diary. Waller led the mounted troops while Major Hannibal Honestus Boone led the others. "Passed through Napoleonville," the private noted. "The ladies waved flags at us as we passed. We reached camp about sundown. All willing and anxious to stop as our carts had no springs to them and consequently rode very hard." The trip accomplished little. "Not up in time to have any fun." A few days later the Texans trundled back to Thibodaux, and from there they rode to Bayou Beouf near Brashear City. Here, Waller at last taught his men how to be soldiers. "A huge quantity of orders was received today," Craig grumbled. "All very tight and strict and which will discommode many of us Texas Cavalry."[14]

While the Federals remained relatively quiet, Taylor worked through Mouton to forge a competent force in the region, and officers held the Confederate Army in Southwest Louisiana to much higher standards than they had previously. The marriage of the 10th and 12th Battalions was tempestuous. Many resented the fact that authorities promoted Lieutenant Colonel Franklin Clack of the 12th to colonel of the composite 33rd Infantry Regiment, even though he had brought fewer men into the new unit than the majority's favorite, Lieutenant Colonel Valsin Fournet. These hard feelings, aggravated by cultural clashes between the men from New Orleans men and their Cajun compatriots, led to insurrection. Fist fights and threats became commonplace, as did desertions. Unchecked, this simmering turmoil threatened to turn deadly.

On October 19 Mouton ordered his old regiment, the recently arrived 18th Louisiana, to move from their camps of instruction near Berwick Bay, load onto a train, and join him at Terrebonne Station. From there they continued on to Bayou des Allemands. After unloading from the cars, the regiment formed up, weapons ready, and Mouton addressed the sullen garrison. "Gen. Mouton . . . exposed to them the folly and impropriety of attempting to obtain redress of grievances by mutiny," wrote a Louisiana soldier. The speech had the desired effect, and the uprising subsided, but officers and observers alike realized that they could never make these two very different commands come to love each other. The 33rd Louisiana would eventually vanish in favor of the two small battalions that had composed it.[15]

Aggravated by this setback, Mouton continued his attempts to mature and professionalize his army while his commander, General Taylor, looked to the strategic picture and took measures to protect his vulnerable back from a surprise attack from the Gulf of Mexico. Berwick Bay and its outlet to the sea through Atchafalaya Bay remained largely undefended. Confederates had moved channel markers and built obstructions to slow any Union advance, but a determined enemy naval expedition by this route would not only cut Mouton off

View from the streets of Vicksburg west over the city docks toward the Louisiana shore. The Confederate garrison here would rely on food coming from that direction to sustain them against Union attacks. Old Courthouse Museum, Vicksburg, Mississippi.

but also win control of the Teche and Atchafalaya—and the interior of Louisiana. Louisiana riverboat pilots knew that, given sufficient water, steamers could follow a cut-off route from the Mississippi at the mouth of the Red River and down the Atchafalaya to Berwick Bay and the ocean. Union gunboats, it stood to reason, could make that trip in reverse with serious implications for Confederate control of the Father of Waters.

Taylor made arrangements to defend these waterways. He gathered an ersatz bayou fleet to defend the watery web that laced the District of Western Louisiana. Captain E. W. Fuller received orders to move the large river steamer *J. A. Cotton* from its hiding place in Little River, some thirty miles east of Alexandria, to Brashear City for refitting as a partially ironclad gunboat. Major Brent sent aboard a battery of one 32-pounder, two 24-pounders, and a rifled field piece to arm the vessel, while workers packed cotton bales around its engines, boilers, and machinery. This warship would patrol Berwick Bay and spar with any Federal vessels attempting an ascent. Three other much smaller steamers served alongside. The little CSS *Segar* was little more than a dispatch and scout boat, while the lightly armed steamers CSS *Hart* and *Darby* served as transports. At the other end of Taylor's territory, two vessels on the Red River completed the Confederate fleet. Formerly an ocean going tug, the CSS *Webb* now sported iron and cotton armor, a massive rifled cannon on its bow, and stout timbers that turned it into a formidable ram. It was Taylor's mightiest ship. Its consort was the CSS *Grand Duke*, another riverboat turned warrior. The steamer *Music* still steamed along in the lower Red River, the upper Atchafalaya, and down the Mississippi to Port Hudson.

Taylor, after securing the cooperation of Governor Moore, had one other task ahead. Mouton was to disband the various parish militias in the Lafourche District, and their members were to report to conscription camps for reassignment to regular Confederate regiments. "As fast as their places could be supplied by regular organizations in the Confederate service, I made arrangements to cause them to be disbanded," Taylor reported. His study of military history, as well as recent events, led him to believe that militia was unreliable at best, and that "employing troops in the vicinity of their own homes" would only produce unsteady soldiers when battle came. In the coming weeks, Taylor's orders would be the final solution to the months-long problem of calling up the militia. Moving them out of the area might at least make them useful elsewhere in the Confederacy.[16]

October passed as a relatively quiet time for the men in Taylor's command. For the next few weeks the Confederates enjoyed almost uncontested control of the region. Confident in his assessment of Union intentions, Taylor ordered Waller's Texans, in camps near Brashear City, to Lake Charles to guard against naval incursions up the Calcasieu River. They would also welcome the arrival of new horses from Texas. "A dispatch was received from Major Boone stating that we were . . . to be remounted," crowed Private Craig, "which news was received with immense joy. All ready."[17]

On the Lafourche Confederate troops lounged among pleasant settings, with local citizens tending to their needs. "What a happy time we passed during the stay of the Confederates here," reminisced Helen Dupuy. On the Mississippi slaves dug embrasures into the levee for use by field guns to harass shipping. By the second half of October Taylor had made the rounds of his troops and felt comfortable enough with the progress of his command that he left Mouton at Berwicks Bay for a new errand. He traveled east to a meeting with Lieutenant General John C. Pemberton, newly in command of the growing citadel of Vicksburg, to discuss how their armies might best cooperate to keep the Mississippi River in Confederate hands.[18]

Taylor made a thorough tour of his state en route. He lingered more than a week at New Iberia and saw to the safety of the salt mine at Avery Island on Bayou Petit Anse. He next went to Alexandria, where he attempted to procure supplies, then moved on the same errand to Monroe. From here he traveled eastward to the Mississippi, a trip totaling more than two hundred miles. As he neared the great river, he encountered some additional reinforcements for his army, the 28th Louisiana Infantry under Colonel Henry Grey. "Without much instruction and badly equipped, its material was excellent," wrote Taylor. "Colonel Grey was instructed to move by easy marches to the Teche."[19]

At Vicksburg he renewed his acquaintance with General Pemberton, whom he had first met on the Niagara Frontier fifteen years before, and they discussed strategy. "It was of vital importance to control the section of the Mississippi receiving the Red and Washita Rivers," Taylor wrote. "By so doing connection would be preserved between the two parts of the Confederacy, and troops and supplies crossed at will." Taylor pointed out his army's ability to affect the outcome of events east of the river, claiming that his campaign in the Lafourche District had forced the Union evacuation of Baton Rouge. The two went on to discuss the need to bolster Port Hudson into as strong a citadel as Vicksburg. Pemberton agreed. As the two parted, Taylor promised to forward supplies to both forts. Louisiana and Texas would feed the garrisons that would defend the Confederate portion of the Mississippi River. Taylor just needed enough troops to defend this lifeline.[20]

CHAPTER TEN

SIBLEY'S BRIGADE

*We were on our way to Louisiana with the expectancy of
keeping the enemy from . . . making raids into Texas.*
Private H. C. Wright, 4th Texas Cavalry

Considering the showdown brewing in Louisiana, Henry Hopkins Sibley's Brigade of New Mexico veterans was naturally the object of much speculation by both Federals and Confederates. Union war planners had been impressed by the brigade's prowess on the western battlefields and tried to track it after its return to Texas, wary of the effect these veteran reinforcements might have in their next post. The brigade's soldiers speculated about their next theater of operations, but of one thing they were certain: they wanted nothing more to do with General Sibley. All hoped for a new leader worthy of their sacrifices.

Both Federals and Confederates were baffled in their efforts to track this force, because neither side really knew where the brigade had gone. Upon their return from New Mexico that summer, Sibley's staff had posted at Marshall, Texas, in the northeast corner of the state. They had dutifully reported their presence to Lieutenant General Theophilus Holmes, commander of the Department of the Trans-Mississippi in Little Rock. Sibley's officers had hoped to be called to

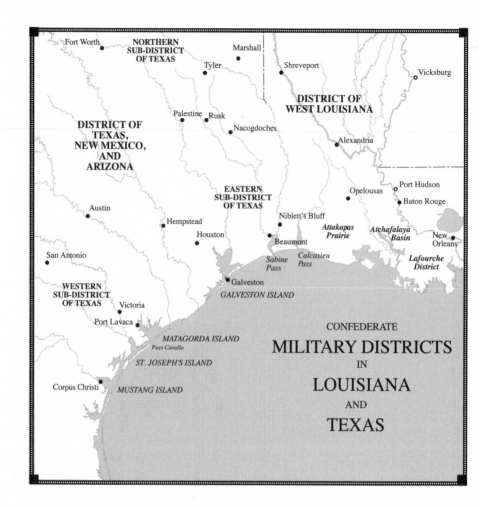

Fort Worth
NORTHERN
SUB-DISTRICT
OF TEXAS

Marshall

Tyler

Shreveport

Vicksburg

DISTRICT OF
WEST LOUISIANA

Palestine Rusk

DISTRICT OF
TEXAS,
NEW MEXICO,
AND
ARIZONA

Nacogdoches

Alexandria

EASTERN
SUB-DISTRICT
OF TEXAS

Opelousas

Port Hudson

Baton Rouge

Austin

Hempstead

Niblett's Bluff

*Attakapas
Prairie*

*Atchafalaya
Basin*

New
Orleans

Houston

Beaumont

San Antonio

*Sabine
Pass*

*Calcasieu
Pass*

*Lafourche
District*

WESTERN
SUB-DISTRICT
OF TEXAS

Victoria

Galveston

GALVESTON ISLAND

Port Lavaca

MATAGORDA ISLAND
Pass Cavallo

ST. JOSEPH'S ISLAND

CONFEDERATE

MILITARY DISTRICTS

IN

Corpus Christi

MUSTANG ISLAND

LOUISIANA

AND

TEXAS

Virginia, but the men in the ranks and the line officers who led them had dissipated like vapors.

Sibley in fact lobbied for a Virginia assignment when he arrived in Richmond for his court-martial. That fall, a telegram from Adjutant General Samuel Cooper seemed to confirm the success of Sibley's request. Senator Lewis T. Wigfall of Texas had specifically requested that five regiments be sent to the Army of Northern Virginia: three from Sibley's Brigade joined by the 23rd Texas Cavalry and the 2nd Texas Partisan Rangers.[1]

Holmes ignored that order. He needed Sibley's Brigade and the other two regiments as a bargaining tool. At almost the same time, requests for reinforcements began buffeting Holmes's headquarters from Taylor in Louisiana and Pemberton at Vicksburg. Holmes was more than happy to volunteer the shadow of Sibley's Brigade for all these assignments—he had never even seen it and no one could tell him how many troops it counted—as a signal of his willingness to cooperate. Holmes needed soldiers himself: he planned to invade northwest Arkansas by year's end, so he jealously guarded the other two regiments. General Robert E. Lee and the Army of Northern Virginia would have to make do with the Texans they had, Holmes decided, but Pemberton could gladly have Sibley. "General Holmes informs me that he cannot send a single man from his army, but will send Sibley's cavalry brigade from Texas," Pemberton wrote to President Jefferson Davis in November. "That will help Vicksburg but little." Holmes received credit for being accommodating, but Pemberton had refused the gesture. The onus was now on the defender of Vicksburg to find troops from some other quarter, since those Holmes offered did not suit him.[2]

At this, President Davis took a personal interest. He sided with Pemberton. "I am disappointed," he wrote to Cooper, "by a renewed attempt to withdraw Sibley's brigade from the special service for which is was designed." Cooper took the hint. "Sibley's Brigade is not wanted at Vicksburg," he telegraphed Holmes. "Order it to report to General Taylor in West Louisiana." Of all the potential reinforcements for Louisiana, these mounted troops held the most promise for an immediate impact. So, the president of the Confederate States determined the fate of the scattered New Mexico veterans. The final disposition of Sibley's Brigade mattered little to Holmes. Better the two regiments he had in hand over three who could not be located.[3]

The veterans of Sibley's Far West misadventure found little joy being in such demand when orders reached their homes commanding them to reassemble the brigade after their impromptu furlough of the last few months. Few were enthusiastic about resuming the contest. Nevertheless, starting in late September, the various companies began gathering in local enclaves before riding on to regimental camps. Bearing the new designation "cavalry" instead of the outdated "mounted volunteers," the 4th, 5th, and 7th regiments returned to war.

In Victoria Alfred Petticolas reluctantly said goodbye to his friends. "The order was given to fall in. Being desirous of remaining to dinner,

Nearly a decade apart in age, Robert Thomas Williams, left, and John Williams, right, were both veterans of the New Mexico campaign as members of Company E, 4th Texas Mounted Volunteers. When the younger brother fell ill in Santa Fe, his older sibling stayed behind during the Confederate retreat to nurse him back to health. Union troops captured them on April 20, 1862, and escorted them overland to Missouri and from there by rail to Camp Douglas, Chicago. The two returned to Confederate lines after being exchanged at Vicksburg in September. They made it back to Milam County, Texas, just in time to rejoin their command as Sibley's Brigade returned to active service. Courtesy Don A. Schroeder, Dallas, Texas.

I did not fall into ranks but stayed down at Mrs. Shirkey's and kept out of sight of the Captain till he had gone," he wrote. After enjoying the last home-cooked meal he would have for some time, he went out into the yard and prepared to leave. "After dinner I saddled up Stonewall, my horse, a full blooded Spanish pony, very heavy built." He then turned to say farewell. "I took leave of Mrs. Shirkey and family with regret for they have been very kind to me." Soon, Petticolas would resume his place as fifth sergeant of Company C, 4th Texas Cavalry. "I . . . was rather low spirited—thinking of the kind friends I had left behind."[4]

A similar scene unfolded in Milam County. Fred Wade, a six-foot-three-inch native of Canada, spent his last evening at home with comrades, enjoying the adoration of some local maidens. "The girls gave us a farewell party," he remembered. "[They] made two pidgins full of honey cookies [and] coffee out of parched acorns, wheat and okra . . . and gave each of us a pair of socks that they had knit themselves." All through the night, the teenagers visited and played parlor games.[5]

At first light, though, the young men knew they had to go. "The horses were saddled at daylight and the girls rode with us. . . . On reaching our parting place we all got off our horses, joined hands and sang *God be with You Till we Meet Again.*" After tenderly helping the girls to remount, Wade and his seven companions said their goodbyes. "If there was a dry eye among the sixteen of us, I did not see it," he wrote. "Some of the girls rode off with their faces in their hands. Three out of the eight boys never saw their sweethearts again." He and his companions rode on to rejoin Company E, 4th Texas Cavalry.[6]

After his service in New Mexico Theophilus Noel of Company A, 4th Texas, returned to Richmond, Texas, but did not like what he saw. As he visited familiar haunts, he marveled at the number of able-bodied men still at home. He described them as "those who took to wearing spectacles after the passage of the 1st Conscript Law. Anything to keep out of the service, you know; that you may shun danger of being struck by an enemy's bullet." Noel considered these fellows to be beyond contempt and accused them of "swindling, cheating," and fraud. He saved some venom, though, for Confederate agents serving in the cotton bureau. "Wives were told when their cotton was being pressed and taken from them that it was to get supplies, medicine and clothing for the army. There are many men belonging to this brigade who have had their cotton pressed . . . [but] have never drawn one stitch of clothing from the government," he wrote. "Although they have fought in every battle and have always had a gun, yet never a grain of powder, lead, or caps have they used that was imported by cotton or the Cotton Bureau."[7]

The orders took longer to find the men of the 5th Texas. William Randolph Howell of Company C delayed leaving his home in Plantersville, Texas, until mid-October, waiting on specific instructions as to where to rejoin his regiment. He had been back on his farm since July 23. "It is useless to remark," he noted, "I enjoyed that time."[8]

Changing orders and unclear intentions caused a huge amount of confusion as to where the brigade would be resurrected. Some headed for Marshall, only to be redirected to one of several other towns in East Texas. Eventually, a majority of the men made their way to Cypress City, the 4th Texas Cavalry rendezvous, and to Hempstead, bivouac of the 5th and 7th regiments. Upon arriving at camp, the troops found a critical lack of supplies as well as many new soldiers—volunteers and conscripts—who had yet to be trained.[9]

H. C. Wright of Company F, 4th Texas Cavalry, joined his friend and brother-in-law, John Poe, as they left their homes in Polk County. "Mounted again on good horses, with recovered health and spirits, again we left our home and loved one for the thrilling scenes of war," he wrote. "This time we had no foolish notions that the war was only a frolic and would soon be ended. We now comprehended its seriousness and knew that many of us would never return again to our homes." His arrival in camp was cheered, as he had been left for dead near El Paso. "I met with a hearty greeting from old friends whom I had not seen since they left me in New Mexico," Wright remembered. He also learned his next destination. "We were on our way to Louisiana with the expectancy of keeping the enemy from holding that country in peace and making raids into Texas."[10]

Wright also noted many new faces among his comrades. "I also formed the acquaintance of the many new recruits who had been called by the conscript law to enlist," he remembered. "Some, indeed, were young fellows who gladly enlisted, but a good many were men of middle age, now obliged to leave their wives and children for the hazards of war."[11]

The presence of the newcomers bothered many of the New Mexico veterans. After reviewing who had arrived back in camp, Private Wade noticed too many new faces for his liking. "[They] went in the service when forced in by the conscript law," he noted. He expressed chagrin at how many boastful would-be warriors had now suffered a change of heart. "Many of the most fiery play soldiers skipped to Mexico. We had slackers those days as well as now."[12] Friction and animosity were common as the regiments rebuilt. "We veterans and the conscripts were not very harmonious," Wade added. "We called them featherbed militia."[13]

John W. Watkins of Marlin, Texas, volunteered to join the brigade, leaving his young wife at home. He took his place in the ranks of the decimated Company B, 5th Texas Cavalry. His new comrades had been among those who had made the lancer charge at Val Verde six months before. When he arrived in camp, he mimicked the veterans' disdain for unwilling enlistees who had been forced into the army. "There is a regiment of conscripts at this place," he wrote home. "They have houses built for them while the rest of us have to do without tents."[14]

One group of soldiers conspicuously missing were the men who served the trophy cannons of the Val Verde Battery. Taken at their namesake battle, the two remaining 6-pounders and two 12-pounder howitzers had been engraved with the names of the men who—often at the cost of their lives—had seized them, constituting the only tangible gains of the entire New Mexico campaign. Served by volunteers largely drawn from the 5th Texas Cavalry who had taken the guns, this unit had a special *esprit de corps* that comes from the fire of battle. Instead of gathering his men near Houston, Captain Joe Sayers had already overseen their repair in and now led the battery to Louisiana.[15]

In addition to the tensions between veterans and recruits, volunteers and conscripts, there remained the question of who was in charge. The men almost unanimously disliked Sibley, but for the time being, he was conveniently out of the way in Richmond. Several candidates vied for the interim post.

Even though the campaign in New Mexico had been an unmistakable disaster, the brigade had spawned heroes. One of the biggest winners was William Read Scurry, formerly lieutenant colonel of the 4th Texas Mounted Volunteers. Considered the architect of victory at Glorieta, Scurry had received the wreathed stars of a brigadier general as reward from his government. He left his old comrades behind and headed to Galveston to command the garrison at that critical point. It was rumored that he might lead the brigade once it left Texas, no matter its destination. Colonel William Steele of the 7th Texas also received advancement to brigadier general, but he bolted from the brigade to serve on other fields. Famous for his rear-guard defense of Confederate Arizona, Steele departed for an independent command in the Indian Territory.

The acting command of the brigade devolved to its senior colonel, James Reily of the 4th Texas. To the rank and file he was virtu-

Colonel James Reily had been many things in his life, including a Republic of Texas soldier, a Whig politician, and a consul to St. Petersburg, Russia. A leading member of Houston society, he naturally gained high rank when Texas raised troops for the Confederacy, leading the 4th Texas Mounted Volunteers in Sibley's Brigade. He missed the chance of gaining a reputation heroic or otherwise during the failed New Mexico campaign. Author's collection.

ally unknown. Certainly no one had seen him fight. The reason for this was clear enough; Colonel Reily had served on detached duty as a diplomat in Mexico during the campaign. Even so, he maintained his position as senior colonel of the brigade and as head of the 4th Texas Cavalry. Now he was in charge.

Despite his lack of battle experience, Reily boasted sterling credentials as a leader. Born to a prosperous Ohio family in 1811, he graduated from Miami University at age eighteen and then moved on to Transylvania University in Lexington, Kentucky, where he earned a law degree and a reputation for oratory. There he met and married Ellen Hart Ross, a distant relative of Henry Clay. They moved to Texas during the revolution, and in the summer of 1836 Reily served as major on the staff of General Thomas Rusk. Two years later Reily was Rusk's law partner, residing in Nacogdoches. He moved to Houston in 1838 after Rusk's election to chief justice of the Texas Supreme Court. The two maintained their partnership for another year. Reily eventually entered executive branch politics, serving as a diplomat to the United States in the second Houston administration. After annexation, he returned to law.[16]

Reily was also a product of the turbulent 1850s. While practicing law, he was an important voice in the small but vocal Whig Party. He left that crumbling organization over the issue of slavery and became a Democrat, winning a seat in the Texas legislature. As a reward for his support of James Buchanan, the wealthy and urbane Reily received an appointment as consul to Russia, but he did not find that nation to his liking and instead moved to St. Louis to practice law. During the secession crises, Reily returned home to Houston, boldly supported disunion, and went so far as to raise a company of volunteers. "Col. Reily is a true and loyal citizen of Texas," trumpeted the Austin *Texas State Gazette* in March 1861, "and a man of decided talents."[17]

Sibley made Reily his first pick for brigade leader for the New Mexico Campaign, but the general had coveted his pen as much as his sword. Because of Reily's foreign service experience, Sibley sent him to establish diplomatic relations with the northwestern Mexican states. As a result, Reily missed any chance of fighting, glory, or infamy in the New Mexico Campaign. Now Sibley answered charges before a tribunal; Reily remained.

Colonel Arthur Pendelton Bagby now commanded the 7th Texas, having been promoted up one grade to replace Steele. An attorney and son of an Alabama governor, he, too, had never heard the whistling of bullets in New Mexico. He was a

Colonel Arthur Pendleton Bagby was the son of a governor of Alabama. He was also a West Point graduate and served in the 8th U.S. Infantry at Fort Chadbourne on the Texas frontier. He left the army, returned to Mobile to practice law and then moved to Gonzales, Texas, just prior to the Civil War. He served as second-in-command of the 7th Texas Mounted Volunteers in New Mexico and killed many bottles of whiskey during the campaign, but he never fought the Federals. Author's collection.

veteran of another sort of combat that seemed to plague the Confederacy. While reportedly drunk one evening in Doña Ana, Arizona, Bagby had threatened to shoot an uptight subordinate. From that point on Bagby had fought to defend his reputation in a court-martial. Having emerged relatively unscathed, he resumed his place among the brigade field officers.

Colonel Tom Green led the 5th Texas Cavalry. Oddly absent from the list of promotions to brigadier general like Scurry and Steele, he had also won laurels in New Mexico, equal to or greater than those of his promoted compatriots. Green had achieved victory when the chaotic battle of Val Verde appeared lost. "I cannot commend Green too highly to the favorable consideration of the Executive," Sibley had written in his report to Jefferson Davis. Indeed, the commander of the Confederate Army of New Mexico had given Green high praise. "General Sibley, after the battle was over, complimented me in presence of all the field officers in the Brigade in such eulogistic terms that my face almost burst with shame," Green wrote to a friend, "stating publicly that the Battle of Val Verde has made me a brigadier, that there would be <u>no doubt</u> of my commission as soon as his report reached Richmond."[18] He had reason to be optimistic. A raft of letters endorsed by such men as the chief justice of the Texas Supreme Court, the state comptroller, the state treasurer, and the Confederate war tax collector for Texas all recommended his promotion.[19]

The honor never came. When the hoped for rank failed to materialize, Green correctly considered this a great insult and realized that public opinion had somehow turned against him. He had left Texas in October of 1861 a bona fide hero with the overwhelming confidence of his neighbors and countrymen but had returned under a cloud. Gone were the accolades. Now, the most respected and widely read newspapers in the state published thinly veiled smears of his character. He was, they argued, one of the reasons that the New Mexico Campaign had ended in such catastrophic failure. Alcohol, these stories murmured, was a weakness for the colonel.[20]

As a result, the gossip insisted, Green's unmistakable bravery and bold leadership had faltered. He was a frequent visitor to Sibley's headquarters in Albuquerque, and some argued, a frequent visitor to Sibley's medicine chest. Rumors had Green drinking with Sibley while other officers in the brigade continued the campaign. Scurry, a mere lieutenant colonel at the time, led the army—including half of Green's regiment—at the Battle of Glorieta on March 28. Sibley remained sauced in Albuquerque, and Green hovered with his command nearby, out of danger. The two men, the grumblers argued, had left active campaigning and combat to their subordinates in favor of lounging about—booze addled—in the safety of town.

When events made obvious that the Texans would have to retreat from New Mexico for want of supplies, the chatter turned nasty. "It is hoped," wrote a disgruntled captain in the brigade, "that there will be some courts-martial and courts of inquiry." While not prepared to name individuals and risk insubordination, the captain made clear his sentiments. "Let the people of Texas see whether certain persons can . . . stay in comfortable quarters in towns soaking themselves with *rum and whiskey* while others are doing the work. I could a tale unfold," the captain fumed, "that would make Texas too damned hot to hold some men, that up here have been carrying high heads."[21] As Green learned when he arrived back in Texas, this captain and his various home front allies had been hard at work.

Tom Green was a veteran of San Jacinto and campaigns against Mexicans and Indians, as well as a bona fide Texas hero and one of Austin's most admired residents. As colonel of the 5th Texas Mounted Volunteers, he saved the Confederate army at the Battle of Val Verde. Even so, he came back from the New Mexico campaign under suspicion of being a drunk. He set out to purge this stain on his reputation with the cleansing fire of battle. Author's collection.

Green had never been wounded in combat, but in the summer of 1862 the blows he received were crueler than shot and bayonet, for they came from the pens and lips of his fellow Texans. "To my great surprise I found some anonymous scribblings in the newspapers depreciating me and extolling Scurry to the skies, and putting words in his mouth he only dreamed of uttering—in fact making the most absurd and mendacious statements not even founded in truth, to glorify Scurry and depreciate me so far as my management was concerned." Green brooded over the fact that he was made the scapegoat, while two junior officers received promotions. "Tell me what in the name of God I have done," Green begged his friend, fellow Texan, and political ally John H. Reagan, the Confederate postmaster general.[22] The New Mexico adventure ended poorly. Even so, Green wrote, "I believed that I at least had come out of it unscathed by the tongue of slander, with the universal confidence of the army."[23]

Despite this, Green must have known what was being said about him. "I have heard I was accused of drinking on the campaign," he wrote to Reagan. He admitted to drinking "occasionally" while at Sibley's headquarters in Albuquerque, but also adamantly claimed that he never swallowed "a drop when near the enemy." Those who saw him surprised by the enemy while at a fandango near Peralta, New Mexico, might have argued the point. Either way, he was quick to claim that he had mended his ways. "Since the New Mexico Campaign I have not drunk liquor at all and I never intend to take another drink during the war," he sputtered. "If I have been charged with the habit of getting drunk it is basely false. The people and soldiers of Texas would promote me if they had a chance."[24]

The postmaster general, though, was not so sure. Before he advanced his friend's claim in the halls of government at Richmond, Reagan asked for outside endorsements for Green. The responses were guarded. "Whatever his habits were before—and I have never known him [to] drink to excess—he is now resolutely abstentious and have no doubt he will remain so during his continuance in the service," wrote one witness. While not an outright endorsement of Green the soldier, this sort of statement did at least allay fears that Green, although a drinker, was not an obvious drunk like Sibley. Even so, the whiff of alcohol would retard Green's promotion for many months.[25]

For the time being, Green would have to be satisfied at the head of his regiment. Wounded and smoldering, the colonel held a guarded opinion of his new commander, Reily. "I have known him in Texas for 20 years," he wrote. "He is a man of talents and a speaker but has no reputation in Texas as a soldier or officer."[26]

The soldiers in Reily's own regiment harbored doubts about their untried military chieftain as well. Upon arriving at the 4th Texas camps at Millican, Texas, Reily ordered his command into a hollow square formation. Standing in the middle, he harangued the troops over complaints by local citizens regarding missing livestock and general plundering. "When you boys were in New Mexico, in the enemies' country, I thought you were the finest lot of soldiers I ever saw," the colonel yelled. "Now you are in your own country, you steal everything you can get your hands on. I am going to put a stop to it." His solution was to order strict camp discipline. "I am going to double guard duty. A sentinel on post knows no man. When a man approaches your post," Reily bellowed, "he must give the pass word or you shoot to kill." Thoroughly chastised, the warriors of the 4th Texas returned to their tents grousing about the dressing down. The scolding especially stung the honor of the young troops, as Reily's budding teenage daughter was on hand to witness the spectacle.[27]

But the rank and file had ways of humbling their officers. Shortly after the incident, a group of conspirators heard that Reily and his family had traveled to a local planter's for supper and would be returning after dark. A handful of the bolder pranksters decided to post a heavy picket near the road the colonel would travel. Private Bill Henderson spotted the buggy as it approached and stepped boldly into the middle of the lane. "Halt! Advance with the password," the brazen soldier yelled.[28]

"I am Colonel Riley, let me pass," was the reply. Instead, Henderson ordered the officer to dismount from the vehicle and to wait there until the sergeant of the guard could arrive and verify his claim. Eventually, the guards declared themselves satisfied as to the colonel's identity and allowed him to pass into camp.[29]

The next morning, the soldiers sat nervously around their breakfast fires waiting for Reily's reaction. All knew he was a disciplinarian, and most suspected he was a martinet of the worst stripe. Soon an orderly from headquarters summoned Henderson to Reily's tent. The doomed private turned to his messmates with obvious intent. "I'm not going," he told his friends. "I won't go to the guardhouse." The other soldiers convinced Henderson to answer the inquiry, arguing persuasively that he had only followed orders.[30]

Henderson went to the tent, as commanded, but received a shock upon his arrival. "[Reily] caught me by the hand and said 'Bill, you are my sort of a soldier. If I had an army like you, I could take Washington and end the war,'" the bewildered Henderson related. After this unexpected congratulation Reily brought a jug of whiskey out from under his bed and summoned his daughter to fetch a glass, sugar bowl, and spoon. "Honey, here is a *soldier*," Reily said, introducing Henderson to the girl. Twelve-year-old Ellen Reily then put two spoonfuls of sugar into the glass, filled it with whiskey, and stirred it coyly. As she passed him a glass, "her fingers touched my hand," Henderson remembered. "Blissful thrills ran all over me," despite the fact she was half his age. Reily allowed the soldier to finish his drink then sent him back to camp, saying "Bill, when you want another dram, come here.[31]

CHAPTER ELEVEN

TEXAS INVADED

We flank the rebellion
Massachusetts governor John A. Andrew

D espite the best intentions of the Confederate government and the needs of Richard Taylor, Sibley's Brigade would not be going to Louisiana, at least not yet. They were needed closer to home. On September 22, the same day the 21st Indiana was skirmishing with Rebels near Donaldsonville, Union warships prowling the Texas coast—four-hundred miles west of the Mississippi River—ushered in the next phase of the great contest in the region.

While Taylor looked for Yankee aggression in the Lafourche District and hoped that troops from west of the Sabine would come to his aid, Confederates neglected to consider bolder Federal ambitions. It soon became clear that Texas would suffer next. If the Texas coastal defenses fell and Union troops went ashore, the Rebels leaders of the Lone Star State would have problems aplenty and Taylor would be on his own. Union gunboats and blockaders would neatly snip the supply line to Vicksburg and Port Hudson at its origin.

The presence of the enemy on the coast was nothing new. Admiral David G. Farragut's ships—mostly inferior sailing vessels that could

Five Union warships, including the USS Arthur *(right) and the USS* Sachem *(second from right) as well as the USS* Belle Italia, Reindeer, *and* Corypheus *shell the Confederate positions at Flour Bluff defending the town and harbor of Corpus Christi.* The Battle of Corpus Christi *by Thomas Noakes, painting on display at the Inez Sterling Adams South Texas Historical Gallery, Corpus Christi Museum of Science and History.*

be spared from more important work on the Mississippi—had been exploring the Texas coast for months and knew its inlets and sounds by sight and reputation. A flotilla composed of the schooners USS *Corypheus*, USS *Reindeer*, the sloop USS *Belle Italia*, the bark-rigged USS *Arthur*, and the small screw steamer USS *Sachem* first struck at Corpus Christi in mid-August 1862. They destroyed five commercial boats of various sizes in the bay and surrounding waters and drove the garrison at Corpus Christi's Flour Bluff from its guns. Within weeks, the U.S. Navy made prizes of several blockade runners in the vicinity, thus proving the worth of this peripheral campaign while adding new ships to Farragut's fleet. Now the navy would try to drive a wedge between Texas and Louisiana.

Farragut ordered his captains to try their luck at Sabine Pass, a waterway that controlled the entrance to Sabine Lake on the Texas-Louisiana border. A successful reconnaissance would temporarily close this haven for blockade runners and determine the course Farragut might follow in the future. If possible, it might even work as an invasion route for a campaign to interdict the flow of men and supplies heading east.

The eastern horizon was slowly turning gray on September 24, 1862, when two small schooners silently glided into Sabine Pass, Texas, to begin the contest. Offshore, the silhouette of a steamer paced the horizon, watching over its smaller consorts like a protective mother. Slowly, deliberately, the two sailing vessels tacked into position more than two-and-a-half miles away from a small earthwork flying the Stars and Bars of the Confederate States. As the Union bluejackets steered their vessels with wind and tide, Texan gunners stood to their guns and watched the doughty sailing craft maneuver. As the orange sun crested the horizon in a blaze of light, the Federal ships slowed their progress, and the Stars and Stripes flapped fitfully in a moderate breeze. The naval officers on board had demanded the surrender of the fort the day before, but had been rebuffed. Now they would press their case with iron.

The Confederates on shore saw the flash and smoke first, then heard the telltale "pop-boom" carry across the water as a solid shot whirred toward their position. A white blossom of water and a few skips marked the shortfall of the twenty-pound shot. Next, a deeper, growling rumble announced the launching of the first of three massive mortar rounds, each falling progressively nearer the Texans.

For most of the untried artillerists in the muddy fort, this was the first time anyone had deliberately tried to kill them. Exhilarated by this harmless introduction to war, the Texans, mostly twenty-year-olds from the surrounding region, gamely replied. Their twin heavy 32-pounders and antique medium 32-pounders bucked and lurched as their crews estimated the distance to the offending vessels. The Rebels shots, too, smacked the water and nothing else. After nearly a dozen such exchanges, both sides fell silent, each out of range of the other. For the rest of the day the Texans watched as the Union crews, straining at their anchor cables, kedged their warships closer toward shore for a better shot while being careful to stay out of range. The Union vessels were the schooner USS *Rachel Seaman* and the mortar boat USS *Henry Janes,* and their crews were under orders to reduce the Rebel earthwork or to drive the garrison from its guns.

Gunners on both sides renewed the duel at 5 p.m. Within minutes, the seemingly playful salutes of the morning were replaced by firing in deadly earnest. "In course of a half hour, they got the exact range of our battery, and began to drop 13-inch shells all around us," wrote Sergeant H. N. Conner of Company A, Speight's Battalion. High trajectory mortar rounds spiraled over and among the Texan position, trailing sparking, smoky tails. Some rounds burst overhead; others landed solidly in the fort, showering the Rebels with mud and debris. [1]

Conner noted the destruction in his diary. The large projectiles were "partly tearing away our walls, injuring [the] barracks in [the] fort, and tearing up the breastworks dreadfully," he wrote. The 20-pounder rifles of the *Rachel Seaman* sent shot zipping into and past the fort. Despite the noise of explosions and the impact of iron on mud—not to mention the distractions of white hot shell fragments spinning through the air—none of the Texans were hit.[2]

Out-ranged and out-gunned, the Texans could only endure. "Finding that our guns did no damage, we ceased firing," Connor continued. Without a way to reply, some of the more reckless clambered up the parapet and waved their hats in defiance at the vessels in the distance. Most sensibly sought cover. "The men took refuge under shelter of the walls," Connor recorded, "and lie close, and 'hope for a better time coming.'" The bombardment lasted the rest of the afternoon, with increasing effect.[3]

Nightfall and thunderstorms ended the three-hour fight. Although unable to dismantle the Texan position that day, the Union ships had forced its gamecock garrison to duck. As dusk lengthened and lightening flashed across the sky, the two Union schooners ceased firing and slipped away, toward the Gulf of Mexico and their escort.

Inside the Confederate works Major Josephus S. Irvine, San Jacinto veteran and commander of the post at Sabine Pass, and Captain K. D. Keith of Company B, 1st Texas Heavy Artillery, debated the morrow's course of action. Clearly the enemy had the advantage in artillery, having tossed 20-pounder parrot rounds into the Rebel works with impunity. The mortar, too, provided cause for alarm. Without an effective means of responding to the Union naval threat, resistance appeared futile.

Near midnight, rain-soaked reinforcements interrupted the officers and their gloomy deliberations. Twenty-six infantrymen from

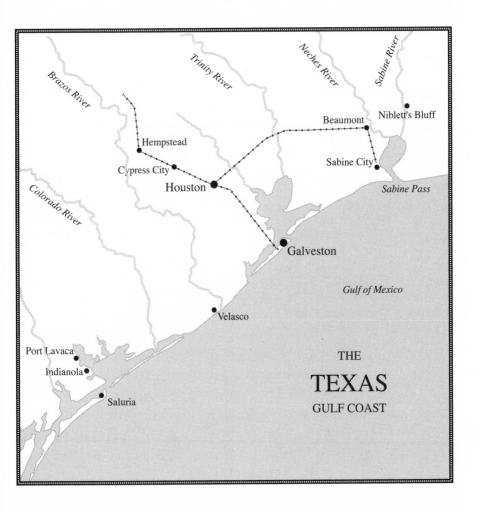

Company E of Ashley Speight's 11th Texas Battalion arrived under the command of Captain G. W. O'Bryan, having marched for hours in the driving rain. While encouraging to the rain-sodden and bomb-addled garrison, these newcomers did not change the equation. In addition to the threat of being pounded into mush, all understood that this meager outpost was vulnerable to being cut off. Union vessels might pass the battery, move up the bay—Sabine Lake—and land troops to block a Rebel retreat. With enemy soldiers between them and safety, the garrison would then have to evacuate via the only other route— the long beach road to Galveston, subject to bombardment from ships in the gulf.

Frederick Crocker was a civilian-turned-warrior, joining the West Gulf Blockading Squadron with the temporary rank of volunteer lieutenant. In this capacity, he participated in patrolling the shores of Texas, earning praise and promotion for service in those waters. Among the ships he commanded were the USS Rachel Seaman, Kensington, *and* Clifton. *He left the navy at the end of the war. Author's collection.*

At a 2 a.m. council of war, the consensus appeared to be in favor of immediate evacuation, and Major Irvine ordered his fort abandoned. Before leaving, Captain Keith's Texans spiked their artillery and destroyed any public property that could not be carried away. Falling in with Captain O'Bryan's footsore infantry, the Confederates left their fort to the U.S. Navy.

The next morning, the Union ships arrived back on station and discovered that they had silenced the Texan fort. Navy gunners hastened the last few defenders on their way as a detachment landed to investigate the smoldering ruins. Acting-Master Frederick Crocker ordered the *Rachel Seaman* up Sabine Lake to spread additional mischief in the area. Within days Union shore parties from these and other ships, including the USS *Kensington,* raided from the lakefront to within a few miles of Beaumont. The key bridge on the railroad leading to Sabine Pass fell to their torches and guns, as did the town of Sabine and most of the buildings along the waterfront.[4]

Panic swept Beaumont. Southern engineers ordered obstructions placed in the mouths of the Neches and Sabine rivers to avoid Union raids up those streams. When news reached the Confederates that enemy naval officers had attempted to purchase beef from citizens, Rebel horsemen ran all the livestock in the vicinity deep into the thickets of the interior.

News of the victory at Sabine Pass drew Admiral David Farragut's full attention. "The importance of Sabine Pass to the Rebels appears to have been entirely underrated by us," a Union naval officer aboard the USS *Kensington* wrote the admiral. "The quantity of goods of all kinds, and munitions of war that have been run in here has been enormous, and large quantities of cotton have been exported." In an ominous tone, the officer also noted the still-lethal force lurking in the upper part of Sabine Lake. "There are now lying above at least eight steamers and six schooners, large quantities of cotton, and quite a force of troops."[5]

Farragut faced new options in light of this news. The admiral, still frustrated from his failures on the Mississippi, decided to reinforce the success of his Union sailing ships on the Texas coast. While Butler sparred with Taylor in the Lafourche District, Farragut and the navy would expand Union control in the Gulf of Mexico. He ordered Commander William Renshaw with four powerful steam propelled gunboats, USS *Westfield, Clifton, Harriet Lane,* and *Owasco,* deeper into the western gulf to scout out the enemy strength and search for more opportunities to harass Texans.

Renshaw understood that Galveston was clearly the key to a permanent lodgment in Texas. Not only was it the largest city in Texas, but its capture would be a severe blow to Rebel morale.

William B. Renshaw was a son of the sea, having entered the navy in 1831. His father, James, had served in the War of 1812 and named his son after William Bainbridge, the legendary commander of the USS Constitution. *William Renshaw was one of Captain David G. Farragut's favorite officers. Massachusetts Commandery, Military Order of the Loyal Legion Collection, U.S. Army Military History Institute, Carlisle, Pennsylvania.*

In addition, the city was on an island, making it easier for the legless navy to defend their gains. Without much additional effort, Farragut reasoned, a blockade could be swiftly and strictly enforced on the Texas coast with the capture of this single point. Its port facilities, once in Union hands, would provide the navy with a forward base of operations, putting the entire Texas littoral in range of Union raiders.

To Renshaw's eye, Galveston seemed poorly guarded for such an important place. At one time, however, four Confederate batteries, including positions on Boliver Point, Fort Point, and Pelican Spit, swept

The USS Westfield *had been a New York ferryboat before the war but became part of the mortar flotilla operating against the Confederate Mississippi River forts. When efforts there stalled in the summer of 1862, the gunboat headed for Texas. Naval Historical Center.*

the channel and bay, while a battery at San Luis Pass at the southwestern tip of the island closed that approach. Most of the emplaced guns were old 24- and 32-pounders, but William Pitt Ballinger, one of the city's leading citizens, had also shepherded an 8-inch and 10-inch Columbiad from east of the Mississippi to stiffen the city's defenses. San Jacinto hero Sidney Sherman commanded at first, to be succeeded by John C. Moore. Ultimately Joseph J. Cook, Naval Academy graduate and future colonel of the 1st Texas Heavy Artillery, took command of the fortifications.

General Paul O. Hébert, Confederate commander of the District of Texas, New Mexico, and Arizona, did not believe that these few batteries could adequately cover the city, and earlier in the year he had ordered all the guns removed to safety on the mainland. A fort built on Virginia Point would be the new line of defense for the state. Galveston and its residents lay abandoned on their island. Not surprisingly, the political storm he created led to indecision and bad compromises. Citizens insisted that the Confederate heavy guns be deployed in small parcels, each incapable of doing more than soothing the population's anxieties. By the fall of 1862 the Texan guns remained dispersed, exposed, and largely symbolic along Galveston Bay.

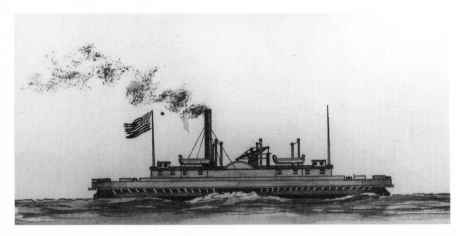

Designers had planned for USS Clifton *to be a ferryboat in the waters around New York City, but instead she entered service as a gunboat almost immediately after being launched. The* Clifton *fought up the Mississippi in 1862 and took damage from the guns of Vicksburg. Once repaired, the steamer was Texas-bound. Naval Historical Center.*

Commodore Renshaw did not know of this strategic blunder, so he arrived off Galveston on October 4 and boldly demanded the surrender of the city instead of simply shooting his way in—erring on the side of caution. At daybreak on October 5, 1862, the commodore ordered Commander J. M. Wainwright to take his vessel, the USS *Harriet Lane*, over the sandbar and into Galveston Bay with a flag of truce to receive the enemy reply. This officer could also investigate and learn what the navy faced at Galveston, since surely the town would not give up without a fight. Renshaw remembered that this incursion was, after all, merely a reconnaissance in force.

A shot from the 10-inch Columbiad on Fort Point at the tip of Galveston Island answered the ship's advance. The *Harriet Lane* dropped anchor and signaled for a boat from shore. After none appeared, Wainwright impatiently dispatched his executive officer Albert Lea ashore in his own boat. The Confederates were unhappy to see the Union officers and hurried them back to their ship after a terse interview. Wainwright, again left waiting, grew stormy as he spied a small Confederate boat, flying a Rebel flag and not a flag of truce, slowly and clumsily making its way from shore. After watching the craft creep forward, the Union officer preemptively ordered his anchors weighed and turned his vessel about, deciding

The USS Harriet Lane *had been in the revenue service before the Civil War. This vessel participated in the opening drama at Fort Sumter before serving as Captain David Dixon Porter's flagship in operations against New Orleans and Vicksburg. Naval Historical Center.*

that the Texans were definitely bluffing, probably stalling, and possibly plotting.

Daylight was waning, and the Federal commanders realized that they had to act promptly or the Texans would have all night to develop their plans. Renshaw, perplexed by Wainwright's report of the events near shore, decided the issue at once. He ordered his steamer captains to dash over the bar and past the puny Fort Point battery. Any skipper who could was to deal with the erratic Confederate dispatch boat en route to the docks of the city. Renshaw would lead the battle line aboard the *Westfield,* followed by *Owasco,* and *Harriet Lane.* The recently arrived mortar schooner *Henry Janes* would be towed in by the *Clifton* and would lob heavier rounds if needed.

When the Union ships steamed into range, the gunners on Fort Point opened fire, sending a 10-inch round whirring past the *Westfield.* Sailors aboard the flagship wigwagged a signal to the rest of the fleet, and Renshaw's bluejackets returned the saucy Texan insult with the combined weight of some twenty naval guns. A shell from the *Owasco* burst directly over the Rebel battery, and its once-bold Texan gunners,

The USS Owasco *was one of the navy's rapidly built "ninety-day gunboats" and served in the campaigns against New Orleans and Vicksburg before heading to the Texas coast. U.S. Navy Historical Center.*

men of the 1st Texas Heavy Artillery, either fled or fell maimed or dead. "The Secesh made a regular skedaddle without taking time to reload their gun," observed Private Henry Gusley, a marine aboard the *Westfield*. Subsequent rounds dismounted the Rebel gun, one shot striking it full on the muzzle. The Rebel launch, suddenly energetic and well-handled, sprinted for home, eager to be clear of the duel. The line of Union ships then paraded into the harbor, barely concerned by the ineffective fire of a pair of 24-pounders nearer town.[6]

Renshaw now grew even bolder. He ordered his ships anchored near the city, white flags hoisted again, and ordered a cease-fire. While the Yankee anchor chains rattled into the water, the Rebels responded by sending their boat back out bearing army officers to determine Renshaw's intentions. The Union commodore demanded the unconditional surrender of the city. After much posturing on both sides—mostly about the etiquette of flags of truce—each side agreed to an armistice. Renshaw granted Confederate authorities four days to remove women, children, and foreigners from the town, after which time he would take the city, by force if necessary. With their single heavy gun lying in a heap on Fort Point, Confederate authorities realized that

An 8-inch Columbiad in an earthen emplacement similar to that which would have guarded the entrance to Galveston Bay. Library of Congress.

their hand was fairly played and ordered Galveston's evacuation. For the next four days Rebel forces and their tools of war streamed out of the city. Renshaw had unexpectedly captured Galveston.

On October 8, 1862, the Civil War came to Texas in a dramatic way. The once remote enemy was anchored in Galveston Bay after firing barely a shot. Unlike the angry mobs of New Orleans just six months before, only a few Galvestonians watched as one hundred blue-coated sailors and marines disembarked onto Kuhn's Wharf and headed for the center of town, escorted by the city's firemen dressed in full uniform. No one interrupted the men as they approached the newly constructed customs house, where the mayor of Galveston handed Captain Jonathan M. Wainwright of the *Harriet Lane* the keys to the building. "The Mayor . . . expressed his pleasure at seeing the city once more about to pass into the hands of the Union," Gusley wrote. Marines ascended the stairs to the roof and, as the citizens looked on, the Stars and Stripes, a flag that had not flown above the city for more than eighteen months, unfurled to bite the breeze. Thirty minutes later the flag came down and the Federal landing party returned to its boat, completing the symbolic capture of the port.[7]

The residents of the most important city in Texas seemed happy to welcome the arrival of the Yankees. "Altogether it was quite a gala occasion," Gusley continued. "When we marched back to the boats nearly every one of our muskets was decorated with flowers, which the women and children gave to us. Of the people of Galveston we must say," the Pennsylvanian concluded, "that a more respectable and well behaved set we have not seen." For the sailors and marines who had marched through the hostile streets of New Orleans six months before, this was a welcome change.[8]

Commander Jonathan M. Wainwright II had commanded Captain David Dixon Porter's flagship, the USS Harriet Lane, *during the campaign to capture New Orleans. The son of the Episcopal bishop of New York, Wainwright joined the navy in 1837 and proved to be popular and successful—traits that put him in important roles during the Civil War. Naval Historical Center.*

This disaster outraged Confederate Texans. Thomas Jefferson Chambers, a tough old Texan revolutionary and founder of the state, expressed his disgust to Secretary of War George W. Randolph in a letter reprinted in the Houston newspaper. "My worst fears have been realized; the coast of the chivalrous state of Texas has been surrendered to the enemy, without a blow struck in its defense," he complained. "I cannot express the deep grief, the shame, the crushing humiliation, with which I was overwhelmed at the reception of this disastrous intelligence, when this deep disgrace was inflicted upon her proud escutcheon." The Yankee gunboats steaming about Galveston Bay had bruised Texan honor. "Where was the proud Texas chivalry displayed

William B. Renshaw and the USS Westfield lead the way into Galveston Bay, with the USS Owasco and Harriet Lane following astern. The USS Clifton is towing in the mortar schooner Henry Janes. Nestell Collection, Nimitz Library, U.S. Naval Academy, Annapolis, Maryland.

at the Alamo, San Antonio, Concepcion, San Jacinto, Oak Hills, Elkhorn, Williamsburg, the Chickahominy, Manassas, Sharpsburg—upon every bloody field where her sons have been present?"[9]

Chambers was willing to concede that, in some arenas, Yankee expertise may have been superior to Texan nerve. "Alas!, it was crushed beneath the weight of a West Point science, and a military genius not her own! Be this her apology and her consolation, however sad and humiliating."[10]

Although Commodore Renshaw might have chuckled at the reference to West Point, the problems he faced were far from humorous, and his military genius would be taxed for a solution. Union army reinforcements would be a long time in coming; after all, he had not actually intended to capture the town. Now that he had, the affront to Texan honor aside, he now had to hold the city he had so easily taken. The two-mile railroad bridge connecting the island to the mainland ran across water too shallow to be patrolled by his ships, and it would have to be left standing, he reasoned, or the city's population would starve. His fleet could control the town with their guns, he believed, but at least a few hundred infantrymen would be required for patrol and shore security. Renshaw was quick to send a celebratory message to Admiral Farragut in New Orleans announcing his bloodless achievement. He also requested that troops be dispatched to hold this surprise conquest.[11]

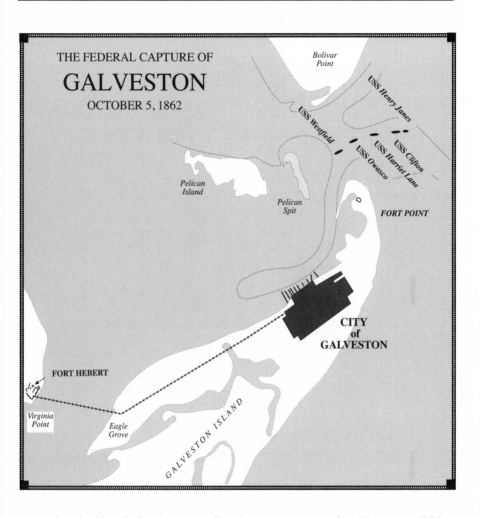

THE FEDERAL CAPTURE OF

GALVESTON

OCTOBER 5, 1862

Bolivar
Point

USS Henry Janes

USS Westfield

USS Clifton

USS Harriet Lane

USS Owasco

Pelican
Island

Pelican
Spit

FORT POINT

**CITY
of
GALVESTON**

FORT HEBERT

Virginia
Point

Eagle
Grove

GALVESTON ISLAND

Federal officials had reason for their optimism that Texas could be brought back into the Union in short order. "From deserters and others flying for the terrors of the conscription (which they are rigidly enforcing at the point of the bayonet), I am of the opinion that we have at last captured a place with strong Union proclivities among the lower and middle classes," Renshaw reported. "The reign of terror that has prevailed during months past would, I should think, taint the loyalty of the most rabid of the rebel citizens." These Texans were tired of the privation of war and would embrace the old flag, but they feared the Rebels and would only act upon their sentiments if the Federal authorities could guarantee their safety. "The people say that all they want is be sure of the support of the Government," Farragut

The symbol of Federal authority in Galveston, the U.S. Customs House. Rosenberg Library, Galveston, Texas.

wrote from aboard the USS *Hartford* to Major General Benjamin Butler, commander of army forces in the Department of the Gulf. Naval officers stressed the need for troops to be sent to complete the conquest.[12]

Butler agreed with that goal. "I should be glad if General Weitzel should be able to move against Texas, and would suggest that an appropriate base of operations would be through Galveston," he wrote to Major General Henry Halleck, "but I have hardly a regiment which I can spare to hold it."[13]

If the troops could be found to man a base on the island, the time was certainly ripe for such a move. Cracks in secessionist solidarity were evident throughout the Lone Star State. Rumors of dissension among the population in the interior trickled into Federal headquarters, including rumblings of a genuine uprising of German Texans in nearby Austin County. The political reorganization and realignment of the state was more than wishful thinking and apparently not far off. For the weeks just prior to the Federal capture of Galveston, Union conspiracies in north Texas and the western Hill Country had led to paranoia and internecine bloodshed. All the omens boded well for a successful return of Federal authority to Texas. It, like southern Louisiana, could become a crucible and laboratory of reconstruction policies.

Two men who were undoubtedly encouraged by the news were Texas Unionists Edmund J. Davis and Andrew Jackson "Colossal Jack" Hamilton. Both men had left the state to become advocates of the loyal citizens they left behind. Both were native southerners, and both were men of influence and wealth. In the summer of 1862, both men had toured northern cities, speaking of the plight of their fellow Texans. On the day Galveston fell, Hamilton was in Washington, D.C., for an interview with the president. Within weeks, the Texan was a federal brigadier with authority to raise troops. By the end of October Hamilton plotted his triumphant return to his homeland while his accomplice, the recently commissioned Colonel Davis, enlisted the first recruits in the 1st Texas Cavalry (U.S.) from among refugees in New Orleans, under the proud eye of Ben Butler.[14]

Colonel Edmund J. Davis, a native of Florida, spent most of his early adulthood in South Texas, living in Corpus Christi, Laredo, and Brownsville. When secession fever hit Texas, he backed Sam Houston's Unionist position. His views eventually caused him to flee the state in the summer of 1862; he traveled to Washington, D.C., where he earned his commission and orders to raise a regiment of Texas Unionists. Courtesy of Denis Gaubert, Thibodeaux, Louisiana.

Back in Butler's home state of Massachusetts, Governor John A. Andrew must have relished the news from his fellow Bay State men then operating along the margins of the Gulf of Mexico. The governor had always seen the conquest of Texas as critical to the Union war effort. With the backing of influential businessmen from his state, he argued that this remote region was "the state easiest to take and hold, with larger public consequences dependent upon such action than any other." Andrew wrote an outline of his argument and delivered it

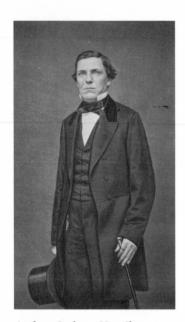

Andrew Jackson Hamilton had been a successful Texas politician in the antebellum period. Forced from the state in the summer of 1862 because of his Unionist sentiments, he became an ardent and vocal advocate for a Federal invasion of Texas. He got his wish. Library of Congress.

to Gustavus V. Fox, the assistant secretary of the Navy. "We flank the rebellion . . . we open the way out for cotton . . . we cut off future annexations in the interest of the Rebels." He also suggested that a rail line could be run from the coast to Missouri, thus by-passing the Deep South states. "These points are urged . . . by leading commercial men and capitalists."[15]

Andrew might have been interested in industry and commerce, but he was better known for his aggressive abolitionist views and saw a chance to prove his beliefs. "Instead of loyal men leaving Texas, as they are now doing," he wrote, "they will remain, and in a few years will fill Texas with a European immigration, which will demonstrate, as the Germans are now doing, that cotton can be raised without slaves." Even more immediately, a successful lodgment between Matagorda Bay and Sabine Pass would allow the U.S. government to begin the demolition of chattel labor forever. "Events will no doubt educate the people and the next Congress to a wise solution of all questions which may afterward arise in connection with slaves and slavery in an exceptional state . . . like Texas." Andrew believed that this place held the keys to future domestic tranquility for the nation. "By such seizure and treatment . . . we shall have at the end of the war material guarantees that will prevent any compromise or settlement as to make . . . another rebellion possible." In short, he argued, that capturing Texas would forever crush any future attempts to expand the institution of slavery—a leading cause of the current conflict. Without Texas, there could never be a Confederate empire in the Southwest.[16]

The fall of 1862 was gloomy in Texas. Galveston, the largest city in the state, remained in Federal hands as its forward base. Texan citizens and soldiers feared invasion, and enemy warships preyed upon its coast. Friends and family lay dead on the distant battlefields of Virginia, Tennessee, Arkansas, and New Mexico. The Lone Star State's heroes had been slain: Albert Sidney Johnston, Ben McCulloch, Benjamin Franklin Terry, William P. Rogers, and countless others who had been just as dear now filled soldiers' graves. Unionists, too, grew bolder as Federal forces came closer. A general feeling of pessimism gripped the Confederate population.[17]

Governor John Albion Andrew of Massachusetts had a keen interest in two things: arming former slaves and invading Texas. James Lorenzo Bowen, Massachusetts in the War, 1861-1865 *(C.W. Bryan & Co., 1888).*

CHAPTER TWELVE

UNION OFFENSIVE

Oh de Lawd's name be praised!—We knowed you'd come.
Recently freed slave woman, Ascension Parish, Louisiana

U nion war planners congratulated themselves on the *coup de théâtre* at Galveston. Commander W. B. Renshaw's expedition had not only closed the Texas coast but also, they speculated, it virtually guaranteed that no Texas reinforcements would be heading to Louisiana. "They are under the impression that a large force of ours is on the way to invade Texas," Renshaw reported from Galveston, noting that across the bay "they are concentrating troops at that point to meet them." Butler could now finish off Richard Taylor without threat of interference from the west. While the navy captured the largest city in Texas, the army had not been idle. The 21st Indiana's late-September reconnaissance in force, coupled with the reports of the Mississippi gunboat commanders, convinced Butler that peace on the Father of Waters would come only when the Lafourche District was scoured clean of Confederates.[1]

"This whole country is alive with troops and field artillery," Lieutenant Francis A. Roe wrote to Admiral Farragut from the USS *Kathadin,* as he skirmished with Rebels around Donaldsonville on Septem-

An 11-inch Dahlgren amidship. Notice the different types of projectiles at the feet of the two officers: a cluster of grapeshot is on the right, a shell strapped to a wooden sabot is in the middle, and what appears to be a powder bag is on the left. Library of Congress.

ber 29. "In a few hours," he continued, "the enemy can muster one or two thousand men at almost any point on the West Bank of the river." The naval officer also emphasized the quality of these Rebels: "These troops are not all composed of guerillas, but regulars and militia troops are combined with them. They are exceedingly vigilant and active." Roe ended his report by proposing a plan of action: "I earnestly trust that General Butler will give us a regiment or so of good troops and allow us to clean out Donaldsonville, which I regard as the piratical resort of all the bad men of the country."[2]

Brigadier General Alfred Mouton's troops had also changed their tactics. Confederate field batteries moved behind the cover of the river levee, gauging their movements by spotters' reports as to Union shipping and gunboat movements. Any enemy vessels patrolling upriver from New Orleans toward Baton Rouge would receive a pummeling. With water levels low, these southern cannons had a twenty-foot height advantage and could sweep the Union vessels with canister shot. Two vessels under Lieutenant Commander George M. Ransom, USS *Kineo* and USS *Katahdin*, churned upriver to investigate the substance of these rumors, calling again at Donaldsonville. On October 20 sailors and marines entered the town, questioned local residents and slaves, and brought back disturbing news. Not only was the countryside filled with Rebels, but all the local Unionists had evacuated or fled. Only resentful secessionists remained. Once away, gunners lobbed eleven rounds into the woods above the town to drive away some mounted Confederates. Building steam, the two-ship flotilla headed up the Mississippi River toward Plaquemine and Bayou Goula, mindful they were pushing deeper into enemy territory.[3]

The clash between these vessels and Mouton's Confederates came quickly. Two miles above Donaldsonville, Union sailors spotted clusters of enemy horsemen. Union gun commanders ordered their big 11-inch Dahlgrens and 30-pounder Parrots brought out for action. While lookouts tracked the movements of these horsemen, the crews of both vessels braced themselves. Within moments, bullets from concealed sharpshooters whizzed across the decks, splintering wood and causing bluejackets to duck for cover. The navy guns answered in a flurry of smoke and fire, shelling the area where the horsemen had last been spotted, and spraying the levee with grape shot. After several minutes, Lieutenant Roe ordered the *Katahdin* to cease firing. No Rebels remained in sight, and apparently none had been hit. The *Kineo* and *Katahdin* continued their upstream glide to Plaquemine.[4]

At dawn on October 21, the Federals sent a shore party into Plaquemine to search for signs of the enemy. A friendly overseer at a nearby plantation revealed that Confederates had indeed attempted to ambush the ships and would do so again as they passed back toward Donaldsonville. Equipped with this knowledge, Ransom ordered his crews to battle stations and began his return trip, prowling for the insolent enemy.[5]

The Confederates obliged by opening fire near the same positions they had held the previous day. This time, however, they brought their cannons. A volley from four field guns, shooting from masked embrasures cut into the levee, sent projectiles screaming over the decks of the *Kineo*. Other than a holed bulwark, some tangled hammocks, severed rigging, and a missing officer's hat, this hostile Rebel salute achieved little. Then came the small arms fire. Bullets tapped into deck and mast, keeping the crewmen dodging. By the time the Federal gunners unleashed their broadsides against the Confederates, the southern cannons and sharpshooters had disappeared. Ransom ordered his ships to come about and continued to shell the levee and the trees beyond for several more minutes, but with no effect.[6]

The vessels persisted in their patrol downriver toward New Orleans. At the sight of every bend in the river or suspicious location, Union gunners plastered the area with shell and grapeshot. The Confederates may not have interdicted the river, but their hit-and-run tactics had made the Union sailors and their skippers nervous. Bluejackets landed below Donaldsonville and cut the telegraph line, reporting the presence of freshly cut embrasures here as well. The Rebels, it appeared, planned to keep up their mischief. Roe took a moment to record a few lines in his journal: "We are now constantly under fire of this covert kind as we pass up and down the river. The troops and guns are concealed and watch for us to pass along and fire and flee. Sharpshooters (I suppose the assassins are called) occupy treetops and take deliberate aim at our decks. We now regularly fight our way up and down the river."[7]

Reports like these convinced Butler that the time had come to settle the issue of who was in charge of the banks of the Mississippi. He had growing confidence in his army and needed little urging from the navy to attack the enemy; he had in mind a general offensive that would whip the Rebels and end the cycle of brush fights at burned-out river towns. For the first time since arriving in Louisiana, Butler believed New Orleans was relatively safe. No Confederate attacks from east of the river, which he had feared ever since the Battle of Baton Rouge in August, had materialized. In fact, the enemy on that bank had abandoned the offensive and had begun constructing a massive fortification at Port Hudson, effectively surrendering any initiative they once held. With the Rebels turning to picks and shovels instead of cannons and bayonets, Butler turned his attention to conquering the west bank.

After consulting with Admiral David Farragut in early autumn, Butler was ready to deliver the decisive stroke to seize and occupy the
Lafourche District. Since security of the Mississippi clearly depended
upon control of both banks, the officers planned a three-pronged invasion that would utterly destroy Taylor's command and banish Rebel
hopes in Louisiana forever.

Butler's principal sledge in this hammering attack would be a four-
thousand-man "Reserve Brigade" of infantry. These troops—the 12th
and 13th Connecticut, the 75th New York, the 1st Louisiana (U.S.), and
the 8th New Hampshire, along with the 1st Maine and 6th Massachusetts artillery batteries—would travel aboard eight transports. Butler
also dispatched the three companies of the nascent 1st Louisiana
(U.S.) Cavalry and another from the 2nd Massachusetts Battalion to
scout ahead of the force. These troops, covered by the gunboats USS
Kineo, Itasca, and *Sciota,* would land near Donaldsonville and head
southward along Bayou Lafourche.

A second column would move in from Algiers. The battle-bruised
veterans of the 8th Vermont would push down the line of the Opelousas Railroad to link up with the Reserve Brigade at Thibodaux. Accompanying these New Englanders would be the 1st Louisiana Native
Guards, African Americans who would repair the railroad and fight if
needed.[8]

Should these army columns fail, Butler planned a backup strategy
that required the cooperation of Admiral Farragut. The general would
dispatch a force to swing in behind Mouton from the sea and cut off
his retreat by capturing Brashear City. When New Orleans capitulated,
several useful steamers fell into Union hands. Butler had turned four
of them—the *Diana, Kinsman, Estrella,* and *Calhoun*—into gunboats
to support his infantry. Farragut released crews from his warships to
man the vessels, and placed a rising star, twenty five-year-old Lieutenant Commander Thomas McKean Buchanan, in command of the
flotilla. His uncle Franklin Buchanan, a Confederate naval officer, had
already made history commanding the CSS *Virginia* in the first duel of
ironclads at Hampton Roads the previous March.

The USS *Diana* had become a decent gunboat. Union carpenters
rebuilt the one-time side-wheel steamer into a light draft warship ca-

A sketch of the USS Diana *from a naval officer. She was part of the booty that came into Union hands with the capture of New Orleans. Nestell Collection, Nimitz Library, U.S. Naval Academy, Annapolis, Maryland.*

pable of prowling about in the bayous and swamps of Southwest Louisiana. It had churned these same blackwater streams—Bayou Lafourche, Bayou Teche, the Atchafalaya River—as a merchant vessel in time of peace. Under Union control the ship would return, this time to hunt Confederates. Careful thought had gone into the ship's remodeling. *Diana's* casemate had been armored with iron rails, allowing it forward protection should it nose into a Rebel ambush. In addition to the defensive protection, the vessel mounted a 20-pounder Parrot Rifle in a bow pivot, ready to return the fire of assailants.

Carpenters similarly converted the other vessels. The USS *Kinsman,* classified by the navy as a "small side-wheel combatant—4th rate," was a 245-ton bayou transport that had been a Rebel supply vessel before its capture and transformation into a rakish little gunboat. The screw steamer USS *Estrella*—a captured blockade runner—dwarfed these two riverboats. Its sixty-man crew served a battery of five guns, including a 30-pounder Parrot in a bow pivot. Buchanan made the largest vessel in the flotilla, the medium side-wheeler USS *Calhoun,* his flagship. This ship had previously flown the Confederate flag as a privateer but had fallen prey to the U.S. Navy near the mouth of the Mississippi. Nearly seventy Union sailors now lived aboard the

The USS Estrella *is on the left of this drawing of Union warships off Pensacola. English-built, she was fast and seaworthy. Naval Historical Center.*

Calhoun and were prepared to use its three heavy guns to combat the rebellion in Louisiana.

Butler had great confidence in his ad hoc navy. The four vessels were to leave New Orleans heading downstream simultaneous to the army's push upstream. With luck and diligence, the gunboats would clear the Mississippi, pass along Louisiana's Gulf Coast, splash up the lower Atchafalaya River, and arrive at Berwick Bay in time to cut off any Rebel retreat. Packed tightly aboard the transport *St. Mary's* as a landing force, the scrappy 21st Indiana would serve on board as sharp-shooters.

Butler handpicked the man to lead this expedition: Brigadier General Godfrey Weitzel, a twenty-seven-year-old Cincinnati German trained at West Point. Having graduated second in the class of 1855, Weitzel's first appointment in the Engineer Corps had, ironically, been to build, upgrade, and restore the fortifications protecting New Orleans. In 1859 he returned to his alma mater as an assistant professor of engineering. When the war broke out, Weitzel, with his knowledge of key fortifications, joined Butler's staff as his chief engineer.

The USS Calhoun *started the war as a Confederate privateer, capturing a half dozen sailing vessels including the* John Adams, Mermaid, *and* Panama *off the mouth of the Mississippi. Confederate authorities decided that she made a better blockade runner, sailing her out of Berwick Bay and New Orleans to Cuba with cargos of sugar and cotton in exchange for gunpowder, weapons, merchandise, medicines, and coffee. The* Calhoun's *luck ran out on January 23, 1862, when the USS* Samuel Rotan, Rachel Seaman, *and* Colorado *cornered the vessel near the Southwest Pass of the Mississippi and ran her aground. The Southern crew set the ship afire before escaping to shore. Fast-acting Federals boarded, doused the flames, and added the steamer to their inventory of gunboats operating in Louisiana waters. Confederate commanders predicted that the* Calhoun, *in Union hands, would "prove a great pest on the coast, as she is very fast and of light draft," adding that her loss was "an unfortunate piece of business." Naval Historical Center.*

After the fall of New Orleans, Weitzel assumed the de facto role of Butler's second in command and served as acting mayor for the city.

The young officer had served impressively. To help win the affection of his subject citizenry, Weitzel launched a campaign to clean up New Orleans by managing trash and sewage, thus improving health and livability during the summer of 1862. But true glory came on the battlefield, and Weitzel was eager to test himself. Butler arranged to promote the talented young soldier to brigadier general to lead the Lafourche expedition. No one in the Union army would regret the choice.

His plans and leaders in place, Butler felt confident of success. "I can easily hold this portion of Louisiana, by far the richest, " he wrote to General-in-Chief Henry Halleck. Butler also announced that he would build upon the navy's victories and "extend the movement so far as to substantially cut-off all supplies from Texas to the enemy this coming winter." Butler fully understood the relationship between The Lone Star State and the Confederate efforts along the lower Mississippi.[9]

Brigadier General Godfrey Weitzel was a very capable engineer and a keen organizer. He was General Benjamin Butler's most important lieutenant in the field. Library of Congress.

The Lafourche Campaign began in earnest on October 24, as the transport and gunboats flotilla pulled away from the docks at Camp Carrollton late in the afternoon. Crowds of observers lined the banks of the river as on board, bands played from the decks and pennants streamed from the rigging. At Camp Parapet, the men of the sloop of war *Portsmouth* climbed into the rigging to cheer on the expedition. "We all felt very happy," Captain Frank Godfrey of the 1st Louisiana Cavalry noted, "and thought we had made a good start."[10]

Timing was crucial to this complicated, combined-arms operation involving converging columns operating in difficult terrain. As Butler's ambitious invasion began, clusters of ships peeled away in opposite directions from the New Orleans wharves as carloads of soldiers, black and white, swayed down the railroad tracks across the river. If all went according to plan, the land elements would meet four days later in Thibodaux, with General Mouton's Confederates locked between them.[11]

The next morning broke cold and foggy as Weitzel landed his men at the Winchester Plantation, six miles below Donaldsonville. The cavalry trotted ahead, scattering Rebel pickets, while the gunboats continued upstream to put the town under their guns. By midday Butler's Yankees entered Donaldsonville's deserted streets. This was the first active service for Captain John William De Forest and the 12th Connecticut, and the sight of the "once flourishing little town" pro-

Captain John B. Hubbard, General Godfrey Weitzel's assistant adjutant general, whom he described as "the best officer I ever had or ever saw." A native of Hollowell, Maine, Hubbard was the son of a former governor of that state and a graduate of Bowdoin College; he had plans to practice law in Portland. When the war started, he joined the 12th Maine as a lieutenant before transferring to Weitzel's staff in time to plan the invasion of the sugar parishes. Courtesy of Denis Gaubert, Thibodaux, Louisiana.

vided their first taste of war. "Destruction had befallen it," the captain related, and it had become "a desert of smoke blackened ruins." Black laborers unloaded supplies from the transports, soldiers patrolled the town, and the men of the 1st Louisiana—assigned to garrison the place—knocked together quarters from scavenged lumber.[12]

Delays forced Weitzel to spend the night in the town instead of several miles down the road, as he had planned. "My regiment slept on the floor of a Catholic church," De Forest noted, adding, "I ate my supper off a tombstone in the cemetery." Other troops quartered in various public buildings, hotels, and private homes.[13]

The invaders also spent their time looting. Weitzel expressed remorse. "I have violated one of the first principles of campaigning, never to encamp in a village when one can just as well remain outside," he is reported to have said. Other officers were amazed at the destruction. Much of the town had already been plundered by the navy, but the remainder "might as well have been burned," wrote one Federal, "for the soldiers . . . made wasteful havoc with the furniture and windows of those [houses] that were standing."[14]

The gray October day on which the Union troops arrived was unseasonably blustery, cold, and rainy. "Nature was in unison with our feelings," wrote plantation mistress Josephine Pugh from her home Woodlawn, responding to the news that traveled quickly down Bayou Lafourche. "It was very cheerless, and our hearts were heavy with the tiding . . . that the Yankees had landed."[15]

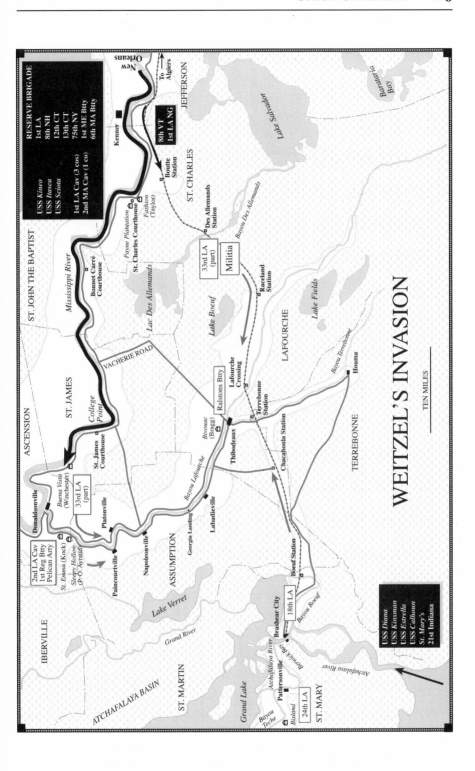

WEITZEL'S INVASION

TEN MILES

The Church of the Ascension of Our Lord Jesus Christ in Donaldsonville, Louisiana. Completed in 1843, it was the second sacred structure to stand on the site. In the fall of 1862, it would house Union troops. State Library of Louisiana.

Word of the Union invasion arrived at General Alfred Mouton's headquarters in Thibodaux late that same day, catching him off guard. Mouton's troops remained badly scattered and his commander, Richard Taylor, was away from his headquarters and unavailable for consultation. That evening Mouton mounted his horse and rode toward Donaldsonville to ascertain Yankee intentions. He met Colonel William G. Vincent's command falling back down the bayou after having abandoned its camp at St. Emma. Convinced that this was not a mere raid and that the enemy was bent on invasion, Mouton reversed his course, dispatching orders to his far-flung commands to rally at Winn's Plantation two miles north of Labadieville.[16]

The Confederate forces in Southwest Louisiana flowed in modest gray streams toward Thibodaux. Vincent fell back with his 2nd Louisiana Cavalry as well as the 33rd Infantry and Semmes's Battery—in all, about nine hundred men and four guns. The 18th Louisiana Infantry moved up by rail from Brashear City about forty miles from the rally point, and the 24th "Crescent" Regiment, a mere shadow organization

Donaldsonville in ruins. What the navy hadn't finished in August, repeat visits by U.S. troops helped complete, creating "a desert of smoke blackened ruins." State Library of Louisiana.

of fewer than 150 men, loaded onto transports in New Iberia, more than eighty miles away, for a ride down the Teche. Ralston's two-gun Mississippi Battery moved out from Thibodaux. By the afternoon of October 26, Mouton's forces assembled at a hastily chosen location near Georgia Landing.[17]

Mouton planned his stand with Bayou Lafourche bisecting his intended battlefield. On the afternoon of October 26, the 18th and 24th Louisiana infantry settled into a drainage ditch behind a stout rail fence that bordered Texana Road. Their position fronted five hundred yards of open fields west of the bayou. Ralston's battery moved into position on their right. In all, little more than five hundred men covered two hundred yards from the bayou to the wooded swamp on their left, with a one-hundred man detachment of the 2nd Louisiana Cavalry in reserve. East of the bayou, men from the 33rd Louisiana, the 2nd Louisiana Cavalry, a small remnant of the Terrebonne militia and Semmes's battery formed a line, nearly nine hundred strong, in position with their compatriots across the way.[18]

A Louisiana cemetery. "I ate my supper off a tombstone," wrote Captain John William De Forest of the 12th Connecticut.

The Confederate plans made good use of the terrain. West of Bayou Lafourche, a swampy expanse of timber, the Black Marais, protected the left and allowed a way to work around the Union flank as the bluecoats made their way across the open fields fronting the Texana Road. East of the Lafourche, cane fields would mask any Confederate movements, and cleared ground lay between cropland and a thick woods on the Rebel right. In the narrow confines of this battlefield, Mouton hoped to hold the Federals in place while he sent detachments of mounted troops to envelop their line and gain the enemy rear. Mouton placed his cannons in the center on either bank in position to make crisscrossing sweeps over the open channel of the bayou against any advancing forces. A spotter atop a sugar house would wig-wag targeting information to the batteries. By using a combination of ambush, harassing artillery fire, and mounted flankers, Mouton hoped to bewilder the oncoming Yankees. Once the northerners fell into confusion, he would order his veteran infantry into an assault and drive the

Woodlawn Plantation, home of William and Josephine Pugh, survived the war, but the fortune that sustained it did not. By the time of this 1930s photo, the once stately mansion was a derelict shell. It would be completely gone a decade later. Library of Congress.

enemy from the field and into the waiting pistols and shotguns of the Rebel cavalry.

Mouton's plan was deeply flawed. His forces on either bank could not reinforce the other. Despite Taylor's orders, the Confederates had never completed a portable bridge that would have allowed each wing of the divided command to support the other. Instead, such coordination between Mouton's forces would only come across the Labadieville Bridge, more than a mile to the rear of the Confederate line. In the midst of battle, the time it would take to traverse this two-mile round trip might prove disasterous, the fatigue it would induce demoralizing. In addition, Mouton—plagued by old wounds and chronic rheumatism due to the cold weather—established his headquarters back at Oak Wood Plantation in Labadieville, "physically unable to go to the front." His troops, shivering in the ditch alongside Texana Road, were equipped with obsolete weapons.[19]

Weitzel's orders for the conduct of the campaign, by contrast, reflected the thoroughness of an engineer. The 1st Louisiana Infantry and three gunboats would hold Donaldsonville. The general ordered two enormous Mississippi flatboats into Bayou Lafourche. Towed by mules and crewed by black polemen, these barges would become a portable bridge for the men of the Reserve Brigade, allowing their regiments to cross the bayou and respond to threats from either bank. The 8th New Hampshire and Company C of the 2nd Massachusetts Cavalry Battalion crossed the bayou to its west, or right descending bank. On the east, or left descending bank, three independent companies of Louisiana cavalry preceded the 75th New York, the 12th and 13th Connecticut, and two batteries of artillery, the 1st Maine Battery, and the 6th Massachusetts.[20]

While Mouton assembled his veterans, Weitzel's inexperienced troops tramped along the bayou road toward the Rebel position, feeling the discomforts of life on campaign. "The men," wrote De Forest, "quite unaccustomed to field service, complained of the weight of the knapsacks." The officer was appalled at their lack of road discipline. "The troops marched like greenhorns, straggling about the road, the levee, the fields, and taking advantage of every discoverable cut-off."[21]

The first day of the invasion passed with little more than skirmishing. Soldiers sank or torched any bridges or boats along the way. By evening, the Federals had reached Napoleonville.[22]

The troops had encountered signs of distress along their line of march. "We passed pretty residences, flourishing plantations and endless flats of waving cane," De Forest observed. "But the owners of this comfort and wealth were not visible; not a vehicle, not even an equestrian appeared on the highways." At one point in the march, the Yankee column encountered a planter still living on his estate. Described as a "tall, cadaverous man with lank iron-grey hair and the voice of a camp meeting preacher," the southerner harangued the passing army. "Ah boys! Boys! You don't know what awaits you," he hollered. "You are going to defeat and rout and slaughter. Better turn back while you can! Better turn back!"[23] The cocky New Englanders of the 12th Connecticut remained unmoved. "Some of the youngsters yelled impertinences to him," recalled Captain De

This Harper's Weekly *image depicts the impression that many Northerners had of the jubilant bands of slaves that flocked to the army.*

Forest, "and he stalked solemnly into his house, leaving our impenitent array to its fate."[24]

Although the region seemed deserted of whites, its black inhabitants welcomed Weitzel's army as a liberating host. "'God bless you, massas!' they cried," a Federal observed. Many of these former slaves marched along with the column, eager to serve. One said, "Oh de Lawd's name be praised!—We knowed you'd come—Ise a gwine 'long with you." Captain H. B. Sprague of the 13th Connecticut noted that the refugees also carried plunder: "Negroes . . . joined us, bringing with them mules, turkeys, furniture, and bundles of clothing." Some of the northerners had cruel fun with the adoring throng. Captain De Forest noted that former field hands were "ready to do anything for their deliverers and submitted unmurmuringly to the tricks and robberies which were practiced upon them by our jokers and scapegraces."[25]

Captain Godfrey, a conscientious abolitionist, felt a touch of regret for the naiveté he witnessed. "Their happiness was to be of such short duration," he wrote home later. "Dependent, and ignorant as the mass of them were, they were soon to suffer so much, and to learn that the price of liberty was great." He had seen how his fellow soldiers had treated freedmen in the preceding months. "Those whom they now so gladly looked upon as deliverers, were men more of less like those they had left and they like many before them were only to exchange masters."[26]

Young Helen Dupuy watched in horror as U.S. troops and runaway slaves came up to her home. "They insulted us and took the horses, the cattle, the sheep, and the hogs," she recorded. The troops did not enter the house but demanded that the women provide them with water. When the soldiers moved on, the slaves of Sleepy Hollow plantation went with them. "On awakening the next morning we found that there did not remain a single person of that race, neither house servants nor field hands." Dupuy, for perhaps the first time in her life, had to work the fields that had for years been the source of her family's wealth.[27]

CHAPTER THIRTEEN

GEORGIA LANDING

Your firing didn't hurt us, but your coming on and yelling scared us.
Confederate Prisoner

T he unusually wet, frosty dawn of October 27 ushered in a day of heated combat. Mouton's Confederates, unseen in their am-bush positions, tried to catch a quick nap, having suffered in the freezing weather the night before. Upstream, Weitzel's Federals continued their steady tramp down the bayou road, mindful that the enemy was at hand, but uncertain where he might be hiding. Around noon, Captain Solon Perkins's Massachusetts sharp-eyed cavalry van-guard on the west bank of Bayou Lafourche spied some of the Confederates milling about, alerting Brigadier General Godfrey Weitzel that the Rebels may have chosen to make a stand on the Texana Road leading to Georgia Landing, just above Labadieville. Skirmishers from the 8th New Hampshire advanced, confirmed the enemy's presence—behind a fence bordering the opposite side of the field—and returned amid the erratic popping of muskets, confident they had counted all the enemy's guns. Whole once more, the regiment formed a line of battle on the edge of the woods facing the naked furrows ahead, its left side anchored on the bayou levee.

The officers of the 8th New Hampshire believed this to be a screening force for Mouton's army which, if the Confederate general was a good judge of geography, would be positioned nearer to the Labadieville bridge. A good push would brush these gray skirmishers aside, and the advance of Weitzel's army could proceed. But the New Hampshirites had miscalculated. Despite the Federals' confidence, most of the southerners had yet to fire their weapons and reveal themselves. Directly ahead of the 8th New Hampshire lay not a picket line, but the well-concealed guns of Ralston's Mississippi Battery, supported by the 18th Louisiana and the 24th Louisiana.

The men of the 8th New Hampshire stepped out smartly from the woods for what they thought would be a parade-style advance. Instead, they marched unsupported into the guns of two veteran regiments supported by artillery and met a blistering response. The New Englanders wavered as the Confederate fire tore at the Yankee ranks. Rolling volleys rippled along the cypress fence bordering the Texana Road. Three of the 8th's color guard fell, but brave replacements seized the staffs, and the flags continued to face the enemy. A cannon ball whooshed overhead, snapping the pole bearing the national colors, and the banner fluttered toward the ground. Several soldiers surged forward to gather up the stricken fabric, but the color bearer, having recovered from the shock, dove forward to recover his flag. "No you don't," the soldier told his eager comrades as he picked up the red, white, and blue folds. "He rose and moved on, flaunting the stars and stripes," reported an observer.[1]

Despite this bravado, the regimental line shivered, shuddered, and then ground to a halt as the soldiers lost their nerve under the constant smacking of Confederate bullets. Lieutenant Colonel O. W. Lull ordered his New Hampshirites to rapidly form a double column and retreat to the safety of the woods they had left. Rather than making a neat maneuver, however, the men stumbled grudgingly backward, "slowly, crouching, broken, somewhat disorganized, but still fighting, the men blazing away here and there without orders."[2]

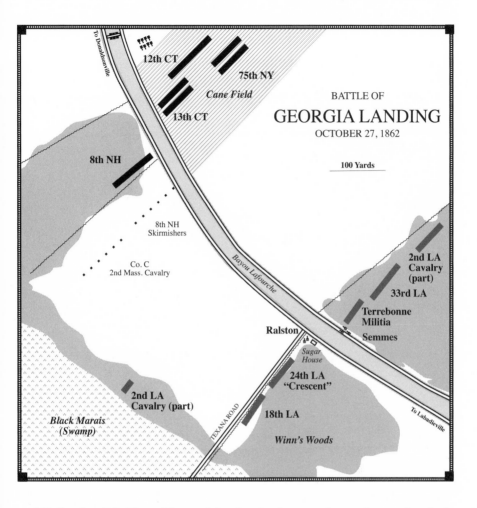

While the 8th New Hampshire backed away from the ambush it had stumbled into, Federal cavalry found Rebels on the east bank of Bayou Lafourche preparing a similar reception. Weitzel sent troops on that side to investigate, and the 75th New York and 13th Connecticut deployed into a line of battle and plunged into the cane field that separated them from the suspected enemy. The guns of the 6th Massachusetts Battery rumbled up the bayou road. Aside from the 8th New Hampshire's battle across the bayou, "there was little noise beyond the breaking of the stalks as we vainly endeavored to keep in line," Captain Sprague recounted. The regiments' flags bobbed above the cane, the only visible marker of the advance. The difficult terrain broke the once well-ordered lines into roughly parallel clumps of men.

Captain John Quincy Adams Warren commanded Company E, 8th New Hampshire at the Battle of Georgia Landing, where he was killed. A native of Nashua, he was the first resident of that community to die in the Civil War. Courtesy of Denis Gaubert, Thibodaux, Louisiana.

When the scattered commands emerged from the field, no Rebels were in sight. The men of the 2nd Louisiana Cavalry and the 33rd Louisiana Infantry had disappeared.[3]

Weitzel sensed a trap and ordered his left-bank regiments to retreat. Mouton had tried to lure him into two fights, but Weitzel would only have one. He would fight this battle on the bayou's west bank. "Not being attacked, we were ordered to fall back," a Connecticut private reported. The Yankees' improvised bridge now became decisive as it swung across the bayou. Gangs of black men—recently freed slaves now in the service of their liberators—hacked and chopped at the levee in order to create a road for the passage of men and guns. This task accomplished, Weitzel ordered his two Connecticut regiments to assist the 8th New Hampshire while the 75th New York guarded the east bank.[4]

The 12th Connecticut dropped their knapsacks, detached two companies to guard the army's wagons, and led the way over Bayou Lafourche. "With drums beating and fifes screaming and banners flying we tramped along, listening to the slow *pumming* of artillery two miles away," remembered Captain De Forest. The column came under fire as it crested the levee and clattered across the flatboats. "A surprisingly loud, harsh, scream passed over us, ending in a sharp explosion and a splashing in the water," the captain continued. "I was not alarmed, but rather relieved and gratified. If they can't aim better than that they are welcome to fire all day, I innocently thought." At that moment the Rebels were firing blindly, but their spotters, atop sugarhouses along the bayou, watched as flags wigwagged the Union movements. A second shell landed closer, splattering water on some of the men. Even so, some of the rookie soldiers still paused to fill their canteens from the bayou. "My chief anxiety," De Forest remembered, "was lest I should wet my feet in the sloppy bottom of the boat."[5]

Once across, one of Weitzel's aides directed the regiments to deploy for battle. The men of the 8th New Hampshire, happy to see their comrades, reformed their line in the safety of the woods. Next came the 12th and the 13th Connecticut, each unit shaking out two companies of skirmishers to cover the advance. In nervous ranks the soldiers received their orders. "Beyond the wood is an open field," a Union staff officer bellowed. "You will cross that and drive the enemy from his position."[6]

This second Union advance became a deadly parody of a drill field parade. The

Sergeant Leonard K. Andrews, Company C, 12th Connecticut Infantry. This resident of New Haven would serve for most of the war, eventually becoming first sergeant of his company. When the call came for the regiment to reenlist in late 1864, he went home. Courtesy of Denis Gaubert, Thibodaux, Louisiana.

three New England regiments made steady progress, halting periodically to redress their line when it was broken by fences, brambles, or ditches. As they neared the edge of the woods, the Rebels fired on the easy targets. "A shell screamed over our heads, passing through the lower branches and sending down a shower of leaves," De Forest wrote. The men of the 12th Connecticut instinctively ducked, causing a rapid ripple to convulse the regiment. Other Rebel rounds followed in quick succession.[7]

Still the untried Federals advanced. The regiments encountered a "stout fence of cypress posts and rails" at the edge of the open field, and they clambered over it, knocked it down, and filed around it. After reforming their lines in the open, and under long-range fire, the Yankees continued their drive, with the sheltering woods behind them and a killing field ahead. The enemy lay five hundred yards away. Among the furrows were scattered the collapsed forms of dead and dying blue coats.[8]

Private Thomas Daley, Company C, 12th Connecticut Infantry. A resident of Hartford, he soldiered with the "Charter Oak Regiment" for all of its three years of hard marching and fighting. In November 1864, he reenlisted for the war, earning a second stripe as corporal in the 12th Connecticut Battalion Veteran Volunteer Infantry. Courtesy of Denis Gaubert, Thibodaux, Louisiana.

The Rebel line rolled out blossoms of smoke and flame. "It was not a volley but a file fire; it was a continuous rattle like that which a boy makes in running a stick along a picket fence," De Forest remembered. "The sharp *whit whit* of bullets chippered close to our ears. In the field before us puffs of dust jumped here and there; on the other side of it a long roll of blue smoke curled upward; to the right of that the grey smoke of artillery rose in a thin cloud. . . ."[9]

The men of the 8th New Hampshire had seen this before. After clearing the woods, the rattled regiment froze, then lay down to avoid the Rebel volleys. After the bullets passed overhead, a captain leapt to his feet to rally his men and continue the advance. "I jumped up to follow him," a soldier recalled, "when I saw a hole puff through his back and he dropped dead instantly, being shot through the heart. I dropped also, thinking it a bad place to stand in all alone."[10]

The fire unnerved some Connecticut men. The bearer of the state flag in the 12th regiment simply turned on his heels and headed for the rear. "He did not look wild with fight," De Forest noted. "He simply looked alarmed and resolved to get out of danger." The captain threatened the shirker with his sword, pushing him back into the front rank.[11]

Shaking off the shock of first combat, the Yankees continued to attack. The Confederates shivered the Union line with two more crisp volleys, injuring more New Englanders. "At the second volley, hearing on my right a sharp crash of broken bone, followed by a loud 'Oh' of pain and horror, I glanced that way and saw Color Sergeant Edwards fall slowly backward, with blood spirting from his mouth and a stare of woful [sic] amazement in his eyes," De Forest recalled. A bullet had knocked in his front teeth and exited behind his left jaw. The stricken soldier clung to the national colors as he fell, dazed. A nearby corporal—a veteran of service in the British Army—dragged the flag out of the sergeant's hands, "jumped to the front, and strode onward, tranquilly chewing his tobacco."[12]

The U.S. troops halted in midfield to take their turn at shooting Rebels. "There was a general feeling of relief, near akin to delight, when the lieutenant colonel's clear, metallic voice pealed out, 'Halt! Fire by file! Commence firing!'" De Forest wrote. The eager soldiers let loose all at once instead of firing the regulated volley their commander requested. "In the next second every one was loading his piece as if his life depended on the speed of the operation."[13]

This violence had been liberating. The 12th Connecticut surged forward, heedless of their lieutenant colonel's demands. "We had been drilled long enough under fire, and we broke away," De Forest admitted. "He might as well have ordered a regiment of screeching devils to halt." The men simply moved forward, loading and shooting at will in a rolling, firing, advance. The once orderly lines gave way to clumps and arcs. Two ranks became three as the troops crowded and closed their lines.[14]

Weitzel, dressed in a sky-blue greatcoat and calmly smoking a cigar, moved among the mobs to restore order. A huge gap had opened in the Union line between the Nutmeg regiments, and the 8th New Hampshire, nearest the bayou, had broken down entirely, with its parade-ground evolutions forgotten in the face of combat, and its men on the ground. Weitzel ordered that demoralized regiment to withdraw while signaling the 13th Connecticut, still in good order, to file to the left oblique and take its place. The 12th responded as well, straightening its line as it moved ahead. "Both regiments poured in an unceasing fire," wrote a Connecticut officer, "all the while marching steadily forward."[15]

The point of decision had arrived. On the left of the Confederate line the Terrebonne Militia emerged from its hiding place in the swamp and moved down the Texana Road to flank the right side of the Union line. "Without forming or halting they opened a hasty sidelong fire, and then broke for the neighboring thickets, disappearing like young partridges," De Forest crowed. The militia had fired their one shot and fled. This encouraged the New Englanders who, still moving and firing, stepped confidently to within one hundred yards of Mouton's steadier Confederates.[16]

But these southerners broke, too. "Swarms of men in gray uniforms sprang out of the ditch which had sheltered them, and fled at full speed . . . jumping over each other like panic-stricken sheep," De Forest wrote. "At this sight the Twelfth raised a scream of exultation and redoubled its uproar of musketry. Just then a stunning volley, the voice of the Thirteenth coming into action, rang out on our left."[17]

Both regiments rushed to the stout cypress fence—"splintered, riddled, honeycombed" by Yankee bullets—and fired blindly into the woods where the Rebels had gone. The northerners could not believe their luck. "The enemy had vanished like a dream," De Forest marveled. "I was amazed at the feebleness of the Southern resistance and could not imagine that we had already won the battle." Blue cavalry galloped forward to pursue the routed enemy, and infantry skirmishers jumped the fence and pushed into the woods. The few Rebels remaining in the ditch held up "all they had of dirty white in token of surrender." The enemy had melted away.[18]

After little more than an hour's sharp skirmishing, Brigadier General Mouton's army had disintegrated and with it Rebel hopes in the Lafourche District. Weitzel had bought victory at Georgia Landing at the price of eighteen dead, seventy-four wounded, half of whom were in the 8th New Hampshire. The Rebels lost five killed, eight wounded, and nearly two hundred missing. They also lost their nerve. One Rebel prisoner explained the disaster to his captors: "Your firing didn't hurt us, but your coming on and yelling scared us."[19]

Mouton stirred into action as he watched his shattered army stream past the windows of his headquarters. He rallied what he could of his defeated army at Labadieville, intending to offer Weitzel another battle. As he busied himself for a resumption of the contest, couriers arrived bearing news of the other Union columns converging on the region. Mouton recognized his peril, and these same Rebel riders turned around and galloped away from Oak Wood Plantation bearing orders for all Confederate forces to fall back on Terrebonne Station

This scene of railroad tracks, locomotives, and wharves—while not in Louisiana—was typical of the facilities and structures that would have stood at Brashear City. The Confederates would wreck all they could as they evacuated up Bayou Teche. Library of Congress.

south of Thibodaux. Confederate troops and parish militias abandoned Boutte, Des Allemands, and Vacherie, destroying key bridges and abandoning supplies. The slow progress of the evacuations and the steady approach of the enemy prompted the jittery Mouton to direct all units to continue to Brashear City, the last remaining exit to the Lafourche District.[20]

Weitzel's victorious troops arrived at Thibodaux about noon on October 28, their band playing both "Yankee Doodle" and "Dixie." "It was with inexpressible pride that we bore the blue flag of Connecticut and the hated Stars and Stripes through the half-deserted streets, keeping step to the music," wrote Captain Sprague. A Catholic priest watched as the marchers passed. "What an army!" he wrote. "A veritable band of looters and drunkards—the officers as well as the men in the ranks. The officers are in general rather polite as long as one flatters them, otherwise they are uncouth and disgustingly vulgar."

After clearing the town Weitzel moved another mile down the bayou and camped at Acadia Plantation, waiting for the column from Algiers and the navy to close the trap.[21]

Their thirty-four mile march had the unintended consequence of clearing the region of its black labor force. "The whole country as far as the eye could reach in our rear . . . was full of carts piled full to overflowing with wooly heads, little and big, men and women . . . all blessing the pretty Yankees," observed Captain Godfrey. "The consequence is that all the plantations are left without hands, and millions of dollars worth of sugar cane are going to ruin for want of hands to gather it."[22]

Mouton's entire defense of the region unraveled in fewer than forty-eight hours. The general panic following the battle at Georgia Landing spread rapidly, and most of the few state militia remaining in the field fled to their homes, confirming Confederate suspicions about their steadiness. Mouton rallied his army at Brashear City on October 29 and ordered them to embark upon an orgy of destruction. Realizing that this depot would soon be in the hands of the enemy, Rebel officers directed their men to burn, scatter, and destroy all supplies and munitions that could not be sent across Berwick Bay. This order doomed the locomotives, rolling stock, and bridges of the Opelousas Railroad.[23]

Mouton had managed to slip out of not just one but two Yankee snares. Every obstacle imaginable had delayed the 8th Vermont and 1st Louisiana Native Guards. High grass had grown over the unused tracks, blocking the path of the Union train and forcing the soldiers to unload and clear the brush. Past Boutte the retreating Rebels had destroyed every culvert and bridge on the route. The Vermonters and their Native Guard allies would not arrive in Thibodaux until November 2, five days behind schedule.

The U.S. Navy, too, missed its quarry. Mechanical problems and a shortage of sailors had caused Buchanan's squadron to lose valuable time in clearing the Mississippi. Arriving in Atchafalaya Bay on October 29, the ships had to find and mark the winding channel, since the Rebels had shifted or destroyed all navigation aids. The next day Buchanan's steamers captured a small Rebel sloop but were engaged at

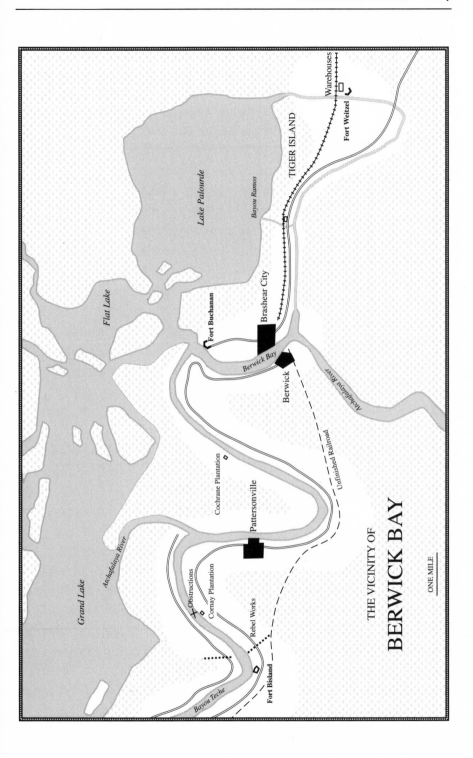

THE VICINITY OF

BERWICK BAY

ONE MILE

long range by the Rebel paddle wheeler *Hart*. The Union ships also kept running aground.

Mouton, even more jittery, wanted Taylor to come and improve the deteriorating Confederate situation. "I . . . had the honor of submitting a brief statement," Mouton wrote that evening, describing his dispatch of an outline of the recent reverses along Bayou Lafourche, "in the meantime urging upon General Taylor the necessity of his presence here." The next morning, Mouton sent an additional message by separate courier urging the district commander to come immediately. The small Confederate army at Brashear City seemed cornered, and Mouton appeared frozen by a growing sense of panic. His inability to make an independent decision, and perhaps his fear of Taylor's famous wrath would, if unchecked, mark the end of Mouton's command.[24]

Messages from the *Hart* at midday on October 30 confirmed Mouton's fears of the Yankee naval presence and his imminent peril. Regaining his senses with the arrival of this dire news, Mouton hurried his men across Berwick Bay that evening under the covering protection of the *Hart* and CSS *Cotton*. By the following afternoon, Buchanan's USS *Kinsman* and USS *Estrella* steamed into Berwick Bay, still sparring with the CSS *Cotton* but forty-eight hours short of victory. Mouton's army remained, but the issue of control in the Lafourche District had been settled in the Yankees' favor.

Although the victory was not total, the Federals had won much. On the morning of November 2 the 21st Indiana unloaded and occupied Brashear City, amazed at the destruction. The Confederates had burned ninety-eight cars along the Opelousas Railroad. The locomotives lay in heaps, victims of deliberate head-on collisions. The long bridges over bayous Ramos and Beouf had burned. For the next month, U.S. troops labored hard to rebuild the devastated facilities and reopen the railroad to Algiers. Weitzel would not pursue Mouton further—at least, not yet.

Taylor was already nearby and heading toward the scene of action when Mouton's breathless dispatches arrived. The Confederate commander arrived to meet his defeated and demoralized army near Pattersonville as it retreated up Bayou Teche. After receiving a more substantial report from his Acadian subordinate, Taylor believed that, aided by the bayou gunboats, a successful stand could be made and the panic arrested. Conceding the loss of the Lafourche District, Taylor set his jaw to keeping the invaders out of the Teche country and issued orders that the Confederate Army would retreat no further. Mouton agreed.

Taylor chose the Bisland Plantation, which was eighteen miles by road from Berwick Bay, to be the centerpiece of his defense. Colonel Valery Sulakowski, Mouton's chief engineer, laid out an impressive defensive line. This Polish veteran of the Austrian army had immigrated to New Orleans before the war. Appointed colonel of the 14th Louisiana, he had led the unit to the peninsula of Virginia where he attempted to instill discipline and drill into an otherwise disorderly regiment. He earned a repuation as a severe martinet and his troops grew to despise him. Sulakowski eventually gave up on his command, resigned his commission in disgust, and returned to New Orleans in March 1862. As events proved, he was just in time to witness the capture of the city by Ben Butler's Federals. Sulakowski made an appointment with the enemy general and offered his services, but the wily Yankee mistrusted the saucy foreigner and instead enrolled him on the list of registered enemies. Within months Sulakowski found himself under escort and banished from the city. A man without a country, the Pole made his way to Mouton's command. Once there, he put his famous temper and keen engineering eye to work—once again—for the Confederate cause.

Gangs of slaves constructed a line of earthworks where southern soldiers would resist an invasion. A redoubt, appropriately named Fort Bisland, on the right descending (or south) bank commanded the bayou five miles upstream from Pattersonville.[25] From there, soldiers and slaves extended breastworks one thousand yards on both sides of the Teche, their ends anchored in the surrounding swamps. Deep furrows and tangles of unharvested sugar cane in the fields fronting these works would provide natural obstacles to any advancing enemy infantry and would keep them in the rifle sights for a few moments longer.[26]

The Confederates also prepared positions and obstacles between Berwick Bay and Bisland Plantation to serve as impediments to a

Union land or naval invasion. Fresh earth dug from rifle pits lined the bayou near the junction of the Teche and the Atchafalaya River. At Cornay's Bridge, two miles in front of Bisland, laborers sank the steamer *Flycatcher* and a brick-laden schooner sideways in the stream. Massive, ancient live oaks felt the bite of the ax as they toppled into the Teche, helping to form a latticework of iron-and-wood snags to hinder enemy navigation. Taylor's gunboats and transports retreated behind these barriers like badgers in their burrows.

While Taylor hurried to put his command onto a defensive footing, the U.S. Navy pressured the dispirited Rebels. At dawn on November 3 Commodore Buchanan sent the *Diana* upstream to locate the retreating enemy. When that vessel returned at mid-morning with a report that the CSS *Cotton* was waiting for them, he ordered his entire four-ship squadron up the Teche to clear the obstructions as quickly as they were made and to hunt down the Confederate gunboats. The squat, heavy USS *Calhoun* led the parade, followed by the long and lanky *Estrella*. The two little paddle wheelers, *Diana* and *Kinsman*, followed. The ships churned up Berwick Bay, made a port turn into the Atchafalaya, cleared Pattersonville a dozen miles upstream, and then veered to port into Bayou Teche. The 21st Indiana waited on board, ready to lend a hand at the guns. Just around the first bend of Bayou Teche, fourteen miles into the journey, the Federal ships caught sight of their quarry.

At half past one in the afternoon the duel opened, seemingly one-sided. Twenty-seven Union guns opposed seven. Rebel shot and shell pummeled the flagship *Calhoun,* including one round that flung a soup tureen and a roast beef into the paddle wheel. A second shot bent the wheel shaft, and another passed completely though the hull. Buchanan's gunners returned fire, and the commander personally sighted the bow gun. After only three shots, that weapon, a 30-pounder Parrot rifle, broke loose from its deck mounts. This malfunction, coupled with the loss of the bell wires by which commands were passed to the engine room, prompted Buchanan to order his ship to back away. Below deck a 32-pounder lay broken by a shot, and the ship's paint lay splashed like the black blood of a demonic monster around a splintered storage locker. The commodore signaled the

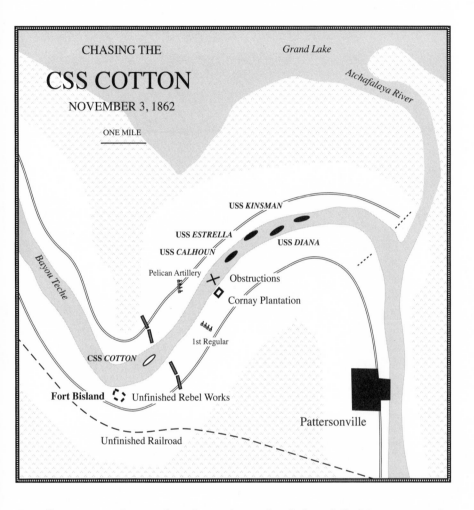

CHASING THE

CSS COTTON

NOVEMBER 3, 1862

ONE MILE

Grand Lake

Atchafalaya River

USS *KINSMAN*

USS *ESTRELLA*

USS *CALHOUN*

USS *DIANA*

Pelican Artillery

Obstructions

Cornay Plantation

Bayou Teche

1st Regular

CSS *COTTON*

Fort Bisland   Unfinished Rebel Works

Pattersonville

Unfinished Railroad

Estrella to move forward and continue the fight while his men made repairs.[27]

The *Cotton,* despite the growing intensity of the uneven contest, was ready for the newcomer. "They came up in full confidence of overpowering numbers," wrote Captain E. W. Fuller, the Confederate skipper. "The shot and shell literally rained down on and about our boat, several striking us but without doing serious damage. We returned their fire, my brave boys cheering frequently."[28]

The *Estrella* passed into the lead and closed the range to the enemy. "One, more adventuresome than the rest," Fuller reported, "steadily steamed up the bayou." Rounds from the Rebel guns careened into the starboard bow of the ship, knocking along the length of the boat

A Harper's Weekly *illustration of the fight between the CSS* Cotton, *in the rear, and the* USS Calhoun, Estrella, *and* Kinsman *downstream. The USS* Diana *is not pictured.*

and causing havoc. Within minutes the Union ship was in trouble. Two gunners lay dead, and the pilot reported the ship unmanageable. A round had passed through the ship's guts and had severed the wheel ropes connected to the rudder. Lieutenant Commander Augustus P. Cooke commanded his ship to run to the shore, where it stuck into the bank and listed to such a degree that its guns were no longer in the fight. With the *Estrella* out of action and the USS *Calhoun* temporarily indisposed, the two riverboats would now have their turn.

These smaller vessels fared little better. At first, fortune favored the attackers as the *Cotton's* rounds glanced off the iron on the forward portion of their casemates. The crew of the *Diana,* while preparing to open fire, discovered that the traversing mounts for their heavy Parrot rifle were jammed and the gun could not be pivoted. Thus effectively unarmed, they withdrew, taking a parting hit in the stern as they left. This left the USS *Kinsman* alone in the fight. The boat paddled gamely toward Cornay's Bridge to face its enemy only to discover that nearly a dozen field pieces were hidden along the banks, raking it *en enfilade.* Mouton had devised an ambush, and the Yankee vessels had moved into it.[29]

The *Kinsman* suffered. Some fifty-four shots of various caliber hit the ship, knocking its hull and upper works into pieces. A solid shot crashed deep into the heart of the vessel, smashing into the magazine and scattering ammunition about the chamber. Rebel projectiles killed one sailor and wounded five others. The pilot's leg was mangled. In addition cannon balls and shells opened the steamer up to the water of the bayou, and it began to sink.[30]

The *Cotton* and the field batteries had made a lethal team. Gunners from Semmes's First Regular Battery threw the weight of their pieces into the fight, which was their first real action since the Battle of Baton Rouge. This combat was the inaugural fight for a new organization, Captain Thomas Faries's Pelican Artillery, which had been created with recruits from St. James Parish whose Mississippi River homes in the Lafourche District now lay behind enemy lines. This battery would see important service in the coming months.[31]

By mid-afternoon the Confederates had fared well in the fight. The *Cotton* had been struck, but none of the impacts had inflicted any serious damage. The field batteries did not lose a man before they retired to refill their empty caissons. Time, though, was against them. In the bayou Captain Fuller received news that he was out of ammunition. "When victory seemed to be within our reach, it was announced that we had no more cartridges," he wrote. Some of his crew made ersatz powder sacks by shearing off their pants legs, filling them with loose powder, and tying each end. This effort provided only enough firepower to affect an escape. "Retreat," sighed Fuller, "was all that remained for us." The battle was over, for the time being, and the Confederates settled for a draw.[32]

Unaware of his enemy's straits, Buchanan salvaged what he could of the botched Union attack. Despite its useless bow gun, the USS *Calhoun* charged forward and allowed the *Kinsman* to limp down the Teche to safety, its pumps working furiously as its crew bailed by hand. Boldly, Buchanan ordered his ship to turn hard to starboard, placing it across the bayou so that all his port broadside guns could fire. But before he could attack the *Cotton*, the Confederate steamer retreated out of sight, leaving the Yankees in control at Cornay's Bridge. The battle had lasted two hours. The Federals frittered away the rest of the day in unsuccessful attempts at clearing the obstructions, and with night approaching, Buchanan ordered his squadron back to Brashear City.[33]

Neither side wanted to settle, however. The following day Buchanan returned to Cornay's Bridge with the *Calhoun* and *Estrella*, seeking battle. No enemies appeared and the ships withdrew before nightfall. At 10:30 a.m. on November 5 Buchanan's ships approached the contested area a third time and were met with a shot from the *Cotton*, hiding around a point upstream. Both the *Estrella* and *Calhoun* fought the elusive Rebel for an hour, but they withdrew after the Parrot rifle on the bow of Buchanan's flagship broke again, this time the victim of an enemy solid shot.

The Federal sailors gave up. "I can do nothing until General Weitzel arrives," Buchanan wrote. "They are now strongly posted at the obstructions, and although I can drive them off, I can not work at them." Final victory at Cornay's Bridge would take the assistance of the Union army.[34]

Having abandoned its attempts to destroy the *Cotton*, the U.S. Navy busied itself with other targets in the region while the army consolidated its position at Brashear City. The first objective was to obtain salt, a vital strategic commodity. The *Diana* and *Kinsman* raided along Bayou Petit Anse, trying to reach the Avery Island salt works, perhaps the finest deposit of the valuable mineral in the entire Confederacy. The notorious Louisiana tides worked against the vessels, as did the rifles of Colonel Edwin Waller's 13th Texas Cavalry Battalion. The Cane Cart Cavalry, still rebuilding after its humiliation at Bonnet Carré in September, had been ordered to the works to discourage landing parties. Skirmishing continued for four days, starting on November 8, but with little success for the Federals. A week and a half later, they returned to Petit Anse, this time with the steamer *St. Mary's* loaded with the crack 21st Indiana. The Confederates met this threat by dispatching Faries's Pelican Artillery to strengthen the defenses. After a long-range and largely harmless duel, the Yankee ships departed. The Federals and Confederates faced a stalemate.

The immediate crisis past, Taylor wrestled with the peculiar geography of his department as he shifted his thinking to defense.

"Penetrated in all directions by watercourses when the Mississippi was at flood, my 'district' was especially exposed," Taylor wrote. "Every little bayou capable of floating a cock-boat called loudly for forts and heavy guns." Having given up the Lafourche District, the Confederates had lost the buffer that protected Louisiana's interior from the ravages of war. Taylor realized the enemy was now at the gates, and in a few days or weeks at best, the Federals would follow up their successes by moving farther into the state.[35]

The greatest advantage the enemy could gain was the capture of his fleet, and with it the Union forces could project power deep into Confederate territory. Taylor clearly needed fortifications to protect his command from invasion. Although acutely interested in the activities along the Teche, he was also responsible for the comprehensive defense of his department. Due to the nature of the terrain, a failure in one arena would make the other indefensible, especially given the waterborne mobility of his enemy. He doled out his inadequate ration of heavy guns as best he could. Two 32-pounders went to defend the Washita River, and two more went to the minor defenses at Barbin's Landing on the Red River dubbed Fort Taylor. Similarly, "the presence of gunboats on Berwick's Bay made it necessary to protect the Atchafalaya for access to the Red and Washita could be had by it," Taylor wrote. He decided to build a small battery, named Fort Burton, on Butte La Rose, "the only place for many miles not submerged when the waters were up. The country between it and the Teche was almost impassable even in the dry season—a region of lakes, bayous, jungle and bog."[36]

The Confederate strategic situation in Louisiana neared a crisis point. Taylor knew that Mouton and his army had proven inadequate to defend the Lafourche District from a determined Federal invasion. Now they would have to cover an even more extensive front against an increasingly powerful enemy. Taylor understood that the forces at hand could not adequately cover every avenue of approach, and the terrain did not allow for easy concentration of widely scattered forces. Taylor could only hope for time. With a little luck and the backing of the calendar, perhaps he could repair his army, gather a fleet, add reinforcements, and once again challenge the foe.[37]

CHAPTER FOURTEEN

BEAST BUTLER

Everything looking like war, not as it is in New England,
but as it is in the South.
Captain John Franklin Godfrey, 1st Louisiana Cavalry (U.S.)

E ven though it had lost its momentum in southwest Louisiana, the U.S. Navy continued to prowl the waters of the western Gulf of Mexico. If naval raids could rattle the nerves of Texas authorities, they would withhold reinforcements, undermining the Confederate position in Louisiana. When Godfrey Weitzel's troops started their campaign against Alfred Mouton in the Lafourche District, W. B. Renshaw sallied from Galveston with his two ferryboats-turned-gunboats, the *Westfield* and the *Clifton,* on a raid west along the Texas coast. The ships turned into Matagorda Bay, hunting blockade runners and seeking out fresh provisions and Unionist sentiment. A Confederate schooner, the *Lecompte,* fell prey to the prowling warships, as did a few bales of cotton. Enterprising sailors harvested oysters, ducks, and geese from the coast, but in their forays they discovered very little pro-Union sentiment, despite earlier reports. "Patriotism was high in Texas," sneered Private Henry Gusley aboard the *Westfield.* "Most decidedly they do not love the Yankees as well as they professed they did in '46. Comment is useless—we leave the subject in disgust."[1]

After thrashing about Matagorda Bay for four days Renshaw decided to square off against the Confederate defenders in the region. Leading his two lightest draft vessels, the *Westfield* and the *Clifton,* on October 31—the same day Mouton had abandoned Brashear City— Renshaw moved to shell Port Lavaca, a minor sanctuary for small blockade runners. The Union commodore informed the Texan garrison commander, Major Daniel D. Shea, of his intentions to destroy the town, allowing ninety minutes for civilians to be removed.

After the allotted time, the Federals moved toward shore and engaged Shea's two Confederate batteries. "They returned the fire quite vigorously with round and rifle shot, showing us both good guns and good gunnery," a Union observer noted. Luck worked against the bluejackets. As dusk approached, the *Westfield*'s heaviest gun, the 100-pounder Parrot on its bow, broke, crippling the ship's firepower. Unable to throw his heaviest shells against the enemy, Renshaw fretted as the battle sputtered to an inconclusive skirmish. Frustrated, he ordered his ships to move out of range for the night. The next day he resumed the battle, hoping that the enemy had fled. When he discovered the Texan gunners still ready to fight, Renshaw ordered his ships back into Matagorda Bay and out of action.[2]

He had other reasons to retreat from the fight. In this noisy but fruitless episode, Renshaw learned some of the dangers of navigating Texas waters. His flagship, the *Westfield,* seemed destined to find every one of the region's ubiquitous sandbars. While maneuvering against the Confederate batteries at Port Lavaca, his pilot had grounded the ship a half dozen times. After each episode the crew of the *Clifton* diligently brought their ship alongside and dragged the flagship to safety, leading one Federal wag to designate the *Clifton* as Renshaw's personal tugboat. But every sailor aboard both boats understood the dangers of being aground and under the enemy's guns. Early on November 5 Renshaw and his two vessels reentered Galveston Bay, their expedition over.

Other frustrations plagued Renshaw's command in Galveston Bay. When Union sailors went ashore at Point Boliver to forage for fresh provisions, they were ambushed and shotgunned by Confederate cavalrymen. In another instance, Texans snared a navy launch and crew that ventured too close to shore. Renshaw knew that his sailors and Marines were vulnerable to such tactics, but he remained confident that Galveston was, and would continue to be, indefensible for the Rebels. Nevertheless, he wondered why he should continue suffering losses covering the city until infantry could garrison it. He wrote Farragut to request that Galveston be abandoned—temporarily—until infantry could land and capture the city permanently.

He had reason for concern. Prudence required him to anticipate the enemy's next move, and rumors among the sailors in Renshaw's flotilla indicated that the Confederates seemed to be plotting an attack. "We hear," wrote Gusley, "that a rebel ram has been discovered at the head of the bay. This latter, however, we consider doubtful." Farragut would not be budged by mere speculation, and he refused to yield ground so easily earned. He responded to Renshaw by announcing that ground troops were already heading straight toward Texas aboard transports from New England.[3]

That was good news, and Renshaw proudly reported the effects of the Union efforts at both ends of his theater of war: "Great alarm and excitement has been caused at Houston, in this state, and among the military generally, by the movements of General Weitzel." Renshaw took note of the relationship between battles in Louisiana and morale in Texas. According to the commodore, reports arrived that families were already fleeing Houston in anticipation of a Union offensive. "The fear of his movement has had the good effect of staying their attack upon us, and of further movements at Sabine Pass, I am convinced," wrote Renshaw. He also chartered a boat, the *Island City,* at government expense to move a dozen recruits to New Orleans for the 1st Texas Cavalry, along with Unionist refugees from Galveston. Of the last he wrote, "Some of the men have had prices placed upon their heads, and all of them are obnoxious to the enemy."[4]

Farragut's promise of Union reinforcements was quickly verified. Word had already arrived that a massive seaborne expedition, fitting out in New York under Nathaniel P. Banks, was heading to the Lone Star State. Besides tens of thousands of men, the story went, the U.S. government was also sending Brigadier General Andrew Jackson Hamilton as Unionist governor to reestablish political control.[5]

While the Texans fretted over these rumors of imminent invasion, other Union naval expeditions pounded away at their jangled nerves. Taking a cue from the raid up Bayou Petit Anse in search of the Avery Island salt works, the commander of the USS *Morning Light,* Acting Master John Dillingham, led a foray against a newly established salt works at Cedar Lake, near Velasco, Texas, on November 27. Sailors lowered three boats of raiders, who made short work of the "machinery, carts, and implements," reported Dillingham. They also destroyed "several tons of salt which was packed in hide bags for inland transport." The entire landing party returned to the sailing vessel without incident. Kettles, tubular boilers, workshops, and twenty thousand pounds of salt lay ruined.[6]

The next morning, Dillingham decided to strike at a smaller satellite operation four miles down the beach. His vessel was a classic clipper ship—deep draft, all sails and no steam—which kept him from coming in closely, due to the fickle nature of tides and wind. The sailors and marines who set off in smaller boats were therefore not able to benefit from the ship's covering cannons on its gun deck.[7]

As they had the day before, the Federals pulled their boats out of the surf and set about their raid, but this time mounted Texans, eager to exact revenge, met the shore party. The Yankees fled to their boats with the horsemen riding hard behind them. One sailor spun around and surrendered immediately, but his shipmate fell in a blast of buckshot—one round piercing his lung and another breaking his neck as it passed through his mouth. Five other bleeding raiders neared their boats, sporting a variety of cuts and bruises from the Texan weapons.[8]

When all seemed lost for the handful of Federals on shore, a fresh breeze filled the sails of the *Morning Light,* allowing Dillingham to put the beach under his guns. The booming of cannons sounded salvation for the bullet-riddled raiders, and the Texan riders wheeled their horses and fled. "We most effectually routed them," Dillingham crowed. His executive officer, Henry Washburn, stood amazed as crews hauled the boats back aboard: "Nearly all in the boats were slightly wounded and the boats completely riddled with balls or slugs." Indeed, carpenters counted twenty-four holes in one craft, with nearly a dozen spent bullets rattling around in its bottom. The Texans might be jittery, but they would still kill trespassers on their beaches.[9]

Even so, by the end of November 1862 the United States appeared on the cusp of decisive victory in the western Gulf of Mexico. Union warships, enforcing the blockade, made frequent captures off of the coasts of Louisiana and Texas. Weitzel's troops occupied the Lafourche District, and a gunboat fleet patrolled the mouth of the Atchafalaya River and the lower stretches of Bayou Teche. Sabine Pass lay blocked. Along the Mississippi Donaldsonville and nearby towns upriver housed Union garrisons. Galveston, already fallen, would soon feel the tramp of Union infantry. From New Orleans to Corpus Christi, the Federal noose tightened. The Union victories in southwest Louisiana and southeast Texas had shifted the Confederates onto the defensive and frozen them in place.

With the enemy apparently cowed, the Federals had to tend to a growing list of chores. The U.S. Army and Navy, armed with the strategic initiative they had earned with gunfire and blood, took steps to ensure that the lower sugar parishes and Galveston would remain in Union hands should the Rebels try to retake the land. Ceasing their pursuit of Mouton's battered army, the Federal infantry took time to dig fortifications, reorganize their commands, and harvest the abundant property—both strategic and otherwise—of their newly conquered province.

Federals also faced the enormous issue of a large displaced population. The stakes in the war had changed in mid-September, when President Lincoln issued the preliminary Emancipation Proclamation, converting the conflict into a war to end slavery. As of January 1863, the document read, all slaves in areas still in rebellion would be forever free. This pronouncement, coupled with the First and Second Confiscation Acts, passed in 1861 and 1862, would unfasten the foundations of Southern civilization.

Sensing that a new age had dawned, freed slaves swarmed every movement of the Federal army. At Brashear City, the Confederates had abandoned some four hundred wagonloads of African American laborers, leaving the Yankees to feed, house, and employ them. Already reports arrived at Weitzel's Thibodaux headquarters telling of rampant, predato-

Union successes in the field, coupled with the announcement of the Emancipation Proclamation, accelerated the flight of slaves away from their masters and into Federal lines. Harper's Weekly.

ry plundering by this ever-growing mass of refugees. This issue, as much as any, retarded the otherwise lightening successes of the army.[10]

"Now, what should I do with them?" Weitzel asked on November 1 in a letter to Major George C. Strong, General Butler's assistant adjutant-general and chief of staff. Weitzel's frustration cried from every page of his dispatch: "I already have twice as many negroes in and around my camp as I have soldiers within." The United States, in its haste to invade the South and capture the region, had no firm policy on how to handle the multitude of former slaves who would hail the arrival of the Union troops as the "Year of Jubilo." Once these workers left the plantations and the southern labor system, they turned to the government to supply their needs. "I cannot feed them," Weitzel wrote, mindful of the rations needed to sustain his own army. "As a consequence, they must feed themselves."[11]

With no means of support, many freedpeople resorted to theft and scavenging, resulting in the concomitant unsettling of the white population. Some former slaves, tasting the first sweetness of liberty, did not readily distinguish between loyal or rebel planters. "The community, of whom already quite a number have taken the oath of allegiance, is in great terror," Weitzel reported of the white southerners. This frightened populace came to his headquarters, hoping for same-race sympathy and begging for weapons with which to defend their homes. Weitzel felt unenthusiastic about this proposition—after all, he was in an enemy country.[12]

Neither did Weitzel agree with Butler's experiment in arming former slaves. He found the presence of the Louisiana Native Guard in the Lafourche District disruptive and distasteful. "I cannot command those negro regiments," Weitzel wrote. "The commanding general knows well my private opinions on this subject. What I stated to him privately, while on his staff, I now see before my eyes." To this German engineer, the sight of African American troops only emboldened the masses of displaced slaves. He thought that once they had seen men like themselves armed and participating in the battle for freedom, these former hands would never be content to go back to their fields. They, for the first time, would feel empowered.[13]

"Since the arrival of the negro regiments symptoms of servile insurrection are becoming apparent," Weitzel warned. He also added that he could not police the entire region without dangerously scattering his command. Was he to defeat the Rebels or become a new master, he wondered. Black troops, he argued, were a bad influence: "I cannot assume the command of such a force, and thus be responsible for its conduct. Its moral effect in this community . . . is terrible." He noted the defenseless nature of the conquered population. "Woman and children, and even men, are in terror. It is heart rending, and I cannot make myself responsible for it."[14]

Many men in the ranks of Weitzel's regiments agreed. "They keep the jail full most of the time with a motley group interspersed with negro soldiers of whose behavior there are endless complaints of burning, stealings, ravishings and lesser crimes," wrote Lieutenant Dana W. King of the 8th New Hampshire Infantry. "They are termed 'The Louisiana Native Guards,' ostensibly freedmen of color, but we know that slaves are in their midst." Certainly, the officer reasoned, Union leaders would soon "disband them or put them under iron rule, or to garrison some fort away from civilization."[15]

THE MAN WHO WON THE ELEPHANT AT THE RAFFLE.
Gen. Weitzel—"BUT THE QUESTION IS, WHAT AM I TO DO WITH THE CREATURE?"
[See Gen. Weitzel's Report to Gen. Butler, on capturing several hundred wagon-loads of Niggers.]

A contemporary editorial cartoon captured the essence of General Weitzel's dilemma, as well as that of other Union officers opering in the South, on policies for dealing with the influx of liberated slaves. They were, so the cartoon suggested, like "the man who won the elephant at the raffle." American Antiquarian Society.

Neither Benjamin Butler nor his chief of staff shared such concerns, arguing instead that the Union forces, whether white or black, were not to blame for the dangers facing the civilians in Weitzel's jurisdiction. "The responsibility rests upon those who have begun and carried on this war," Major Strong lectured. It was not the black troops who had upset this social order, but the presence of Union troops in general. "Does not this state of things arise from the very fact of war itself?" Strong queried. "Did you expect to march into that country, drained as you say it is by conscription of all its able-bodied white men without leaving the negroes to show symptoms of survile [sic] insurrection? You are in a country where now the Negroes outnumber the whites ten to one. Upon reflection, can you doubt that the same state of things would have arisen without the presence of a colored regiment?"[16]

Strong even had a specific case in mind to illustrate his impatience with Weitzel's squeamishness. "General Bragg is at liberty to ravage the homes of our brethren of Kentucky because the Union army of Louisiana is protecting his wife and his home against his Negroes," Strong snorted. "Without that protection, he would have to come back to take care of his wife, his home, and," he added, "his negroes."[17]

Weitzel's superiors urged him to revisit the conclusions he had drawn from the scenes he had witnessed. "You say that there have appeared before your eyes the very facts, in terror-stricken women, children, and men which you had before [only] contemplated in theory. Grant it," wrote Strong, "but is not the remedy to be found in the surrender of the neighbors, fathers, brothers, and sons of the terror-stricken woman and children, who are now in arms against the Government within 20 miles of you?" Once these Rebels surrendered and returned peacefully to their homes, he argued sarcastically, "you will be able to use the full power of your troops to insure their

Few in Federal service believed more in harnessing the military potential of the southern slave population than Major George C. Strong. General Butler's principal lieutenant was a native of Stockbridge, Vermont, and a graduate of West Point. He would eventually earn promotion to brigadier general and lead black troops against Battery Wagner in South Carolina, where he would be seriously wounded. He died weeks later from tetanus. Library of Congress.

safety from the so-much-feared . . . servile insurrection." If the Confederates refused to yield, "whatever may ensue is upon them, and not upon you or upon the United States. You will have done all that is required of a brave, humane man to avert from these deluded people horrible consequences of their insane war upon the Government."[18]

An image from Harper's Weekly *showing Butler sitting "in imperial dignity in his judgment seat" at his palatial New Orleans headquarters.*

Headquarters in New Orleans seemed baffled as to why the plight of the white inhabitants should impact the military operations in the region. Strong, for one, saw the social disorder as something to be desired. "When was it ever heard before," the major continued, "that a victorious general, in an unsurrendered province, stopped in his course for the purpose of preventing the rebellious inhabitants of that province from destroying each other?" He considered Weitzel's compassion misguided and terror a Union ally. "As a military question, perhaps the more terror-stricken the inhabitants are that are left in your rear the more safe will be your lines of communications." Strong, at the urging of Butler, ordered the field commander to continue his active campaigning and to ignore the social issues in the wake of the army. "I do not see how you can turn away from an armed enemy before you to protect or defend the wives and children of those armed enemies from the consequences of their own rebellious wickedness."[19]

This said, Butler instructed Strong to provide Weitzel with a policy for dealing with the issue of uprooted African Americans. "Of course there will be no more difficult subject for you to deal with than the negroes," the chief of staff wrote Weitzel. Congress had already declared that slaves fleeing Rebel masters were free once they arrived within Union lines. "But the question recurs, 'What shall we do with them?'" Butler's solution, as expressed by Strong, was simple: put them back to work. "It is our duty to take care of them, and that can include employment. Put them as far as possible upon plantations; use every energy to have the sugar crop made and preserved for the owners that are loyal," he advised, "and I do not mean by loyalty [mere] lip service."[20]

Weizel's report illustrated a yawning need for a national policy regarding freed slaves, and Butler urged his superior, Major General Henry Halleck, to give some sort of ruling. "General Weitzel brings up the interesting question of the war," Butler wrote. "The President and yourself are aware that I am wholly without guide on this matter." There was no national policy in regards to the future of freed slaves, and army commanders in Virginia, the Carolinas, Tennessee, Arkansas, and Mississippi were cobbling together an inconsistent array of solutions across the various theaters of war. In fact, Butler made his own de facto policy in southwest Louisiana based on local needs.

He had written to his government before requesting an opinion—but had received silence. More than a year previously, while serving in Virginia, Butler had unilaterally coined the phrase "contraband" in regard to runaway slaves entering U.S. lines. His actions at that time influenced the passage of the First Confiscation Act, which declared slaves to be weapons of war, but stopped short of defining their status as human beings, laborers, and combatants. Now, Butler acted again. Without sought-for guidance, he decided on his own to further shape the destiny of freedmen by arming African Americans, justifying his plan by noting, "No communication disapproving of that organization has been received, I must therefore take it to be approved."[21]

This issue had come up before, and the government consistently failed to provide guidance. When Union forces occupied New Orleans, planters south and east of the city found themselves behind Union lines and abandoned by their slaves. Most signed the oath of loyalty then promptly petitioned Butler for redress. To address these needs, Butler negotiated an accord between planters and their former slaves that established a system of wage labor, including rules as to length of workweek, wages paid, and restrictions on punishments. Military provost marshals and civilian and military patrols regulated the arrangement and responded when insubordination or agitation warranted corrective measures. Now Butler ordered that this system be adapted to the conditions of the conquered Lafourche country.[22]

So instead of finishing off the Confederates militarily and eliminating the remnants of Mouton's army, Weitzel spent his energy, and that of his soldiers, in reorganizing the labor system in his area of operations. "Let the planters make arrangements to pay their negroes $10 a month for able-bodied men," Strong advised Weitzel, "$3 to be expended in clothing, and so in proportion."[23] Lieutenant George Smith, a Union officer in the 1st Louisiana Infantry at Donaldsonville, reported that the former slaves were returning to work and were being paid and fed. "This was a nice arrangement," he added, "and opened the way for self-support to thousands that otherwise would be an expense to the government."[24]

There remained, however, the question of what to do with the plantations abandoned by their secessionist owners. In most cases leasing agents, including such finance firms as the Charles A. Weed Factioning Company, took control of the forfeited properties and operated the farms on behalf of the United States. These contractors hired black labor at a dollar a day—much better than plantation wages—to bring in the crops and ship them to government warehouses, thus resuscitating the plantation economy. The United States had itself become one of the new masters.[25]

As Weitzel had feared, not all slaves returned happily to their former homes. At the David Pugh plantation near Thibodaux, the returning laborers did not immediately settle into their old routines. "The Negroes who had returned under the terms fixed upon by Major-General Butler," Weitzel reported, still arguing his case, "without provocation or cause of any kind, refused this morning to work, and assaulted the overseer and Mr. Pugh, injuring them severely; also a gentleman who came to the assistance of Mrs. Pugh." He also reported trouble in the Houma area: "The entire community thereabout are in hourly expectation and terror of a general rising."[26]

Even so, none of the dire scenarios that Weitzel forecasted came to pass. Union troops remained in the area, and the tension of the early days of freedom soon reverted to the drudgery of agricultural routine. U.S. troops spent the next few weeks in garrisons throughout the newly won region and oversaw the transformation of Louisiana society. They also made sure that the bounty of the land made its way into friendly hands. "Our present orders, according to camp rumor," grumbled Captain De Forest, "are to stay here until every hogshead of sugar in the Lafourche country has been sent to New Orleans."[27]

The Butler plan promised to yield several benefits. When all went well and a tense but workable accord emerged between owner and laborer, the fields of the Lafourche region would once again be productive. Produce useful to the Union war effort would be funneled out of the region and through New Orleans to market. The issue of what to do with the freed slaves would be settled. Abolitionists would have a laboratory by which they could illustrate their theories about the success of a wage labor system in a soon-to-be defeated South, and the proceeds of the sale of commodities would help finance the entire operation. All told, there were fifty thousand to sixty thousand former slaves who would now form the backbone of this new arrangement.

Above all, however, Butler's plan would bring about the de facto abolition of slavery in this conquered province. From that point, there could never be a turning back, and the Confederacy's chief vulnerability would be clearly exposed. Slavery was the Rebel Humpty-Dumpty. Once it had been broken by Union conquests, there was very little chance of the South putting it back together again, no matter the war's outcome.

Even so, Butler wanted Weitzel to disentangle himself as quickly as possible from the issues of black troops and unrestrained freedmen because practical military issues still required attention. First, Butler formally organized the newly conquered region into the Lafourche District of the Department of the Gulf and set Weitzel in command. Next, Butler ordered the railroad to be rebuilt and restored and civilian employees put back on the job to keep this vital link open. Third was the issue of defending the region from disruptive Rebel incursions. Butler's staff directed Weitzel to construct fortifications at Donaldsonville and Brashear City. These two points guarded the most likely invasion routes and would be held by stout earthen works. Weitzel tried to refuse the command of the Lafourche District because of the presence of black troops. His superiors ignored him. "The commanding general does not doubt that everything that prudence, sagacity, skill, and courage can do will be done by you, general," Strong wrote, "to prosecute the campaign you have so successfully begun."[28]

In response to these orders, Weitzel's instincts toward the military offensive succumbed to the requirements of the issues at hand. Scores of soldiers and former slaves commenced the creation of Fort Butler, across Bayou Lafourche from the city of Donaldsonville. At first the soldiers of the 1st Louisiana Infantry put down their rifles and picked up their spades to begin the effort. Lieutenant John C. Palfrey, a West Point trained engineer with family ties to the region, arrived to design the redoubt. Soon, white soldiers gave way to an army of black laborers as huge numbers of freedmen found government jobs swinging picks and pushing shovels.[29]

With Mouton and his Confederates lingering just a few miles away on Bayou Teche, and at Butler's command, Weitzel ordered that his position at Berwick's Bay and Brashear City be transformed into a fortified depot and base of future operations. Workers attacked the mud of Tiger Island to build a line of redoubts stretching from the north shore bordering Grand Lake, along the margins of Berwick's Bay, and to a stout star-shaped fortification that could protect the town of Brashear City and defend against naval approaches from the Gulf of Mexico. They also erected bastions along the railroad. New earthworks marked the crossing of the tracks across Bayou Ramos, a few miles behind Brashear City, and at the trestle spanning Bayou Beouf that connected Tiger Island with the rest of the Lafourche District.

Butler had one other major request for Weitzel. He needed help in securing Galveston and wanted the best troops in the department to handle the chore. "I wish to disengage McMillan's regiment as early as it can be dispensed with, if at all," wrote Strong, "to hold Galveston." The 21st Indiana, perhaps the hardest-hitting regiment in southwest Louisiana, was bound by boat for Texas, should Weitzel agree.[30]

This last appeal revealed Butler's larger designs in the region. Planning for the military occupation of Texas, the wily general also asked Admiral Farragut to transport Unionist refugees from Matamoros, Mexico, to Galveston. "It will be improper to enlist even

The customs and habits of Louisiana's slave population were a constant source of fascination and comment by the Union troops who had brought them their liberty. Frank Leslie's Illustrated Newspaper.

Americans as soldiers on Mexican soil," he wrote to U.S. Consul Leonard Pierce Jr., "but there can be no impropriety in sending Americans to do their duty to their country." He would dispatch Colonel E. J. Davis and his embryonic 1st Texas Cavalry to the city to enlist these newcomers into Federal service and begin the reassertion of U.S. control over the rebellious state. This island beachhead, Butler believed, would serve as a catalyst and draw out loyal men from among their secessionist oppressors.[31]

With his Texas scheme percolating in the background, Butler returned again to his Louisiana project. He personally toured the Lafourche region in mid-November, pleased with the disruption he viewed. The earthen citadels rising at Donaldsonville and Brashear City guarded a region in the chaotic throes of rapid evolution to a wage labor system and the end of a centuries-old way of life.

A throng of freed slaves congregated at every U.S. camp, and with this multitude came the entire cross-section of black plantation culture. "Many negroes flocked in . . . bringing their manners and customs with them," observed Lieutenant George Smith of the 1st Louisi-

One of the solutions that Benjamin Butler found for managing the throngs of freed slaves was to have them labor on public works projects. This image shows efforts at rebuilding levees on the Mississippi River. Frank Leslie's Illustrated Newspaper.

ana at Donaldsonville. "In one house some old gray-headed patriarch would hold forth in a religious discourse to a noisy and delighted audience. Further along might be heard the banjo and the fiddle. . . ." Some white soldiers also took notice of the "sable virgins of Africa," leading to liaisons between these former slaves and their liberators. "This last as may well be imagined formed the principal attraction," Smith wrote, "and not infrequently these sable nymphs would be led off by a partner in uniform."[32]

The soldiers implementing the evolving national policy toward conquered slave-owning territories and its inhabitants became witnesses to the disorienting and bewildering effects of the conflict in this region. Among the abandoned plantations, Captain Godfrey, on various scouts with the cavalry, witnessed the hard hand of war in the sugar parishes. "Poor people, many of them no doubt think they are fighting for a good cause," he wrote to his parents. "I felt sad on entering houses and seeing the desolation that prevailed, furniture turned topsy turvy, beautiful paintings thrown down and broken, and everything looking like *war*, not as it is in New England, but as it is in the South."[33]

At one ransacked estate Captain Godfrey saw a glimpse of the manner of people he was fighting. Among the debris he found a bundle of letters sent home by a Rebel at the front but hastily abandoned by his parents in their flight. "The house of the young man . . . is a nice plantation cottage, elegantly furnished, . . . and the owners are evidently wealthy," he noted. Even so, this rich man's son served as an enlisted man. Godfrey shipped the letters back to Maine as a curiosity for his family. "You can see by his letters that he is a private and that he suffered hardships that [even] our tough backwoodsmen would complain of, and [yet] his letters are cheerful, even on his sick bed, as if he were enjoying himself." Godfrey marveled at the Confederate soldier's determination. Perhaps the war would be over soon, he wrote enviously, "if all our rich young men were as willing and earnest in the North as he is for the South."[34]

Second Lieutenant Edward B. Hall, a twenty-two-year-old Boston merchant, had come to Louisiana as a line officer in Company B, 26th Massachusetts Infantry, but moved into staff work as adjutant of a newly formed Louisiana cavalry regiment. He would later take command of Company F, 1st Louisiana Cavalry as its captain until leaving the army in early 1865. Courtesy of Denis Gaubert, Thibodaux, Louisiana.

Landowners who remained along Bayou Lafourche coped as best they could with their change in fortune. "The planters left the woods where they had hidden themselves, but they had nothing left with which to feed their families," wrote Helen Dupuy at Sleepy Hollow Plantation. "The Yankees had taken the provisions, and the flight of the negroes took away all hope of undertaking a crop." The only path to salvation lay through cooperation with Federal authorities. The once-proud planters could take the oath of allegiance to the United States, recover some laborers, and receive rations, or they could maintain their pride and starve. "They endured that humiliation with the hope of improving their situation until the return of the Confeder-

Everything about Benjamin Butler unsettled the Louisiana Confederates. The heavy-handed tactics of the Union general and his strange appearance earned him the nickname "Beast Butler." Harper's Weekly.

ates," Dupuy continued, "but the Yankees did not keep their promises and did not compel the negroes to return to their masters."[35]

Unknown at the time, this invasion ruined the Louisiana sugar industry. What had promised to be the largest yield in more than three decades rotted in the fields. Instead of harvesting more than three hundred thousand hogsheads of sugar, growers in the thirteen sugar parishes salvaged a mere eighty thousand. Banks and factors in New Orleans and elsewhere had advanced some twenty million dollars to planters to bring in the crop, and now these counting houses collapsed like cards. Within two years a scant half-dozen of these financial institutions would remain of the five hundred that had done business in 1860. With credit annihilated and labor scattered, most sensible planters abandoned sugarcane as a crop and looked for other ways to survive. For a few, this meant falling into the embrace of Federal forces and government policies in exchange for protection from their neighbors and a market for their crop. Only planters close to Mississippi and its gunboats could hope to succeed in following this perilous course.[36]

Butler's remorseless policies aimed at humiliating secessionists, the emerging order of race relations, and the government-sanctioned looting of private property embittered many Louisianans who might otherwise have been sympathetic to northern interests. "General Butler is confiscating about everything in this vicinity," Captain Godfrey wrote from Thibodaux. "He is not very popular among his enemies. . . ." With a little care, this officer grumbled, "he might have drawn out a strong union sentiment in this part of the country."[37]

Back in New Orleans, Butler did not care about the plight of the Lafourche families. He had created a little empire for himself, while coincidentally furthering the cause of human liberty and, at the same time, humbling his enemies. He held forth in majesty, and the seething populace of New Orleans was treated to the daily spectacle of the general's carriage ride to his headquarters "with more pomp and display than I have ever seen accorded to a European monarch," as a Scottish writer observed, "bedecked with all the feathers and tinsel that could be crowded into a major general's uniform." Once in his office, the Scotsman continued, "he . . . sat in imperial dignity in his judgment seat, and pronounced sentences according to his undisputed will on the numerous unfortunate wights who were daily brought before him."[38]

In the end, Butler's arrogant treatment of conquered Louisiana was his undoing; within six months he became a political liability for the Lincoln administration. He irritated his superiors by forcing the issue of enlisting blacks and by his obnoxious attitude toward foreign citizens in New Orleans. He had insulted the Crescent City's women with his infamous General Order number 28, in which he declared that discourteous women would be treated as prostitutes. "The people of Louisiana can never get over that order," Godfrey wrote. "I do not think they will ever get over it . . . especially the ladies."[39]

In fact, Butler had offended Unionists, abolitionists, and his own troops. His reputed plundering and graft were legendary. People grew to hate him. Yet, he seemed blind to it all. Instead of trying to court the favor of his superiors by behaving more discreetly, he boldly requested more troops to expand his growing domain. Butler wanted to drive hard into Texas, upending what he termed the Confederacy's "beef barrel." He was particular, though, about the soldiers he wanted: "Please therefore send me New England troops," he wrote to General Halleck. "The newspapers assure me that there are thousands waiting in Massachusetts." These right-thinking Yankees would be just the cure for the secessionist ailments of Louisiana, he thought, and would be the right sort to drag Texas back into the Union. Unbeknownst to him, thousands of New Englanders, New Yorkers, and a handful of Texan Unionists were already on their way to New Orleans and Galveston—but not for Ben Butler.[40]

CHAPTER FIFTEEN

NATHANIEL P. BANKS

Butler had been literally playing the part of a Persian satrap
Lieutenant Colonel David Hunter Strother

B y November 1862 the Lincoln administration had already run through it patience with Butler, and had surreptitiously anointed Nathaniel Prentice Banks, "The Bobbin Boy of Massachusetts," to replace "The Beast" as the next architect of the war in Louisiana and Texas. These men had a lot in common. Both had been potent political forces before the war. Banks, a civilian soldier, rose from plebeian beginnings as a Massachusetts textile mill worker and, later, during his political career, he made great use of his nickname, "The Bobbin Boy," to emphasize his humble background and win working-class votes. He entered state politics in the 1840s, went to Congress in 1853, and rose to Speaker of the House of Representatives by 1856. Two years later he left the national platform to return to his home state, this time as governor. When disunion occurred, he offered himself and the resources of his state to help President Lincoln win the war. His reward was one

Major General Nathaniel P. Banks looked the part of a soldier. More important, he had impressed the right people. He had won the confidence of Abraham Lincoln by efficiently managing the defenses of the nation's capital. "You have let me sleep in peace for the first time since I came here," Lincoln told him. "I want you to go to Louisiana and do the same thing there." Courtesy of Denis Gaubert, Thibodaux, Louisiana.

of the first commissions as major general of volunteers issued by his nation. Now, Lincoln would swap one political appointee from Massachusetts for another more to his liking.

The choice of Banks seemed to have merit. He was certainly a gifted politician and ally of the administration. His intelligence, skilled oratory, and boundless ambition had taken him far. His politics had the appearance of principle but maintained enough latitude to espouse whatever seemed most likely to get him elected. This politics of expedience served Banks well during most of his public career, and in the 1850s Massachusetts political climate, he positioned himself as a moderate, antislavery Republican. He was essentially a centrist who usually adapted his views to those that would gain him the most political benefit.

During his first year in uniform, however, he discovered that war was trickier than politics and clever opponents often uncovered a military fraud. As a result, his army career had been less stellar than his meteoric rise to command. Confederates under General Thomas "Stonewall" Jackson—including Richard Taylor—had humiliated Banks in the Shenandoah Valley in May and June 1862, leading to the loss of a third of his army. The Rebels, living off captured supplies, dubbed him "Commissary Banks" for his generous abandonement of battlefield booty. Banks, at the head of the XII Army Corps, took another swing at Jackson at the Battle of Cedar Mountain. An injury—his wounded horse had reared and kicked him while he was mounting—removed him from the battlefield.

The first orders that would send him to Louisiana arrived on October 31. While recuperating in Washington and serving as commander of the capital's defenses, Nathaniel P. Banks received instructions to proceed to New York and Boston to raise an army. "This assignment was wholly unexpected by Banks," wrote Lieutenant Colonel Richard B. Irwin, the general's assistant adjutant general. "It was, indeed, unsought and unsolicited, and the first offer, from the President himself, came as a surprise." His command was to be a counterpart to an army being raised in the Midwest by Major General John McClernand, another political appointee. Banks and his new army were to steam to New Orleans to accomplish two objectives: first, secure New Orleans against any Confederate counterattacks; second, operate in concert with McClernand's troops in a great north-south pincher to open the Mississippi River. They would finish the chore started by Farragut, Butler, and Davis earlier in the year. On November 8 Banks received sealed instructions assigning him to command the Department of the Gulf.[1]

The officer maintained the strictest secrecy. When asked where he was bound, Banks responded "Texas." Newspapers, gossips, and spies carried the word south and west. This great deception would allow him to surprise not only the Confederates, but also Butler, who would undoubtedly use any advance warning of his pending replacement to cause political trouble. The northern espionage was thus directed at Federals in New Orleans as well as Rebels in Louisiana and Texas.

The command of this clandestine operation came as a reward from Lincoln to Banks. While in Washington, the general had been relentless in his organization of its defenses. He organized the mobs of unattached stragglers into efficient regiments, completed the fortifications, and provided reinforcements to the Army of the Potomac. Newly raised regiments of heavy artillery garrisoned a necklace of earthworks that protected all avenues of enemy invasion. Banks had become the architect of the capital's security. Lincoln called the Massachusetts general to the White House to commend him. "You have let me sleep in peace for the first time since I came here," the president said. "I want you to go to Louisiana and do the same thing there."[2]

A few days later David Hunter Strother, a Virginian serving as a staff officer with the Army of the Potomac, had an interesting proposition to consider. "At dinner I saw General Banks, who called to me and asked me to sit by him," he wrote in his diary in early November. "He said he was about to be ordered south, perhaps to Texas, and asked me to accompany him." The prospect held great appeal for the artist-turned-army cartographer, and his interest grew the more he studied the potential.

"Texas has plenty of good cotton land and can supply the world," Strother mused. "Free labor applied to cotton raising will succeed, if tried." Strother sensed a great opportunity for ambitious men and saw a future for himself in Texas. "This is then a field to make one's fortune, for we go as military colonists and will, if we please, become the leading men of the land," he wrote. Strother believed that smart Unionists would simply eliminate what he saw as the state's current offensive population and replace it with shrewd northerners. "Driving out Rebels and Comanches will be an easy matter."[3]

The Lincoln administration's deception was only partially successful. Butler grew suspicious of the expedition when informers told him New Orleans gamblers were giving ten-to-one odds that he would be sacked. Perhaps, Butler thought, Banks was on his way to assume field command while he continued administrative control—a course he did not relish. He penned a letter to headquarters asking to be sustained in his present position. "Pray do me the favor to reflect that I am not asking for the command of any other person," he hissed. He simply wanted assurances that his own command "shall not be taken from me in such a manner as to leave me all the burden without any of the results." His future would prove gloomier than he feared.[4]

Meanwhile, Banks forged ahead with his plans, shifting his headquarters to New York to oversee the creation of his army. Most of his command would be assembled from forty thousand troops gathering in Boston, New York, and Baltimore, and would include thirty-nine regiments of infantry, six batteries of artillery, and a battalion of cavalry. More than half these units were essentially stay-at-homes and militia, enlisted by the governors of New York and the New England states as a way of making their militia useful but without obligating their citizens to a full term of service. At the same time, these stay-behind soldiers counted toward their respective states' manpower obligations as ordered by the president the past summer. For many of

The troops coming to finish the job in Louisiana write home while aboard transports, telling relatives in New York and New England all about their adventures in this exotic part of the country. Frank Leslie's Illustrated Newspaper.

Banks's men this appeared to be a grand adventure, a Christmas away from home in a warmer climate, with their patriotic chore concluded before the leaves on the maples changed colors again.

Major General Henry Halleck wrote to Butler, teasing him with the idea that he was being reinforced but maintaining the subterfuge covering the expedition. "You are misinformed in regard to there being any troops in New England ready for the field," he wrote in early November in a half-truth. "For the last two months we have been urging the Governors of States to complete their regiments and send them forward as fast as they are ready. It is hoped that some will be ready to start as soon as the November elections are over." Halleck knew the plan for Butler's fall was already advanced; even so, he maintained appearances and implied that all was well. "Brigadier generals will be sent with these reinforcements." Of course he neglected to mention that Banks was coming as well.[5]

A huge array of ships would ferry this host of men to the sunny, southern latitudes of the Gulf of Mexico. The U.S. Government burdened transportation tycoon Cornelius Vanderbilt with the task of gathering them. "This service Vanderbilt performed with his usual vigor, 'laying hands,' as he said, 'upon every thing that could float or steam,'" wrote Irwin. The soldiers who huddled aboard these leaky and rusty tubs were not as generous. One noted that the transports appropriated included "more than one vessel to which it would have been rash to ascribe either of these qualities." Before long, flotillas steamed away from Boston, New York, and Hampton Roads, Virginia. As the eclectic collection of ships straggled down the East Coast, none of the passengers knew where they were heading, but rumors of Texas buzzed through the ranks as intended.[6]

On December 13 most of the great armada assembled at Ship Island, Mississippi. "Truly grand . . . was the spectacle afforded by the black hulls and white sails of this grand concourse of ships at anchor," Irwin remembered. The next day the combined fleets headed out in line ahead. The sight was magnificent and majestic, wrote Irwin, with "flags flying, bands playing, and decks blue with the soldiers of the Union." When the great expedition turned into the mouth of the Mississippi River, it became apparent to all aboard that Louisiana, not Texas, was the immediate object of the campaign. Far astern, ships bearing the rest of the expedition straggled in for weeks.[7]

On December 14, as the steamer carrying Banks and his staff churned up the Mississippi, the eager passengers lined the railings to catch a glimpse of their new theater of war while Strother conferred with the commanding general. "He opened to me for the first time his views and plan of campaign," he wrote. Banks planned to bring Louisiana back into the Union by creating a feeling of good will toward the United States while politically isolating the secessionists. "On the supposition that Butler's rule was violent and high handed and that some people were suppressed rather than won over," Strother continued, "our policy was foreshadowed as conciliatory. Kindness after the rod is the strong card." Strother remained unconvinced and believed his new chief was naïve: "Knowing the character of the population I am not sure but Butler's policy is the safest. . . ."[8]

Banks also held a trump card. Since the Rebels might be hard to convince of the superiority of northern views, replacing them with a more congenial population might be the answer. Banks observed his troops with pride as they marveled at the semi-tropical paradise they were entering. "Half of these fellows," Banks said to his staff, "who see this blooming land for the first time will never willingly return to their bleak and sterile homes in New England."[9]

Butler, although leery of Banks and his expedition, welcomed the mighty armada with military formality. Artillery salutes from Forts Jackson and St. Philip and Farragut's ships marked its approach, and bands and honor guards met it at the city wharf. Butler had even arranged for a stylish carriage to convey the newcomer to his accommodations. Then, Butler learned the truth. Not only was he to be relieved, but he was also being sent home with no orders for future command.[10]

Having delivered the bad news, Banks and his staff settled into the St. Charles Hotel, established their headquarters, and took a look at Butler's kingdom. Strother walked through the city to investigate the condition of his new surroundings. The levees were bare, "instead of being covered . . . with uncountable wealth of sugar, cottons, and the great staples of northwestern trade," he wrote. He later strolled along the main thoroughfares of New Orleans. "Canal Street, Rue Royal, Hotel St. Louis, to the Old Cathedral, Jackson Square," he wrote, "but little business remained and a few people. The place looked like a decayed city of the Old World. . . ." As he passed by the sculpture of Andrew Jackson fronting the French Quarter, he noticed the kind of sarcastic vandalism that characterized Butler's reign. What had been a monument to the War of 1812 had become a present-minded civics lesson. "Some stonecutters were carving General Jackson's motto on the base of the equestrian statue of the old hero," Strother reported: "'The Federal Union, it must and shall be preserved.'"[11]

He encountered a newspaper reporter and asked him about local conditions. "He answered by an expressive wave of his hand, meaning 'Look around and you see it,'" Strother wrote. When asked about Butler, "He twisted his mouth and winked slyly," Strother recorded. "He gave us to understand that Butler was regarded with great horror." The journalists related the various details of the occupying regime. "Butler had been literally playing the part of a Persian satrap," Strother concluded.[12]

On December 16 Banks officially relieved Butler of command of the Department of the Gulf in a brief headquarters ceremony. Banks and his staff entered the suite of offices and participated in a round of introductions. Butler then passed command over to Banks in a short, prepared address, answered with a speech by the new commander. At that point, Banks left Butler to take farewell of his loyal and long-serving staff. "Several officers wept during the reading," Strother remembered. "The General himself seemed much affected."[13]

Banks, by contrast, seemed resplendent in the moment. At five feet, eight inches tall, the new mastermind of the Department of the Gulf lacked heroic physical stature, but he bore himself regally, spoke formally, and as one observer noted, appeared "stately and attractive" nonetheless. With his uniform impeccable and his demeanor charming, Banks looked the part of a high-minded, noble liberator as he ascended to command.[14]

With "The Beast" now caged, Banks's team completed the transition to the new authority. They soon discovered that Butler's decadence permeated his entire administration. Many of the old regime's staff officers desired to keep their lucrative posts under the new Banks administration. Colonel Strother found Butler's former property agent the most repulsive. "He thought all the property of Secessionists ought to be seized and sold," Strother reported. The newcomer asked him who, exactly, the secessionists were. "All the people here are," he responded. "There are no loyal people." Strother asked, "Then who would you sell to? Would you go on to sell all the property?" Here the Yankee was stymied. The property agent admitted therein lay a dilemma, but also expressed his true sentiments. "In his opinion," Strother continued, "there were no loyal people except in Massachusetts, adding after some hesitation 'and the other New England States.'" The Virginian could not conceal his disgust. "And these are the moles who are to administer government for the United States, a nation embracing all climates, all races, and all ideas."[15]

Butler had unquestionably been corrupt. His prewar career as a criminal defense lawyer had evidently taught him how to succeed as a felon. To cover his shady activities, Butler surrounded himself with trusted cronies and family members who keep his secrets lest they incriminate themselves. Further exposure to Butler's policies revealed even more excesses. "It was clear that the whole system had been one of enormous and unblushing fraud and rapine," Strother observed. Butler's racket evidently knew no bounds, and the enormity of the corruption astounded the newcomers. "United States Volunteer officers were engaged in company with speculators outside the army."[16] A planter downstream complained that Andrew J. Butler, the general's brother, had essentially required a fifty thousand dollar bribe to issue a permit to distill rum. Banks, it was universally hoped, would set a higher standard of deportment for the U.S. army in Louisiana.[17]

An inspection of the New Orleans garrison revealed camps that had fallen into disorder. "The Northern regiments . . . started out clean, trig, with habits of civilized neatness and good health," a Yankee inhabitant of the city reported. "At present they were ragged, dirty, lousy, degraded in apparel and in habits. Their moral character had suffered similar degradation."[18]

The outgoing general took the opportunity to exit with a flourish. In a farewell to the citizens of New Orleans, he declared "I found you captured, but not surrendered; conquered, but not orderly; relieved from the presence of an army but unable to take care of yourselves." He then listed the accomplishments that Union occupation and his tenure had brought to the city. "I restored order, punished crime, opened commerce, brought provisions to your starving people, reformed your currency, and gave you quiet protection, such as you had not enjoyed for many years," he wrote.[19]

A salute from Farragut's flagship, the USS *Hartford*, sounded Butler's departure on Christmas Eve, and his leaving marked the end of one of the most controversial episodes in the history of America's internecine conflict. "The streets during the last few days were gay with the population of the city who have come out like gophers in the sunshine," wrote Strother. "Butler has departed, and I suppose New Orleans will breath freer. . . ."[20]

Ironically, despite his deplorable behavior, Butler made a positive impact on many in the Crescent City and, without doubt, many were sorry to see him leave. Much of what he had written in his farewell address was true. For the poor and powerless, he had been a great hu-

Sailors and marines stand at ease in their dress uniforms while the bosun's mate pipes a signal. A similar crew would have greeted General Butler as he boarded the ship that would take him away from Louisiana. Library of Congress.

manitarian. He had championed the downtrodden and had prevented famine for the indigent by putting many on the government payroll. His support of Weitzel's sanitation policies helped rid the city of disease and had improved, if not saved, the lives of thousands of New Orleans's less fortunate. The seedier aspects of his character, though, put Butler's good works in the shadows of his more glaring excesses.

The question remained, however, as to his successor's suitability to the task Butler had started. "General Banks . . . was a man of a different stamp than Butler, although not very well qualified to take command of the city in the state in which Butler had left it," wrote Scotsman William Watson. "General Banks was a man of milder disposition, and did not find it necessary to lay down any extreme measures or enactments, and he did not himself engage . . . in any acts of extortion or plunder." This observer assumed that the change in administration marked the U.S. government's deliberate change in emphasis regarding

Louisiana. "It was supposed that Butler had sufficiently punished the rebels in New Orleans, and that Banks should act more in the military capacity and take the field and act against the Confederates. . . ."[21]

There was, though, an unexpected repercussion of Butler's departure. "The myriads of speculators who had come to New Orleans during Butler's reign," Watson continued, "now reveled under Banks, who, though he did not himself plunder, seemed unable to check it in others." In the coming weeks and months, these parasites would expand their reach and influence now that Butler's supreme control of illicit trade had been broken. "Louisiana, instead . . . of having one large shark, had now whole shoals of them."[22]

CHAPTER SIXTEEN

ARMIES OF THE GULF

We like the idea of going to Texas very much
Private George Fiske, 42nd Massachusetts Infantry

As a humiliated Benjamin Franklin Butler made his way back to Massachusetts, the new ruler of New Orleans and the coastal littoral had to decide which military project to undertake first. Nathaniel Banks saw many possible targets. His president wanted action up the Mississippi, and his new associates in the navy presented a spectrum of opportunities. David Farragut, a blue-water and big guns advocate, longed for a chance to strike Mobile, but he knew his government would not consent because of more pressing issues, mainly the Rebel citadels upstream. On board the USS *Hartford,* the admiral outlined the situation to his new army colleagues. "He explained the position of Vicksburg and prophesied some more rough work presently," Colonel David Strother recorded.[1]

After mulling over Farragut's report and examining the condition of New Orleans, Banks decided that Port Hudson was the key to victory on the river. Taking Port Hudson would result in a devastating

The U.S. flag flies once again over Louisiana's castle-like capitol in this sketch from Frank Leslie's Illustrated Newspaper.

loss of the Red River supply route, dooming Confederate control of the Mississippi. "That place taken," Strother wrote, "Vicksburg would no longer be tenable." Meanwhile more merciful policies toward the defeated Rebels would bring peace in the conquered territory. "He felt every assurance," added Strother, "that our efforts to establish the counter-revolutionary current here would be successful."[2]

Banks allowed little time to slip by before taking the offensive. On December 17, the day after taking command from Butler, Banks sent 4,500 of his troops to drive off a token Confederate force and reoccupy Baton Rouge. Major General Christopher Columbus Augur, commander of the expedition, ordered his men to rebuild and expand the defenses occupied by General Thomas Williams's men the previous summer. The wrecked Louisiana capital would be the Federal outpost from which a campaign against Port Hudson, just a long day's march away, would be launched. The earthworks would protect this outpost from any aggressive moves by the estimated 12,000 Rebels upstream.

Banks also looked north for news of U.S. operations against Vicksburg, which would inform him of his next course of action in his efforts to coordinate the campaigns.

While they waited for more action, officers throughout Federal-occupied Louisiana began organizing their vast new mob of troops into an army. The War Department designated Banks's command as the XIX Army Corps, composed of four divisions. The first division fell to Major General Augur of Michigan, a West Point-trained infantryman who had been a frontier regular and major before the war and who had served with distinction in Mexico. This forty-one-year-old soldier, who sported enormous sideburns, had fought with Banks at Cedar Mountain, where he received a grievous wound during that rough-and-tumble battle. Now he was in Louisiana as the second-in-command of the new army.

Major General Christopher C. Augur was appointed to West Point from Michigan and was a classmate with Ulysses S. Grant. In Louisiana, he was the senior divisional commander in the newly formed XIX Army Corps. Library of Congress.

One of Butler's men, forty-eight-year-old Brigadier General Thomas West Sherman of Rhode Island, took the second division. Like Augur, he was a West Point-trained regular, frontiersman, and veteran of the Mexican War. He had seen much in his career, from fighting Seminoles in Florida to herding Cherokees to the West. He was cited for gallantry at Buena Vista. At the start of the Civil War he had received one of the first appointments to brigade command, and he served at Port Royal, South Carolina, and later in the advance on Corinth, Mississippi. He had been in Louisiana since August and commanded the defenses of New Orleans.

A famous topographical engineer, fifty-one-year-old Brigadier General William H. Emory of Maryland, commanded the third division. Seven years after his 1831 graduation from West Point, Emory helped to survey the boundary between the United States and Canada.

A native of Newport, Rhode Island, Brigadier General Thomas W. "Tim" Sherman was a veteran of hard fighting across three wars. Library of Congress.

He received two citations for gallantry in the Mexican War a decade later and, after that conflict, helped settle the boundary dispute resulting from the treaty of Guadalupe-Hidalgo. He had already served well in the cause of the Union and would be one of the more capable officers in Louisiana.

The junior divisional commander was another frontier regular, Brigadier General Cuvier Grover, a thirty-four-year-old West Point graduate from Maine. Though too young to have served in the Mexican War, he built an impressive career in the West. Grover was a captain at Fort Union, New Mexico, when secession occurred. There he had served alongside Henry Hopkins Sibley. Grover led a division during the Peninsular Campaign and received high praise, but his command was shot to pieces at Second Manassas by Stonewall Jackson's Rebels. In the aftermath of that disaster he accepted a role in Banks's Louisiana adventure.

Officers shuffled the veteran units of Butler's army into brigades with the northeastern newcomers so as to leaven the green soldiers with steadier troops. This also provided the corps with echelons of experienced colonels to lead the brigades. Banks named Godfrey Weitzel the most senior brigadier in the XIXth Army Corps and placed him second in command of Augur's division. Union Colonel Edward Bacon of the 6th Michigan commented on Weitzel's subordinated role under the new regime: "Having been in favor with General Butler, [Weitzel] is necessarily out of favor at court now, and has very little to do with present plans." This talented officer held his position at Brashear City, ready to defend the Lafourche District against any bold strokes by Taylor, but he was overlooked as an important leader in the coming campaigns.[3]

Throughout Banks's army, however, were soldiers in need of training and discipline. "Two-thirds were . . . new levies," wrote Lieutenant

Colonel Irwin. "Some were armed with guns that refused to go off, others did not know the simplest evolutions." This lack of experience manifested itself repeatedly as the new troops continued to arrive. "In one instance . . . the colonel was actually unable to disembark his men except by the novel command, 'Break Ranks, boys, and get ashore the best way you can.'"[4]

While these blue-clad warriors settled into their camps and drilled beneath the bright Louisiana sky, a number of circumstances conspired to alter the course of the coming campaign and modify the army's plan. "Banks could not communicate with the commander of the northern column," Irwin explained, "and knew practically nothing of its movements." General Halleck had anticipated a quick envelopment of Vicksburg from three directions—Banks from the south along the Mississippi, General Ulysses S. Grant from the east along the line of the Mississippi Central Railroad, and General John A. McClernand from Cairo, Illinois, picking up General William T. Sherman at Memphis and proceeding down river. Instead, Banks discovered the formidable citadel of Port Hudson blocking his path and growing stronger each day. As a result, the coordinated campaign that the U.S. government had anticipated became nearly impossible, at least for the southern thrust. Port Hudson would have to be reduced, or bypassed, for the grand strategy to work.

Blunders, egos, and disasters also caused havoc with Federal plans. Unbeknownst to Sherman, the political general McClernand had planned to supersede him, take away his army, and lead the campaign to open the Mississippi alone. When Grant and Sherman learned of this strategic change, they hurried their plans to try to achieve victory before the usurper arrived. While Grant fixed the Rebel army under

Brigadier General William H. Emory was one of the most famous cartographers and topographical engineers in the U.S. This soldier-scientist had already served in Virginia and Tennessee before following Banks to Louisiana. Library of Congress.

Brigadier General Cuvier Grover, from Maine, was a West Point Graduate and a veteran of service on the frontier. By the time he came to Louisiana, he had already won accolades for his leadership at the battles of Williamsburg and Seven Pines. At Second Manassas, he led a ferocious bayonet charge that broke the Confederate line but ruined his brigade. Library of Congress.

General John C. Pemberton in place near Grenada, Sherman led a swift expedition to try to capture Vicksburg. Grant's diversion failed, resulting in Sherman's bloody repulse at Chickasaw Bayou in late December. McClernand joined him there and assumed overall command as the expedition retreated to Milliken's Bend and Lake Providence on the Louisiana side of the Mississippi. At almost the same time Confederate cavalry under General Earl Van Dorn destroyed Grant's supply base at Holly Springs, forcing him to withdraw as well. The Father of Waters would remain in Confederate hands for at least a few more months, and a cloud settled over Grant and Sherman. Banks so far had avoided such a catastrophe.

Since operations along the Mississippi appeared to be going nowhere, Banks turned to see what could be done in Texas. Butler had ordered the shock troops of McMillan's 21st Indiana to leave Brashear City and go to Galveston, but Wetizel had not yet acted on the directive. Banks concurred with this move, and already had other plans for these steady troopers and ordered them to New Orleans to form a heavy artillery regiment in the style of those around Washington, D.C. In their place the new general dispatched the greenhorn 42nd Massachusetts Infantry, most of whom lay scattered along the route from New England in malfunctioning steamers. The regimental headquarters and three companies arrived at New Orleans, but before they could even unpack, they shoved off again on December 21. Following them within days was the 1st Battery of Vermont light artillery and the seeds of E. J. Davis's 1st Texas Cavalry. Brigadier General Andrew Jackson Hamilton would follow to command this mixed brigade, as well as serve as

Getting newly arrived troops onto dry ground was sometimes difficult. "Break Ranks, boys, and get ashore the best way you can" was one method. Frank Leslie's Illustrated Newspaper.

the military governor of conquered Texas. "We like the idea of going to Texas very much," wrote Massachusetts private George Fisk. "It is a healthy country, and I think we shall have as pleasant a time there as anywhere."[5]

Banks was ready to be shed of Hamilton. The Texan had brought with him a large staff, including men largely nominated and promoted by Massachusetts governor John A. Andrew, a known proponent of turning the Lone Star State into a cotton colony. Hamilton and his cronies had protested loudly when Banks deployed his expedition on the Mississippi instead of heading to Galveston. Now they would have their chance to return triumphantly to Texas. "General Hamilton is surrounded by men who are here for the basest mercenary purpose," Banks reported. "Disappointed in their objects, they have been unsparing in their denunciations of the government and especially of myself. Any representations made by them . . . will be at least, only a partial statement of the truth if they be not entirely false."[6]

At the same time that Banks was building his army near Baton Rouge, another Union army lay in camps on the west bank of the Mississippi in northern Louisiana. This sketch from Frank Leslie's Illustrated Newspaper *is of Lake Providence.*

Banks next turned to the issue of rebuilding Louisiana. Since Butler had tried the hammer, Banks would try reason in the quest to bring the state back into the Union fold and to smooth the transition from slave labor to free labor. With his antebellum political career based upon the cause of free labor, he relished the opportunity to put his theories to work. Banks expanded and modified Butler's policies as he saw fit. Instead of a government monopoly on forfeited plantations, seized properties would now be available for lease on a competitive basis. No longer would Lafourche District planters be coerced into signing an oath of loyalty before being reissued their workers by the government, which would enforce order at the point of the bayonet. Instead, Banks drafted one-year labor contracts that allowed former slaves to choose their employers. At the end of the year these freedmen could choose a different employer. By making labor part of the free market, Banks argued, planters would either treat their hands well or lose them to another farm. Bayonets would no longer be necessary to keep order—the laws of capitalism would see to it instead.

Banks, events would bear out, proved naïve in his understanding of the complex situation in Louisiana and its neighboring state, Texas. The Confederate government had taken measures to counter the threat he and his predecessor posed to southern civilization there and his high-minded approach would face constant friction. Meanwhile, Confederates had also seen the trouble brewing in Texas and were in the process of pushing back against the Federal presence there.

Major General "Prince John" Magruder had already bamboozled the Federals once while serving in Virginia. He would try to do it again in Texas. State House Press.

As Richard Taylor had been Richmond's solution to the problems in Louisiana, now John B. Magruder would serve an identical purpose in the Lone Star State. In early November, while Butler had been consolidating his position in the Lafourche District and advancing his plans concerning Galveston, Magruder had been making his way to Houston, eliciting both hope and suspicion from the people of the Confederate District of Texas, New Mexico, and Arizona. Nicknamed "Prince John" because of his courtly manner and mien, Magruder had proven himself to be a fighter. He won three brevet promotions during the Mexican War and was one of the early Confederate idols. This reputation helped the Texans he had come to protect overlook his foppish behavior. They now expected him to drive the Yankees from their shores.

Magruder was a bona fide Southern hero but, like many others, his trophies had tarnished. Although in 1861 he had successfully commanded southern forces on the peninsula of Virginia, Prince John harbored failings. In May 1862 he had run afoul of General Robert E. Lee, commander of the Army of Northern Virginia, who charged Magruder with several mistakes in the Seven Days Battle around Richmond. The proud Prince John offered his resignation from command; Lee accepted it. Another bothersome rumor claimed that Magruder was a heavy drinker. Many Richmond gossips speculated it was his taste for whiskey that had landed him in the remote department of Texas, far from glorious Virginia.

Despite such stories, Texans came to love Magruder because he arrived ready to fight. Prince John's plan focused, for reasons both military and symbolic, on recapturing Galveston. If he could retake the town before Yankee reinforcements arrived, the Federal plan would unravel and the Confederacy's western flank would be secured.[7]

The change in Union command also provided Confederate general Richard Taylor a two-month respite from Federal pressure in Louisiana. While great blue armies gathered like distant storm clouds to both the north and south, the Confederate citadels at Vicksburg and Port Hudson grew stronger against the day that tempest would break. Rebel disasters on other fronts—in Kentucky, Tennessee, Mississippi, and Maryland—meant that Taylor and his compatriots would have to make due with the forces at hand, shepherding what steamboats, heavy artillery, and other strategic resources they could scrounge. Meanwhile the troops in the Confederate river citadels would rely on Taylor for provisions as well as military cooperation. The imminent invasion of Texas now complicated Taylor's mission, placing an enemy to his rear. Whereas Taylor had once looked west for a steady flow of reinforcements and supplies, he realized now that the Yankees clutched the spigot. The last drip he would receive to help him in Louisiana was a brigadier general sans brigade—Henry Hopkins Sibley.

Perhaps the person most responsible for the New Mexico disaster, in both official and public opinion, Sibley remained separated from his brigade of Texans while preparing a legal defense in Richmond against charges arising from that campaign. Confident of vindication, he hoped that his status as a West Pointer and his reputation from the Mexican War would keep him from disgrace. To Sibley's credit, endorsement letters from his staff and doctors rested in the case file in Adjutant General Samuel Cooper's office. But the file also contained accusations. Captain Alfred Sturgis Thurmond, a nemesis and a tough old veteran of all of Texas's wars, had feuded with the general over strategy in Albuquerque. In fact, they almost came to blows. This confrontation caused Sibley to threaten the captain's arrest and caused

Thurmond to file charges. After a cursory hearing Cooper declined to forward the case to a full court-martial. Instead, he dropped all charges and ordered Sibley back to his command. The Confederacy, at this stage, seemed hesitant to sacrifice a man with Sibley's experience and credentials.[8]

General Sibley packed his bags and headed to Louisiana, assuming that he would arrive there almost simultaneously as his brigade from the west, but he would be disappointed. The general reached the Confederate state capital in Opelousas—alone—on Christmas day. He was shocked to learn that his brigade had not preceded him. He had heard rumors that they might be headed to Vicksburg under the command of his former subordinate, William Read Scurry. He had also heard that Magruder was slow to release them from Texas, with Galveston now in enemy hands. Either

Misunderstood and unappreciated, General Henry Hopkins Sibley had been tossed by circumstances and events beyond his control after the failure of his New Mexico campaign. He also suffered from chronic kidney stones that he medicated with liberal doses of whiskey. He now found himself in charge of a tough position in Louisiana but made the best of it. Library of Congress.

way, Sibley believed, his contacts in Richmond had assured their service in his home state of Louisiana. Instead, only the two-hundred-man Arizona Battalion, under notorious Lieutenant Colonel Philemon T. Herbert, had arrived. This battalion contained undisciplined partisans from New Mexico, Arizona, and California–hard-living frontiersmen and veterans of the campaign in the Far West. Now they were on duty near the Mississippi, watching the enemy.

Sibley wrote Lieutenant General Theophilus Holmes, commanding the Confederate Trans-Mississippi, asking him for an explanation. "While in Richmond, the President impressed upon me the importance of immediate and active operations in this quarter, and that I should meet my brigade at the point designated," he seethed. "I deem it proper to say to you that . . . this part of the State of Louisiana, by far the richest in the Confederacy, is in a lamentably defenseless condition." He went on to tell his department commander that Jefferson Davis himself had assured leading Pelican State citizens that Sibley and his Texans would rescue them. "The people and the authorities had relied confidently upon the Texas troops, promised them so repeatedly by the War Department and the President, for protection," he continued. With no wave of reinforcements coming from west of the Sabine, Louisiana secessionists were losing heart. "The citizens seem to have lost all confidence in themselves and reliance in the assurances of the Government," Sibley penned, "and are fleeing from every quarter and in every direction."[9]

Taylor, looking to shore up his defense of the Mississippi's west bank against an inevitable advance by Banks, assigned his newly arrived one-man army to what he styled the "Department East of Atchafalaya." Its headquarters was at Rosedale on Bayou Grosse Tête, about fifteen miles west of Baton Rouge, and the terminus of a railroad connecting the towns with the Mississippi. Sibley now had jurisdiction over all operations from the hamlet of Simmesport, near the junction of the Atchafalaya and the Red River, to as far south down the Bayou Gross Tête as Yankee garrisons would permit. Awaiting him in this maze of swamp were the scruffy Arizona Battalion, the newly organized 28th Louisiana Infantry under Colonel Henry Gray, the 11th Louisiana Infantry Battalion, and the Labadieville veterans of Battery H, 1st Mississippi Light Artillery—together, nearly one thousand men.[10]

A few additional presents for Rebel Louisiana arrived Christmas week, but their recipients were not at hand. Shortly after Sibley had headed east toward Rosedale to command his patchwork brigade, a shipment of cavalry sabers, cartridge boxes, and pistols arrived at Opelousas to arm his missing Texan horsemen. The paymaster, loaded with funds, also arrived, ready to purchase supplies for a brigade few Louisiana authorities could locate. Everyone connected with this unit seemed uncertain of its whereabouts. The arrival of weapons and pay seemed to herald its coming arrival, but on December 26 only the five-gun Val Verde Battery, the trophy of Sibley's campaign in New Mexico, took up a position at Avery Island, late but welcome. Taylor's frustrations grew as he inventoried the cannons, swords, and shin-plasters of Sibley's Brigade, but not the troops themselves.[11]

The last days of 1862 had seen a return to duty for Sibley. Even so, he, Taylor, and even his Federal enemies still wondered what had become of his infamous Texans. Why were the Arizona Battalion, the Val Verde Battery, and the commanding general on duty in Louisiana when the bulk of the brigade was not? The answer was simple—they had been commandeered.

CHAPTER SEVENTEEN

COTTONCLADS

I want 300 volunteers who are willing to die for Texas,
and who are ready to die now
Colonel Tom Green, 5th Texas Cavalry

Three weeks before Sibley had penned his letter to Theophilus Homes trying to learn the whereabouts of his brigade, General John B. Magruder had simply sidetracked the New Mexico veterans in Texas, ordering them to Houston instead of allowing them to continue to Louisiana. The realignment of the Union war machine in the region had given him, like his compatriot Richard Taylor, time to scheme. Spying an opportunity, Magruder planned to use this lapse of Yankee attention to rid Texas of the Union toehold at Galveston before Banks's anticipated invasion of the Lone Star State made enemy gains irreversible.

Federals in New Orleans rightly feared that the inefficiencies of gathering and deploying the army would only embolden the Confederates. Dawdling by Banks would result in a jab by the Rebels. "To sit still," fretted Union Lieutenant Colonel Irwin as he fidgeted at headquarters in New Orleans, "was to invite attack."[1] His observations were prescient.

To beat the enemy in this great race and to strike while they remained disorganized, Magruder needed troops—as did other

Confederate commands, from Richard Taylor in Louisiana to James Pemberton at Vicksburg. Magruder counted a handful of infantry and cavalry units near the coast as well as several companies of heavy artillerists, and all could be gathered quickly for a strike at Galveston. Even so, these troops were green.

What he wanted were veterans to stiffen the resolve of his skittish soldiers. The only battle-tested warriors nearby were the hard-luck 2nd Texas Cavalry, reorganized from John Robert Baylor's old 2nd Texas Mounted Rifles. His sole remaining option was to commandeer the grumbling and scattered veterans of Sibley's Brigade. Magruder knew he must send them to Taylor as per orders. Even so, they had tarried for so long in his district that Magruder now wrote orders designating that the three tattered regiments should reform in the vicinity of Houston, so that they would be handy for any contingency—offensive or defensive, depending on who won the race for the strategic initiative. Until they crossed the Sabine, he reasoned, they still fell under his jurisdiction.

Besides, Magruder reasoned, a good deal of confusion and contradicting instructions remained as to the command's ultimate destination, and he used this chaos to his advantage. When he took over the command of the District of Texas from General Hébert, Magruder received no clear instructions as to the future disposition of Sibley's Brigade. Therefore, using this veil of ignorance, he informed Colonel S. S. Anderson, assistant adjutant general of the Trans-Mississippi Department, that he "ordered the whole of General Sibley's command to the coast" on December 12. A week later a dispatch from the Trans-Mississippi commander, Theophilus Holmes, which passed Magruder's letter en route, arrived to inform Magruder that the Texas brigade's destination would be Vicksburg. Unbeknownst to any of the commanders at the time, the dispatch was made obsolete in turn by Sibley's orders assigning him to Taylor. Bewildered, Magruder responded peevishly, since he believed that a more immediate threat loomed on his front, given the Federal position at Galveston. "Of course I shall facilitate the movement toward Vicksburg in every way in my power, " he wrote, "unless I receive different orders from General Holmes, who of course knows that General Banks is about to sail with a large force for Texas."[2]

The imminent arrival of Banks and his Union army was certainly on the mind of Texas governor Francis R. Lubbock, and he urged Magruder to disregard Confederate needs and to keep every possible soldier on hand for defense of the state. "There seems to be no doubt that a serious invasion of Texas will be attempted this winter," he wrote. "The . . . troops at this time within the State and the State troops are probably sufficient for its defense." The governor noted that the available troops were in rugged condition. "The brigade known as Sibley's, who may now be considered as veterans, are not half armed, and the same may be said of every other regiment in the state."[3]

Texas Governor Francis R. Lubbock fretted about what he considered an imminent invasion of the Lone Star State by a large Union army. Texas State Library.

Lubbock justified a vigorous defense of Texas. "I do not think I overestimate the importance of Texas to the Confederacy, or the interest the Government should feel in preventing its being overrun by the enemy," he argued. He mentioned the active commerce crossing the Mexican border and the impact it was having on the war effort. He also mentioned the state's value as a source of supplies and manpower. "Her wheat fields and her hog and cattle ranches contribute largely to feed the armies," he wrote. "Her wool and cotton factories clothe them in part; her sons have not been behind the foremost at the call of duty, and have poured out their blood like water upon the battlefields of liberty." He insisted that Texas had supported the Confederacy and now the nation needed to support the state. "She deserves a better fate at the hands of the authorities than to be left with the old men and boys to defend herself, while denied the means of effectually doing it."[4]

Magruder agreed that the governor's fear of invasion was valid and that Richmond likely had no idea of the realities in that arena. Sibley's men and two other regiments, the 2nd Texas Partisan Rangers and the 23rd Texas Cavalry, Magruder wrote, were already designated for service out of state at the very hour the Federals appeared ready to extinguish Confederate control of Texas. "I am in receipt of New Orleans papers stating that General Banks with his staff has arrived," he replied, "from which I am satisfied that a force of at least 20,000 strong is at hand for the invasion of this State." He also told Lubbock of Holmes's orders and his military duty to obey them. "While I have facilitated the movement of these troops in every possible manner, I have sent a letter . . . by courier requesting that the order for the movement be countermanded."[5]

Magruder acted sly in this last maneuver. Waiting for a reply from Little Rock—which could not possibly come before the first of the year—would allow him a few more weeks to plan his offensive. This might allow him time to use Sibley's troops to retake Galveston, then just as promptly send them on their way to the next assignment—military protocol met and military necessity accomplished in one bold stroke.

Magruder also understood the need for plausible deniability if he was charged with failing to follow orders in supporting Taylor, Holmes, or anyone else that coveted Sibley's troops. Conveniently for him, no matter what the crisis was along the Mississippi or in Louisiana, Sibley's old brigade simply was in no shape to move anywhere. Most of the troops were unarmed, as Lubbock had reported. "Sibley's command is very deficient in that particular," reported Magruder, "the men having sold their arms when they retreated from New Mexico to citizens and Mexicans to procure food and clothing, of which they were at one time almost destitute." Of course, their new weapons lay in crates far away in Louisiana.[6]

In the camps of Sibley's Brigade, the troops had little more than rumor to sustain them as they contemplated their futures. If they were to go to Louisiana, as many had heard, why had they had been assembled near Houston? Why not Tyler, Marshall, or Niblett's Bluff on the Sabine River? Most correctly suspected a fight was imminent and probably nearby. Shortly after they reassembled at their new bivouacs, Magurder ordered the men on a tiring sixty-mile ride to Houston. Most expected to face an enemy invasion. Instead, the commanders on the coast ordered the men to reverse the journey and return to their camps.

As December wore on, Magruder realized that Banks was not coming—at least, not yet. Even so, he did not believe it to be a feint so much as a delay. The lack of movement by the Federals provided Magruder with a timely gift, and the wily Confederate shifted his thinking from defense to offense. He issued new instructions for the dismounting of the mounted regiments around Houston, with the men to remain near the Galveston, Houston, and Henderson Railroad. Details peeled off to graze the brigade mounts in nearby pastures while the cavalrymen practiced infantry movements. For the soldiers of Sibley's Brigade, the senseless orders, extra drill, and tighter discipline all pointed to an impending battle.[7]

As the chilly days flitted by, Magruder's campaign to retake Galveston progressed with amazing speed. In the early days of the war the Confederate government had purchased several steamboats in the environs of Galveston Bay capable of carrying troops and supplies. Magruder ordered that four of these craft be sent to Houston and readied for combat. The *Bayou City*, a river steamer serving as a police boat in Galveston Bay, was the largest. The *Neptune*, a former mail packet, was next in size, followed by two smaller vessels, the *John F. Carr* and the *Lucy Gwinn*. At the docks of Harrisburg, workers assembled cotton bales, lumber, and cannon to convert the newly acquired vessels into "cottonclad" rams.[8]

True to his reputation, Magruder planned for an unconventional assault using the tools at hand. The attack against Galveston called for a coordinated land and naval assault. His makeshift gunboats would distract and, with luck, surprise, capture, and destroy key Union warships. Cavalry, artillery, and infantry, meanwhile, would move across the railroad bridge onto Galveston Island. They would attack the fleet and the tiny Federal garrison from the city's streets. The audacity of the attack would give the Texans a brief advantage, Magruder believed, and might tip the balance in his favor.

Magruder's hastily assembled army proved impressive. Captain Armand Wier of Company B, 1st Texas Heavy Artillery, volunteered himself and his men to serve aboard the *Bayou City* as gunners, and Company C manned the guns of the *Neptune*. Circulars in Houston called for volunteers to serve aboard the cottonclads as sharpshooters, riflemen who could pick off Union sailors and guncrews. Magruder sent the untried 20th Texas Infantry, inexperienced 21st Texas Infantry Battalion, detachments of the 26th Texas Cavalry, and the veteran 2nd Texas Cavalry to Virginia Point and across the bridge to Galveston Island. A number of artillery batteries also assembled, bringing with them fifteen rifled and smoothbore field pieces. In addition, the remaining companies of Colonel Joseph J. Cook's 1st Texas Heavy Artillery collected and crewed a half-dozen heavier cannon. The largest gun used by the Confederates would be an 8-inch Columbiad smoothbore mounted on Magruder's signature "railway" ram—a flatcar covered with iron rails and crossties to form a casemated, but mobile, emplacement. Sibley's men would form the reserve, remaining ready to react to circumstances as the fight unfolded.[9]

In the dark, early morning hours of Christmas day—the same day General Sibley had arrived in Louisiana without his command—shrill, brassy notes of bugles announced reveille at 1:00 A.M., awakening the soldiers of his estranged brigade. The men then crammed into three trains that waited on the siding to carry them south. By mid-morning, the long trains arrived in Harrisburg.

As though in a race to see who could bulk up their forces first, U.S. troops from New Orleans arrived in Galveston Bay aboard the steamer *Saxon*. That same Christmas morning several hundred soldiers from companies D, G, and I of the 42nd Massachusetts landed at Kuhn's Wharf. "About nine o'clock [we] drew up at the wharf, where a crowd of citizens has collected to witness our movements," Private George Fiske remembered. "As soon as we stepped upon the wharf, orders were given to send away all citizens. The wharf was soon cleared and we proceeded to occupy a large store-house situated upon the end, in the upper story of which we found splendid quarters."[10]

The Federals in Commodore William Renshaw's flotilla and the men of Colonel Isaac Burrell's infantry detachment expected an attack at Galveston. Confederate cavalry patrols were frequent visitors to the city and, due to necessity, the railroad bridge was still intact. The newly arrived infantry expressed surprise at the strange situation they had inherited. "[Things] are somewhat different from what we had expected to find them," Fiske wrote. "It seems that the rebels par-

Kuhn's Wharf juts out into Galveston Bay where ships unload their cargos. The Union troops sent to garrison the city hedged their bets and fortified the warehouses here, relying on the guns of the U.S. Navy to keep them safe from Confederate attack. Rosenberg Library, Galveston, Texas.

tially occupy the island yet, tho' seldom venturing in any force upon it during the day as it lies under the guns of our fleet. But during the night they have undisputed possession, we having no troops upon the land." Renshaw assured Burrell that all would be right in a a few days. "Our gunboats can easily destroy this bridge, and shell the rebels from Virginia Point, with which it connects, but Commodore Renshaw thinks as we have not sufficient land force to follow up the advantage we had better delay for a few days until more troops arrive," Fiske continued. "Everything seemed quiet in the city, tho' during the night several rockets, roman candles etc. were sent up, supposed to be signals to the enemy."[11]

Even so the northerners remained confident in their ability to fend off the best Magruder might offer. In the channel, five strong gunboats lay at anchor, their thirty heavy guns pointing toward the city and their netting raised to repel boarders. Colonel Burrell's tiny vanguard of an army of invasion, ensconced behind makeshift fortifications at Kuhn's Wharf at the end of 18th Street, would serve as a trip wire should the Confederates try anything bold.[12]

Once again on dry ground after weeks of torturous travel aboard transports from New York, the Massachusetts men prepared their position well. Aware of their exposed position, Colonel Burrell quartered his men in a warehouse on the end of the 150-foot long wharf. Their accommodations were cramped, but the position was immediately under the guns of the fleet. As further protection, Burrell ordered that the planks closest to shore be removed and used to build a

This sketch of the USS Sachem *shows the vessel's distinctive profile, with its funnel aft of its two masts. The gunboat was a veteran of blockade duty on the Texas coast. Nestell Collection, Nimitz Library, U.S. Naval Academy, Annapolis, Maryland.*

stout barricade across the width of the wharf. In addition to providing a breastwork, this action left a protective gap of water between the Federals and any enemy approach. Soldiers constructed a second defensive line, made of bricks, barrels of dry plaster, and lumber taken from inside the warehouse. An opening remained in both walls to allow access to pickets, but huge sacks of cotton seed remained nearby to close them in event of an attack. A single board joined the wharf to the shore.[13]

Even though the mortar schooner *Rachel Seaman* had departed a week before, seeking repairs in New Orleans, a half-dozen warships of various sizes added muscle to this improvised redoubt and seemed to guarantee its safety against all comers. The picturesque and heavily armed USS *Harriet Lane,* anchored in the middle of the channel off 29th Street, was farthest west in the naval battle line. Named for James Buchanan's niece and originally commissioned as a revenue cutter in 1852, the ship had already seen action during the war. Aboard were 130 veteran sailors and marines, serving six guns.[14] A fast, well-built ship, most of her crew considered the *Harriet Lane* the darling of the Galveston Squadron.[15]

Ships like the USS Harriet Lane *and* Owasco *counted on heavy cannons like this 9-inch Dahlgren to defend their gains earned on the coast of Texas. This crew of sailors and a marine are readying the gun for action. Notice the nets raised to protect against boarding. Library of Congress.*

Three other veteran ships hovered closer in to Kuhn's Wharf, giving the infantry a sense of immediate security. One of the vessels, the side-wheel steamer USS *Clifton,* was originally a New York harbor ferryboat; it became Navy property late in 1861 and now added its arsenal of six cannons to the weight of the fleet.[16] The smallest of the Federal warships in Galveston Bay, the schooner USS *Corypheus,* had been a Confederate blockade runner, but since its capture in May 1862 it had flown the Federal colors. The *Corypheus* arrived at Galveston on December 29 with its crew of twenty-eight manned two-pivot guns.[17] On the same day the propeller-driven USS *Sachem* arrived, needing repairs after engaging in a heated duel with Confederates near Corpus Christi. A crew of fifty served *Sachem's* four broadside guns and pivoting rifle. Accompanying these two arrivals was the schooner *Lecompte,* fresh from patrolling Matagorda Bay.[18]

Two other Federal warships, the *Owasco* and the *Westfield,* lay anchored near Pelican Spit, protecting the troop transports from any Confederate vessels that might appear. Powerfully armed, the *West-*

field carried four guns in her broadsides, a pivot gun in the stern, and a sizable pivoting rifle in the bow, recently replaced after its massive 100-pounder Parrot rifle had burst while shelling Port Lavaca.[19] The USS *Owasco,* designed specifically for blockade service, carried a rifled pivot gun in the bow, a pivoting gun amidships, and a howitzer on both broadsides.[20]

Naval officers remained edgy and urged vigilance. Spies, lookouts, and gossip continued to indicate the presence of Confederate warships, perhaps including a powerful ram, roaming Galveston Bay, and a similar fleet near Sabine Pass. Renshaw addressed the sailors and marines aboard *Westfield:* "My lads, I have called you together to tell you there is a rumor afloat that an attempt will be made some of these nights to drive us from the harbor, by some rebel steamers." The commodore urged his crew to remain vigilant and to expect something unconventional. "If we are attacked at all it will be by boats drawing very little water . . . their object will be to board us. If they get alongside before we are ready to receive them, or before our anchor is up, they may stand a pretty good job of succeeding." Renshaw knew that whatever the Confederates had planned, they would fail in a traditional naval duel. If the enemy surprised the fleet at anchor, they might have a chance. "If they catch us napping they may succeed," he concluded, "but if we are wide awake, when they come, I'll be damned if they will."[21]

Renshaw, therefore, had either anticipated or uncovered Magruder's intentions, but he could not know that not everything was going as planned in the Confederate camps. Construction problems on the boats and the lack of enthusiasm by Houstonians to serve as volunteer sharpshooters confounded the naval portion of Magruder's grand design. In order to move the operation along, Colonel Tom Green of the 5th Texas Cavalry and Colonel Arthur Bagby of the 7th Texas Cavalry conceived of a plan to use Sibley's Brigade as sharpshooters aboard the ships. On December 30, the officers went to Houston to discuss the idea with Magruder and, although initially hesitant to risk these veterans on such a forlorn hope, the general agreed. Green and Bagby quickly returned to Harrisburg to gather volunteers and inform brigade commander Colonel James Reily of the change in orders. Green and Bagby reached their camps late in the morning of December 31, but the 4th Texas—Reily's regiment—had already departed by rail for Virginia Point to begin its journey into Galveston.[22]

Nonplussed by the lack of instructions from their immediate superior, the colonels decided themselves that the two remaining regiments of the brigade would provide ample volunteers. Colonel Green ordered the 5th and 7th regiments into line, then addressed the troops: "I want 300 volunteers who are willing to die for Texas, and who are ready to die now. Volunteers will step two paces to the front."[23] The response was so overwhelming that each captain could choose only fifteen men from his company for the duty. The remainder marched to Virginia Point under the command of Lieutenant-Colonel Henry C. McNeil of the 5th Texas and Major Gustav Hoffman of the 7th Texas Cavalry to catch up with Reily and to fill him in on the details.[24]

Magruder understood that his puny ersatz navy was no match for the powerful Union flotilla, but his Texan soldiers and crews were game. Further, since arriving at Houston the Confederate fleet had undergone an amazing transformation. Workers removed the upper cabin, or "Texas," and pilothouse from the CSS *Bayou City*. Cotton bales placed on their sides and stacked three high provided a better than seven-foot high wall, nearly two-feet thick. This was backed by another row of bales lying flat, provided the sharpshooters' two-foot tall firing platforms. Remodeling had given the wooden steamer the rakish look of an ironclad ram, a useful disguise in keeping with Magruder's reputation for using deception to fool his enemies. From all indications, Union observers had taken the bait. The ship might look like an innovative ironclad, but its mode of fighting would be ancient. Two boarding planks, designed to drop onto enemy vessels' decks like a Roman *corvus*, had been constructed alongside the *Bayou City*'s smokestacks. The only modern concession sat in its unprotected bow—a single rifled gun mounted in pivot.[25]

The *Bayou City* would lead a squad of riverboats turned combatants. The CSS *Neptune* also emerged as a cottonclad, its rectangular white "armor" stacked much like a cotton transport of antebellum days. Two field howitzers pointed from its bow. Cotton protected the boiler of the cannonless CSS *John F. Carr*; the CSS *Lucy Gwinn* and CSS *Royal Yacht*, which served as wood tenders for the squadron, were defenseless.[26] Marching away from their camps at noon on December 31, the Confederate volunteer "horse-marines" from Sibley's Brigade, armed mostly with Enfield rifles and shotguns, began their new role as they took their places aboard the ships. After reaching the Harrisburg landing the column divided. The 150 soldiers from the 5th Texas Cavalry moved aboard the *Bayou City*, while 100 men from the 7th Texas Cavalry reported to the *Neptune*, and the remaining 50 boarded the *John F. Carr*.[27]

At the same time, Confederate officers completed the landward battle plans. The ground forces were to divide, with one portion storming Kuhn's Wharf, another taking positions along the Strand, and Sibley's remaining veterans providing the reserve, assembling around the customs house at the corner of 20th and Post Office streets. Artillery, with support from the other assembled regiments, would carry the main attack against the Yankee ships. Magruder divided the 20th Texas Infantry, sending most of the companies to haul the artillery pieces from Eagle Grove to their positions along the Strand. Companies A and B, with troops from the 21st Infantry Battalion and the 2nd Texas Cavalry, carried scaling ladders to assault the Federal position at Kuhn's Wharf.[28]

The dark morning hours of New Year's Day would be the time designated for attack, and Magruder moved his forces into position. Halfway to Galveston, a temporary telegraph station had been built which would serve as the final checkpoint between the two elements of the Confederate attack. Leaving Harrisburg at 2:00 p.m., at dusk five hours later the flotilla approached Morgan's Point, where a rowboat left the shore and pulled hard for the Rebel vessels. On board was a courier bearing Magruder's final communiqué, which ended, "All is ready. The Rangers of the Prairie send greeting to the Rangers of the Sea."[29] Three times Colonel Green read the lines aloud to his men, receiving a volley of cheers each time. As night fell, the boats paddled off into the dark.[30]

Magruder had briefed his naval commanders carefully for he, like his enemy Renshaw, knew that surprise was of the essence: the land forces must initiate the attack. The cottonclads were to approach as close to the Federal fleet as possible without being detected and wait for firing from the island to begin at 1:00 A.M. Magruder also informed his officers that he would press the fight with or without the navy, but under no circumstances was the fleet to start the battle. They were to be a shock to the Yankee gunners, who would be pointing their cannons toward the city while the cottonclads snuck up from behind in the bay.[31]

By midnight, the naval squadron had reached Half Moon Shoals, and the men of Sibley's Brigade were anxious for their first fight as "horse-marines." Nothing in their New Mexico experience had prepared them for service aboard a ship. As the small fleet steamed closer to Galveston, tension grew among the volunteers. A party of officers gathered in a stateroom aboard the *Bayou City* to discuss their chances. One of the men asked Commodore Leon Smith if the cotton bales afforded any protection. The veteran steamboat-man assured them that the Federals' large bore solid shot, shell, and grapeshot would be barely slowed by the barricades. The only option was to close with the Yankee vessels before they fired. After his remark, Colonel Green, with a new concern about his soldiers' welfare, became decidedly serious. The men, perhaps sensing his fears, grew even more nervous. Some aimed for nonchalance. Colorado County privates Tom Kindred and Bill Cribbs went below deck and shuffled their playing cards for what they supposed might be their last game of "seven up."[32]

Leon Smith never held an official naval commission from the Confederate government, but General Magruder trusted the veteran mariner because of his skilled seamanship and daring. He eventually became the de facto commander for the Texas Marine Department, including all Rebel gunboats in Texas waters. Rosenberg Library, Galveston, Texas.

CHAPTER EIGHTEEN

GALVESTON

The pride of the Yankee Navy . . . was the prize of our Cow-boys
Dr. George Cupples
Surgeon on the Staff of General George B. Magruder

Almost immediately General John B. Magruder's ambitious and complicated plan went awry. Lookouts spied the approaching Rebel ships and, weighing anchor and building steam, the Federal fleet quickly prepared for battle. Around 1:00 A.M., after the Confederate steamboats took a position near the west end of Pelican Island, still confident that their approach had gone unnoticed, they saw a number of signal rockets streak skyward from the Yankee ships. Lanterns swung in the rigging: white for "enemy in sight," red for "make ready for action," blue for "order to prayers." With their surprise spoiled, the *Bayou City* and *Neptune* hove to, and their captains held a council of war to decide their next move.

Commodore Renshaw had no doubt of his next move, and his Union flagship, the USS *Westfield*, steamed past Point Bolivar in an attempt to engage the Rebel fleet. Confederate commodore Leon Smith, informed of the enemy gunboats' movements and aware of his own orders, decided not to risk starting the battle. Instead, he commanded his squadron to race back to Half-Moon Shoals, four miles away, hop-

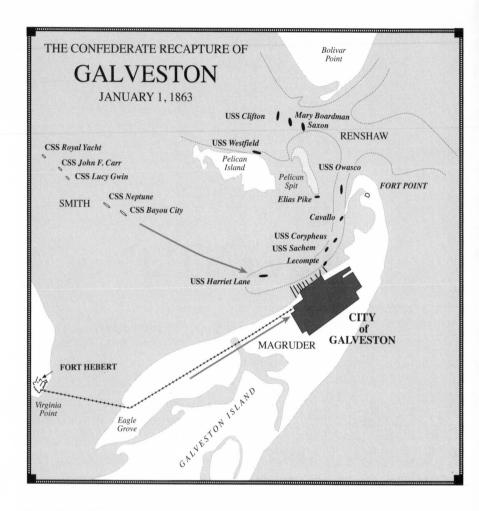

THE CONFEDERATE RECAPTURE OF

GALVESTON

JANUARY 1, 1863

ing that the treacherously shallow Galveston Bay might become an ally. Renshaw pursued the fleeing Rebels, but the *Westfield* soon ran into trouble, grounding on the shoals around Pelican Spit. The Confederates had lured Renshaw into acting rashly and now, with his ship effectively out of action, the Yankee seaman signaled to the USS *Clifton* to tow him out of his predicament.[1]

While the navy fussed about in the bay, reacting to what was assumed to be yet a feint by Confederate gunboats, the Battle of Galveston began in earnest at 4:00 A.M. on New Year's Day with a flash of fire and smoke at the foot of 20th Street. As the cottonclads maneuvered in their cat-and-mouse chase in the bay, Confederate land forces crossed the railroad bridge unnoticed from Virginia Point to the island. After moving his men into their positions, Magruder personally pulled the lanyard of one of Captain Tom Gonzales's field pieces to fire the signal round. "I have done my duty as a private," he said before retiring to his headquarters at Broadway and 24th Street, "now I must attend to that of a general."[2]

The Federal gunners, surprised but not stunned by the salvo of lightweight iron coming from the city, quickly thundered in reply. The USS *Harriet Lane* opened up an intense fire upon the Rebels at the west end of the Strand. Its naval grapeshot loads turned the ship's big guns into devastating shotguns, and disintegrating canister rounds showered the Confederate positions with whistling slugs. The USS *Corypheus* and USS *Sachem* added to the commotion, sending broadside after broadside into the Confederate positions threatening Kuhn's Wharf.

At the Ursuline Convent Dr. George Cupples of Magruder's staff prepared a hospital for the care of the wounded. "The heavens were in a blaze," he reported. "Musketry and heavy guns . . . roaring, rushing, and finally exploding in the air. . . . The wounded began to come in very soon afterward."[3]

Four miles away, Smith could hear the thunder of guns and ordered his ships to action, yelling down the tube to the engine room, "Give me all the steam you can crack on!"[4] As the high-pressure steam engine wheezed and hissed with urgency and the fleet gained speed, the men of the naval expedition looked with amazement at the spectacle unfolding before them. Reports from the heavy guns shook the bay; bursting shells lighted for a brief moment the rigging of the enemy ships; burning fuses made graceful arcs through the air. Muffled explosions from the city streets and the sound of crashing debris added to the hellish cacophony.[5]

On Kuhn's Wharf the Massachusetts infantry received the long-anticipated Rebel attack with coolness that belied their inexperience. A Yankee picket fired at the shadowy figures advancing down the Strand, turned, and ran across the single plank to the safety of the barricade beyond. Inside the warehouse drummers beat the long roll as the Federals scrambled to take their positions for the first combat of their lives. Troops hurriedly moved sacks of cotton seed into the

An eyewitness sketch of the Battle of Galveston as it unfolded. Looking north from the Gulf of Mexico, the artist, a Union officer, indicates the positions of Union ships as, left to right, the USS Sachem, Owasco *(with the large funnel amidship),* Corypheus, *and* Clifton. *This cluster of naval might was defending the exposed position of the 42nd Massachusetts on Kuhn's Wharf. The* Westfield *is aground on Pelican Island in the center of the image, near the landmark Bolivar lighthouse. All alone and vulnerable, the USS* Harriet Lane *can be seen far to the rear as the dark shapes of Confederate steamers close in. Nestell Collection, Nimitz Library, U.S. Naval Academy, Annapolis, Maryland.*

gap and hunkered under cover as round after round of shell and shot came howling overhead. Two men flew backward as a twelve-pound solid shot crashed through the plaster barrels. The warehouse disintegrated in splinters as bullets, canister, and cannon balls perforated its wooden walls. The Rebel gunners assumed they were massacring sleeping Yankees inside.[6]

But the Massachusetts men had boiled out into their positions and kept under cover in the uneven contest, hoping for good results from the navy. When the Rebel fire did not seem to slacken, one captain left his position and stood near the edge of the dock, hollering to the gunners aboard the *Sachem*. "Fire lower, and not so high!" Amazingly, the sailors heard the request over the din of battle and responded promptly and accurately.[7]

Magruder's land attack deteriorated rapidly, because the hoped-for shock had too short a life. The iron storm from the fleet revealed that the Yankee gunners had not been surprised, and their hot projectiles and good aim silenced section after section of the Rebel artillery. On 21st Street, Lieutenant Sidney Sherman Jr. of Company A, 1st Texas Heavy Artillery, son of a famous Texas patriot embarking on his generation's great adventure, had his belly torn open by a piece of grape-shot. "A fine young fellow," Dr. Cupples reported as bearers carried the boy into the convent. "He died in an hour." Even Magruder's largest Confederate gun, the 8-inch "railway ram," had been abandoned. Although they had inflicted some damage on the Federal fleet, the Rebel gunners suffered appalling casualties.[8]

On nearby 18th Street Colonel Joseph J. Cook's storming party had run into trouble as well. The untried men of the 20th Texas broke for cover several times, and heavy cannon fire forced much of the command to seek shelter behind a plank fence. The men of the 42nd Massachusetts, firing their first shots at an enemy, scattered the remaining Rebels with volleys of buck and ball. In desperation, Confederate soldiers pushed one of Gonzales's guns forward and temporarily enfiladed the Kuhn's Wharf position, allowing Cook time to rush his men to the relative safety of a nearby cotton press. With the Federal ships continuing the bombardment, many of the panicked Texans never took the chance of using their scaling ladders. Those who tried found them too short to reach the planks of Kuhn's Wharf. The assault that had been a salient feature of Magruder's plan flashed and faded in an instant.[9]

Officers advanced the reserves. In the middle of Galveston the column of Rebel foot cavalry from the 4th, 5th, and 7th regiments advanced down Broadway, encountering signs of the confusion of battle. "We met Elmore's regiment in full retreat," Fred Wade recalled. "The fire on them from the fleet and a body of soldiers on Kuhn's Wharf was so hot that they threw down their guns and ran." Reily received word from General William Read Scurry to have his men rescue any abandoned ordnance.[10]

The soldiers had gained the center of town when gunners from the USS *Owasco* detected their movements and fired on them. Several rounds of grapeshot passed only a few feet over the column as the troops surged forward to recover the railway ram. "We hitched onto the big Columbiad, but could not stir it," Wade remembered. Not waiting for the *Owasco* to reload and massacre his command, Reily led his troops to safety behind the customs house. "We picked up the guns dropped by Elmore's men and began shooting," Wade said. He had

A fanciful and inaccurate depiction of the fighting along the wharfs and buildings of Galveston. Harper's Weekly.

just fired his rifle and ducked behind the corner to reload when the *Owasco* unleashed another broadside of grapeshot. Dr. S. A. W. Fischer had just passed the private and stepped forward into the street to attend fallen soldiers when a piece of grapeshot passed through his head, temple to temple. The impact knocked the doctor's body halfway across the pavement.[11]

Wade ran to him but quickly returned to cover as his comrades yelled, "lets get to the top of this building and silence that gunboat." A group of Rebel soldiers scampered upstairs, kicking in doors to gain access to the roof. "I was in what seemed like a law office when I saw the brick wall begin to cave in," Wade remembered. Instantly he tumbled to floor in agony; a big shell from a naval gun had nearly been a direct hit. "I looked for my supposed wound and saw the print of a third of a brick on my blouse." As he struggled to his feet, Wade began vomiting violently, which he wrote later, "seemed to relieve me."[12]

The Texans clustered around the customs house scrambled to find something to hide behind, all bravado banished by the deadly blasts of naval gunfire. Private William Randolph Howell of the 5th

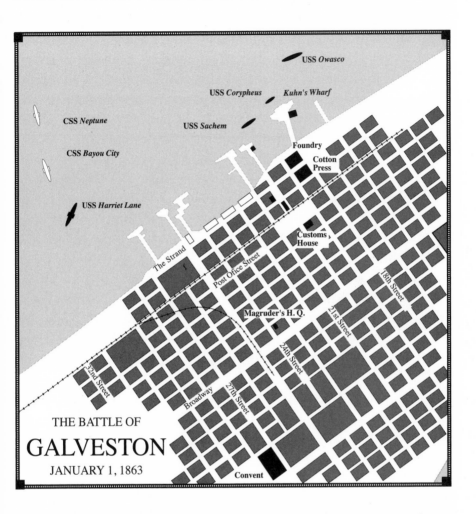

USS *Owasco*

USS *Corypheus*   Kuhn's Wharf

CSS *Neptune*   USS *Sachem*

CSS *Bayou City*

Foundry

Cotton
Press

USS *Harriet Lane*

Customs
House

The Strand

Post Ofice Street

Magruder's H. Q.

18th Street

21st Street

24th Street

32nd Street

Broadway

27th Street

THE BATTLE OF

GALVESTON

JANUARY 1, 1863

Convent

Texas Cavalry remained under cover. Later he wrote his sweetheart that "bombs, balls, grape, and cannisters were flying all around and above me tearing up the earth, smashing up houses and killing and wounding men while the whole atmosphere seemed to be in a blaze. If I had consulted my personal safety, I should have preferred being somewhere else."[13]

Magruder's attack on Galveston had turned into a catastrophe. Increasing numbers of Confederate soldiers left their posts to escape the hail of canister and grape; hundreds scurried for the Gulf shore and the causeway. The general ordered a detachment of Colonel Xavier DeBray's 26th Texas Cavalry to round up the timid and to shoot any soldier who resisted. With no signs of the Confederate naval flotilla,

Magruder felt certain that the barrage would slaughter even more men once daylight came, and he began making plans to end the attack. "Before the appearance of the expected Confederate gunboats, it seems that General Magruder had despaired of their arrival and gave orders that the troops fall back towards the gulf shore," remembered one veteran. "The old fellow sat cross legged, swinging his foot, remarking 'We will have to try them again.'"[14]

The men in the streets of Galveston needed little urging to save themselves. "Then commenced a general skeedaddle," a Texan wrote. "The whole square in front of the courthouse and Trinity Church, then an open plain, was completely covered with the fleeing troops, and they probably made a better time to the rear than the Yankees did at Bull Run. The scene was ludicrous."[15]

Just before dawn, Magruder ordered the remaining crews and guns withdrawn from the Strand, while details from Sibley's Brigade continued to retrieve abandoned cannon. Sunrise found few Rebels along the Strand, and the Federal ships began to slacken the intense bombardment.[16]

As though scripted for dramatic effect, the report from several medium-sized cannons echoed from far off in Galveston Bay. "While the panic was at its height, heavy cannonading was heard on the bay, and everybody knew that the Confederate gunboats were engaged with the enemy," remembered one Rebel soldier. "The fleeing troops halted and soon turned their faces towards the front again, swinging their hats and claiming victory." Smith and his steamboats were making their run to either retrieve victory from disaster or expend themselves in the effort. One man in the 5th Texas Cavalry moved boldly into the open and, in a defiant voice yelled, "Hold Mr. Yank! You've been having everything your own way this morning, but Tom Green and his boys are on hand now and propose to have a little say in the matter."[17]

A second spontaneous, hopeful cheer rang from the city as the longed-for Rebel steamers appeared through the smoke and chilly mist, pressing their tardy attack. The Confederate paddle wheelers, "puffing and snorting from their high pressure steam," according to one Texan sharpshooter, churned through the bay as their cannon roared a second salvo at the Federal ships. As the faintly glowing cannon balls arced through grey sky, most struck the water, but one round from the *Bayou City* hit just behind the *Harriet Lane*'s port wheel, "making a hole large enough for a man to crawl through," according to one witness.[18] Observers in town ran to vantage points to watch the naval battle. "I went up to the third story to see our boats attacking," wrote Cupples. "It was a splendid sight, the blaze of musketry incessant and the vessels and water looking like Stereoscopic views."[19]

Just as Texan hopes rose, events indicated that the gunboat attack was doomed as well. On the third volley from the cottonclads' cannons, the refitted 32-pounder aboard *Bayou City* burst, killing Captain Armand Wier and several of his men. The boat's skipper, Captain Henry Lubbock, did not hesitate—the guns to him were mainly for show and to stiffen the spines of his passengers—but instead steadied his aim for what he intended to be his main attack, despite the billows of smoke coming from the carnage on his bow.

He planned to impale the enemy vessel on the nose of his fragile ship, trading a pawn for a queen. Slightly ahead, the *Bayou City* drove straight ahead for the *Harriet Lane,* its port side a large target for the Rebel assault. Its executive officer, Lieutenant Edward Lea, realized the danger and reversed one of the ship's wheels in order to kick the boat around to the right and present it bow-on to the Rebel attack. At a range of three hundred yards rebel sharpshooters, firing at the maneuvering enemy revenue cutter, drove the Union crew from the forward pivot with a hail of lead while Lubbock ordered his pilot to close with the enemy vessel. The jarring collision did little more than scuff the hull and starboard bow of the Federal warship—the *Bayou City* struck only a glancing blow on the moving ship, shoving it further around.

Lubbock knew immediately that the crash had grievously injured his vessel while doing little to the enemy. The *Harriet Lane*'s hard nose had smashed a portion of the cottonclad's port wheelhouse as the two combatant ships slipped past each other. Though quick-thinking Confederate crewmen dropped the port-side boarding plank to try to lock the antagonists together, the effort was too late, and its target was a few feet out of reach. The board instead dropped hard and slapped into the water, ripping free from its moorings. The battered wheel of the *Bayou City* churned the board into its machinery, causing additional damage. Now the crippled Confederate steamboat could do little more. Its momentum carried it past its target, and its dead left wheel caused it to curve slowly to the left. Lubbock abandoned the assault, and the *Bayou City* limped away toward shore. Yankee sailors, regaining their senses after the confusion of the impact, hurried back to their guns as the *Harriet Lane*'s pilot fought to regain control of the careening vessel and provide them with a clear shot.[20]

He was in for a surprise. The collision had not opened the hull of the *Harriet Lane* to the waters of the bay, but it had caused a troubling wound. The blow had sheared away the *Harriet Lane*'s cathead, part of its anchoring apparatus, causing the massive hook and fifteen fathoms of cable—some ninety feet—to slide into the water. The Union vessel jerked to a crawl as it reached the end of the line, dragging the heavy weight along the muddy bottom of Galveston Bay. The crew saw no immediate way to retrieve it or be shed of it. The additional burden acted as a pivot, causing the ship to swing by the bow, the momentum of its engines now presenting its starboard side toward the attackers but also slinging it stern-first out of the channel. Next the *Harriet Lane* ran aground and skidded sideways to a halt with the bay's sands sliding and crunching beneath its keel. The Union flagship was now immobile and broadside to the axis of the Rebel attack.

Captain William H. Sangster of the *Neptune* saw his opportunity and ordered his ship to finish off the *Harriet Lane* before the wallowing ship could pull free from its predicament. "We had two 24-pounders on board that roared with extraordinary loud report," remembered Private Joseph Faust of the 7th Texas. As the Rebel ship cut to port in an effort to gain a better angle on the Union gunboat, the Texan riflemen opened up. A shot in response from the *Harriet Lane* scattered *Neptune*'s cotton bales and lumber, sending lethal splinters flying among the crew and sharpshooters. "We then opened a frightful rifle-fire on them just as a bomb exploded in our midst and hit many," Faust reported. He, and many of his fellow Germans, became casualties. "H. Sippel dead, and R. Haas seriously wounded. Sylvester Simon, Wilhelm Simon, Fritz Penshorn also were hit by splinters but only slightly.

This Harper's Weekly *image depicts the ramming of the USS* Harriet Lane *by the CSS* Neptune. *What followed next was a point-black gun battle. The damaged CSS* Bayou City *is barely visible in the haze beyond. Naval Historical Center.*

I was hit on the chest by a wood splinter and sank unconscious to the floor," he later recounted. Shrugging off the blow, the wounded *Neptune* closed the distance and slammed hard into the side of the Yankee ship, ten feet behind its starboard paddlewheel, heeling the vessel from the impact and driving it free from the mud.[21]

The struggle between the two crews now began in earnest. The men of the 7th Texas Cavalry fired steadily at every target aboard the Union vessel while Rebel boarding parties tried unsuccessfully to grapple and secure the prize as it drifted lazily away. Union Commander Jonathan M. Wainwright moved around the deck, rallying his sailors until Confederate bullets cut him down. The two ships were in a dilemma. They were too far apart for boarding, but close enough that small arms drove the gunners from the cannons of the superior Union ship. The USS *Owasco,* steaming forward to rescue the *Harriet Lane,* broke the deadlock when its gunners began to find the range, hurling round after round at the *Neptune.*

Meanwhile Sangster discovered that his vessel was sinking. Water poured in through the Rebel steamer's mangled bow and cannon wounds, and he knew he could not make another stab at the *Harriet Lane.* As the surface of the bay churned from enemy cannon fire, the

Lieutenant John Guest, skipper aboard the USS Owasco, *quickly realized that the* Harriet Lane *was in trouble and ordered his vessel to close with the Confederates despite the bullets skittering through the rigging and across his deck. His ship drove off the* Neptune *and appeared to save the day. Author's Collection.*

commander of the *Neptune* ordered his crew to back his sinking vessel away from the *Harriet Lane* and into the shallows off 32nd Street. As the *Neptune* retreated, a point blank shot from one of the *Lane's* 9-inch Dahlgrens blew a huge hole in the cottonclad's bow, causing it to plow water below deck and founder near shore.[22]

With one ship sinking and the other crippled, the Confederate naval attack, like its shore-side counterpart, seemed to be a total loss. "A round of cheers went up on board the *Harriet Lane*, and her men threw their caps into the air with joy, supposing all was ended," a Union veteran remembered.[23]

Lubbock, however, was determined to make another dash at the Federal ship before accepting defeat. The crew of the *Bayou City* cleared its damaged wheel of debris and turned the vessel around, stoking its fires for a renewal of the contest. At the same time, the *Harriet Lane's* jubilant crew returned to their battle stations and attempted to haul in the anchor and free the ship to maneuver. The short violent dash by the resurrected *Bayou City* surprised the Yankee gun crews, who managed to fire only one round at the onrushing cottonclad, sending a solid shot through its wheel house without effect. One hundred yards away, sharpshooters aboard the stricken *Neptune* renewed their firing at the *Harriet Lane* even as saltwater rolled across their gunboat's lowest deck. These Texan Enfields once again scattered the Yankee bluejackets, allowing the *Bayou City* to finish her run unmolested. "While the *Neptune* was going to the bottom," Private Bill Davidson of the 5th Texas Cavalry recalled, "the fate of the day rested on the shoulders of Bagby and his followers. Had their fire slackened one moment, the *Bayou City* could not have turned, and victory would have perched upon the Federal banner."[24]

A Union officer drew this image of the CSS Bayou City *making her second attack on the USS* Harriet Lane *while the CSS* Neptune *limps off in the background. Nestell Collection, Nimitz Library, U.S. Naval Academy, Annapolis, Maryland.*

A deafening crash and tremendous jolt signaled the impact as the ship drove into the port paddlewheel of the Federal vessel. Deck debris tumbled to the right as the stricken ship heeled over from the collision, groaning timbers buckling and breaking as the twisted wheel braces of the *Harriet Lane* impaled the Confederate steamer, locking the antagonists together. Lubbock had finally stuck the *Harriet Lane* a solid blow.[25]

Now, Tom Green's Texans finished the work as they boarded the Federal ship. Cutlass in hand, Smith appeared on the bow of the *Bayou City,* hurried over to the Yankee ship's netting, and cut it free. Clambering over the rail, he looked back and called for his men to follow, then turned to shoot the dying Union commander Wainwright through the forehead at close range, ending that officer's suffering. Rebel gun crews and sharpshooters rushed forward, downing the rest of the net as they tumbled onto the deck of the *Harriet Lane.*

The steamer was strangely silent. Its deck was gouged and scarred from hundreds of Rebel bullets. On the bridge, the Yankee skipper lay mangled; in addition to the bullet in his head, three others had ripped his frock coat, and three had pierced his thigh. Lea was nearby, dying from five bullet wounds to his abdomen. Three other crewmen, two with head wounds and another with his belly peppered by buckshot, lay sprawled and motionless. A Federal sailor meekly stepped out from behind a door, held up his hands, and surrendered the ship. The growing light of morning allowed the spectators on shore to see the entire episode. "The pride of the

Galveston resident George Grover drew what he saw of the battle from town. The Neptune *is swamped to the left; the* Bayou City *and* Harriet Lane *are locked in battle, and the* Owasco *is closing from the right. Rosenberg Library, Galveston, Texas.*

Yankee Navy," crowed Cupples from his third-story roost in town, "was the prize of our Cow-boys."[26]

The pause that followed the ship's capture was short lived as the other Union ship commanders realized what had happened and moved to recapture the *Harriet Lane.* The USS *Owasco,* its bow cannon already firing vigorously, steamed along the Galveston wharves and turned slightly to starboard, one half-mile from the Rebel ships. A powerful 11-inch Dahlgren amidships, already the bane of the men on shore, swung around and fired at the captured vessel, one round smashing a sizable hole in the *Harriet Lane's* stern.[27] The Rebel riflemen scrambled for cover while their gunners attempted to bring the *Harriet Lane's* cannon to bear on the *Owasco,* only to discover that the ship was listing too greatly from the ram attack to be useful now. Sensing the hopelessness of the situation, soldiers of Green's regiment abandoned their own flimsy steamboat for the more substantial but crowded revenue cutter, making a great target for the Federal guns. Furiously, Lubbock demanded that Green prevent the panicked men from deserting the *Bayou City* and leaving it defenseless.

The crew of the *Owasco* fired wildly, trying to scare the Texans away from their prey while protecting their captured comrades from friendly fire. The tactic might have worked save for the fact that the two ships were impaled together, and the Texans could not have run even if they wanted to. Instead, the Rebels grew desperate. "Tom Green's headquarters on that occasion . . . was in front, where the bullets fell thickest," a soldier remembered. The Texan colonel shouted to his men, "Come on boys, and we'll whip them now." Green's heroics rallied about half of his command, who opened a rapid and deadly fire against the *Owasco,* giving it the same treatment they had given the *Harriet Lane.* As bullets whistled through the Union ship's rigging, one Texan noted that "the crowd of men on the *Owasco's* decks seemed to melt like snow under a summer's sun." Smith ordered that the captured crew of the *Harriet Lane* be brought on deck and placed in clear sight of the Union gunners. The commander of the *Owasco,* unwilling to endanger his comrades, and with his gun crews wounded around him, quickly ordered that his engines be reversed and that the vessel be backed out of the range of the deadly Rebel rifles and the treacherous channel to safer water.[28]

The battle again reached a strange stalemate, and a lull settled over the bay. Confederate soldiers hung a white flag from the stern of their prize, but Union ships and soldiers remained present and deadly. Lubbock, a daring bluff in mind, ordered a yawl and crew to carry him toward the enemy fleet under flag of truce, with an officer from the *Harriet Lane* along for the journey. He first approached the USS *Owasco* and asked for the senior commander of the Federal fleet; he was directed toward the USS *Clifton* and its commander, Lieutenant Commander Richard Law. Upon being taken aboard and escorted to a stateroom, Lubbock boldly demanded the surrender of the remaining Union vessels, giving the Federals three hours to decide. The terms of the truce seemed remarkable. Lubbock declared that one Union vessel would be allowed to carry away all the fleet's crews, but the remaining ships and property would be surrendered to the Confederacy. Law agreed to carry the demand to Renshaw, still aboard the grounded *Westfield* out at Pelican Spit.[29]

Lubbock left the *Clifton* and directed his launch toward Kuhn's Wharf. There he met Union colonel Isaac Burrell and explained the naval situation. The Union infantry's great victory appeared to be in jeopardy. Burrell asked for clarification on the terms of the truce and requested to communicate with the vessels of the fleet. Lubbock re-

An image of the fight, with a few embellishments. Frank Leslie's Illustrated Newspaper.

fused but introduced him to General Scurry at the foot of the wharf. As these officers conferred about the changed circumstances, Lubbock headed toward Magruder's headquarters to report.

Down the street the Texans understood that if their bluff failed, they would need the *Harriet Lane* ready to attack the Union fleet, and the truce allowed the Rebels an opportunity to try to untangle the ship from the *Bayou City*. The *John F. Carr*, held in reserve during the battle, attempted without success to drag away the cottonclad. In desperation, commanders ordered the steamboat to simply drag both stricken vessels to the 27th Street Wharf, where men from Green's regiment attempted to rock the boats apart by gathering on the bow. Rebel officers soon concluded that the services of several carpenters and skilled mechanics would be required to straighten out the mess.[30]

The cease-fire also allowed soldiers, surgeons, and hospital stewards to begin the bloody work of gathering and tending the wounded. Near Kuhn's Wharf, a dozen casualties awaited stretchers. Along the Strand, artillerymen with a wide variety of gory canister and grapeshot wounds awaited treatment. Confused clusters of men wandered about, looking for friends among the casualties. Horse-drawn ambulances clattered along, stopping at various points to load casualties. A burial detail, eager to dispose of one shot-mangled corpse, closed up the hole they had dug on the tip of the island.[31]

Twenty-four hours after they had parted, the "Rangers of the Sea" were reunited with the "Rangers of the Prairie," and they started to count brigade casualties. At the 27th Street Wharf, soldiers from the 5th Texas Cavalry carried friends from the *Bayou City*, placing them beside comrades wounded in the city streets. Nineteen-year-old John Hogsett had received his first wound at Val Verde, New Mexico. He had later been captured and then paroled. Now he took a stretcher ride to the hospital at the Ursuline Convent. Lieutenant J. H. Alexander of Palestine had also been wounded at Val Verde, when he was a private. After three promotions and a promising military career, he was taken off the gunboat to be buried. Aboard the *Neptune*, the bodies of eight men from Anderson County, more than half the volunteer squad from Company I, 7th Texas Cavalry, were placed into boats to be carried to shore. Soldiers also removed the splinter-filled body of a German sergeant from New Braunfels. Thirty-three men had been killed or wounded in that regiment alone.[32]

Those unhurt in Sibley's brigade clustered together and congratulated themselves on surviving another fight. "The heroes of Val Verde, Glorieta, Johnson's Ranch, Albuquerque, and Peralta met together at the water's edge," remembered a soldier, "and with one long, loud yell, wrote Galveston on their bullet-torn banner."[33]

Observing the Union ships moving further out into the bay under flags of truce, and sensing that he could no longer count on their support, Burrell surrendered his men to Scurry. At Kuhn's Wharf, the 258 men of the 42nd Massachusetts emerged from behind their solid barricades and marched down the Strand in a column of fours, Burrell in the lead. "When all was ready we were marched off the wharf into the city and among the crowds of rebel soldiers," recorded Private George Fiske of Company D. "I say crowds for they have no ranks–everyone fighting on his own hook like so many Indians."[34]

Galveston resident James E. Bourke rode in a rowboat amid the tumult of battle and sketched this panoramic account of the fight, showing all of its phases. To the left, the USS Clifton *steams near Fort Point, adding its guns to the battle. In the center foreground lies Pelican Island, with the barracks buildings clearly visible. To the left near the channel marker is the supply ship* Cavallo. *Below near the supply dock is the coal bark* Elias Pike, *while the transports* Mary Boardman *and* Saxon *ride at anchor and the USS* Westfield *rests aground to the right. At the top of the image, fighting rages near Kuhn's Wharf where the* Corypheus *and* Sachem *offer close support. Confederate artillery, some located in second-story windows, pound away at the Federal infantry position while some take cover at the cotton press at the base of the wharf. The USS* Owasco *can be seen steaming to the rescue of the* Harriet Lane, *which is set upon by three Confederate cottonclads. Besides the* Neptune *and* Bayou City, *the artist may have included the* John F. Carr *trying to separate the tangled combatants. Rosenberg Library, Galveston, Texas.*

The young man from Medford, Massachusetts, was amazed at the look of the soldiers now claiming triumph, and he marveled at their ersatz equipment. "They had all kinds of arms . . . but the most curious thing about them was their dress," he wrote. "There were no uniforms, but everyone was dressed in home-made clothes. Some were decked out with tassels and feathers like so many indians, and take them together, they appeared like a party

In this detail from George Grover's sketch, details of the CSS Bayou City *reveals a warship easily mistaken for an ironclad ram in the fog, smoke, and haze of battle. Notice the* corvus *boarding plank jutting upward from the cottonclad's deck. Rosenberg Library, Galveston, Texas.*

of savages. Many of them wore blankets which were of all colors and descriptions. Some had only a piece of old carpeting tied on with a string, and some were of nicer material." They looked like ruffians, he thought, compared to the tidy Yankees: "The greater part of them had long hair reaching to their shoulders. Their hats were also of all shapes and sizes, from the deerskin scull cap, to the one-and-a-half-foot brim straw hat. Many had on moccasins instead of shoes."[35]

The Texans could not restrain their delight at having captured the Bay State men. "They were wild with joy at the result of the battle," Fiske noted. "We were the first troops which had landed in their state, and they had captured us at the first attempt. To this I think we owe our kind treatment. How they cheered! None of our good, old yankee hurrahs however, but a sort of war whoop, and on every side resound-

This Harper's Weekly *image of the destruction of the USS* Westfield *accurately shows four Confederate cottonclads, the captured USS* Harriet Lane, *the tender* Royal Yacht, *and the two coaling vessels* Cavallo *and* Elias Pike. *It also shows the tragedy of the sailors killed in the explosion and the debris that would shower Galveston's streets.*

ed their wild, triumphant 'Yah-hoo.' 'Happy New Year' shouted some one. Yes, happy to you but not particularly to us we thought."[36]

In addition to this column others made their way out of the city. Bearers carried the half-dozen blue-coated casualties to waiting carriages. Another group of prisoners marched up 27th Street: the dejected crewman from the *Harriet Lane*.[37]

Aboard the *Westfield* Renshaw was thunderstruck at Lubbock's gutsy demand. Further, given the nature of the proposed terms, perhaps the *Bayou City* was not a cottonclad but an ironclad ram, similar to others guarding harbors around the Confederacy. Certainly only such a monster could have captured the *Harriet Lane*. Renshaw could not be certain what he faced, and the hazy morning light had not clarified the issue. To be safe, he issued orders designed to protect the rest of his command, and he planned to investigate the rumors from the security of the gulf, thus denying the Rebels any additional gains. By mid-morning, with the deadline for the truce approaching, he ordered his fleet to run. He would return to recapture Galveston another day.

The USS *Westfield* would not join the retreat. Renshaw ordered that his grounded flagship be abandoned and directed that a slow match be applied to its magazine. He was among the last to board one of the ship's boats to be rowed to a nearby transport. Nearing safety, Renshaw listened impatiently for the death blast of his former ship. Instead, only silence. Convinced that the match had burned out, the commodore ordered that the rowboat be turned around. The boat came alongside the flagship, and its crew made fast as Renshaw climbed back onto the deck. At almost that same moment, a titanic blast blew apart the commodore and twelve of his crew. Debris from the cataclysm showered the bay and dropped among the Galveston's battle-littered streets more than a mile away.

Before the explosion Lubbock and Green had rowed back to the USS *Owasco* and boarded to learn the decision of the Union navy regarding surrender. The answer came when the ship, still flying a flag of truce, began moving toward the Gulf of Mexico. This was a clear violation of the truce terms, and Lubbock and Green demanded to see Law. When the *Owasco* hove to with the *Clifton*, the Confederates renewed their tirade. Nonplussed, Law offered to take the Texans to see Renshaw, whom everyone assumed was safely aboard one of the transports, but maintained *Owasco*'s steady progress toward the open sea. Lubbock and Green changed their tack and insisted on being permitted to leave. Law assented, slowing down enough for them to board their own boat and cast off before continuing his retreat.

The skipper of the USS Clifton, *Lieutenant Commander Richard L. Law was the ranking surviving officer of Renshaw's squadron and was left holding the bag for the disaster. This distinguished Connecticut-born officer faced a court-martial and was relieved of rank and duty for the rest of the war. Officials later reassigned him and promoted him to commander and later captain. Law retired from the navy in 1886. State House Press.*

Uncertain of the import of the dramatic explosion coming from Pelican Island, and unaware of Renshaw's fate, the Union fleet followed his last orders and headed for the gulf. Upon arriving back at shore Lubbock and Green bellowed orders for the Rebel artillerymen to hurry back to their posts, unlimber their guns, and make what effort they could to stop the Federal exodus. These gunners, however, could do little more than register their smoky protest as the Yankee ships headed to safety. The last of the Union gunboats, the schooner *Corypheus,* put its sheets to the wind and escaped as well, a violation of orders by its Union master who had received word to burn the boat and spike its guns.[38]

Smith believed he could do more, and he ordered all available Confederate ships to pursue. Men from Sibley's Brigade, milling by the 27th Street Wharf, hustled aboard the *John F. Carr* as that flimsy steamer cast off and gathered steam. This unarmored Rebel paddle-wheeler, adding more fuel to its fires, attempted to build up as much speed as possible; the last of the Union ships, however, had already cleared the bar at the mouth of the harbor. The *Carr*'s skipper wisely ended the chase as ocean waves splashed over the boat's lower deck, threatening to flood it.[39] The Union ships escaped, but their unbroken string of successes now lay unraveled. Six hours after it had started, the Battle of Galveston ended.[40]

CHAPTER NINETEEN

THE
TURNING TIDE

The coast of Texas is . . . free.
Governor Francis R. Lubbock

The exploded carcass of the *Westfield*, out on Pelican Spit, sputtered as the remnants of the vessel burned along the waterline. Flotsam bobbed on the surface of Galveston Bay, and debris lay scattered for miles, testimony to the surprising and violent end of the warship. It, like the hopes of a Union reoccupation of Texas, had been wrecked by the Confederate victory at Galveston. John Magruder's bold attack convinced Confederates across the country that hope remained for their eventual success and that the gloomy days of early 1862 had, a year later, been replaced by dash and daring that would eventually win the day. For every victory won by Union arms and iron, Confederates would counter with imagination and enterprise. In time, Federal war planners and politicians would realize the futility of armed coercion and would negotiate a peace. Confederates everywhere took heart that New Year's Day.

Any settlement of the war would come at a price, as the residents of Galveston realized. The streets of their city had been marked by war. Large caliber shot littered the roads. Unexploded shells lay half-buried in the dirt; furrows from heavy rounds cut across the boulevards. Grapeshot and pieces of canister liberally covered the ground. Spent bullets, ripped cartridge paper, and the ephemeral leavings of war were everywhere, but especially around Kuhn's Wharf. Rebel field pieces rested amid the rubble. Limbers and guns sat idle, secreted behind walls and in hedges where their crews or others had dragged them. Buildings along the Strand stood in shambles. For blocks into the city, naval artillery had knocked apart frame houses, widely scattering the debris. The U.S. customs house, completed in 1860 but never occupied, had been wrecked by several direct hits. Projectiles had mangled Perry's Foundry and the Merchants Cotton Press, along with its nearby sheds, where Colonel Joseph J. Cook's storming party had sought refuge. The battle-scarred city had become a symbol for the war-torn nation, now nearly two years into its calamity.[1]

In addition to the morale boost Magruder's victory provided, the physical fruits of the Confederate win at Galveston were impressive. The Eastern Sub-District of Texas gained a welcome bounty of abandoned Federal equipment, including several vessels left by the Federals in their haste to escape. Near the edge of the city Confederate sailors boarded the schooner *Lecompte* and posted a guard. A mile further east along the island the supply boat *Cavallo,* loaded with coal and general merchandise, surrendered. Her three-man crew and a contract merchant offered no resistance. At Pelican Spit Texan officers eyed the battery scattered among the shattered hulk of the *Westfield* hoping to salvage these cannons and add them to the defenses of the city. The crew of the Rebel steamboat *John F. Carr* grappled the anchored supply ship *Elias Pike* and sent aboard a crew.[2]

The battle had been intense, and surgeons and first sergeants from both armies continued the task of counting their casualties. Sibley's Brigade alone suffered seventeen men killed and twenty-eight wounded, some mortally. The other Confederate forces engaged lost ten men killed and another hundred wounded. Federal gunfire killed one civilian in the city and wounded two volunteer sailors from Houston. The

U.S. Navy had also bled. Five Union sailors died aboard the *Harriet Lane,* and an additional twelve were wounded. Sixteen sailors became casualties aboard the *Owasco.* Renshaw and the doomed dozen had gone up with the *Westfield.* The *Clifton* and the *Sachem* each lost one man. Like so many casualties on so many fields over the past twenty months, these dead and wounded became abstractions—the devil's math—in a titanic conflict.[3]

Specific incidents carried with them the tragic symbolism of the war as a whole. Aboard the *Harriet Lane* Lieutenant Commander Edward Lea lay dying on the deck while his father, Major Albert M. Lea, served on shore as an engineer on Magruder's staff. Hearing of his son's distress, the elder Lea came to his side, then sought an ambulance to carry his boy to a hospital. Before the conveyance could be located, the boy expired, breathing out the phrase, "my father is here," as he died.[4]

On the morning after the battle, the importance of the Confederate victory became clear when the Federal steamer *Cambria,* carrying Colonel Edmund Jackson Davis and the 1st Texas Cavalry, appeared in the gulf. On board were several hundred Texan Unionists, with arms and equipment for yet another Federal regiment to be raised from sympathizers in the state.[5] With Galveston as a base, the Yankee soldiers had planned to raid the interior, much like Butler had done after the fall of New Orleans. If they had arrived a few days earlier, Davis's rifles might have influenced the outcome of the battle and kept Galveston in Union control, allowing Federal reconstruction to begin in Texas.[6]

Indeed, the missed opportunities seemed to compound themselves. The Mississippi had nearly been taken six months before, but now the Confederates had a stronger hold on it than ever. Galveston had briefly been a beacon to Unionists in Texas and a ray of hope to politicians in Washington. Just a few months earlier many southerners believed themselves whipped, but now they felt invincible.

Instead of arriving as liberators, Davis and his men simply reminded Confederate Texans what lay at stake at Galveston. Magruder decided to lure the *Cambria* into the bay, complete his victory, and snuff out the symbol of Unionist sentiment. With luck he would add this excellent iron steamer and a renegade Texas regiment to his haul. To perfect the ruse, the U.S. flag floated atop the *Harriet Lane* and another flapped from the customs house to give the appearance that Galveston was still under Union control. Officers on the Yankee ship, convinced of their safety, lowered a boat and dispatched men to find a harbor pilot willing to guide them to the island; Confederates captured these sailors at gunpoint when the launch reached the wharf. Rebels jumped into the boat and rowed back out with a pilot to try to lead the unsuspecting enemy into the bay.

Magruder ordered that the *Harriet Lane* be loaded with riflemen, with its fires raised, in case the operation was compromised. Volunteers from Sibley's Brigade took their places aboard the ship, eager to take another jab at the enemy, but engineers could not fix its damaged wheels. The troops then hustled over to one of the captured sailing vessels, wasting valuable time boarding a boat that would probably never catch up to the Yankee steamer if it were to smoke out Magruder's ambush. By the time the jittery Rebels were ready to sally forth, the crew of the *Cambria* had already brought the bogus pilot on board. Instead of yet another *coup de main*, thorough questioning by vigilant Union officers uncovered the Rebel plot, and the *Cambria* steamed back to sea, the would be Rebel saboteurs now captives.[7]

The Rebels netted prisoners that day as well. One of the Union sailors captured in the Union pilot boat was a deserter, "Nicaraugua" Smith, from a Texas regiment at Galveston. The island's Rebel garrison turned out for his execution the next day. "We were formed in a hollow square," Fred Wade remembered. "Smith was blindfolded and placed on his coffin and the order 'Fire!' was given." The condemned man braced upon the impact of the bullets, then jerked the blindfold from his eyes before falling dead. "We were a mad lot of boys," Wade remembered. This was the first execution most had witnessed, and many felt squeamish over the affair. "Our officers seemed to say 'see what happens to a deserter.'"[8]

Magruder knew that the Federals would be back in force, so he brought slaves to the city to build earthworks and redoubts. Commodore Leon Smith issued another call for sailors, and a number of Sibley's Brigade responded, hoping to avoid odious chores including supervising slaves or even working a shovel themselves; when the *Harriet Lane* underwent her test run, the repairs to the captured warship did not hold and the vessel limped back to dock. On January 7 the blockade of Galveston resumed with the arrival of the USS *Brooklyn.* Two days later that ship and two others shelled the newly erected forts guarding the beach, but with little effect. [9]

The victory at Galveston emboldened Confederate garrisons at other points on the Texas coast. On January 8, 1863, a detail of ten men from Speight's Battalion struck at the Union fleet near the Sabine Pass lighthouse, burning the small side wheel steamer *Dan,* which had been used as a gunboat by the Federals since its capture in the Calcasieu River. "Heavy mist and fog veiled our movements, and in two hours she was left a wreck on the mudflat," wrote Sergeant H. N. Connor. Surprisingly, the other Union ships on hand kept their distance. "The balance of the fleet instead of coming to her aid, put to sea."[10]

The tremors from the Battle of Galveston also thundered through New Orleans, forcing Federal planners into a deep depression. Lieutenant Colonel David Hunter Strother paid a Sunday visit to the USS *Hartford* and "found Admiral Farragut in the dumps about the Galveston affair. His professional pride seemed to be touched and he has ordered a court of inquiry." When he learned the details of the debacle, Strother noted that the *Harriet Lane* could become a menace in the western Gulf while it was in Rebel hands. He also sized up the parties responsible for the disaster. "This affair seems to indicate overconfidence on the part of the naval officers," he noted. "It was certainly well done and well planned by the Confederates."[11]

Even the normally optimistic Nathaniel P. Banks was gloomy, and he predicted that the Union would fail in its efforts to suppress the rebellion. "The General seems to be low-spirited this morning and begins to accept the certainty of the fall of the Republic," Strother wrote. The pessimism spread, as Strother noted: "I do not see myself what ground there is for hope. The confident tone of the Northern press is gone, and the Southern papers are filled with accounts of victories." The staff officer blamed the bungling of the war department and the Lincoln government for these failures. "So the blind Polyphemus, after wasting his strength in gigantic but misdirected efforts to strike the enemy, will lie down and die," he wrote. "What is to come after his death, who can imagine."[12]

By contrast, the news from Texas buoyed confidence across the Confederacy. Magruder received the thanks of Congress, and the names of the principal players became common knowledge in the halls of Richmond. Magruder enthusiastically reported to Governor Francis R. Lubbock that "the coast of Texas is . . . free." There was no longer a Union threat from that quarter. In addition Magruder proudly noted that the Union ships dispatched to reestablish the blockade of the state were first-rate vessels, not the inferior vessels of the past few months, indicating the enemy's newfound esteem for the Texans. These ships, Magruder added, "keep a respectful distance from our shores."[13]

The next phase in the war would require more men, and none were so sought after as Sibley's wandering brigade. A few days after the Battle of Galveston, General Theophilus Holmes's official reply to Magruder arrived in regard to the mid-December query regarding Sibley's men. Holmes simply stated that Magruder had no authority to keep Sibley's men in Texas—the order to send them to Louisiana had come directly from Richmond. Magruder responded cheerfully, relishing the chance to detail the fight at Galveston and assuring his superior that the Texans would soon be on their way to Richard Taylor. "I shall spare no efforts to facilitate the departure of Sibley's brigade," he wrote. "Should the lieutenant-general wish them ordered elsewhere they can be diverted to any other point after reaching New Iberia."[14]

Shortly after this exchange a message arrived for Magruder from the office of President Jefferson Davis that subtlety validated the nearly insubordinate course he had taken. "The boldness of the conception and the daring and skill of its execution were crowned by results substantial as well as splendid," Davis wrote. "Your success has been a heavy blow to the enemy's hopes, and I trust will be vigorously and effectively followed up." The president had another suggestion, perhaps with the military squabbling over Sibley's Brigade in mind: "It is hoped that your prudence and tact will be as successful in allaying domestic discontents as your military ability in retrieving our position

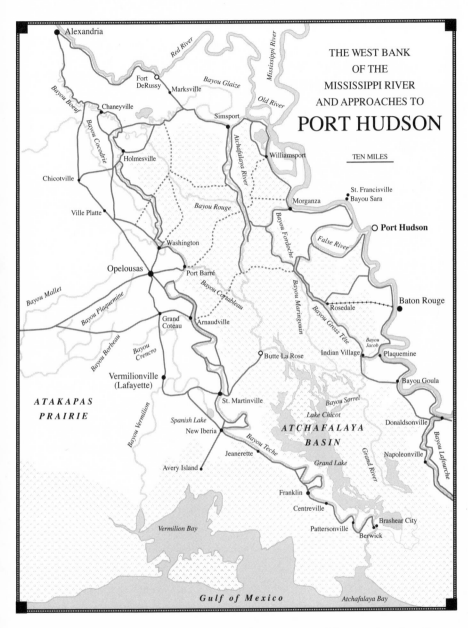

THE WEST BANK
OF THE
MISSISSIPPI RIVER
AND APPROACHES TO

PORT HUDSON

TEN MILES

on the Texas coast." The victory at Galveston would energize the Confederate war effort on the lower Mississippi.[15]

While he waited for his brigade, General Henry Hopkins Sibley settled into his new command on the banks of the Mississippi and assessed his options from his headquarters at Rosedale. His scouts reported troubling news from across the river. In Baton Rouge a fire had gutted the majestic state capital building, leaving the faux castle a ruin of collapsed towers and crenellated walls. The Federal forces in town claimed it was an accident, and it most likely was. Even so, the capitol's destruction seemed like an omen of future destruction for suffering Louisiana. To his credit, Sibley worked aggressively at keeping Federals off his bank of the Mississippi with the tools he had at hand. Observers would watch the Union garrison at Baton Rouge, making notes regarding the passage of Federal vessels up and down the river. Sibley opened a correspondence with newly arrived General Franklin Gardner at Port Hudson—who by coincidence had assumed command just that week. These two newcomers, Gardner and Sibley, would share intelligence and perhaps even troops as they protected the southern gate to what remained of the Confederate Mississippi River.[16]

The terrain in Sibley's department, like most of southern Louisiana, was composed of bayou and swamp. In the north lay the convoluted but critical junction of the Red and the Atchafalaya rivers, the waters of which poured into an ox-bow outlet called Old River before oozing, sediment heavy, into the Mississippi. The rough hamlet of Simsport, just a few miles from this point, marked the only settlement in the area worthy of the term. One road followed the course of the Old River to the Mississippi then turned south, generally running along its western banks all the way to Algiers, opposite New Orleans, passing Port Hudson and Baton Rouge, across the river, en route.

A secondary road ran along the banks of the Atchafalaya river more than thirty miles. Another road intersected it two-thirds of the way south and led from Morganza on the Mississippi some dozen miles east to Port Barré, about twenty miles southwest toward Opelousas and Washington. Off this road another track ran south along the course of Bayou Fordoche to Bayou Grosse Tête. This stream and a road next to it ran parallel to the Mississippi just fifteen miles to the east. Rosedale lay twenty miles south along this route, and ten miles further south was the Chitimacha Indian village. Here, Bayou Plaquemine and a road along its margins led to the river town of Plaquemine. Beyond the Indian village, the road continued along the Grosse Tête

The burned-out shell of the Louisiana capitol, standing like a metaphor for the course of the war on the lower Mississippi. State Library of Louisiana.

until near where that waterway intersected Grand River, the eastern branch of the meandering Atchafalaya. At this junction, Bayou Sorrel split away, leading west, toward Grand Lake. The road ended its southerly course here, in a swamp, and turned east toward the Mississippi, striking it at the town of Bayou Goula. Locals had worked out myriad cut offs and shortcuts to navigate the various swamps and bayous of the region, but all were subject to seasonal inundations. It was ideal country for mounted raids and partisan warfare; for wagons and artillery, it was a nightmare.

This marginal country also harbored a secret. For decades steamboat pilots, barge polers, and pirogue owners knew of an unobvious route connecting Louisiana's western Attakapas Prairie parishes to the Mississippi. Starting at Port Barré near Opelousas, waterborne travelers could move east-southeast down Bayou Cortableau to the Atchfalaya and south down that stream past Butte-a-la-Rose to Grand Lake. Here, instead of heading down to Berwick Bay and the Gulf of Mexico, clever pilots could navigate a tortuous tangle of bayous at the Lake Chicot bulb at the north end of Grand Lake, emerge into Bayou Sorrell, pass east-northeast up that stream to its confluence with Grand River, travel left—north—up Bayou Gross Tête to Bayou Plaquemine, and make a right turn at the Chitimacha village for a seven-mile float to the Mississippi. Pilots found this route tortured, dangerous, and full of snags, but a great way to shave hundreds of miles off a trip from Opelousas to New Orleans. Only a seasoned river man could navigate its confusing maze.

The Federals realized the value of this strip of land between Bayou Gross Tête and the Mississippi, and Union detachments had already occupied most of the river towns on the west banks below Baton Rouge, with gunboats hovering nearby. Within days of Sibley's arrival the first collision of opposing troops in the department east of the Atchafalaya occurred at one of these outposts. Captain Solon Perkins, commanding Company B, 2nd Massachusetts Cavalry Battalion, and already a seasoned veteran of the Department of the Gulf, tangled with Sibley's pickets on December 29 between Plaquemine and the Indian village. Perkins, operating from a base at Bayou Goula and renowned among the people in the region for his ability to fight partisans and guerillas, knew that the Confederates had changed the balance of power along Bayou Gross Tête and that they had probed south to learn what they could. The Massachusetts horsemen skirmished with Sibley's newcomers, but Perkins quickly realized his men were too few and prudently withdrew. The Federals fell back to the Mississippi and signaled a nearby gunboat, the five-gun USS *Katahdin* under Lieutenant Commander F. A. Roe, to heave to for a conference.[17]

The two officers decided on a joint course of action. Perkins wanted to lure the Rebels into a fight then let the navy's lethal guns pound them into mush when they came within range. "This I shall do," agreed Roe. "We have a series of signals agreed upon to operate in conjunction. We shall harass the rebels, and if possible entrap them into a disaster." Roe pondered what this enemy build-up foreshadowed, fearing that a serious raid in the region would spread fear among its residents. "Appearances seem to indicate that the Rebels are meditating a descent," he wrote. Rebel scouts and guerillas had already begun intimidating the local planters. "All those who have taken the oath of allegiance to the United States are threatened with hanging and instant death." Before he and Perkins rallied against the Rebels, Roe requested infantry to reinforce the post at Plaquemine, just in case the enemy pushed their advantage.[18]

The arrival of three companies of the 162nd New York at Plaquemine two days later, on the evening of December 31, 1862, marked the furthest advance to date by Union occupiers on the west bank of the Mississippi in Louisiana. To concentrate Federal strength, Perkins and his horsemen moved up from their base at Bayou Goula to meet the foot soldiers, who arrived at midnight that same evening. The dawn of New Year's Day found Major James Bogart of New York, now in command of the small force, struggling with issues unique to service in Louisiana. "I . . . ask full instructions in regard to citizens," he wrote. "They are mostly of French extraction. Some have taken the oath and some not." There was also the issue of slaves who, as elsewhere in the South, saw the day of their liberty finally at hand with the arrival of U.S. troops. Bogart again needed guidance. "In regard to contrabands," he wrote, "my course so far has been to keep them on their plantations and allow them in no case to gather in the town."[19]

By January 3, Perkins, Bogart, and Roe had accumulated an impressive array of troubling news concerning Confederate intentions. Bogart, new to the service and jumpy from the alien surroundings and the unclear mission, had kept his men on alert for hours. "Information received from citizens, contrabands, and especially from my own cavalry scouts, led me to expect an attack," he wrote. He also knew he was facing a force under Confederate general Sibley estimated to include at least one regiment of infantry, two pieces of artillery, and about five hundred cavalry—a guess close to the mark. He was less certain, though, if these men were the much-feared veterans of New Mexico or some other forces. The Confederates had been probing his lines for the last few nights, leading the USS *Katahdin* to shell the woods beyond Plaquemine as an after dark routine. The only casualties from these noisy probes and responses came when a short fuse caused a naval round to burst over the Federal positions, killing a New York sergeant and wounding two enlisted men.[20]

The next day a second Union gunboat arrived, but Bogart and his Federal forces ashore lost their nerve. "During the morning contrabands came in from Bayou Jacob, Bayou Grosse Tête, and Grand River, all of whom reported the enemy's force much larger than they have been heretofore," he scribbled. Indeed, Gardner may have reinforced

Sibley with cavalry from Port Hudson. Federals on the lookout for Sibley's New Mexico veterans, though, misconstrued this build-up of forces as the arrival of the Texans in force, indicating major Confederate reinforcements. Even the normally steady Perkins believed the Union outpost at Plaquemine was in jeopardy, reporting his opinion that enemy force had grown to more than five thousand men with two batteries of artillery, all entrenched at the Indian village. Bogart requested reinforcements from Baton Rouge. When they failed to arrive within three hours, he ordered Plaquemine abandoned. Sibley had scared away his first opponent in Louisiana. He may have just missed an opportunity to gobble up an isolated Union outpost. Once again, Union forces gave ground.[21]

CHAPTER TWENTY

WHAT OUR FRIENDS MAY EXPECT

The echo of their cannon at Galveston ...
reverberated with glory along the Mississippi
Major General John Bankhead Magruder

The spate of defeats at the beginning of 1863 wearied the Federals. The successes of the previous year, it seemed, had been squandered. Not only had Vicksburg not fallen, but the Confederates had also retaken a length of the river and, by constructing the fortress at Port Hudson, had secured the Red River supply line of Texas beef and grain. What had been a long string of Union successes—the almost unopposed occupation of the Lower Mississippi and Texas—had now come to an abrupt reverse. Fortune seemed opposed to northern ambitions in January 1863.

Private Henry O. Gusley, formerly of the USS *Westfield*, knew something about bad luck. He had evacuated that ship—his home for more

After the disaster at Galveston, the USS Clifton *returned to New Orleans to deliver the bad news and to put in for repairs. Nestell Collection, Nimitz Library, U.S. Naval Academy, Annapolis, Maryland.*

than a year—during the fight at Galveston. He had also watched in horror as his beloved skipper, William Renshaw, and twelve of his comrades had been killed. Now he served aboard the USS *Clifton,* which had traveled to New Orleans for repairs before returning to service near Galveston. On January 10 the ferryboat arrived at its former station but faced an entirely changed situation when it tried to join the Union vessels there. "It being dark when we came upon the fleet lying there, we had some difficulty in making them believe we were really a 'Simon pure' Yankee craft," Gusley wrote. Across the dark waters of the Gulf of Mexico the marine heard drummers beating the crews of the five Federal ships to quarters, and he listened to the gun commanders issue orders to run the cannons into firing positions. For a few moments it looked as though the *Clifton* would fall victim to friendly fire. Despite this tension the nervous men aboard the Union warships eventually stood down. "We soon settled their suspicions," he scrawled, "and for the rest of the night we lay quietly at anchor."[1]

On Sunday, January 11, the Union flotilla off Galveston, eager to undo Magruder's work, readied for a general attack on the town scheduled for the next day. Sailors secured their ships while gun crews drilled at their pieces. This fleet would certainly not suffer the same fate as

Renshaw's little squadron, the Federals believed. The expedition's commander, Captain Henry H. Bell, had already fought his share of Confederates and would err on the side of caution. His flotilla had shelled Galveston the day before, and he learned that Confederate strength there continued to grow, with the emboldened Texans managing to skip a number of rounds beyond the Federal blockade line. Taking stock of that action, Bell planned to smother the newly emboldened southerners with his heavy guns before making a general advance into the bay.

Bell's flotilla claimed many advantages in size and strength. His flagship, USS *Brooklyn*, a large screw sloop, counted ten 9-inch Dahlgrens in each broadside and a crew of more than three hundred men. It was a veteran of Admiral Farragut's attempts against Vicksburg and operations on the Mississippi. The ship

North Carolinian Henry Haywood Bell was fleet captain in the West Gulf Blockading Squadron, one of Admiral Farragut's chief subordinates. Aboard his flagship, the USS Brooklyn, *he went personally to see what could be done to change the navy's luck in Texas waters. Naval Historical Center.*

and its experienced crew would lead the effort to retrieve Galveston. His second largest vessel was the USS *Hatteras*, a five-gun sidewheeler. The small wooden screw steamer *New London* carried five medium-weight guns. Alongside these would be the lighter draft "ninety-day" gunboats *Sciota* and *Cayuga*, each bearing a large 11-inch Dahlgren amidship. Bell believed that the *Brooklyn* could handle the shore batteries while the USS *Clifton* and the others ran past the sandbar and engaged the Confederate gunboats in the harbor.

That afternoon, lookouts aboard the various ships all sang out when sails appeared on the southwestern horizon, causing Bell to ponder his options. The newcomer was arriving from an unexpected quarter. Unsure of whether the ship might be a sizable blockade runner or perhaps Union reinforcements, Bell dispatched the *Hatteras* to investigate the stranger. Just after dark, he received a shocking answer.

Union commanders, already edgy about the defeat at Galveston, were caught off guard by the arrival of the CSS Alabama off the coast of Texas. The USS Hatteras paid the price, being nearly blown out of the water in mere minutes. Harper's Weekly.

The same bad luck that had stalked the Union naval leaders returned to make another jab. The stranger sighted by Bell's fleet was the legendary Confederate raider CSS *Alabama*. Its skipper, Raphael Semmes, had been tipped off to the opportunity of expanding Magruder's victory from accounts in captured Yankee newspapers. Citizens and soldiers alike climbed atop roofs in Galveston and peered from upper stories to watch as flashes began rippling out at sea. Bell, cloaked in a fog of distance and darkness, could not determine what was happening from his vantage point, so he ordered the *Brooklyn* and the *Sciota* to move away from Galveston and out to open water to investigate and await events. All too quickly the distant thunders and lurid flashes faded away, replaced once again by the sounds of surf and wind. A day later Bell learned that he had witnessed the rapid and remorseless destruction of the USS *Hatteras* by the guns of the CSS *Alabama*.[2]

With this fresh surprise, Union naval strategy in the western Gulf capsized. Bell realized that he simply did not have a complete enough picture of the Rebel capabilities to proceed with his assault. He had assumed that the Confederate capacity to resist was more than feeble but less than robust, and he wanted to crush it while he could. But if the unthinkable occurred—a coordinated Confederate naval offensive—with the *Alabama* attacking from the gulf while the *Harriet Lane, Neptune, Bayou City,* and whatever else Magruder had dredged up since sallied out of the bay, his squadron might be severely hurt. Any losses of Union ships were potential gains, from salvage or capture, for the Confederates. Additionally there remained, of course, the persistent rumor of a Texan ironclad. Bell prudently called off his attack and dispatched the *Clifton* to New Orleans with the bad tidings.

This blow caused Admiral David G. Farragut to become myopic. The admiral moved aggressively to restore the navy's prestige, ordering gunboats from Key West to New Orleans to swarm to Texas; perhaps they could corner the *Alabama* or the *Harriet Lane* and retrieve the situation. He also tried to thin out the squadrons operating on the Mississippi and the inland waterways, weakening Louisiana's defenses so that he could reinforce the navy on the Texas coast. For Commodore Thomas McKean Buchanan at Berwick Bay, this meant losing half his ships. General Nathaniel P. Banks protested loudly, insisting that he needed the steamers to protect Brashear City, provide communications in the region, and keep the Rebel gunboats on Grand Lake and Bayou Teche in check. Without them, the enemy would roll back all the gains of the previous year. Farragut relented but signaled that the ships were his to command and that Banks and Buchanan should know they might be ordered away on short notice.

To lessen the impact of such a blow, planners suggested the elimination of the Confederate ships lurking in the bayous, thus easing the threat from a Rebel raid or offensive. With Taylor's naval capability neutralized, Union warships could respond freely to whatever point in the theater appeared most threatened. The guns of Galveston had shaken awake the Union forces at Brashear City; now these Yankees once again went hunting for Rebels to spoil any plots aborning. In particular they wanted to destroy the CSS *Cotton*, not as part of a general advance as had occurred a few months earlier, but simply to cripple Confederate capabilities along Bayou Teche. Union officers in southern Louisiana, because of the Battle of Galveston, had a newfound respect for the enemy.

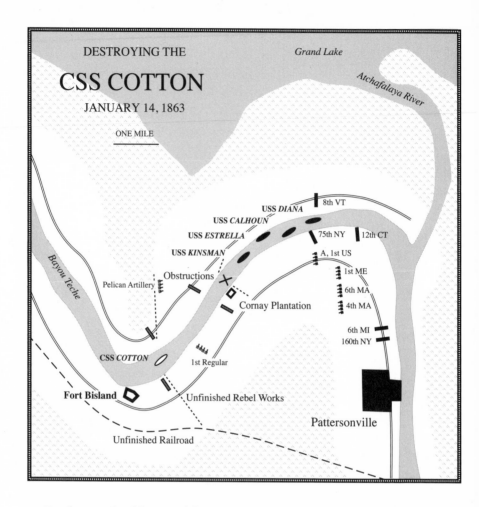

DESTROYING THE

CSS COTTON

JANUARY 14, 1863

ONE MILE

Grand Lake

Atchafalaya River

Bayou Teche

USS *DIANA*   8th VT

USS *CALHOUN*

USS *ESTRELLA*   75th NY   12th CT

USS *KINSMAN*   A, 1st US

Pelican Artillery   Obstructions   1st ME

Cornay Plantation   6th MA

4th MA

6th MI
160th NY

CSS *COTTON*   1st Regular

Pattersonville

Fort Bisland   Unfinished Rebel Works

Unfinished Railroad

Buchanan had learned from his earlier tangles with the Rebel boat that this operation would have to be a well-coordinated blow landed by both army and navy. In the dark morning hours of January 13, 1863, the men of General Godfrey Weitzel's Brigade boarded steamers and made their way to Pattersonville, where the infantry met artillery and cavalry that had traveled overland after being ferried across Berwick Bay. Daylight revealed six regiments of infantry, including the Lafourche Campaign veterans of the 12th Connecticut, 75th New York, 21st Indiana, and 8th Vermont. Two other regiments, the 6th Michigan and the 160th New York, came along as well. Battery A, 1st U.S., 1st Maine, 4th and 6th Massachusetts—four batteries of field artillery—added muscle to the strike force. Captain Richard Barrett's Company

B, 1st Louisiana Cavalry, scouted the country ahead. In the bayou sailors aboard Buchanan's four gunboats prepared to take another turn at skinning the *Cotton* while their comrades ashore kept the enemy pinned down and cowed on both banks.

That afternoon Weitzel's force moved to test the Confederates' strength. Driving the Rebels out of Pattersonville, blue-clad skirmishers advanced for another few miles before pulling up short, in full view of the CSS *Cotton* and its attending army. After a noisy but harmless exchange of cannon and small arms fire, the Federals withdrew, well informed of enemy strengths and dispositions. The whole Union array spent a rainy night at the confluence of Bayou Teche and the Atchafalaya River, ready to deliver their combination of land and water blows in the morning like the flurry of a boxer's fists.[3]

An early start on January 14 brought the Federal command in sight of the majestic *Cotton* as well as its supporting infantry and field guns along the works at Bisland Plantation. Weitzel opened the contest. On the Federal right soldiers of the 8th Vermont fanned out of their columns into a line and moved up the east bank. Sixty men picked from that regiment and from the 75th New York moved ahead on the opposite bank. They were acting as sharpshooters, with orders to kill the Rebel gunners aboard the enemy boat. Weitzel deployed the rest of his infantry to cover the Louisiana riflemen. In the center of the Union line Buchanan ordered his ships to move forward, quickly outdistancing the soldiers on land as they thrashed through fields of cane and corn.

Buchanan should have waited a bit longer, and his audacity proved disastrous. Confederate infantry lining the banks, as yet unthreatened by Weitzel's approach, freely peppered the Union ships and drove their exposed gun crews to seek cover. The field guns of the Pelican Artillery and the heavy guns of the *Cotton,* as well as the rifles of its onboard infantry sharpshooters, confused the Federal boat captains as bullets and balls rattled and crashed among the ships' woodwork and casemates.

The iron-armored *Kinsman* dashed into the lead and moved boldly toward Cornay's Bridge to close the distance on the Rebel steamer and slug it out at close range. The Confederates had planned for that, however, and the waters of Bayou Teche erupted in a geyser of smoke, fire, and spray as the *Kinsman* shuddered from the explosion of an under-water torpedo, which detonated just six feet from its hull and blasted apart a ship's boat. "Her consort was shivered into a thousand pieces, and she was made entirely submerged by a sheet of water which filled the air," an observer aboard the *Diana* reported. The southern trap had worked, and the Union vessel, though still intact and not leaking, no longer had a working rudder. During the short interlude after the blast, a bullet entered the *Kinsman*'s pilothouse, striking its commander in the shoulder. With fate clearly against it the now unwieldy gunboat, un-controllable except by alternating its paddlewheels, limped down-stream and out of the fight. Sailors with sweeps and gaffs probed the water for other mines and found a second device—with 125 pounds of powder—poised for another victim. They were able to disarm it.[4]

Buchanan chose another gunboat to throw into the fight and sig-naled to the *Estrella* to move ahead. The response from its skipper— that the fire from the rifle pits was too intense to make headway— sent the commodore into a rage. Buchanan would not wait for the army to dress its battle lines and clear the banks; the navy could handle the hardest part of this chore on its own. Buchanan took the skipper's timid response as a disgusting amalgam of cowardice and insubordination, and he ordered the *Estrella* to move aside and let him pass. The commodore would take the *Calhoun* into the fight and finish it himself.

As the gunboat neared the obstructions, the commodore stepped on deck to observe the navigation hazards with his spyglass and to check for more torpedoes. Confederate riflemen, only about 150 feet away, could not believe their luck. One sharp-eyed Rebel put a bullet through Buchanan's right temple, and the commodore flung his spy-glass over his shoulder with a jerk and cried out, "Oh God!" as he dropped to the deck. One of the engineers aboard was standing on the bridge beside Buchanan when the fatal bullet struck. "He fell like an ox, and as he fell I saw a blood spot the size of a half dollar in front of his right ear and from it the blood began to flow," he said. "So quick was it all that the spot was visible to me before the blood came."[5]

Bullets also peppered the rest of the ship. The pilot fell wounded, and the *Calhoun* drifted into the west bank. The engineer, now in charge, dove for cover behind a ventilator and yelled down the tube to reverse the engines. As the sailors moved to respond, more than a dozen fell dead or wounded as the vessel backed down Bayou Teche at an angle before grounding by its stern on the opposite bank. The constant pinging and whirring of bullets pinned down the ship's gun crews, forcing them to serve the guns in rushes, careful to take cover between loading, aiming, and firing. Rebel bullets also ricocheted below decks. "The only steam gauge we had was shot away," one crewman wrote. "A musket ball was embedded in the iron of the steam drum."[6]

The current pushed the perforated *Calhoun* back into the stream and carried it out of danger. The engineer breathed easily at last, glad to be out of danger. He also noticed five holes in the ventilator, all meant for him. "I went down on the gun deck, pretty well scared," he recalled. "The woodwork was riddled with bullets."[7]

A fourth Union gunboat, the USS *Diana,* hove to near the disabled *Calhoun* and joined the fight. The sharpshooters from the 8th Vermont clattered down gangplanks to neutralize the Rebel snipers on the ground. "We were not long in leaving that boat, and had just stepped on shore when she was riddled with a shower of iron and lead," remembered Corporal Rufus Kinsely. The Vermonters fired a few shots at the Louisianans before lunging straight at their rifle pits in a rolling, loose-ordered charge. The Confederates fled back to the safety of their own lines, but thirty-seven raised their hands in surrender to the impetuous Yankees.[8]

The crews of the Union ships, clearly vulnerable to small arms fire, could now catch a breath. They relaxed even more as they watched the enemy gunboat withdraw. The *Cotton* had expended nearly all its energy fending off the Union ships. The intensity of the battle had forced the gunners to fire all their artillery cartridges. Captain Fuller ordered the crew to cut off their trouser legs, fill them with gunpowder, and tie the loose ends as an ersatz answer to the predicament, but the effort took time. As the Confederate sailors ripped their pants, a growing wave of blue-clad infantry approached from ahead.[9]

General Weitzel and the army would finish this fight. Around 10 a.m. soldiers from the 75th New York and 8th Vermont began a determined drive up both banks of the bayou, scattering Rebel skirmishers and cavalrymen like so many flushed quail. Lieutenant Colonel James McWaters attempted to rally his Louisiana horsemen until a bullet cut him down. With the Rebels flushed into the open and out of the way, the Vermonters and their New York comrades moved in on the *Cotton*. Three artillery batteries also rumbled into place, ready to add the weight of their guns to the fight. When they were within rifle range, the northern skirmishers cleared the *Cotton*'s decks and in part avenged the treatment given to the *Calhoun*. Among the first to fall was the vessel's second-in-command, Lieutenant Henry Kennedy Stevens, who had recently commanded the CSS *Arkansas* at the Battle of Baton Rouge. Wood splinters and shiny silver splashes dotted the *Cotton*'s rusted rail armor as the steady spattering of bullets increased in ferocity. Within minutes, many of the Rebel crew lay dead or dying, and its commander, the intrepid Captain Fuller, had been hit in both arms. The pilothouse lay abandoned and the vessel lazily bumped its bow into the east bank.[10]

Union troops closed in on the increasingly inert *Cotton*. An officer from the 75th New York stood on the bank opposite the steamer and ordered it to strike its colors. Instead a Rebel rifleman shot the Yankee through the heart. At almost the same time, the guns of the Pelican Artillery galloped to the rescue, unlimbering and firing in an effort to brush away the swarming Federal skirmishers. On the east bank, two Confederate 10-pounder Parrots flung twenty rounds at the skirmishers of the 8th Vermont, "filling the air with bursting bombs and solid shot, which mowed the cane on every side," Kinsley remembered. On the west bank, two 6-pounders treated the 75th New York to a limber chest full of spherical case, causing the Union advance to shudder to a halt, then slowly to back up. Temporarily saved, the crippled but resourceful Fuller regained the helm of the *Cotton* and gallantly steered the vessel with his feet as it backed away from the fight.[11]

The Federal troops surged to catch the retreating vessel, but the opportunity had passed. The ungainly *Cotton*, reversing awkwardly up the bayou, retreated under cover of the Rebel field batteries. Comrades helped Fuller off the vessel onto a waiting transport, and Lieutenant E. T. King of the St. Martin's Rangers took the helm. This errand completed, the *Cotton* returned downstream to cover the Confederate

The CSS Cotton's *last battle. A sketch from* Frank Leslie's Illustrated Newspaper *depicting Union sharpshooters getting within range of the elusive Confederate gunboat.*

cannons that had saved it. The ship, however, met a storm of projectiles from Union batteries and infantry, now drawn up in force. Seeing the enemy in control of both banks and the Pelican Artillery safely withdrawn, King decided against renewing the struggle. The Union troops gave up the chase when they came into range of the redeployed southern field pieces and the heavy howitzers at Fort Bisland.[12]

The Federals owned the field and planned to finish their job on the morrow. That night Weitzel dispatched orders designed to ready his small army to renew the struggle at sunrise. Crews aboard the naval flotilla probed for torpedoes and grappled with the obstructions in Bayou Teche, intending to use first light to clear a path for their gunboats to glide up the stream in pursuit of what would certainly be a Rebel force in full and panicky retreat. By mid-morning, they believed, the *Cotton* and the redoubt at Bisland would be under their guns—if not destroyed—and Mouton's army would be scattered.[13]

Mouton had reason to fear the next day's battle. His fortifications were incomplete, and his forces were inadequate to defend them against Weitzel's regiments and gunboats. His men were outnumbered, and he believed he had been whipped. He conveyed his new plans to the *Cotton*'s captain. "I received orders to immediately report to General Mouton at headquarters," King wrote. Mouton ordered that the guns from the *Cotton* be dismounted and put into the works. The giant steamer was to be scuttled to provide yet another line of obstructions to discourage the Union fleet—a sacrifice to save the army. While King understood the logic, he did not agree with the decision, and he did not want the chore. "I remonstrated against this on the ground that I had risked my life to save the boat," he added, "and any person could do that as well as I could." Mouton insisted, stating that King would know best how to situate the vessel to cause the greatest blockage in the bayou.[14]

That night King obeyed, commanding a skeleton crew aboard the *Cotton* to take the vessel on its "funeral trip down the bayou." As it neared the Union lines, crewmen knocked holes in the bottom of the hull, and King gave the wheel a hard turn, sending the vessel obliquely across the channel. It settled quickly. The departing Rebel crew torched the works still above water before rowing back to safety.[15]

After the battle against CSS Cotton, *Weitzel had twenty-five wounded soldiers to transport several miles back to Brashear City. Medical personnel used a large raft on Bayou Teche to gently float the injured back to the hospital.* Frank Leslie's Illustrated Newspaper.

"The *Cotton*, which had become the pet and pride of our community," lamented a writer for the *Houston Tri-Weekly Telegraph*, "is no more. . . . Baptized in blood . . . invincible to her enemies, the idol of her friends," the writer continued, the *Cotton* had been killed by a Confederate pen, which "swept into annihilation what tempests of shot and shell and fire had failed to scathe. She now lies a gloomy wreck upon the water, though lost and abandoned, defiant in her loneliness, and still, as she was when afloat, a barrier to the advancing foe."[16]

When daylight revealed that the Confederate nemesis lay dead, Weitzel decided that the renewal of the Union attack was unnecessary. He had never intended to invade the Teche country; he merely wanted to destroy the *Cotton*. Triumphantly he ordered his army back to Brashear City. "We have accomplished the object of our expedition," he telegraphed from his headquarters. "The C. S. gunboat *Cotton* is one of the things that were."[17]

The effort to destroy the *Cotton* on January 13-14 had resulted in a sharp little fight and had achieved much. Rebel rifles and cannons killed or wounded some three dozen Union soldiers and nearly that many sailors. Union weapons had done their chores as well. Five Confederates died and another ten were wounded onboard the late Rebel steamer. On shore ten Confederates fell and more than fifty of their sharpshooters surrendered to the skirmishers of the 8th Vermont and 75th New York.[18]

As intended, the loss of the *Cotton* was a serious blow to Taylor's plans along Bayou Teche. As long as she had remained afloat, Union gunboats moved with caution on that stream and into Grand Lake. "The *Cotton*, which was the only boat we had for the defense of the Teche and one that had done more fighting than any in the Confederacy, was foolishly destroyed by our own officers," lamented King. Her mobile guns would be missed, although King and the St. Martin's Rangers used them to build "The Bull Battery," an ox-drawn siege train. This innovation aside, Taylor needed reinforcements more than ever so that he could challenge Union control of the region. He looked again toward Texas.[19]

Instead of being underway for Louisiana, though, Sibley's men still lingered in the Lone Star State. With the thrill of combat behind them, these warriors once again spiraled into boredom, tomfoolery, and misdemeanor. Discipline—never their strong suit—unraveled. While dawdling at Galveston, these bored troops turned to women and liquor to enliven their stay.

A week after the battle Lieutenant John Coleman of Falls County, a survivor of the disastrous New Mexico lancer charge at Val Verde, tested his fate by accompanying a group of brother officers from the brigade bent on mischief. Finding an untended carriage—it turned out to be General Magruder's—the officers climbed in and headed for an assignation house on the beach. When they arrived, however, the proprietress informed them that no women remained.

Undaunted, the group searched the house anyway and found a large store of brandy, which they took as a consolation prize. As their drinking party grew loud, two neighbors fearing burglary opened fire on the looters. The officers quickly poured out of the building and approached the offending strangers. As one of the neighbors raised his gun to fire, Coleman fired a shot, grazing the man's head. Staggered, the civilian tried to shoot again, prompting Coleman to send a second bullet into the citizen's shoulder. For this incident the lieutenant was demoted and transferred out of the brigade into a conscript regiment.[20]

Sibley's Brigade also buzzed with gossip about the battle. Rumors and innuendo from other regiments infected the camp; rival units suggested that the brigade's men in the land attack were cowards and had joined the general panic at the height of the fight. Other rumors accused Colonel Reily of losing control over his men, leading to a rout. Colonel Green, very sensitive to such matters, chafed under accusations that his men, too, had broken under fire aboard the *Bayou City* and that their colonel had exercised poor leadership.[21]

Other Texans called the men of Sibley's Brigade thieves. Someone had profited handsomely from the battle—fourteen Enfields and several articles of clothing disappeared from the gun crew of the *Bayou City*. When Captain Lubbock left his ship during the battle to arrange the truce, he left behind his shotgun and a brace of pistols. Presumably someone in the brigade now had these items.[22]

Despite these smudges on their honor, the press and other Texans heaped laurels on the brigade. The men from the sunken *Neptune,* who continued their devastating and constant firing even as the ship went down, received credit from some observers for the success of the sea-borne attack. Magruder commended Colonel Bagby of that regiment in his official report. Colonel Green, also mentioned in dispatches, saw his reputation restored, as he emerged as one of the fight's principal heroes.[23]

The accolades continued. Grateful citizens of Hempstead presented a warhorse to Green. A committee of the town's leading citizens offered the animal out of "their high appreciation of your services upon the battlefield of New Mexico, and of your late brilliant achievement in the capture of the enemy's vessels at Galveston," they wrote. "You have long been known to Texas as one of her most chivalric sons. Your command composed of the choicest spirits of the land—and under your leadership—were expected to win honors. The expectations of your countrymen have not been disappointed." The whiskey stains upon his reputation were fading.[24]

A week later Green wrote a note of thanks for their generosity. "I accept the fine charger as a compliment to the brave officers and men who have served under my command as . . . their representative." He generously shared the tribute. "I am indebted to their gallantry and good conduct for whatever of credit may attach to me." He ended with a promise: "Be assured that the conduct of the gallant 5th Texas Mounted Volunteers in the New Mexican Campaign and in the recent campaign to Galveston is an indication of what our friends may expect of us in the future."[25]

For their part, the men of the 4th Texas would be serving under a new banner. Matilda Young and Charlotte Allen, leading women in Houston, presented a handmade "Texas-pattern" Confederate battle flag to the regiment. On its folds were embroidered "Val Verde, Glorieta, Peralta, Galveston," and "Galveston Bay." In a brief address the women declared that the regiment's "weather-beaten banner that has so often floated upon Arizona breezes and beneath New Mexican skies, might with just propriety claim the inscription." It was time to furl the unit's old Stars-and-Bars and replace it with this new emblem. "Houston feels that it is her privilege to present to you," the ladies continued, "and to your brave officers and men, this flag, commencing as you did the new year with two victories, whose deathless names shall soon entwine proudly and gracefully with those of the glorious days of the Republic of Texas."[26]

Their presentation also came with an Old Testament style exhortation. "Our prayer is, that this banner may go before you as the pillar of fire and the cloud did before the Israelites, leading you to fresh triumph over the foe, leading you all safely at last to the promised land of a peaceful, united independent, liberated, Confederacy."[27]

Under these new flags, the men of the 4th, 5th, and 7th Texas cavalries at long last moved away from the coast and set their eyes on Louisiana. Colonel Reily wrote an admiring note to Magruder as means of farewell. "There is not an officer or man in the brigade that does not feel proud of having fought under your immediate command," he gushed. "We separate with sorrow from a hero who has learned us how to conquer both on land and water."[28]

Veterans of other Texas regiments on faraway fields, however, had had their fill of Galveston talk. Private Jim C. Murray, writing from the camps of Hood's Texas Brigade in Virginia, thought the whole affair had been overstated. "I suppose the people of Texas will never get done blowing about the fight at Galveston," he wrote his mother. "Some say they almost go into fits when they meet a man who was in the fight. [From] all I can hear it was quite a small affair. We have lost as many men out of our company in one fight as was killed then[,] and then it was no new thing to march that many to death. What would they do to make sure of us?"[29]

Battles in Texas continued to dominate southern newspapers and the public imagination for a little while longer, especially since Magruder had ordered another creative strike against the Yankees on the Texas coast. By employing similar tactics as he used in his triumph at Galveston, the Virginian would clear Sabine Pass of Union blockaders. Major Leon Smith dutifully traveled by rail to Beaumont to oversee the refitting of two steamers, the *Josiah H. Bell* and the *Uncle Ben*, into cottonclads.

Men of Speight's Battalion and the 2nd Texas Cavalry would get their chance to act as sharpshooters and boarders. Sergeant H. N. Connor received orders to round up some of his men. "Twenty-five men [were] called for from our company to go aboard the Bell as sharpshooters," he wrote, noting that "there [are] about 100 men from other regiments already aboard." His soldiers drew lots to see who would go. "I myself among the fortunate ones [who] drew prizes."[30] Gunners from Company F, 1st Texas Heavy Artillery manned a rifled 68-pounder on the *Bell* and two 12-pounders on the *Ben*. Major Oscar M. Watkins of Magruder's staff held overall command of the operation. The targets of this offensive were the two vessels blockading the pass, the eight-gun USS *Morning Light*, a converted clipper ship, and the lightly armed schooner *Velocity*, a former blockade runner.

On January 21 the Rebel boats ventured onto peaceful seas, their steam-driven paddles churning the water as they headed for their becalmed victims. Union sailors, catching sight of the Confederate vessels, stretched canvas across their yards to try to escape. Slowly their ships responded, and a steady stern chase ensued. The *Josiah H. Bell* and the *Uncle Ben* pursued the Yankee vessels for thirty miles, and after hours of pursuit they finally closed to within two miles. Captain Frederick Odlum and Lieutenant Dick Dowling, serving a re-bored 8-inch rifle on the deck of the *Bell*, opened fire. The first shot careened off the *Morning Light*'s main mast. A second shot drilled a hole in the ship's boat. Subsequent shots splintered the clipper's decks and fouled its rigging, slowing the vessel even more. Captain John Dillingham, commanding the *Morning Light*, ordered that his ship be turned around to combat the pesky Rebels with his broadside of four guns, but their nimble Confederate vessel avoided the Union battery's sights.

When the Texans closed to within rifle range, the Federal ships were doomed. Enfields cleared *Morning Light*'s deck, hitting thirteen of its crew in the first few minutes of the fusillade. The ship's guns were now useless and abandoned. Dillingham ordered that his magazines be flooded and the colors struck. The *Velocity* surrendered soon after. The Rebels took them both in tow, yet another blow to Union prestige.

The *Morning Light* was too deep to clear the bar at the mouth of Sabine Pass, so the Texans dismantled her at sea. The scrapping came to an abrupt halt on January 23 as three Union gunboats hove into sight. Gunners aboard the *Josiah H. Bell* finished off the *Morning Light* with their cannon before their steamer sped away to safety. The doomed Yankee clipper burned rapidly. Sergeant Connor marveled at the majesty of the whole spectacle. "It was quite a beautiful scene," he wrote. "The gunboats coming rapidly from one point; the flames springing from all parts of the beautiful ship, and the *Bell* steaming in with a heavy column of black smoke from her chimney." The *Morning Light* burned well and sank quickly, its loaded guns cooking off as they became heated, a final salute from a dying warrior–and a final insult to Union prestige in the western Gulf.[31]

In General Orders Number 45 Magruder praised his men with his usual immoderate flair. The war's entire course in Louisiana and Texas, he believed, had been reversed by his recent efforts. The initiative now rested with the Confederates, and the time to liberate the Pelican State was at hand. He would send his Lone Star horse marines to save the day. "The echo of their cannon at Galveston and Sabine had not died away ere they were taken up . . . along the Mississippi," he crowed.

"The whole country has been electrified by the daring and skill of Texans." He had grown to love his rough-hewed amateurs, and knew that they would make their presence felt in the coming weeks. "The commanding general of the Army of Texas is confident," he boasted, "that his troops will . . . astonish still more their enemies and world by such evidences of skill and audacity as shall make the word 'Texan' a better word than 'Spartan.'"[32]

CHAPTER TWENTY-ONE

TWO YEARS AFTER SECESSION

America seems perishing of madness
Julia LeGrand, New Orleans, Louisiana

O n January 26, 1863, two years to the day after Louisiana had plunged into its experiment at disunion, Governor John Albion Andrew of Massachusetts stood in an office in Washington, D.C., eager to see the fulfillment of some long-held ambitions. Secretary of War Edwin M. Stanton, seated at his desk, scrawled out an official order authorizing the governor to raise additional volunteers from his state to help dismantle the Confederacy. The document began with permissions authorizing the creation of artillery units to defend Massachusetts's forts and infantry units to be composed of volunteers who would serve for three years' duty in the South. Stanton then leaned aside as Andrew, pen in hand, moved forward to add the phrase, "and may include persons of African descent organized into separate corps." As the governor stepped away and resumed his watchful stance, Stanton leaned back to finish the document with the usual directives to bureaus of supply, transportation, staff, and ordnance to support this effort. He then signed his name.[1]

This document lay pregnant with importance for the future course of the war and the nation that would emerge after the blood and dust of the conflict had settled. Within weeks a new African American regiment, the 54th Massachusetts, emerged. Beyond the creation of this soon-to-be famous regiment, bound for glory in South Carolina, lay the truth that Northern war planners and social reformers had united and managed to transform a clumsy Federal effort to suppress a state-led insurrection into a referendum on the entire American experiment. These first state-raised black troops were more than just riflemen; they represented a point of no return for both Union and Confederate causes.

The existence of the 54th Massachusetts also marked the triumph of those who would remake the republic. Scott's anaconda continued its constrictions, but its victim continued to squirm. President Abraham Lincoln remained vigilant in his search to detect in the South's conquered portions a loyal element who would support his increasingly untenable belief that secession had been unpopular. Men like Andrew, however, had different issues at heart, and they had achieved their goal. The nation that would emerge on the far side of the war, whether whole or in pieces, would be a new creation.

Nowhere in the South would this social and political revolution have more import than in Louisiana. Secession in the Pelican State had begun as something less than total revolution. It had felt like a dangerous adventure, full of romance and chivalry, in the heady days of 1861, but the gloss had worn away in less than a year as hardship and mourning became frequent visitors to Louisiana homes. Then came the disaster at New Orleans. Only the miracle at Vicksburg in the summer of 1862—the repulse of Admiral David Farragut's ships—had provided a shadow of hope that the southern cause, which had grown increasingly expensive in blood and treasure, might be salvaged.

The summer of 1862 had been Lincoln's time in purgatory as he imagined the possible collapse of the republic the voters, at least those in the North, had entrusted to him. In his desperation for options to limit the rebellion's successes, he expanded the ability of Union troops to bring fire and sword to the stubborn South in hopes of finally shocking it back to its senses. Smoke-blackened ruins now dotted Dixie, and plunder and contraband made their way into northern lines as the hardness of battle came into full view. Total war, waged upon the inhabitants of those areas considered disloyal, became a new tool for impressing the folly of secession upon the Confederates.

With each burning house, with every seizure of sugar or cotton, the investment made by secessionists grew dearer. The stakes in the awful card game became too large to abandon, with each passing day and each new atrocity—real or perceived. To fold at this point would be to admit foolishness; to quit now would be to discard the memories of better times and happy homes. Any admission of guilt would be dishonorable; the ghosts of so many robust young men would return to haunt those who lost faith. At the very least, the political tensions that had started the war remained unresolved. If they had been reason enough to go to war then they were reason enough to prosecute the war to a successful conclusion, many southerners decided. The conflict had grown steadily more ugly. Nowhere had the Federals presented a more lurid demonstration of their resolve, and their ability to increase the pressure on secessionists, than in Louisiana during the summer and fall of 1862.

Even so, leaders and soldiers across the Confederacy had remarkably risen to the challenge after having nearly collapsed just a few months earlier. A new paladin, General Robert E. Lee, had punished and confused the Federals in Virginia, resuscitating the hopes of what had been a moribund nation. Similarly, General Richard Taylor had served as *beau gallant* of Louisiana, a knight-errant sent to slay a beast bent on terror and corruption. His efforts, though limited in success, had at least registered a blow on the scaly belly of the Union leviathan. General John Magruder had even managed to break off one of the creature's horns and cause it pain with his bold stroke at Galveston. These soldiers and the blows they struck had not ended the war; instead, they had prolonged it with all its attending horrors.

Now that Stanton's order allowed African Americans to serve in their own regiments, reconciliation was made impossible. One nation would have to receive a mortal wound before the fight could end. The

The days after emancipation saw much celebrating by former slaves, including these freedmen at a dance. The harsh realities of their new situation would catch up with them quickly. Frank Leslie's Illustrated Newspaper.

black men enlisted into the service of the United States could never return to their antebellum status; they must conquer or die. Likewise, no negotiated terms could ever reweave the unraveled fabric of southern society. The people of the South, white and black, could never view each other the same way again. Southerners who might have considered a settlement of the political irritants that had precipitated secession now saw military victory as the only guarantee of their futures, believing that Yankee politicians had intentionally turned their human property against them. There could be no Confederate half measures now.

Julia LeGrand of New Orleans had certainly experienced a change of heart during the two years of conflict. One by one her slaves had deserted her, often taking family possessions as they left, and had joined a growing throng of transient and rowdy free persons loitering about the city. "I once was as great an abolitionist as any in the North . . . [and] placed black and white upon the same plane," she confided to her journal. "But my experience with negroes has altered my way of thinking and reasoning. It was when we owned them in numbers that

For many former slaves, freedom was bewildering. Eventually, thousands made their way to major urban centers like New Orleans to start a new life. Library of Congress.

I thought they ought to be free, and now that we have none, I think they are not fit for freedom."[2]

This member of the Crescent City's gentry watched as her community changed after the Federal invasion. The racial harmony that LeGrand imagined had existed in the past now degenerated into suspicion and animosity. Northern radicals, she reasoned, were the root of the present evil. "The abolitionists are the Jacobins of America. They have not shown any kindness to the poor negroes, either; they die by hundreds from disease engendered by unaccustomed hardships and exposure, also starvation," she wrote. "The suburbs and odd places in and about this city are crowded with a class never seen until the Federals came here—a class whose only support is theft and whose only occupation is strolling the streets, insulting white people, and living in the sun. This is really the negro idea of liberty."[3]

She could not reconcile her observations of occupied New Orleans to the high blown rhetoric of the Unionists and their radical allies. All of the destruction and heartache seemed pointless; to her, the object of abolitionist hopes seemed unworthy. "These creatures whom fanatics are pitying . . . and for whose possible benefit it is pretended that Federals troops are sent to die," she hissed, were not worth the catastrophe created on their behalf. "America," she concluded, "seems perishing of madness."[4]

Nearly 175 miles away in Alexandria Clarissa Hewitt—the once-pampered mistress of Creole Plantation near Donaldsonville—settled her family into their lives as refugees, more determined than ever that the Federal invaders must be turned back. After fleeing the Union troops in May 1862, the wealthy southerner had lurked aboard a steamer among the bayous of the sugar parishes before finally lighting in temporary quarters on the Red River that fall. She made do with little food, poor housing, and considered plain clothes and simple household items rare luxuries. By winter, though, she and her family had righted themselves and made their home in a rented house in Alexandria. Clarissa even enrolled her youngest daughter, Clarice, and her nephew in the local schools. The New Year, she believed, would return them all safely home, and this nightmarish episode would become simply an adventure that would grow with the telling.

Clarissa's husband, James, had managed to bring with him a large quantity of sugar, which he used as barter. Not only did he see to his family, but also he hoped to shuttle food and materials of war for a renewed Confederate effort in Louisiana. "His great desire is to get together by means of his sugar a supply of provisions for some of our Army posts that are beginning to feel the want of food, owing to the blockade," his wife recalled. James Hewitt, a native of New York, personally oversaw the gathering of supplies for the Confederate Mississippi River fortifications. This saccharine cache might have furnished capital for him to resuscitate his future fortunes, but only Rebel successes in the field would allow the family to return to their land near Donaldsonville.

The Hewitts had more than their fortunes riding on the outcome as well. They had also given three sons to the Confederate cause: one served with Robert E. Lee in Virginia, one fought with the Army of Tennessee, and the third was inside the works at Port Hudson. "How the Southern women suffer, thinking of our dear brave young sons, who have been brought up in the greatest luxury and ease, many fighting in the ranks of our Army, enduring the greatest hardships and priva-

Civil War New Orleans from the album of Sergeant Major Marshall Dunham, 159th New York. A view north from the upriver side of the 700 block of Canal Street looking downriver toward the 800 block and the intersection with Bourbon Street. The city is enjoying an early-morning calm—a few stores are still shuttered, and very few people are on the streets. Marshall Dunham Photograph Album, Mss 3241, Louisiana and Lower Mississippi Valley Collections, LSU Libraries, Baton Rouge, Louisiana.

tions. We know that they are doing it without a murmur and we are proud of their brave and unselfish lives."[5]

The spirit of defiance glimmering in the hearts of Louisiana women contrasted starkly with the gloom attending their new nemesis, Union general Nathaniel P. Banks. He understood that the circumstances of his campaign had now changed dramatically, especially with the disasters in Texas. The loss of the Union toehold in the western gulf would haunt him until the end of the war. "Galveston, as a military position, was second only in importance to New Orleans or Mobile," he wrote. "I regarded the loss of Galveston in its consequences . . . as the most unfortunate affair that occurred in the department. The possession of this island and its military occupation would have been of great importance to the Government in all operations in that part of the country. It would have held a large force of Rebel troops in the vicinity of Houston, enabled us to penetrate the territory of Texas at any time, or to concentrate our forces on the Mississippi." He had hoped to keep the Texans pinned down west of the Sabine River. Now he feared they were coming for him.[6]

Indeed, the Confederates of Louisiana would not have to face Banks and his Federal invaders alone in the coming months. Having won Galveston, the Texas soldiers would literally ride to the rescue. Sam Houston, the hero of San Jacinto and veteran Lone Star warrior, sensed that the military initiative had shifted. "Most sincerely we do trust that a new era has now dawned upon us," he wrote from his sickbed in Huntsville. The old general—ousted from his office as governor because he would not take an oath of loyalty to the Confederacy—was dying. Even so, his war-blood was up as he remembered the stirring days of a quarter century before. The men he had led along the banks of Buffalo Bayou against the forces of Santa Anna in 1836 had been the fathers and grandfathers of this Confederate generation. Houston had once been a stubborn Unionist, but like so many men of conscience, he remained true to his home state when it seceded. Houston's friends and neighbors had nearly all embraced the cause, right or wrong, and his own son had been wounded at Shiloh under the stars and bars of the nascent Confederate States of America. Now, the old warrior believed, the world would see what homespun Lone Star soldiers could achieve. "You will find that all Texans want," he mused, "is a general who is capable of leading them to victory."[7]

The old general's assessment would be tested in the coming months, but the previous two years had upended most notions of how the war would play out. What had started as a national political impasse turned violent had grown into an full scale rebellion. Even so, Federal arms nearly prevailed in the first year of conflict as Southern ardor cooled amidst the reality of Union strength and Confederate vulnerabilities. The days of easy secession and fire-eating tantrums had faded into the past, replaced by the realities of death and destruction. Political principles had withered and grown muted in the face of the realities of war. Louisiana was beginning to learn the cost of its stand, as was Texas, both in terms of blood and treasure.

This photograph of Federal-occupied New Orleans is looking south, with the upriver portion of the city off to the right. The broad Mississippi levee in the background is crowded with hogsheads of sugar and materials of war in long columns radiating from the water's edge. Union transports crowd the landings; in the distance, mortar schooners, their tree-branch camouflage still attached to masts and spars, await their opportunity for another crack at Confederate forts upstream. Marshall Dunham Photograph Album, Mss 3241, Louisiana and Lower Mississippi Valley Collections, LSU Libraries, Baton Rouge, Louisiana.

The government of Abraham Lincoln, too, had grown wiser in its two years of suppressing the move for independence in the South. The president had assumed lukewarm support for the secessionists among the general populations of the Confederate States. His plan to defeat the enemies on the field and reassert Union control had nearly succeeded only to be replaced by a growing dread that military campaigns alone would not suffice to restore the nation. Lincoln's decisions of the summer of 1862 would turn the blue armies and navies from liberators into occupiers as increasingly heavy-handed tactics alienated the once-loyal citizens of southern states. The longer the war ground on, the more bitter the legacy, the more complete the change, the more altered the future of the nation. The unexpected consequences of the Union's approach to the rebellious South exacted an even greater price in men, machines, and morale. Even so, Lincoln had decided: if the war could not be won quickly, it would be won totally and decisively.

There lay an irony at the end of these two years of escalating suffering. Confederate successes on the field prolonged the war and increased the chances that all the South claimed to be fighting for would, in the end, have to be sacrificed for victory. Union failures, on the other hand, injected hatred and spite into the conflict, increasing southern resistance and requiring even more hard handed straining to break the back of the rebellion. By early 1863, neither side could back down, neither side had a clear path out of the Hell that they had crafted. For the people of Louisiana, their role in this tragedy had grown too familiar, too clear. Yet, the suffering had only begun.

NOTES

Chapter 1

[1] John Dimitry, *Louisiana and Arkansas,* Volume X of Clement A. Evans, ed., *Confederate Military History: A Library of Confederate States History, in Twelve Volumes, Written by Distinguished Men of the South, and Edited by Gen. Clement A. Evans of Georgia* (Eleven volumes, Atlanta: Confederate Publishing Company, 1899), 11-12.

[2] William Watson, *Life in the Confederate Army: Being the Observations and Experiences of an Alien in the South during the American Civil War* (New York: Scribner and Welford, 1888), 87-88; Thomas O. Moore to William H. Gist, October 26, 1860, in Records of Louisiana State Government, 1850-1888, National Archives Microfilm Publications, M-359, Roll 4. See also Charles B. Dew, "Who Won the Secession Election in Louisiana?" *Journal of Southern History* 36 (1970): 18-32.

[3] Dimitry, *Louisiana and Arkansas,* 12, 22; Dew, "Who Won the Secession Election in Louisiana?" 18; Thomas O. Moore, *Special Message of Thomas O. Moore, Governor of the State of Louisiana to the General Assembly, December 1860* (Baton Rouge: n.p., 1860), 5.

[4] Dimitry, *Louisiana and Arkansas,* 15; Charles L. Dufour, *The Night the War was Lost* (New York: Doubleday, 1960; repr., Lincoln: University of Nebraska Press, 1994), 25.

[5] Charles B. Dew, "Who Won the Secession Election in Louisiana?" 18-32.

[6] Walter Prichard, "The Effects of the Civil War on the Louisiana Sugar Industry," *Journal of Southern History* 5 (August 1939): 316-17.

[7] A recent work on the peculiarities of Louisiana politics in the antebellum period is John M. Sacher, *A Perfect War of Politics: Parties, Politicians, and Democracy in Louisiana, 1824-1861* (Baton Rouge: Louisiana State University Press, 2003).

[8] Dimitry, *Louisiana and Arkansas,* 22.

[9] Watson, *Life in the Confederate Army,* 87-88.

[10] Ibid.; Prichard, "Effects of the Civil War on the Louisiana Sugar Industry," 317.

[11] Watson, *Life in the Confederate Army,* 87-88.

[12] Ibid.

[13] Dimitry, *Louisiana and Arkansas,* 25.

[14] Julia LeGrand, *The Diary of Julia LeGrand, New Orleans 1862-1863,* ed. by Kate Mason Rowland and Mrs. Morris L. Croxall (Richmond, Virginia: Everett Wadley Company, 1911), 75.

[15] T. Michael Parrish, *Richard Taylor: Soldier Prince of Dixie* (Chapel Hill: University of North Carolina Press, 1992), 104; *Official Journal of the Proceedings of the Convention of the State of Louisiana,* February 2, 1861 (New Orleans, 1861).

[16] Parrish, *Richard Taylor* , 104; *Official Journal of the Proceedings of the Convention of the State of Louisiana,* February 2, 1861 (New Orleans, 1861).

[17] *Official Journal of the Proceedings of the Convention of the State of Louisiana,* March 21, 1861 (New Orleans, 1861); Dufour, *Night the War was Lost*, 31.

[18] Tom Green to Nathan Green, February 12, 1861, Tom Green Papers, West TexasCollection, San Angelo State University, San Angelo, Texas.

[19] George Winston Smith, "Some Northern Wartime Attitudes Toward the Post-Civil War South," *Journal of Southern History* 10, No. 3 (August 1944): 255; "The Redemption of Virginia," *New York Times,* April 28, 1861.

[20] Abraham Lincoln, *Message to Congress in Special Session, July 4, 1861,* in Carl Van Doren, ed., *The Literary Works of Abraham Lincoln* (Norwalk, CT: Easton Press, 1980), 190-91.

[21] Ibid., 197.

[22] Ibid., 198.

[23] Ibid., 201.

[24] William Lloyd Garrison to Oliver Johnson, April 19, 1861, William Lloyd Garrison Papers, Boston Public Library.

[25] "Letters of General Thomas Williams, 1862," *American Historical Review* 14 (January 1909): 309.

[26] Smith, "Some Northern Wartime Attitudes," 255; Thomas H. Turner to Hamilton Fish, November 28, 1860, Fish Papers, Library of Congress.

[27] Allen R. Millett and Peter Maslowski, *For the Common Defense: A Military History of the United States of America* (New York: Free Press, 1984), 161; Timothy D. Johnson, *Winfield Scott: The Quest for Military Glory* (Lawrence: University Press of Kansas, 1998), 226; Winfield Scott to George B. McClellan, May 3, 1861, in U.S. War Department, *The War of the Rebellion: A Compilation of the Official Records of the Union and Confederate Armies* (128 vols., Washington: 1880-1901; repr., Gettysburg: National Historical Society, 1972), series 1, vol. 51, 369-70. Hereafter cited as *OR*, with all references to Series 1.

[28] Archer Jones, *Civil War Command and Strategy: The Process of Victory and Defeat* (New York: Free Press, 1992), 21; Winfield Scott to George B. McClellan, May 3, 1861, *OR*, vol. 51, 369-70; Millett and Maslowski, *For the Common Defense,* 161.

[29] Millett and Maslowski, *For the Common Defense,* 162.

[30] Johnson, *Winfield Scott,* 226.

[31] Dufour, *Night the War was Lost*, 55.

[32] Claude LeGrand, 7th Louisiana Infantry, to Dearest Sisters (Julia and Virginia LeGrand), Thursday, May 30, 1861, reproduced in LeGrand, *Diary*, 25-26.

[33] "Letters of General Thomas Williams, 1862," 312.

[34] Dufour, *Night the War was Lost*, 122.

Chapter 2

[1] George W. Cable, "New Orleans Before the Capture," in *Battles and Leaders of the Civil War,* eds. Robert U. Johnson and Clarence C. Buel (New York, 1887-8. Reprint, Secaucus, NJ: Castle, 1987), vol. 2, 19.

[2] LeGrand, *Diary,* 45.

[3] Cable, "New Orleans Before the Capture," 21.

[4] Frances Fearn, ed., *Diary of a Refugee* (New York: Moffat, Yard, 1910), 11-13.

[5] Ibid.

[6] Prichard, "Effects of the Civil War on the Louisiana Sugar Industry," 318.

[7] An outstanding book on the fall of Confederate New Orleans is Charles L. Dufour's *The Night the War was Lost.*

[8] "Letters of General Thomas Williams, 1862," American Historical Review 14 (January 1909): 314.

[9] The 4th Wisconsin, the 30th and 31st Massachusetts, the 6th Michigan, and the 9th and 12th Connecticut.

[10] Two batteries from Massachusetts and one from Vermont.

[11] Benjamin F. Butler to Secretary of War, May 8, 1862, *OR,* vol. 6, 506; David C. Rankin, ed., *Diary of a Christian Soldier: Rufus Kinsey and the Civil War* (New York: Cambridge University Press, 2004), 93.

[12] Benjamin F. Butler to Secretary of War, May 8, 1862, *OR,* vol. 6, 506. The 21st Indiana carried Merrill Rifles, a breech-loading weapon equipped with a detachable sword bayonet and praised for its accuracy. See Earl J. Coates and Dean S. Thomas, *An Introduction to Civil War Small Arms* (Gettysburg, PA: Thomas Publications, 1990), 33.

[13] As quoted in Robert S. Holzman, *Stormy Ben Butler* (New York: MacMillan, 1954. Repr., New York: Collier Books, 1961), 78; see also Dick Nolan, *Benjamin Franklin Butler: The Damnedest Yankee* (Novato, California: Presidio Press, 1991) and Chester G. Hearn, *When the Devil Came Down to Dixie: Ben Butler in New Orleans* (Baton Rouge: Louisiana State University Press, 1997).

[14] Helene Dupuy, "Memorable Days and Various Notable Circumstances During the Civil War in the United States in the State of Louisiana from 1861-1865," Alcee Fortier, transcriber (unpublished manuscript, Louisiana State University, Louisiana and Lower Mississippi Valley Collection, Hill Memorial Library), 2.

[15] Christopher G. Peña, Scarred by War: Civil War in Southeast Louisiana (Bloomington, IN: Authorhouse, 2004), 84-90.

[16] As quoted in Barnes Lathrop, "The Lafourche District 61-62: A Problem in Local Defense," *Louisiana History* 1 (Spring 1960): 119.

[17] Fearn, *Diary of a Refugee,* 13-16.

[18] Ibid.

[19] Ibid.

[20] A recent source that narrates the entire career of the Fox is Andrew R. English, *Chasing the Fox: The Chronology of a Blackade Runner* (Baltimore: Gateway Press, 2004).

[21] John D. Winters, *The Civil War in Louisiana* (Baton Rouge: Louisiana State University Press, 1963), 150-1; Peña, *Scarred by War,* 84-93.

[22] Rankin, *Diary of a Christian Soldier,* 96.

[23] "Letters of General Thomas Williams, 1862," 315.

[24] As quoted in Dufour, *Night the War was Lost,* 331.

Chapter 3

[1] As quoted in Terrence J. Winschel, *Vicksburg: Fall of the Confederate Gibraltar* (Abilene, TX: McWhiney Foundation Press, 1999), 20.

[2] "Letters of General Thomas Williams, 1862," 317.

[3] Winters, *Civil War in Louisiana*, 104-5.

[4] Edward T. Cotham Jr., ed., *The Southern Journey of a Civil War Marine: The Illustrated Notebook of Henry O. Gusley* (Austin: University of Texas Press, 2006), 73.

[5] Ibid.

[6] Winters, *Civil War in Louisiana*, 103-4; "Letters of General Thomas Williams, 1862," 318.

[7] Cecil B. Eby Jr., ed., *A Virginia Yankee in the Civil War: The Diaries of David Hunter Strother* (Chapel Hill: University of North Carolina Press, 1989), 136.

[8] Winters, *Civil War in Louisiana*, 125-48.

[9] Watson, *Life in the Confederate Army*, 434.

[10] Holzman, *Stormy Ben Butler*, 80;

[11] Holzman, *Stormy Ben Butler*, 93; Mary Boykin Chesnut, *A Diary from Dixie, as written by Mary Boykin Chesnut, wife of James Chesnut, Jr., United States Senator from South Carolina, 1859-1861, and Afterward an Aide to Jefferson Davis and a Brigadier-General in the Confederate Army* (New York: D. Appleton, 1905), 183.

[12] As quoted in Holzman, *Stormy Ben Butler*, 85.

[13] Holzman, *Stormy Ben Butler*, 82.

[14] LeGrand, *Diary*, 40; Marion Southwood, *Beauty and Booty: The Watchword of New Orleans* (New York: M. Doolady, 1867), 57.

[15] LeGrand, *Diary*, 40, 43, 45; Southwood, *Beauty and Booty*, 57.

[16] James K. Hosmer, *The Color Guard: Being a Corporal's Notes of Military Service in the Nineteenth Army Corps* (Boston: Walker and Wise, 1864), 163.

[17] As quoted in Robert F. Pace, "'It Was Bedlam Let Loose': The Louisiana Sugar Country and the Civil War," *Louisiana History* 39 (Fall 1998): 389. A fine work that captures the feel and importance of the entire sugar region during this era is Charles P. Roland, *Louisiana Sugar Plantations During the Civil War* (1954. Reprint, Baton Rouge: Louisiana State University Press, 1997).

[18] As quoted in Dufour, *Night the War was Lost*, 332.

[19] As quoted in Dufour, *Night the War was Lost*, 334.

[20] As quoted in Dufour, *Night the War was Lost*, 335, 349.

[21] Theophilus Noel, *A Campaign from Santa Fe to the Mississippi: Being a History of the Old Sibley Brigade from Its First Organization to the Present Time; Its Campaigns in New Mexico, Arizona, Texas, Louisiana and Arkansas in the Years 1861-2-3-4*, eds. Martin Hardwick Hall and Edwin Adams Davis (Houston: Stagecoach Press, 1961), 56-7.

[22] Ibid.

[23] The best book on the New Mexico Campaign, if I do say so myself, is Donald S. Frazier, *Blood and Treasure: Confederate Empire in the Southwest* (College Station: Texas A&M University Press, 1995).

[24] David B. Gracy II, ed., "New Mexico Campaign Letters of Frank Starr, 1861-1862," *Texas Military History* 4, no. 3 (Fall 1964): 181-84.

Chapter 4

1   Dupuy, "Memorable Days," 2; Jefferson Davis to Thomas O. Moore, June 26, 1862, *OR*, vol. 15, 767-68.

2   Davis to Moore, June 26, 1862, *OR*, vol. 15, 768.

3   Winters, *Civil War in Louisiana*, 150-51.

4   Thomas O. Moore to George Randolph, June 25, 1862, *OR*, vol. 15, 766.

5   Winters, *Civil War in Louisiana*, 151.

6   Moore to Randolph, July 8, 1862, *OR*, vol. 15, 774. Moore specifically called for the courts-martial of Captain William Taylor and Colonel Francis C. Wilkes of the 24th Texas Cavalry. Both of these soldiers went on to have important Civil War careers, and ended the war serving with the remnants of Hiram Granbury's Brigade in the Army of Tennessee.

7   Edward T. King to William Jones, editor, *New Iberia Times Democrat*, June 27, 1910, William Jones Letters, 1862-1863, Manuscript Section, Howard-Tilton Memorial Library, Tulane University (hereafter cited as William Jones Letters); Peña, *Scarred by War*, 92-93.

8   King to editor, *New Iberia Times Democrat*, June 27, 1910, William Jones Letters; Rankin, *Diary of a Christian Soldier*, 99-100.

9   Rankin, *Diary of a Christian Soldier*, 99-100; Peña, *Scarred by War*, 100-101.

10   J. K. Gaudet to R. C. Martin, June 28, 1862, Martin-Pugh Papers, Box 3, No. 265, Allen J. Ellender Archives, Ellender Memorial Library, Nicholls State University, Thibodaux, Louisiana (hereafter cited as Martin-Pugh Papers).

11   William B. Ratliff to R. C. Martin, June 26, 1862, Martin-Pugh Papers, Box 3, No. 262.

12   J. K. Gaudet to R. C. Martin, June 28, 1862, Martin-Pugh Papers, Box 3, No. 265.

13   Ibid.

14   W. W. Pugh to R. C. Martin, July 8, 1862, Martin-Pugh Papers, Box 3, No. 268.

15   For the best discussion of this episode and period see Barnes Lathrop, "The Lafourche District in 1862: Militia and Partisan Rangers," *Louisiana History* 1, no. 3 (Summer 1960): 230-44.

16   Moore to Randolph, July 8, 1862, *OR*, vol. 15, 773-74.

Chapter 5

1   Daniel E. Sutherland, "Abraham Lincoln, John Pope, and the Origins of Total War," *Journal of Military History* 56, No. 4 (October 1992): 568-74.

2   As quoted in Sutherland, "Abraham Lincoln, John Pope, and the Origins of Total War," 574, 580.

3   LeGrand, *Diary*, 88.

4   Sutherland, "Abraham Lincoln, John Pope, and the Origins of Total War," 574; Winters, *Civil War in Louisiana*, 125-48.

5   Sutherland, "Abraham Lincoln, John Pope, and the Origins of Total War," 574; Winters, *Civil War in Louisiana*, 125-48.

6   "Letters of General Thomas Williams, 1862," 325.

7   Cotham, *Southern Journey*, 81.

8   D. G. Farragut to the people of Donaldsonville, no date, enclosed with "Report of the Committee of Citizens Residing on the Right Bank of the Mississippi, parishes of Ascension and St. James," August 11, 1862, U.S. Naval War Records Office, *Official Records of the Union and Confederate Navies in the War of the Rebellion* (27 vols., Washington: Govt. Print. Office, 1894-1922), Series 1, vol. 19, 142-43. (Hereafter cited as *ORN* with all references to Series 1.)

9   Cotham, *Southern Journey,* 91.

10 One of the better discussions of the burning of Donaldsonville and its aftermath can be found in Christopher Peña's *Scarred by War: Civil War in Southeast Louisiana* (Bloomington, IN: Authorhouse, 2004), 104-13.

11 For a closer view of Governor Thomas O. Moore and his role in the Civil War, see Edwin Adams Davis, *Heroic Years: Louisiana in the War for Southern Independence* (Baton Rouge: Louisiana State University Press, 1964); Van D. Odom, "The Political Career of Thomas Overton Moore, Secession Governor of Louisiana," *Louisiana Historical Quarterly* 26 (October 1943): 975-1054.

12 Winters, *Civil War in Louisiana,* 123; Benjamin F. Butler to Secretary of War Edwin M. Stanton, May 8, 1862, *OR,* vol. 6, 506.

13 Benjamin F. Butler to Secretary of War Edwin M. Stanton, September 1862, *OR,* vol. 15, 559; Richard Nelson Current, *Lincoln's Loyalists: Union Soldiers from the Confederacy.* (Boston: Northeastern University Press, 1992), 90-91.

14 John Franklin Godfrey, *The Civil War Letters of Captain John Franklin Godfrey* (South Portland, ME: Ascensius Press, 1993), 14, 16.

15 H. H. Boone, "Maj. Boone's Report," In Camp, Col. Norwood's Plantation, to Richard Taylor, May 26, 1863, as printed in *The Bellville Countryman,* August 8, 1863, 2.

16 Current, *Lincoln's Loyalists,* 96-97.

17 Godfrey, *Civil War Letters,* 23.

18 Ibid.

19 Benjamin F. Butler to Edwin M. Stanton, Secretary of War, August 14, 1862, *OR,* vol. 15, 548-49; Butler to Major General Henry Halleck, August 27, 1862, *OR,* vol. 15, 556.

20 C. Peter Ripley, *Slaves and Freedmen in Civil War Louisiana* (Baton Rouge: Louisiana State University Press, 1976), 40-42.

21 Two important works on this topic are Ted Tunnell, *Crucible of Reconstruction: War, Radicalism, and Race in Louisiana, 1862-1877* (Baton Rouge: Louisiana State University Press, 1984) and William F. Messner, *Freedmen and the Ideology of Free Labor: Louisiana, 1862-1865* (Lafayette: Center for Louisiana Studies, 1978).

22 Ripley, *Slaves and Freedmen in Civil War Louisiana,* 44-45.

23 P. G. T. Beauregard to Ed Gotheil, August 15, 1862, *OR,* vol. 15, 799.

Chapter 6

1   Donald S. Frazier, Blood and Treasure: Confederate Empire in the Southwest (College Station: Texas A&M University Press, 1995), 146-47.

2   *Houston Tri-Weekly Telegraph,* March 26, 1862.

3   Spurlin, *Waller's 13th Texas Cavalry Battalion,* 33-34.

4   Ibid., 37-45.

5   Ibid.

6   Reverend Pere Charles Menard, Annals of the Church of St. Joseph, April 24, 1991, in *The Bayou Catholic,* as quoted in Chris Peña, *Touched by War: Battles Fought in the Lafourche District* (Thibodaux, LA: C. G. P. Press, 1998), 196.

7   Taylor, *Destruction and Reconstruction,* 108; Parrish, *Richard Taylor,* 245.

8   *OR,* vol. 15, 802.

9   Ibid.

10 The only biography of Taylor is T. Michael Parrish, *Richard Taylor: Soldier Prince of Dixie* (Chapel Hill: University of North Carolina Press, 1992); see also Richard Taylor, *Destruction and Reconstruction: Personal Experiences of the Late War* (New York: D. Appleton, 1879).

11 R. L. Pugh to Mary Williams Pugh, December 16, 1862, R. L. Pugh Papers, Lower Louisiana and Mississippi Valley Collection, Hill Memorial Library, Louisiana State University, Baton Rouge, Louisiana.

12 Peña, *Touched by War,* 114.

13 Taylor, *Destruction and Reconstruction,* 139.

14 Taylor, *Destruction and Reconstruction,* 139; Edward T. King to William Jones, editor, *New Iberia Time Democrat,* June 27, 1910, William Jones Letters.

15 Taylor, *Desruction and Reconstruction,* 140-41.

16 Fearn, ed., *Diary of a Refugee,* 17-18.

17 As quoted in Jefferson Davis Bragg, *Louisiana in the Confederacy* (Baton Rouge: Louisiana State University Press, 1941), 255-56; Parrish, *Richard Taylor,* 246-47.

Chapter 7

1   Barnes Lathrop, "Federals Sweep the Coast: An Expedition into St. Charles Parish, August, 1862," *Louisiana History* 9 (Winter 1968): 62-68; Stephen Thomas to H. W. Birge, *OR,* vol. 15, 132.

2   Barnes Lathrop, "Federals Sweep the Coast: An Expedition into St. Charles Parish, August, 1862," *Louisiana History* 9 (Winter 1968): 62-68.

3   Thomas to Birge, September 3, 1862, *OR,* vol. 15, 132.

4   Arthur W. Bergeron, *Guide to Louisiana Confederate Military Units, 1861-1865* (Baton Rouge: Louisiana State University Press, 1989), 163-66; Richard Taylor, *Destruction and Reconstruction: Personal Experiences of the Late War* (New York: D. Appleton, 1879), 109-110.

5   Taylor, *Destruction and Reconstruction,* 109-110.

6   Taylor, *Destruction and Reconstruction,* 139.

7   George R. Morris, "The Battle of Bayou des Allemands," *Confederate Veteran* 34 (1910)14.

8   Ibid.

9   Ibid.   This is essentially the route now covered by Louisiana Highway 20 from the town of Chackbay to Vacherie.

10 Parrish, *Richard Taylor,* 255; Robert Butler to his sister, September 22, 1862, Benjamin F. Butler Papers, Manuscript Division, Library of Congress.

11 Winters, *Civil War in Louisiana,* 155-56; Morris, "Battle of Bayou des Allemands," 14.

12 As quoted in Morris, "Battle of Bayou des Allemands," 14.

13 Stephen Thomas to R. S. Davis, September 6, 1862, *OR,* vol. 15, 134-35.

14 Rankin, ed., *Diary of a Christian Soldier,* 106; Stephen Thomas to R. S. Davis, September 6, 1862, *OR,* vol. 15, 134-35.

[15] Rankin, ed., *Diary of a Christian Soldier,* 106; Stephen Thomas to R. S. Davis, September 6, 1862, *OR,* vol. 15, 134-35. Private L. J. Ingalls received the Congressional Medal of Honor for his actions at Boutte Station.

[16] Stephen Thomas to R. S. Davis, September 6, 1862, *OR,* XV: 134-135.

[17] Ibid.

[18] Ibid. The steel 1.5-inch Ellsworth Rifle fired a solid two-pound, three inch-long lead bolt and was the only breach loading cannon manufactured in the United States in the course of the war and very few were issued. These light cannons usually found their way into cavalry and garrison units and served a useful counter-battery guns due to their excellent range. Five authentic examples survive today.

[19] Winters, *Civil War in Louisiana,* 156.

[20] Ibid.

[21] Rankin, ed., *Diary of a Christian Soldier,* 107.

[22] Charles Spurlin, *West of the Mississippi with Waller's 13th Texas Cavalry Battalion CSA* (Hillsboro, TX: Hill Junior College Press, 1971), 47; C. C. Cox, "Reminiscences of C. C. Cox," *Southwestern Historical Quarterly* 6 (January 1903): 219.

Chapter 8

[1] Spurlin, ed., *Waller's 13th Texas Cavalry Battalion,* 47; Cox, "Reminiscences," 219.

[2] Spurlin, ed., *Waller's 13th Texas Cavalry Battalion,* 48; R. N. Weisiger, Daybook 1862, pg. 83-85, Victoria Regional History Center, HC-114-4p. 83-86, Victoria College, Victoria, Texas.

[3] *Overton (TX) Sharp Shooter,* May 31, 1888.

[4] *Ibid.*

[5] *OR,* vol. 15, 135-37; Cox, "Reminiscences," 219; Spurlin, ed., *Waller's 13th Texas Cavalry Battalion,* 48.

[6] *OR,* vol. 15, 135-37; Cox, "Reminiscences," 219; Spurlin, *Waller's 13th Texas Cavalry Battalion,* 48.

[7] *OR,* vol. 15, 135-37; Cox, "Reminiscences," 219.

[8] R. N. Weisiger, Daybook 1862, pg. 86.

[9] Cox, "Reminiscences," 220 ; Spurlin, *Waller's 13th Texas Cavalry Battalion,* 48.

[10] *Overton (TX) Sharp Shooter,* May 31, 1888.

[11] Cox, "Reminiscences," 220; Spurlin, *Waller's 13th Texas Cavalry Battalion,* 48; R. N. Weisiger, Daybook 1862, pg. 86

[12] Cox, "Reminiscences," 220; Spurlin, *Waller's 13th Texas Cavalry Battalion,* 49.

[13] Morris, "Battle of Bayou des Allemands," 14. Lieutenant Achille Bougere was a native of the region, and was serving as an officer in the 30th Louisiana Infantry stationed at Port Hudson. He was apparently assigned to Taylor to aid in this operation.

[14] *Overton (TX) Sharp Shooter,* May 31, 1888.

[15] Cox, "Reminiscences," 220-21.

[16] Spurlin, *Waller's 13th Texas Cavalry Battalion,* 49.

[17] Cox, "Reminiscences," 221; Spurlin, *Waller's 13th Texas Cavalry Battalion,* 49 ; R. N. Weisiger, Daybook 1862, pg. 90.

Chapter 9

1   Dupuy, "Memorable Days," 4.
2   *OR*, vol. 15, 568-69.
3   Ibid.
4   Ibid.
5   Peña, *Touched by War*, 157; Bergeron, *Louisiana Confederate Military Units*, 130-132.
6   C. W. Raines, *Year Book for Texas, 1901* (Austin: Gammel Book Company, 1902), 362; "Confederate Papers Relating to Citizens or Business Firms, 1861-1865, Publication Number M346, National Archives and Records Administration.
7   Taylor, *Destruction and Reconstruction*, 108, 165; Ezra Warner, *Generals in Gray: Lives of the Confederate Commanders* (Baton Rouge: Louisiana State University Press, 1959), 222-23; Noel, *Santa Fe to the Mississippi*, 78.
8   Peña, *Touched by War*, 165-65; Taylor, *Destruction and Reconstruction*, 113.
9   Peña, *Touched by War*, 164.
10   *OR*, vol. 15, 176-177, 820; Peña, *Touched by War*, 164.
11   Cox, "Reminiscences," 222.
12   Peña, *Touched by War*, 158; *OR*, vol. 15, 800; Winters, *Civil War in Louisiana*, 157.
13   *OR*, vol. 15, 142.
14   Spurlin, *Waller's 13th Texas Cavalry Battalion*, 53-54.
15   Arthur W. Bergeron, Jr., ed., *Civil War Reminiscences of Major Silas T. Grisamore, CSA* (Baton Rouge: Louisiana State University Press, 1993), 94-96; Peña, *Touched by War*, 164 ; Bergeron, *Louisiana Confederate Military Units*, 145-146.
16   *OR*, vol. 15, 175.
17   Spurlin, *Waller's 13th Texas Cavalry Battalion*, 55.
18   Dupuy, "Memorable Days," 6.
19   Taylor, *Destruction and Reconstruction*, 115.
20   Ibid., 116.

Chapter 10

1   Theophilus Holmes to J. C. Pemberton, November 25, 1862, *OR*, vol. 22, pt. 1, 897-98; Samuel Cooper to Jefferson Davis, November 29, 1862, *OR*, vol. 22, pt. 2, 767.
2   J. C. Pemberton to Jefferson Davis, November 28, 1862, *OR*, vol. 22, pt. 2, 767; Holmes to Cooper, December 5, 1862, *OR*, vol. 17, pt. 2, 784.
3   Jefferson Davis to Samuel Cooper, no date, *OR*, vol. 15, pt. 2, 767; Cooper to Holmes, November 29, 1862, *OR*, vol. 17, pt. 2, 768; Cooper to Pemberton, November 29, 1862, *OR*, vol. 22, pt. 1, 899.
4   Alfred Petticolas Diary, vol. 3, September 12 to October 23, 1862 (unpublished typescript in possession of Don Alberts, Rio Rancho, NM).
5   F. S. Wade, "Tales of Early Days in Texas" (unpublished memoir typescript in possession of Rosalind Wade Brinkley, Elgin, TX), 41.
6   Ibid.
7   Noel, *Santa Fe to the Mississippi*, 55-56.
8   William Randolph Howell Diary, July 23-October 30, 1862, William Randolph Howell Papers, Barker Texas History Center. (Hereafter collection cited as Howell Diary, repository cited as BTHC.)

9   Noel, *Santa Fe to the Mississippi,* 61; Martin Hardwick Hall, *The Confederate Army of New Mexico* (Austin: Presidial Press, 1978), 13-40; Frank Calvert Oltorf, *The Marlin Compound: Letters of a Singular Family* (Austin: University of Texas Press, 1968), 111.

10 Henry C. Wright, "Reminiscences of H. C. Wright of Austin," 53-54, BTHC.

11 Ibid.

12 Wade, "Tales of Early Days in Texas," (unpublished memoir, typescript in possession of Rosalind Wade Brinkley, Elgin, TX), 40.

13 F. S. Wade, "Reconstruction Days: A True Story of the Early Days" (unpublished memoir, typescript in possession of Rosalind Wade Brinkley, Elgin, TX), 19.

14 John M. Watkins to Irene Watkins, Camp Terry, October 1, 1862, Marlin, Texas, Watkins Letters, Confederate Research Center, Hillsboro, Texas.

15 The Val Verde Battery was composed of the cannons captured from Union Captain Alexander McRae at the Battle of Val Verde, New Mexico, on February 21, 1862. Originally there had been three 6-pounder field guns, two 12-pounder howitzers, and a 12-pounder mountain howitzer. One of the 6-pounders was subsequently lost in battle, more than likely being a cannon reportedly struck on the muzzle and destroyed at the Battle of Glorieta on March 28, 1862. After the New Mexico campaign, the remaining guns received new fittings, harness, and paint at the shop of A. Eickel of New Braunfels, Texas, during September 1862. One 12-pounder howitzer bore the inscription, "Val Verde, Major Lockridge, Captain Adair, Feby 21/61," while its twin read "Val Verde Lt. Col. Sutton." The two 6-pounders had markings that read simply "Captured at Val Verde, Feby 21/62." The oldest cannon—one of the howitzers—had been cast in 1842 while the other guns all carried 1846 dates. See C. W. Raines, *Year Book for Texas, 1901* (Austin,: Gammel Book Company, 1902), 362.

16 Hall, *Confederate Army of New Mexico,* 52.

17 *Austin Texas State Gazette,* March 20, 1861.

18 Sibley to Cooper, February 22, 1862, *OR,* vol. 9, 506; Green to Reagan, November 13, 1862, Green Papers, West Texas Collection, San Angelo State University.

19 Royal T. Wheeler, C. N. Johns, C. N. Randolph, and George J. Durham to Jefferson Davis, September 5, 1862, Compiled Military Service Record of Thomas Green, Records of the Adjutant General's Office, National Archives, Washington, D.C.

20 Green to Reagan, November 13, 1862, Green Papers; Martin Hardwick Hall, ed., "An Appraisal of the 1862 New Mexico Campaign: A Confederate Officer's Letter to Nacogdoches," *New Mexico Historical Review* 51 (October 1976): 332.

21 Green to Reagan, November 13, 1862, Green Papers; Hall, "Appraisal of the 1862 New Mexico Campaign," 332.

22 Tom Green to John H. Reagan, November 13, 1862, Green Papers

23 Ibid.

24 Ibid.

25 Wheeler, C. N. Johns, Randolph, and Durham to Davis, September 5, 1862, Compiled Military Service Record of Thomas Green, Records of the Adjutant General's Office, National Archives, Washington, D.C.

26 Tom Green to Nathan Green, September 24, 1861, Green Papers, West Texas Collection, San Angelo State University.

27 Wade, "Reconstruction Days," 15.

28 Ibid.

29 Ibid.
30 Ibid., 16
31 Ibid.

Chapter 11

1   W. T. Block, ed., "The Diary of 1st Sergeant H. N. Connor," September 24, 1862,
    http://www.wtblock.com/wtblockjr/diaryof.htm. Printed and in possession of
    the author.
    W. T. Block, ed., "The Diary of 1st Sergeant H. N. Connor," September 24, 1862.
3   Ibid.
4   Ibid.
5   *ORN*, vol. 19, 225
6   Cotham, *Southern Journey*, 106.
7   W. B. Renshaw to David G. Farragut, "Report of Commander Renshaw, U.S. Navy,
    commanding USS *Westfield*," October 5, 1862, *ORN*, vol. 19, 259-260; Charles W.
    Hayes, *Galveston: History of the Island and the City* (Austin: Jenkins Garrett Press,
    1974), 1:524; Cotham, *Southern Journey*, 106.
8   Cotham, *Southern Journey*, 107.
9   *Houston Tri-Weekly Telegraph*, Extra, June 23, 1863.
10 Ibid.
11 Renshaw to Farragut, October 5, 1862, *ORN*, vol. 19, 259-60.
12 Renshaw to Farragut, October 8, 1862, *ORN*, vol. 19, 255-60; Farragut to Butler,
    October 28, 1862, *ORN*, vol. 19, 318.
13 *OR*, vol. 15, 159.
14 Current, *Lincoln's Loyalists*, 98-99.
15 Andrew to G. V. Fox, November 27, 1861, *OR*, vol. 15, 412.
16 Andrew to G. V. Fox, November 27, 1861, *OR*, vol. 15, 412. For a discussion of
    Confederate ambitions in the American Southwest, see Frazier, *Blood and
    Treasure*.
17 Robert M. Franklin, Speech to Camp Magruder United Confederate Veterans,
    April 2, 1911, Galveston, Texas, 4, Texas and Local History Collection, Rosenberg
    Library, Galveston, Texas (repository cited as TLHC); Warner, *Generals in Gray*,
    131-32; Hayes, *Galveston*, 1:525; Clement Evans, ed., *Confederate Military History:
    A Library of Confederate States History, in Twelve Volumes, Written by
    Distinguished Men of the South, and Edited by Gen. Clement A. Evans of Georgia*
    (Atlanta: Confederate Publishing Co., 1899), 11:78; John B. Magruder to Samuel
    Cooper, February 26, 1863, *OR*, vol. 15, 211-212.

Chapter 12

1   *ORN*, vol. 19,259.
2   F. A. Roe to David G. Farragut, September 29, 1862, *ORN*, vol. 19, 215-16.
3   *ORN*, vol. 19, 313, 315, 437.
4   Ibid., 110-11.
5   Ibid.

6   Ibid., 111.

7   Ibid., 111-13.

8   Barnes F. Lathorp, "Invasion," *Louisiana History* 2 (1961), 175-77.

9   *OR*, vol. 15, 158-59.

10   Godfrey, *Civil War Letters*, 27.

11   Lathorp, *Invasion*, 175-77.

12   John William De Forest, *A Volunteer's Adventures: A Union Captain's Record of the Civil War*, ed. James H. Croushore (Baton Rouge: Louisiana State University Press, 1996), 55; Godfrey, *Civil War Letters*, 28-29.

13   De Forest, *A Volunteer's Adventures*, 55; Peña, *Touched by War*, 155-56.

14   Peña, *Touched by War*, 177; George G. Smith, *Leaves from a Soldier's Diary: The Personal Record of Lieutenant George G. Smith, Co. C, 1st Louisiana Regiment Infantry Volunteers [White] During the War of Rebellion* (Putnam, CT: n.p., 1906), 30.

15   As quoted in Peña, *Touched by War*, 172.

16   *OR*, vol. 15, 176.

17   Ibid.

18   *OR*, vol. 15, 176; Peña, *Touched by War*, 174.

19   *OR*, vol. 15, 176; Peña, *Touched by War*, 174-75; Bergeron, *Reminiscences of Major Grisamore*, 98.

20   Diary of Homer B. Sprague, 13th Connecticut, April 14, 1863, vol. 2, 79-80, Papers of Homer B. Sprague, Manuscripts Division, Library of Congress, Washington, D.C.; De Forest, *A Volunteer's Adventures*, 55.

21   De Forest, *A Volunteer's Adventures*, 55-56.

22   *OR*, vol. 15, 168.

23   De Forest, *A Volunteer's Adventures*, 56.

24   Ibid.

25   Diary of Homer B. Sprague, 13th Connecticut, April 14, 1863, vol. 2, 79-80, Papers of Homer B. Sprague, Manuscripts Division, Library of Congress, Washington, D.C.; . De Forest, *A Volunteer's Adventures*, 56.

26   Godfrey, *Civil War Letters*, 33.

27   Dupuy, "Memorable Days," 7.

Chapter 13

1   John M. Stanyan, *A History of the Eighth Regiment of New Hampshire Volunteers* (Concord, New Hampshire: Ira C. Evans, 1892), 142; Peña, *Touched by War*, 181; Sprague Diary, 85-86.

2   Stanyan, *Eighth Regiment of New Hampshire Volunteers*, 142; Sprague Diary, 85-86.

3   Peña, *Touched by War*, 182-85.

4   Peña. *Touched by War*, 182, 186; *New York Times*, "Further Details of the Operations of General Weitzel," November 20, 1862; De Forest, *A Volunteer's Adventures*, 58.

5   De Forest, *A Volunteer's Adventures*, 58-59.

6   Ibid., 60.

7   Ibid., 61, 62.

8   Ibid., 62.

[9] Ibid.

[10] Stanyan, *Eighth Regiment of New Hampshire Volunteers*, 145-46; Peña, *Touched by War*, 185.

[11] De Forest, *A Volunteer's Adventures*, 63.

[12] Ibid., 64.

[13] Ibid., 65.

[14] Ibid., 65

[15] Peña, *Touched by War*, 188-89; Sprague Diary, 86-90.

[16] De Forest, *A Volunteer's Adventures*, 66.

[17] Ibid., 67.

[18] De Forest, *A Volunteer's Adventures*, 66-67; Stanyan, *Eighth Regiment of New Hampshire Volunteers*,144-45; Peña, *Touched by War*, 190.

[19] De Forest, *A Volunteer's Adventures*, 70.

[20] *OR*, vol. 15, 177.

[21] Sprague Diary, 92; Charles Menard, Annals of the Church of St. Joseph, April 2, 1991, *Bayou Catholic*; Peña, *Touched by War*, 196.

[22] Godfrey, *Civil War Letters*, 20.

[23] *OR*, vol. 15, 178-79.

[24] *OR*, vol. 15, 179.

[25] The Teche winds generally northwest to southeast. For purposes of this book, the left bank is the north bank, the right bank is the south bank.

[26] Felix Robert Collard, "Reminiscences of a Private, Company G, 7th Texas Cavalry, Sibley Brigade, C.S.A." (unpublished typescript, 1923, in possession of Don Alberts, Albuquerque, NM), 13; Alfred Mouton to Edward Surget, May 2, 1863, *OR*, vol. 15, 396-97; C. M. Horton Diary, April 11, 1863, Civil War Papers, Box 20, Folder 2, LHA.

[27] *ORN*, vol. 19, 332.

[28] *ORN*, vol. 19, 336.

[29] *ORN*, vol. 19, 327, 330-31.

[30] *ORN*, vol. 19, 328, 330-31.

[31] *ORN*, vol. 19, 337-38.

[32] *ORN*, vol. 19, 336.

[33] *ORN*, vol. 19, 328.

[34] *ORN*, vol. 19, 331.

[35] Taylor, *Destruction and Reconstruction*, 140-41.

[36] Ibid.; Steven M. Mayeux, Earthen Walls, Iron Men: Fort DeRussy, Louisiana, and the Defense of Red River (Knoxville: The University of Tennessee Press, 2007), 7-9.

[37] Ibid.

Chapter 14

[1] Cotham, *Southern Journey*, 114.

[2] *ORN*, vol. 19, 800; Cotham, *Southern Journey*, 115.

[3] Cotham, *Southern Journey*, 116.

[4] W. B. Renshaw to D. G. Farragut, December 15, 1862, *ORN*, vol. 19, 431-32.

[5] Current, *Lincoln's Loyalists*, 97-98.

[6] *ORN*, vol. 19, 380.

[7] *ORN*, vol. 19, 381.

8   *ORN*, vol. 19, 381.
9   *ORN*, vol. 19, 381.
10   Peña, *Touched by War*, 198.
11   *OR*, vol. 15, 170.
12   *OR*, vol. 15, 170.
13   *OR*, vol. 15, 171-72
14   *OR*, vol. 15, 171-72.
15   Stanyan, *Eighth Regiment of New Hampshire Volunteers*, 156.
16   *OR*, vol. 15, 165.
17   *OR*, vol. 15, 166.
18   *OR*, vol. 15, 165.
19   *OR*, vol. 15, 165-166.
20   *OR*, vol. 15, 162-63.
21   *OR*, vol. 15, 162.
22   Ripley, *Slaves and Freedmen in Civil War Louisiana*, 44-45.
23   *OR*, vol. 15, 165.
24   Smith, *Leaves from a Soldier's Diary*, 35-37.
25   Ripley, *Slaves and Freedmen in Civil War Louisiana*, 45.
26   Peña, *Touched by War*, 202; Pugh incident in *OR*, vol. 15, 172.
27   De Forest, *A Volunteer's Adventures*, 73.
28   *OR*, vol. 15, 166.
29   Smith, *Leaves from a Soldier's Diary*, 34; Peña, *Touched by War*, 201.
30   *OR*, vol. 15, 163.
31   Current, *Lincoln's Loyalists*, 97; Benjamin Butler to Leonard Pierce, Jr., November 12, 1862, *OR*, vol. 15, 591-92.
32   Smith, *Leaves from a Soldier's Diary*, 34-35.
33   Godfrey, *Civil War Letters*, 20-21.
34   Ibid.
35   Dupuy, "Memorable Days," 8.
36   Prichard, "Effects of the Civil War on the Louisiana Sugar Industry," 319.
37   Godfrey, *Civil War Letters*, 20-21.
38   Watson, *Life in the Confederate Army*, 407.
39   Godfrey, *Civil War Letters*, 23; *OR*, vol. 15, 158-59.
40   *OR*, vol. 15, 158-59.

Chapter 15

1   Richard B. Irwin, *History of the 19th Army Corps* (New York: G.P. Putnam's Sons, 1893), 54-55.
2   Ibid., 56.
3   Eby, *A Virginia Yankee*, 127, 130.
4   Nolan, *Benjamin Franklin Butler*, 220-21.
5   Halleck to Butler, November 3, 1862, *OR*, vol. 15, 589.
6   Irwin, *History of the 19th Army Corps*, 59.
7   Ibid., 57, 59.
8   Eby, *A Virginia Yankee*, 134-35.
9   Ibid., 134.
10   Nolan, *Benjamin Franklin Butler*, 222.

[11] Eby, *A Virginia Yankee,* 136, 139.
[12] Ibid., 135.
[13] Ibid., 136.
[14] James G. Hollandsworth, Jr., *Pretense of Glory: The Life of General Nathaniel P. Banks* (Baton Rouge: Louisiana State University Press, 1998), 19.
[15] Eby, *A Virginia Yankee,* 138.
[16] Ibid., 141.
[17] Ibid., 141.
[18] Ibid., 141.
[19] Nolan, *Benjamin Franklin Butler,* 222.
[20] Eby, *A Virginia Yankee,* 139.
[21] Watson, *Life in the Confederate Army,* 440.
[22] Ibid., 441.

Chapter 16

[1] Eby, *A Virginia Yankee,* 137.
[2] Ibid., 137.
[3] Edward Bacon, *Among the Cotton Thieves* (Detroit: Freer Press Steam Book and Job Printing House, 1867), 149.
[4] Johnson and Buel, *Battles and Leaders,* 588.
[5] As quoted in Edward T. Cotham, Jr., *Battle on the Bay: The Civil War Struggle for Galveston* (Austin: University of Texas Press, 1998), 83, taken from Richard A. Atkins and Helen Fiske Atkins, eds., *Civil War Journal of George M. Fisk of Medfield, Massachusetts* (Syracuse, New York: no publisher, 1962), 11.
[6] As quoted in Francis R. Lubbock, *Six Decades in Texas* (Austin: Ben C. Jones, 1900), 449.
[7] Douglas Southall Freeman, *Lee's Lieutenants* (New York: Charles Scribner's Scribner's Sons, 1944), 1:15, 608-11; Warner, *Generals in Gray,* 207-8. For items relating to Magruder's drinking, see Charles W. Trueheart to Anne Tompkins Trueheart, February 21, 1863, Trueheart Family Papers, TLHC (hereafter cited as Trueheart Papers). Minetta Altgelt Goyne, *Lone Star and Double Eagle: Civil War Letters of a German-Texas Family* (Fort Worth: Texas Christian University Press, 1982), 81; Hayes, *Galveston,* 1:525; Evans, *Confederate Military History,* 11:78; Magruder to Cooper, February 26, 1863, *OR,* vol. 15, 211-20. For Magruder's designs for Texas, see Robert M. Franklin Speech to Camp Magruder United Confederate Veterans, April 2, 1911, p. 7, TLHC;
[8] Thompson, *Henry Hopkins Sibley,* 309-10.
[9] Henry Hopkins Sibley to Theophilus Holmes, December 25, 1862, *OR,* vol. 15, 910-11.
[10] Ibid.
[11] Henry Hopkins Sibley to Theophilus Holmes, December 25, 1862, *OR,* vol. 15, 910-11; Sibley to Gardner, February 4, 1863, *OR,* vol. 24, pt. 1, 339.

Chapter 17

[1] Irwin, *History of the 19th Army Corps,* 51.
[2] John Bankhead Magruder to Anderson, December 12, 1862, *OR,* vol. 15, 897; Magruder to Anderson, December 19, 1862, *OR,* vol. 15, 902.

[3] Lubbock to Magruder, December 6, 1862, *OR*, vol. 15, 896.

[4] Ibid.

[5] Magruder to Lubbock, December 21, 1862, *OR*, vol. 15, 903-4.

[6] Magruder to Samuel Cooper, December 9, 1862, *OR*, vol. 15, 894.

[7] Don E. Alberts, *Rebels on the Rio Grande: The Civil War Journal of A. B. Peticolas* (Albuquerque: University of New Mexico Press, 1984), 62; Peticolas Diary, September 12-14, 1862, typescript in possession of Don Alberts, Rio Rancho, New Mexico; John Bankhead Magruder, "General Order Number 16," December 12, 1862, Moritz Maedgen Papers, Texas Collection, Baylor University, Waco, Texas.

[8] Franklin Speech, 4-5; Hayes, *Galveston*, 1:550-51; Magruder to Cooper, February 26, 1863, *OR*, vol. 15, 212.

[9] Richard B. Irwin, "The Capture of Port Hudson," in *Battles and Leaders of the Civil War*, eds. Johnson and Buel, 3:586-87; Marcus J. Wright, *Texas in the War, 1861-1865*, ed. Harold B. Simpson (Hillsboro, TX: Hill Junior College Press, 1965), 39-49; Hayes, *Galveston*, 2:552-53; Magruder to Cooper, February 26, 1863, *OR*, vol. 15, 213.

[10] Atkins and Atkins, *Civil War Journal of George M. Fiske*, 15.

[11] Ibid.

[12] Franklin Speech, 6; Charles A. Davis to William Schouler, January 10, 1863, "Report of Lieutenant Davis, U.S. Army, Adjutant Forty-second Massachusetts Infantry," *ORN*, vol. 19, 457-59; Hayes, *Galveston*, 1:548. The 42nd Massachusetts Infantry was inexperienced, having recently arrived from Readville, Massachusetts, where the regiment had been raised. The remaining seven companies were still in transit at this time.

[13] William S. Long to D. C. Houston, January 10, 1863, "Report of Assistant Engineer Long, U.S. Army," *ORN*, vol. 19, 459; Magruder to Cooper, February 26, 1863, *OR*, vol. 15, 213; Hayes, *Galveston*, 1:547; Franklin Speech, 7; E. Jarvis Baker, Speech to Benjamin Stone, Jr., Post 68, Grand Army of the Republic, 1882, E. Jarvis Baker Memoirs, BTHC (hereafter cited as Baker Speech).

[14] The *Harriet Lane* carried two 9-inch and two 32-pound smoothbores in each broadside, a 9-inch pivot gun forward of her wheels, and a 20-pounder rifled pivot gun in the bow.

[15] Franklin Speech, 6; G. V. Fox to Acting Rear-Admiral David D. Porter, February 6, 1863, *ORN*, vol. 24, 242-43; Magruder to Cooper, February 26, 1862, *OR*, vol. 15, 213; H. H. Bell Diary, February 28, 1863, *ORN*, vol. 19, 745; Naval Historical Center, Department of the Navy, *Dictionary of American Fighting Ships* (Washington, D.C.: Government Printing Office, 1975-1981), 3:250.

[16] Four 32-pounders and two 9-inch Dahlgren smoothbores.

[17] A 24-pounder howitzer in the stern and a 30-pounder Parrot rifle in the bow.

[18] *Sachem* carried two 32-pounders in each broadside and a 20-pound Parrot rifle in the bow. Franklin Speech, 6; Magruder to Cooper, February 26, 1863, *OR*, vol. 15, 213; Naval Historical Center, *American Fighting Ships*, 6:220-21; Hayes, *Galveston*, 2:131, 193.

[19] Four 8-inch and one 9-inch Dahlgren smoothbores, and one 100-pounder Parrot rifle.

[20] *Owasco* carried one 20-pounder Parrot rife, one 9-inch Dahlgren in pivot, and two 24-pounder howitzers. Franklin Speech, 6; Magruder to Cooper, February 26, 1863, *OR*, vol. 15, 213; Naval Historical Center, *American Fighting Ships*, 7:236; Hayes, *Galveston*, 5:192.

[21] Cotham, *Southern Journey*, 118-19.

22 Noel, *Santa Fe to the Mississippi*, 63; "Battle of Galveston Described by Veteran: A Member of Company A, Fifth Texas Cavalry, Tells Story," *Galveston Daily News*, January 5, 1914; Magruder to Cooper, February 26, 1863, *OR*, vol. 15, 212-14.

23 "Battle of Galveston," *Galveston Daily News*, January 5, 1914.

24 Noel, *Santa Fe to the Mississippi*, 63; Joseph Faust to Hermann Seele, December 29, 1862, Joseph Faust Papers, BTHC (collection hereafter cited as Faust Papers); Howell Diary, December 31, 1862, Howell Papers.

25 *Bayou City* carried a refurbished 32-pounder, converted into a rifle; The howitzers aboard the *Neptune* were 24-pounders.

26 Alexander Pitt, "Answers of Alexander Pitt, a witness brought before the Commissioner by the Marshall," *In the Matter of the Confederate States of America vs. the Gunboat Steamship called the "Harriet Lane,"* September 12, 1862, C.S.A. Prize Commission Papers, 29 (hereafter cited as *C.S.A. vs. "Harriet Lane,"*), TLHC; Hayes, *Galveston*, 2:551; Franklin Speech, 4-7; Magruder to Cooper, February 26, 1863, *OR*, vol. 15, 212; J. W. Lockhart to his wife, January 7, 1863, published in "This is the 51st Anniversary of Battle of Galveston: Only Handful of Survivors of that Historic Event Living Today in the City—Search Brings to Light a Long-Ago Letter," *Galveston Daily News*, January 1, 1914, 3.

27 Franklin Speech, 5-6; Noel, *Santa Fe to the Mississippi*, 65.

28 Franklin Speech, 7; Hayes, *Galveston*, 2:552-53; "Lockhart Letter," *Galveston Daily News*, January 1, 1914.

29 Franklin Speech, 7.

30 "Battle of Galveston," *Galveston Daily News*, January 5, 1914, 3.

31 Hayes, *Galveston*, 2:552; Henry S. Lubbock, "Answers of Henry S. Lubbock, a witness brought before the Commissioner by the Marshall," *C.S.A vs. "Harriet Lane,"* 6.

32 Franklin Speech, 6; "Battle of Galveston," *Galveston Daily News*, January 5, 1914; Hall, *Confederate Army of New Mexico*, 141-48.

Chapter 18

1 Franklin Speech, 6-7; Hayes, *Galveston*, 2:553; Lubbock, "Answers," *C.S.A.* vs. *"Harriet Lane,"* 6; Henry Wilson to Farragut, January 6, 1863, "Report of Lieutenant-Commander Wilson, U.S. Navy, commanding USS *Owasco*," *ORN*, vol. 19, 439; Daniel Phillips, "Answers of Daniel Phillips, a witness brought before the Commissioner by the Marshall," *C.S.A. vs. "Harriet Lane,"* 27. The signal book from the *Harriet Lane* was captured, but it is unknown whether the blue lanterns were hung on purpose or by mistake.

2 Hayes, *Galveston*, 2:553.

3 Dorman H. Winfrey, ed., "Two Battle of Galveston Letters," *Southwestern Historical Quarterly* 65, (October 1961), 252.

4 Hayes, *Galveston*, 2:553.

5 "Tom Gonzalesís Artillery: Record of Jan. 6, 1863, Transmitting Artillery Captainís Report of Battle of Galveston," *Galveston Daily News*, January 5, 1914; Hayes, *Galveston*, 2:553, 556-57; Noel, *Santa Fe to the Mississippi*, 64; Howell to Sallie Patricks, January 19, 1863, Howell Papers; A. T. Spear to Farragut, January 2, 1863, "Report of Acting Master Spear, U.S. Navy, Commanding U.S. Schooner Corypheus," *ORN*, vol. 19, 438.

6   Anonymous diary of a Union soldier, January 1, 1863, TLHC; Davis to Schouler, January 10, 1862, *ORN*, vol. 19, 458; Long to Houston, January 10, 1862, *ORN*, vol. 19, 460; Baker Speech, 20.

7   Anonymous diary of a Union soldier, January 1, 1863, TLHC.

8   Dorman, ed., "Two Battle of Galveston Letters," 252.

9   Baker Speech, 21; Hayes, *Galveston*, 2:555, 571; Magruder to Cooper, February 26, 1863, *OR*, vol. 15, 214, 217; Noel, *Campaign from Santa Fe to the Mississippi*, 65; "Lockhart Letter," *Galveston Daily News*, January 1, 1914. See also Franklin Speech, 7. "Buck and Ball" loads consisted of one round bullet packed with three buckshot and were common ammunition for most smoothbore muskets. Other accounts of the battle suggest that the Texans attempted unsuccessfully to scale the enemy works, although there is no enemy confirmation of this story.

10 Wade, "Reconstruction Days," 20

11 Dorman, ed., "Two Battle of Galveston Letters," 254. 256; Wade, "Reconstruction Days," 20.

12 Wade, "Reconstruction Days," 20.

13 Noel, *Santa Fe to the Mississippi*, 64; Howell to Patricks, January 19, 1863, Howell Papers.

14 William Lott Davidson, C. C. Linn, and Phil Fulcrod, "The Battle of Galveston and Movements of the Brigade in 1863," *The Overton* (Texas) *Sharpshooter*, June 14, 1888, 1.

15 William Pitt Ballinger Diary, January 3, 1863, William Pitt Ballinger Family Papers, TLHC (hereafter cited as Ballinger Diary); H. M. Trueheart to Mary Trueheart, January 22, 1863, Trueheart Papers; Davidson, Linn, and Fulcrod, "The Battle of Galveston and Movements of the Brigade in 1863," 1

16 Hayes, *Galveston*, vol. 2:556, 559; William Pitt Ballinger Diary, January 3, 1863; H. M. Trueheart to Mary Trueheart, January 22, 1863; Noel, *Santa Fe to the Mississippi*, 65; Magruder to Cooper, February 26, 1863, *OR*, vol. 15, 214-15.

17 *The Houston Tri-Weekly Telegraph*, January 7, 1863; Davidson, Linn, and Fulcrod, "The Battle of Galveston and Movements of the Brigade in 1863," 1

18 Franklin Speech, 8.

19 Dorman, ed., "Two Battle of Galveston Letters," 254.

20 Franklin Speech, 8; "Battle of Galveston," *Galveston Daily News*, January 14, 1914; James S. Palmer, Melancton Smith, and L. A. Kimberly to Farragut, January 12, 1863, "Proceedings of Court of Inquiry," *ORN*, vol. 19, 448; Lubbock, "Answers," *C.S.A. vs. "Harriet Lane,"* 7; Sangster, "Answers," *C.S.A. vs. "Harriet Lane,"* 13; Hayes, *Galveston*, 2:556-57. The refitted 32-pounder aboard *Bayou City* burst on its third shot, killing Captain Armand Wier and several of his men.

21 Faust to Seele, January 1, 1863, Faust Papers; Sangster, "Answers," *C.S.A. vs. "Harriet Lane,"* 15.

22 Noel, *Santa Fe to the Mississippi*, 66; Franklin Speech, 8; Hayes, *Galveston*, 2:556-57.

23 Charles Palfrey Bosson, History of the Forty-second Regiment Infantry: Massachusetts Volunteers, 1862, 1863, 1864 (Boston: Charles, Knight, and Company, 1886), 102.

24 Davidson, Linn, and Fulcrod, "The Battle of Galveston and Movements of the Brigade in 1863," 1.

25 Lubbock, "Answers," *C.S.A. vs. "Harriet Lane,"* 7-8; Franklin Speech, 8; "Battle of Galveston," *Galveston Daily News*, January 14, 1914, 3; Hayes, *Galveston*, 2:556-57.

26 Franklin Speech, 8; "Battle of Galveston," *Galveston Daily News*, January 14, 1914; Noel, *Santa Fe to the Mississippi*, 66; Thomas N. Penrose to J. M. Foltz, February 26, 1863, enclosure in "Report of Casualties," *ORN*, vol. 19, 443; Hayes, *Galveston*, 2: 556-57, 574; Dorman, ed., "Two Battle of Galveston Letters," 253

27 Wilson to Farragut, January 6, 1863, *ORN*, vol. 19, 439; Palmer, Smith, and Kimberly to Farragut, January 12, 1863, *ORN*, vol. 19, 450.

28 Lubbock, "Answers," *C.S.A. vs. "Harriet Lane,"* 8; James V. Riley, "Answers of James V. Riley, a witness brought before the Commissioner by the Marshall," *C.S.A. vs. "Harriet Lane,"* 17; Magruder to Cooper, February 26, 1863, *OR*, vol. 15, 215; Franklin Speech, 9; Wilson to Farragut, January 6, 1863, *ORN*, vol. 19, 439; Davidson, Linn, and Fulcrod, "The Battle of Galveston and Movements of the Brigade in 1863," 1.

29 John Y. Lawless, "Answers of John Y. Lawless, a witness brought before the Commissioner by the Marshall," *C.S.A. vs. "Harriet Lane,"* 32-34; Franklin Speech, 9.

30 Magruder to Cooper, February 26, 1863, *OR*, vol. 15, 215; Sangster, "Answers," *C.S.A. vs. "Harriet Lane,"* 16; Hayes, *Galveston*, 2:559, 567-68; "Lockhart Letter," *Galveston Daily News*, January 1, 1914, 3.

31 Hayes, *Galveston*, 2:567-68; Noel, *Campaign from Santa Fe to the Mississippi*, 160-69; Faust to Seele, January 1, 1863, Faust Papers.

32 (Houston) *Tri-Weekly Telegraph*, January 5, 7, 1863; Dorman, ed., "Two Battle of Galveston Letters," 256; Hall, *Confederate Army of New Mexico*, 277.

33 Davidson, Linn, and Fulcrod, "The Battle of Galveston and Movements of the Brigade in 1863," 1

34 Atkins and Atkins, Civil War Journal of George M. Fiske, 19.

35 Ibid.

36 Ibid, 20.

37 "Lockhart Letter," *Galveston Daily News*, January 1, 1914; Davis to Schouler, *ORN*, vol. 19, 458; Isaac S. Burrell, January 23, 1863, "Unofficial statement of Colonel Burrell, commanding Forty-second Regiment Massachusetts Volunteers," *ORN*, vol. 19, 462.

38 William L. Burt to Nathaniel P. Banks, no date, *ORN*, vol. 19, 456; Magruder to Cooper, February 26, 1863, *OR*, vol. 15, 216; Phillips, "Answers," *C.S.A. vs. "Harriet Lane,"* 28.

39 Lawless, "Answers," *C.S.A. vs. "Harriet Lane,"* 34; Riley, "Answers," *C.S.A. vs. "Harriet Lane,"* 19; Magruder to Cooper, February 26, 1863, *OR*, vol. 15, 216.

40 Several important articles touch on various aspects of the battle of Galveston. These include Charles C. Cumberland, "The Confederate Loss and Recapture of Galveston, 1862-1863," *Southwestern Historical Quarterly* 51 (October 1947) 109-130 and Alwyn Barr, "Texas Coastal Defense, 1861-1865," *Southwestern Historical Quarterly* 65 (July 1961) 1-31. Other articles of interest are Louis Tuffly Ellis, "Maritime Commerce on the Far Western Gulf, 1861-1865," *Southwestern Historical Quarterly* 77 (October 1973) 167-226; H. A. Trexler, "The Harriet Lane and the Blockade of Galveston," *Southwestern Historical Quarterly* 35 (October 1931) 109-123 and David P. Marvin "The Harriet Lane," *Southwestern Historical Quarterly* 39 (July 1935) 15-20. Two master's theses have also been written on the subject: Ruby Lee Garner, "Galveston during the Civil War" (master's thesis, University of Texas, Austin, 1927) and Paeder Joel Hooverstol, "Galveston in the Civil War" (master's thesis, University of Houston, 1950).

Chapter 19

1   Howell to Patricks, January 19, 1863, Howell Papers; Hayes, *Galveston*, 2:555, 569-70; Magruder to Cooper, February 26, 1863, *OR*, vol. 15, 218.
2   Lawless, *C.S.A. vs. "Harriet Lane,"* 34; Magruder to Cooper, February 26, 1863, *OR*, vol. 15, 216; Palmer, Smith, and Kimberly to Farragut, January 12, 1863, *ORN*, vol. 19, 450.
3   Foltz to Farragut, January 8, 1863, "Report of Casualties," *ORN*, vol. 19, 442; Hayes, *Galveston*, 2:567-68; Magruder to Cooper, February 26, 1863, *OR*, vol. 15, 216. One of the duties of the first sergeant was to call roll and make company reports concerning casualties. See William J. Hardee, *Hardee's Rifle and Light Infantry Tactics, for the Instruction, Exercises and Manuevers of Riflemen and Light Infantry* (New York: J. O. Kane, 1862), 125.
4   David G. McComb, *Galveston: A History* (Austin: University of Texas Press, 1986), 77.
5   This regiment was often referred to by Texas Confederates as the "First Texas Traitors." Its regimental surgeon, Malek A. Southworth, had served in the same capacity for the 4th Texas Cavalry in New Mexico.
6   Banks to Henry W. Halleck, "Report of Major-General Banks, U.S. Army, transmitting detailed report of Major Burt, of Governor Hamilton's staff," January 7, 1863, *ORN*, vol. 19, 454-55; Magruder to Cooper, February 26, 1863, *OR*, vol. 15, 219; C. M. Mason to Edmund P. Turner, "Report of Major Mason, C.S. Army, regarding attempt to entice Federal army transport Cambria into Galveston Harbor," January 8, 1862, *ORN*, vol. 19, 827-28.
7   Oltorf, *The Marlin Compound*, 113-14; Hayes, *Galveston*, 2:582-83; Magruder to Cooper, February 26, 1863, *OR*, vol. 15, 219-20.
8   Wade, "Reconstruction Days," 21.
9   Hayes, *Galveston*, 2:583-84; "Lockhart Letter," *Galveston Daily News*, January 1, 1914, 3; Noel, *Santa Fe to the Mississippi*, 67.
10 Block, ed., "Diary of 1st Sergeant H. N. Connor," January 8, 1862.
11 Eby, *A Virginia Yankee*, 143-44.
12 Ibid., 144.
13 Francis R. Lubbock, *Six Decades in Texas: Or, Memoirs of Francis Richard Lubbock, Governor of Texas in War Time, 1861-63. A Personal Experience in Business, War, and Politics* (Austin, Texas: Ben C. Jones & co., printers, 1900), 453.
14 Anderson to Magruder, January 2 1863, *OR*, vol. 15, 922; Magruder to Anderson, January 9, 1863, *OR*, vol. 15, 936; Magruder, January 14, 1863, "Address to the Army of Galveston," *ORN*, vol. 19, 467; Noel, *Santa Fe to the Mississippi*, 67; Howell Diary, January 14, 1863, Howell Papers.
15 Davis to Magruder, January 28, 1863, *OR*, vol. 15, 211.
16 In early January, Gardner seemed willing to send Sibley the cavalry from Port Hudson, even though he knew he would probably never get them back. See Gardner to Major Waddy, January 12, 1863, *OR*, vol. 15, 942-43. A dispatch between Pemberton and Gardner refused to allow troops to pass from Port Hudson to the West Bank. See Pemberton to Gardner, January 16, 1863, *OR*, vol. 17, Part 2, 837.
17 F. A. Roe to James Alden, December 29, 1862 *OR*, vol. 15, 192.
18 Ibid.
19 James H. Bogart to Lew Benedict, January 2, 1863, *OR*, vol. 15, 193.
20 Bogart to Benedict, January 3, 1863, *OR*, vol. 15, 193.
21 *OR*, vol. 15, 196-97.

Chapter 20

1   Cotham, *Southern Journey*, 131.
2   Hayes, *Galveston*, 2:583-84; "Lockhart Letter," *Galveston Daily News*, January 1, 1914, 3; Noel, *Santa Fe to the Mississippi*, 67.
3   Rankin, *Diary of a Christian Soldier*, 117.
4   Ibid., 118.
5   *ORN*, vol. 19, 520.
6   Ibid.
7   Ibid.
8   David C. Rankin, ed., Diary of a Christian Soldier: Rufus Kinsley and the Civil War (New York: Cambridge University Press, 2004), 118.
9   Morris Raphael, *The Battle in the Bayou Country* (Detroit: Harlo Press, 1975), 70.
10 Taylor, *Destruction and Reconstruction*, 143.
11 *ORN*, vol. 19, 521; *ORN*, vol. 19, 522-23; Raphael, *Battle in the Bayou Country*, 71; Rankin, *Diary of a Christian Soldier*, 118.
12 Raphael, *Battle in the Bayou Country*, 70.
13 *ORN*, vol. 19, 521.
14 Edward T. King to William Jones, June 27, 1910, William Jones Letters.
15 Raphael, *Battle in the Bayou Country*, 72; *Houston Tri-Weekly Telegraph*, February 2, 1863; Edward T. King to William Jones, June 27, 1910, William Jones Letters.
16 Raphael, *Battle in the Bayou Country*, 72; *Houston Tri-Weekly Telegraph*, February 2, 1863.
17 *ORN*, vol. 19, 517.
18 *ORN*, vol. 19, 522; *ORN*, vol. 19, 523-524.
19 Edward T. King to William Jones, June 27, 1910, William Jones Letters.
20 Oltorf, *Marlin Compound*, 114-15. Conscript regiments were thought to be composed of shirkers and cowards, and therefore association with one was not commonly sought.
21 Noel, *Santa Fe to the Mississippi*, 67; "Battle of Galveston," *Galveston Daily News*, January 5, 1914, 3; Ballinger Diary, January 3, 1863; Charles W. Trueheart to Anne Tompkins Trueheart, February 21, 1863, Trueheart Papers.
22 Riley, "Answers," *C.S.A. vs. "Harriet Lane*," 19; Lubbock, "Answers," *C.S.A. vs. "Harriet Lane*," 12.
23 Noel, *Campaign from Santa Fe to the Mississippi*, 67; "Battle of Galveston," *Galveston Daily News*, January 5, 1914, 3; Ballinger Diary, January 3, 1863; Charles W. Trueheart to Anne Tompkins Trueheart, February 21, 1863, Trueheart Papers.
24 *Houston Tri-Weekly Telegraph*, January 23, 1863.
25 Ibid.
26 *Houston Tri-Weekly Telegraph*, February 16, 1863
27 Ibid.
28 Reily to Magruder, January 31, 1863, *OR*, vol. 15, 970.
29 Jim C. Murray to "Mother," May 11, 1863, typescript from original, in private possession of Michael Murray, Austin, Texas.
30 Block, ed., "Diary of 1st Sergeant H. N. Connor," January 20, 1862.
31 Ibid., January 23, 1862.
32 Magruder, General Orders No. 45, March 11, 1863, *OR*, vol. 15, 238-39.

Chapter 21

[1] Edward McPherson, *The Political History of the United States of America during the Great Rebellion* (Washington, D.C.: Philip and Solomons, 1865), 279; James Freeman Clarke, *Memorial and Biographical Sketches* (Boston: Houghton, Osgood, 1878), 44.

[2] LeGrand, *Diary,* 110.

[3] Ibid., 112.

[4] Ibid., 102.

[5] Fearn, ed., *Diary of a Refugee,* 23-24.

[6] Nathaniel P. Banks, April 6, 1865, *OR,* vol. 26, pt. 1, 6-7.

[7] Sam Houston to John B. Magruder, as quoted in Lubbock, *Six Decades in Texas,* 452.

BIBLIOGRAPHY

Unpublished Primary Sources

Manuscript Collections
Boston Public Library, Boston, Massachusetts
    William Lloyd Garrison Papers
Eugene C. Barker Texas History Collection, Center for American
    History, University of Texas, Austin
    E. Jarvis Baker Memoirs
    Joseph Faust Papers
    William Randolph Howell Papers
    Henry C. Wright Memoir
Allen J. Ellender Archives, Ellender Memorial Library, Nicholls State
    University, Thibodaux, Louisiana
    Martin-Pugh Papers
Library of Congress, Washington, D.C.
    Hamilton Fish Papers
    Homer B. Sprague Papers
Louisiana and Lower Mississippi Valley Collection, LSU Libraries,
    Baton Rouge, Louisiana
    Robert O. Butler Papers
    Helene Dupuy Diary
    R. L. Pugh Papers
National Archives, Washington, D.C.
    Thomas Green, Compiled Military Service Record
    Records of Louisiana State Government, 1850-1888, Microfilm

Publications, M-359, Roll 4
Confederate Papers Relating to Citizens or Business Firms, 1861-1865, Microfilm Publications, M-346
Rosenberg Library, Galveston, Texas
  Anonymous diary of a Union soldier, January 1, 1863
  C.S.A. Prize Commission Papers
  William Pitt Ballinger Family Papers
  Robert M. Franklin Speech
  Trueheart Family Papers
Harold B. Simpson Confederate Research Center, Hillsboro, Texas
  John M. Watkins Letters
Texas Collection, Baylor University, Waco, Texas
  Moritz Maedgen Papers
Tulane University, New Orleans, Louisiana
  C. M. Horton Diary, Civil War Papers, Box 20, Folder 2, Louisiana Historical Association Collection
  William Jones Letters, 1862-1863, Special Collections, Howard-Tilton Memorial Library
Victoria Regional History Center, Victoria College, Victoria, Texas
  Daybook 1862 of Captain R. N. Weisiger, HC-114-4, File 8.
West Texas Collection, San Angelo State University, San Angelo, Texas
  Tom Green Papers

Government Documents

Naval Historical Center, Department of the Navy. *Dictionary of American Fighting Ships.* 8 vols. Washington, D.C.: Government Printing Office, 1975-81.

Official Journal of the Proceedings of the Convention of the State of Louisiana. New Orleans, 1861.

U.S. Naval War Records Office. *Official Records of the Union and Confederate Navies in the War of the Rebellion.* 27 vols. Washington, D.C.: Government Printing Office, 1894-1922.

U.S. War Department. *The War of the Rebellion: A Compilation of the Official Records of the Union and Confederate Armies.* 128 vols. Washington, D.C.: Government Printing Office, 1880-1901.

Newspapers

Austin Texas State Gazette
Bellville Countryman
Galveston Daily News
Houston Tri-Weekly Telegraph
New York Times
Overton (TX) Sharp Shooter

Published Primary Sources

Alberts, Don E. *Rebels on the Rio Grande: The Civil War Journal of A. B. Peticolas*. Albuquerque: University of New Mexico Press, 1984.

Atkins, Richard A., and Helen Fiske Atkins, eds. *Civil War Journal of George M. Fiskeof Medfield, Massachusetts*. Syracuse, NY: n.p., 1962.

Bacon, Edward. *Among the Cotton Thieves*. Detroit: Freer Press Steam Book and Job Printing House, 1867.

Bergeron, Arthur W., Jr., ed. *Civil War Reminiscences of Major Silas T. Grisamore, CSA*. Baton Rouge: Louisiana State University Press, 1993.

Block, W. T., ed. "The Diary of 1st Sergeant H. N. Connor." Available online at http://www.wtblock.com/wtblockjr/diaryof.htm. Original in private collection.

Chesnut, Mary Boykin. *A Diary from Dixie, as written by Mary Boykin Chesnut, wife of James Chesnut, Jr., United States Senator from South Carolina, 1859-1861, and Afterward an Aide to Jefferson Davis and a Brigadier-General in the Confederate Army*. New York: D. Appleton, 1905.

Cotham, Edward T., Jr., ed. *The Southern Journey of a Civil War Marine: The Illustrated Notebook of Henry O. Gusley*. Austin: University of Texas Press, 2006.

Cox, C. C. "Reminiscences of C. C. Cox." *Southwestern Historical Quarterly* 6 (January 1903): 204 - 235.

De Forest, John William. *A Volunteer's Adventures: A Union Captain's Record of the Civil War*. Edited by James H. Croushore. Baton Rouge: Louisiana State University Press, 1996.

Doren, Carl Van, ed. *The Literary Works of Abraham Lincoln.* Norwalk, CT: Easton Press, 1980.

Eby, Cecil B., Jr., ed. *A Virginia Yankee in the Civil War: The Diaries of David Hunter Strother.* Chapel Hill: University of North Carolina Press, 1989.

Fearn, Francis, ed. *Diary of a Refugee.* New York: Moffat, Yard, 1910.

Godfrey, John Franklin. *The Civil War Letters of Captain John Franklin Godfrey.* South Portland, ME: Ascensius Press, 1993.

Goyne, Minetta Altgelt. *Lone Star and Double Eagle: Civil War Letters of a German-Texas Family.* Fort Worth: Texas Christian University Press, 1982.

Gracy, David B., II, ed. "New Mexico Campaign Letters of Frank Starr, 1861-1862." *Texas Military History* 4, No. 3 (Fall 1964): 169-88.

Hall, Martin Hardwick, ed. "An Appraisal of the 1862 New Mexico Campaign: A Confederate Officer's Letter to Nacogdoches." *New Mexico Historical Review* 51 (October 1976).

Hosmer, James K. *The Color Guard: Being a Corporal's Notes of Military Service in the Nineteenth Army Corps.* Boston: Walker and Wise, 1864.

Irwin, Richard B. *History of the 19th Army Corps.* New York: G.P. Putnam's Sons, 1893.

Johnson, Robert Underwood, and Clarence Clough Buel, eds. *Battles and Leaders of the Civil War.* 4 vols. New York, 1887-88. Reprint. Secaucus, NJ: Castle, 1987.

LeGrand, Julia. *The Diary of Julia LeGrand, New Orleans 1862-1863.* Edited by Kate Mason Rowland and Mrs. Morris L. Croxall. Richmond, VA: Everett Wadley, 1911.

"Letters of General Thomas Williams, 1862," *American Historical Review* 14 (January 1909): 304-28.

Lubbock, Francis R. *Six Decades in Texas.* Austin: Ben C. Jones, 1900.

Moore, Thomas O. *Special Message of Thomas O. Moore, Governor of the State of Louisiana to the General Assembly, December 1860.* Baton Rouge: n.p., 1860.

Morris, George R. "The Battle of Bayou des Allemands." *Confederate Veteran* 34 (1910): 14-16.

Noel, Theophilus. *A Campaign from Santa Fe to the Mississippi: Being a History of the Old Sibley Brigade from Its First Organization to the Present Time; Its Campaigns in New Mexico, Arizona, Texas, Louisiana and Arkansas in the Years 1861-2-3-4.* Edited by Martin Hardwick Hall and Edwin Adams Davis. Houston: Stagecoach Press, 1961.

Rankin, David C., ed. *Diary of a Christian Soldier: Rufus Kinsey and the Civil War.* New York: Cambridge University Press, 2004.

Smith, George G. *Leaves from a Soldier's Diary: The Personal Record of Lieutenant George G. Smith, Co. C, 1st Louisiana Regiment Infantry Volunteers [White] During the War of Rebellion.* Putnam, CT: n.p., 1906.

Southwood, Marion. *Beauty and Booty: The Watchword of New Orleans.* New York: M. Doolady, 1867.

Spurlin, Charles, ed. *West of the Mississippi with Waller's 13th Texas Cavalry Battalion CSA.* Hillsboro, TX: Hill Junior College Press, 1971.

Stanyan, John M. *A History of the Eighth Regiment of New Hampshire Volunteers.* Concord, NH: Ira C. Evans, 1892.

Taylor, Richard. *Destruction and Reconstruction: Personal Experiences of the Late War.* New York: D. Appleton, 1879.

Watson, William. *Life in the Confederate Army: Being the Observations and Experiences of an Alien in the South during the American Civil War.* New York: Scribner and Welford, 1888.

Secondary Sources

Barr, Alwyn. "Texas Coastal Defense, 1861-1865." *Southwestern Historical Quarterly* 65 (July 1961): 1-31

Bergeron, Arthur W. *Guide to Louisiana Confederate Military Units, 1861-1865.* Baton Rouge: Louisiana State University Press, 1989.

Bragg, Jefferson Davis. *Louisiana in the Confederacy.* Baton Rouge: Louisiana State University Press, 1941.

Clarke, James Freeman. *Memorial and Biographical Sketches.* Boston: Houghton, Osgood, 1878.

Coates, Earl J., and Dean S. Thomas. *An Introduction to Civil War Small Arms.* Gettysburg, PA: Thomas Publications, 1990.

Cotham, Edward T., Jr. *Battle on the Bay: The Civil War Struggle for Galveston* (Austin: University of Texas Press, 1998.

Cumberland, Charles C. "The Confederate Loss and Recapture of Galveston, 1862-1863." *Southwestern Historical Quarterly* 51 (October 1947): 109-30.

Current, Richard Nelson. *Lincoln's Loyalists: Union Soldiers from the Confederacy.* Boston: Northeastern University Press, 1992.

Davis, Edwin Adams. *Heroic Years: Louisiana in the War for Southern Independence.* Baton Rouge: Louisiana State University Press, 1964.

Dew, Charles B. "Who Won the Secession Election in Louisiana?" *The Journal of Southern History* 36 (1970): 18-32.

Dimitry, John. *Louisiana and Arkansas.* Vol. 10, *Confederate Military History: A Library of Confederate States History, in Twelve Volumes, Written by Distinguished Men of the South, and Edited by Gen. Clement A. Evans of Georgia.* Edited by Clement A. Evans. Atlanta: Confederate Publishing Company, 1899.

Dufour, Charles L. *The Night the War Was Lost.* New York: Doubleday, 1960. Reprint, Lincoln: University of Nebraska Press, 1994.

Ellis, Louis Tuffly. "Maritime Commerce on the Far Western Gulf, 1861-1865." *Southwestern Historical Quarterly* 77 (October 1973): 167.

Roberts, O. M., and J. J. Dickison. *Texas and Florida,* Vol. 11, *Confederate Military History: A Library of Confederate States History, in Twelve Volumes, Written by Distinguished Men of the South, and Edited by Gen. Clement A. Evans of Georgia.* Edited by Clement A. Evans. Atlanta: Confederate Publishing Company, 1899.

Frazier, Donald S. *Blood and Treasure: Confederate Empire in the Southwest.* College Station: Texas A&M University Press, 1995.

Freeman, Douglas Southall. *Lee's Lieutenants.* 3 vols. New York: Charles Scribner's Sons, 1944.

Hall, Martin Hardwick. *The Confederate Army of New Mexico.* Austin: Presidial Press, 1978.

Hardee, William J. *Hardee's Rifle and Light Infantry Tactics, for the Instruction, Exercises and Manuevers of Riflemen and Light Infantry.* New York: J. O. Kane, 1862.

Hayes, Charles W. *Galveston: History of the Island and the City.* 2 vols. Austin: Jenkins Garrett Press, 1974.

Hearn, Chester G. *When the Devil Came Down to Dixie: Ben Butler in New Orleans.* Baton Rouge: Louisiana State University Press, 1997.

Hollandsworth, James G., Jr. *Pretense of Glory: The Life of General Nathaniel P. Banks.* Baton Rouge: Louisiana State University Press, 1998.

Holzman, Robert S. *Stormy Ben Butler.* New York: MacMillan, 1954. Reprint. New York: Collier Books, 1961.

Johnson, Timothy D. *Winfield Scott: The Quest for Military Glory.* Lawrence: University Press of Kansas, 1998.

Jones, Archer. *Civil War Command and Strategy: The Process of Victory and Defeat.* New York: Free Press, 1992.

Lathrop, Barnes, ed. "Federals Sweep the Coast: An Expedition into St. Charles Parish, August, 1862." *Louisiana History* 9 (Winter, 1968): 62-68.

Lathrop, Barnes. "The Lafourche District 61-62: A Problem in Local Defense," *Louisiana History* 1 (Spring 1960): 99-129.

Lathrop, Barnes. "The Lafourche District in 1862: Militia and Partisan Rangers." *Louisiana History* 1 (Fall 1960): 230-244.

Marvin, David P. "The Harriet Lane." *Southwestern Historical Quarterly* 39 (July 1935): 17-19.

Mayeux, Steven M. Earthen Walls, Iron Men: Fort DeRussy, Louisiana, and the Defense of Red River. Knoxville: The University of Tennessee Press, 2007.

McComb, David G. *Galveston: A History.* Austin: University of Texas Press, 1986.

McPherson, Edward. *The Political History of the United States of America during the Great Rebellion.* Washington, D.C.: Philip and Solomons, 1865.

Menard, Pere Charles. "Annals of the Church of St. Joseph," *The Bayou Catholic*, Thibodaux, Louisiana, April 24, 1991.

Messner, William F. *Freedmen and the Ideology of Free Labor: Louisiana, 1862-1865.* Lafayette: Center for Louisiana Studies, 1978.

Millett, Allen R., and Peter Maslowski. *For the Common Defense: A Military History of the United States of America.* New York: Free Press, 1984.

Nolan, Dick. *Benjamin Franklin Butler: The Damnedest Yankee.* Novato, CA: Presidio Press, 1991.

Odom, Van D. "The Political Career of Thomas Overton Moore, Secession Governor of Louisiana." *Louisiana Historical Quarterly* 26 (October 1943): 975-1054.

Oltorf, Frank Calvert. *The Marlin Compound: Letters of a Singular Family.* Austin: University of Texas Press, 1968.

Pace, Robert F. "'It Was Bedlam Let Loose': The Louisiana Sugar Country and the Civil War." *Louisiana History* 39 (Fall 1998): 389-409.

Parrish, T. Michael. *Richard Taylor: Soldier Prince of Dixie.* Chapel Hill: University of North Carolina Press, 1992.

Peña, Christopher G. *Scarred by War: Civil War in Southeast Louisiana.* Bloomington, IN: Authorhouse, 2004.

Peña, Christopher G. *Touched by War: Battles Fought in the Lafourche District.* Thibodaux, LA: C. G. P. Press, 1998.

Prichard, Walter. "The Effects of the Civil War on the Louisiana Sugar Industry." *The Journal of Southern History* 5 (August 1939): 315-32.

Raines, C. W. *Year Book for Texas 1901.* Austin: Gammel Book Company, 1902.

Raphael, Morris. *The Battle in the Bayou Country.* Detroit: Harlo Press, 1975.

Ripley, C. Peter. *Slaves and Freedmen in Civil War Louisiana.* Baton Rouge: Louisiana State University Press, 1976.

Roland, Charles P. *Louisiana Sugar Plantations During the Civil War.* 1957. Reprint. Baton Rouge: Louisiana State University Press, 1997.

Sacher, John M. *A Perfect War of Politics: Parties, Politicians, and Democracy in Louisiana, 1824-1861.* Baton Rouge: Louisiana State University Press, 2003.

Smith, George Winston "Some Northern Wartime Attitudes Toward the Post-Civil War South." *Journal of Southern History* 10, no. 3 (August 1944): 253-74.

Sutherland, Daniel E. "Abraham Lincoln, John Pope, and the Origins of Total War." *Journal of Military History* 56, no. 4 (October 1992): 568-74.

Thompson, Jerry. *Henry Hopkins Sibley: Confederate General of the West.* Natchitoches, LA: Northwestern State University Press, 1987.

Trexler, H. A. "The Harriet Lane and the Blockade of Galveston." *Southwestern Historical Quarterly* 35 (October 1931): 109-23.

Tunnell, Ted. *Crucible of Reconstruction: War, Radicalism, and Race in Louisiana, 1862-1877.* Baton Rouge: Louisiana State University Press, 1984.

Warner, Ezra. *Generals in Gray: Lives of the Confederate Commanders.* Baton Rouge: Louisiana State University Press, 1959.

Winschel, Terrence J. *Vicksburg: Fall of the Confederate Gibraltar.* Abilene, Texas: McWhiney Foundation Press, 1999.

Winters, John D. *The Civil War in Louisiana.* Baton Rouge: Louisiana State University Press, 1987.

Wright, Marcus J. *Texas in the War, 1861-1865.* Edited by Harold B. Simpson. Hillsboro, TX: Hill Junior College Press, 1965.

Theses

Garner, Ruby Lee. "Galveston during the Civil War." Master's thesis. University of Texas, Austin, 1927.

Hooverstol, Paeder Joel. "Galveston in the Civil War." Master's thesis. University of Houston, 1950.

INDEX